Canada's Residential Schools

Volume 2

Canada's Residential Schools:
The Inuit and
Northern Experience

———

The Final Report of the
Truth and Reconciliation
Commission of Canada

Volume 2

Published for the
Truth and Reconciliation Commission

by

McGill-Queen's University Press
Montreal & Kingston • London • Chicago

2015

Truth and Reconciliation Commission of Canada

Website: www.trc.ca

ISBN 978-0-7735-4653-0 (v. 2 : bound).   ISBN 978-0-7735-4654-7 (v. 2 : paperback).

Printed in Canada on acid-free paper

An index to this volume of the final report is available online. Please visit http://nctr.ca/trc_reports.php

Library and Archives Canada Cataloguing in Publication
Truth and Reconciliation Commission of Canada
[Canada's residential schools]
    Canada's residential schools : the final report of the Truth and Reconciliation Commission of Canada.

(McGill–Queen's Native and northern series ; 80–86)
Includes bibliographical references and index.
Contents: v. 1. The history. Part 1, origins to 1939 — The history. Part 2, 1939 to 2000 — v. 2. The Inuit and
    northern experience — v. 3. The Métis experience — v. 4. The missing children and unmarked burials
    report — v. 5. The legacy — v. 6. Reconciliation

Issued in print and electronic formats.
ISBN 978-0-7735-4649-3 (v. 1, pt. 1 : bound).   ISBN 978-0-7735-4650-9 (v. 1, pt. 1 : paperback).
ISBN 978-0-7735-4651-6 (v. 1, pt. 2 : bound).   ISBN 978-0-7735-4652-3 (v. 1, pt. 2 : paperback).
ISBN 978-0-7735-4653-0 (v. 2 : bound).   ISBN 978-0-7735-4654-7 (v. 2 : paperback).
ISBN 978-0-7735-4655-4 (v. 3 : bound).   ISBN 978-0-7735-4656-1 (v. 3 : paperback).
ISBN 978-0-7735-4657-8 (v. 4 : bound).   ISBN 978-0-7735-4658-5 (v. 4 : paperback).
ISBN 978-0-7735-4659-2 (v. 5 : bound).   ISBN 978-0-7735-4660-8 (v. 5 : paperback).
ISBN 978-0-7735-4661-5 (v. 6 : bound).   ISBN 978-0-7735-4662-2 (v. 6 : paperback).
ISBN 978-0-7735-9817-1 (v. 1, pt. 1 : ePDF).   ISBN 978-0-7735-9818-8 (v.1, pt. 1 : ePUB).
ISBN 978-0-7735-9819-5 (v. 1, pt. 2 : ePDF).   ISBN 978-0-7735-9820-1 (v. 1, pt. 2 : ePUB).
ISBN 978-0-7735-9821-8 (v. 2 : ePDF).   ISBN 978-0-7735-9822-5 (v. 2 : ePUB).
ISBN 978-0-7735-9823-2 (v. 3 : ePDF).   ISBN 978-0-7735-9824-9 (v. 3 : ePUB).
ISBN 978-0-7735-9825-6 (v. 4 : ePDF).   ISBN 978-0-7735-9826-3 (v. 4 : ePUB).
ISBN 978-0-7735-9827-0 (v. 5 : ePDF).   ISBN 978-0-7735-9828-7 (v. 5 : ePUB).
ISBN 978-0-7735-9829-4 (v. 6 : ePDF).   ISBN 978-0-7735-9830-0 (v. 6 : ePUB)

1. Native peoples—Canada—Residential schools. 2. Native peoples—Education—Canada.
3. Native peoples—Canada—Government relations. 4. Native peoples—Canada—Social conditions.
5. Native peoples—Canada—History. I. Title. II. Series: McGill-Queen's Native and northern series ; 80–86

E96.5.T78 2016   971.004'97   C2015-905971-2
                                           C2015-905972-0

Contents

Canada's Residential Schools

Volume 2

Introduction

Residential schooling in Canada's North deserves its own consideration for a number of reasons.

First, its history is more recent than that of residential schooling in the rest of the country. As late as 1900 there were only two residential schools north of the sixtieth parallel. By 1950 there were only six residential schools and one hostel in the North. This slow growth reflects the fact that while the overall goals of the Canadian government's Aboriginal policy were to assimilate, civilize, and Christianize, this policy was not applied in a uniform manner. Where there was no pressing demand for Aboriginal lands, the federal government delayed taking on the obligations that Treaties created. This was particularly true in the North. As long as there was no prospect of economic development or of the arrival of large numbers of non-Aboriginal settlers, the federal government was not prepared to negotiate with northern Aboriginal peoples. Nor was it interested in establishing reserves or residential schools—or any sort of school, for that matter. Were it not for the work of Roman Catholic and Anglican missionaries, residential schooling would have no history north of the sixtieth parallel before 1950.

A second distinct feature of the situation in the North was the fact that, in the years after 1950, the Canadian government did not simply extend the existing southern residential school system into northern Canada. Instead the federal government created a system of day schools and hostels under the direction of Northern Affairs rather than Indian Affairs. This system was intended from the start to be integrated into, not separate from, the public school system of the day. Unlike the southern schools, the northern schools made no attempt to restrict admission to First Nations students, so Métis and Inuit, along with a number of non-Aboriginal students, also attended them. At the end of the 1960s, these schools were transferred from the federal government to the governments of the Northwest Territories and the Yukon.

That jurisdictional transfer gave rise to a third difference between residential schooling in the South and in the North. From 1970 to the system's windup in the late 1990s, residential schools were administered by northern governments. Residences were located in both of the territorial capitals of the period, and residential schooling was the subject of far more political attention and understanding than in the rest of the country. During the system's later years, former residential school students were serving as premiers and ministers of northern governments.

Residential schooling in the North also played a major role in the rapid transformation of the region's traditional, land-based lifestyles and economies. The tremendous distances that Inuit and some First Nations and Métis children had to travel to school meant that, in some cases, children were separated from their parents for years. The establishment of day schools and what were termed small hostels in over a dozen communities in the eastern Arctic led many parents to decide to settle in those communities on a year-round basis so as not to be separated from their children. The large hostels in the western Arctic and Churchill, Manitoba, and later in Iqaluit (Frobisher Bay), brought a generation of Aboriginal youth from different regions and backgrounds into contact with one another. Many of these individuals would go on to play leading roles in the creation of the new territory of Nunavut in 1999.

Finally, because Aboriginal people made up the majority of the population in two of the three northern territories, the per capita impact of the schools in the North is higher than anywhere else in the country. And because the history of these schools is so recent, not only are there many Survivors today, there are also many living parents of Survivors. For these reasons the intergenerational impacts and the legacy of the schools, both the good and the bad, are particularly strongly felt in the North. There were also northern institutions with unique histories in the overall residential school story. Grandin College in Fort Smith and the Churchill Vocational Centre in northern Manitoba—and the staff who worked in these schools—are often cited for the positive roles that they played in developing and encouraging a new generation of Aboriginal leadership in the North. The legacy of other schools, particularly Grollier Hall in Inuvik and Turquetil Hall in Igluligaarjuk (Chesterfield Inlet), is far darker. These schools were marked by prolonged regimes of sexual abuse and harsh discipline that scarred more than one generation of children for life.

While the northern experience was unique in some ways, the broader themes remain constant. Children were taken from their parents, often with little in the way of consultation or consent. They were educated in an alien language and setting. They lived in institutions that were underfunded and understaffed, and were prey to harsh discipline, disease and abuse. For these reasons this is not the only volume of the historical report to address northern issues. The thematic chapters in other parts of this report include northern examples in their discussion of the residential school experience. The issue of sexual abuse in the northern residences, for example, is given its fullest discussion in the portions of the report that deal directly with abuse. The hostels that the Anglican Church established for Métis students in the Yukon are detailed in the separate section on the Métis experience of residential schooling.

The history of residential schooling in the North has been divided into two sections. The first deals with the era before 1960, a period best described as the missionary era. It starts with an overview of Canadian government policy in the North, followed by a survey of missionary activity and northern residential schooling in the nineteenth century, and by two chapters on the era of the mission schools in the Northwest Territories. The first of these chapters is a chronological and thematic history; the second draws on a number of memoirs written by former students to capture a sense of life in the schools. A thematic and chronological history of the schools in the Yukon follows.

The decline of the missionary schools overlapped with the assertion of federal authority in the North after 1950. For that reason, the second section of this report deals with the history of residential schooling in the North after 1950, which parallels the evolution of democratic governance in northern Canada, the historical redrawing of the map of Canada to create a new territory of Nunavut, and the essential participation of many northern residential school Survivors in that evolution as they assumed important roles in running the governments they had previously criticized, and then went on to influence and redesign. These same Survivors have been at the vanguard of educational reforms in recent years and are now ensuring that all northern students, Indigenous and non-Indigenous alike, are learning about northern Aboriginal history, including the Treaties and the residential school era, as part of their mandatory core curriculum. Through their example, they are influencing and challenging the rest of Canada to do the same.

Mission schools in the North: 1867 to 1960

CHAPTER 1

An era of neglect: Canadian government policy in the North before 1950

The Canadian government's interest in the North until the Second World War was extremely limited. Much of the North was acquired in 1870 in the transfer of Rupert's Land and the North-Western Territory to Canada. Until 1876, the North-West Territories included all of present-day Alberta, Saskatchewan, Yukon, the Northwest Territories, and Nunavut, as well as much of present-day Manitoba, Ontario, and Québec.[1] As settlement increased, new provinces were created out of the territories, portions of the territories were added to existing provinces, and the territories were subdivided. Today, northern Canada is made up of three territories: Yukon (created in 1898), the Northwest Territories (the name was changed from the North-West Territories in 1906), and Nunavut (created in 1999). Portions of Québec and Labrador that extend into the Ungava Peninsula also make up part of the northern Inuit traditional homeland and are properly considered part of the Canadian North. The Québec portion of the Canadian North is known as Nunavik, while the Newfoundland and Labrador portion is known as Nunatsiavut.

In the late nineteenth century the northern portion of the territories was subdivided on several occasions into a variety of administrative districts, including Ungava, Mackenzie, Yukon, and Franklin. Canada north of the sixtieth parallel is over 3.9 million square kilometres, about one-third of the entire Canadian land mass. It is home to members of the Tlingit, Athapaskan, and Inuit (or Eskimo-Aleut) language groups.[2]

The discovery of gold in the Yukon in 1898 led to the establishment of a separate Yukon Territory. The federal government appointed a commissioner as head of government and an advisory council, composed largely of white southerners, to serve as the governing body. While the gold boom saw tens of thousands of people come to the region and hundreds of millions of dollars of gold shipped out of the country, it was short-lived. By 1911, Dawson City, home to 16,000 people in 1898, had a population of only 2,500.[3]

In 1903, in response to the presence of American whaling stations in the Far North, Royal North-West Mounted Police posts were established at Fort McPherson and Herschel Island, thereby asserting Canadian sovereignty in the Arctic.[4] In 1905 the provinces of Alberta and Saskatchewan were created out of the southern portions of the old North-West Territories and Manitoba's northern border was extended to the sixtieth parallel. At the same time the federal government amended the *North-West Territories Act*, allowing for the appointment of a territorial commissioner who would govern the territory with an appointed council. The first commissioner was Lieutenant Colonel Fred White, a former Mounted Police comptroller. On his death in 1918, White was replaced as territorial commissioner by W. W. Cory, the deputy minister of the interior.[5]

The Yukon went into economic decline after the Klondike gold rush, while the North-West Territories remained, from the Canadian government's perspective, an unknown land: its features were unmapped, its people uncounted.[6] Well into the twentieth century, First Nations and Inuit people of the territories continued to organize their own communities and maintain their own lifestyles, although they were involved in the fur trade and affected by disease.[7]

No Northwest Territories council was appointed until 1920, when the government was spurred into action by the discovery of oil at Norman Wells near the Arctic Circle. The following year, a Northwest Territories and Yukon Branch was established within the Department of the Interior. Under the supervision of Branch Director O. S. Finnie, the first permanent federal government offices in the Northwest Territories were established in Fort Smith, just north of the Alberta border.[8] The Canadian Arctic Expedition of 1913 to 1918 was one of the government's first efforts to map the islands of the western Arctic and conduct a study of the Inuit.[9] In 1922 the government began conducting annual patrols in the eastern Arctic, providing limited medical services and carrying out scientific surveys.[10] Both the patrols and the police presence were primarily intended to assert sovereignty, not to address the needs of the people of the territory.[11]

Throughout the 1920s the members of the Council of the Northwest Territories were all officials of the Department of the Interior or of the Mounted Police. Their meetings were held in Ottawa.[12] Aboriginal people, who constituted the vast majority of the territorial population, had no direct ability to influence the council.[13]

Only two Treaties were negotiated in the Northwest Territories: Treaty 8 and Treaty 11. Treaty 8 covered much of northern British Columbia, Alberta, and Saskatchewan as well as a portion of the western North-West Territories. It was reached in 1899 in response to the presence of prospectors drawn north by the Klondike gold rush. First Nations people were forced into negotiating this Treaty in 1898 when they refused to allow police and trappers into the Fort St. John area without a Treaty. The federal government chose to leave the First Nations of the Yukon out of the Treaty since it was believed the gold rush would not lead to a permanent settlement. The land around Great Slave Lake, however, was thought to hold considerable potential for long-term mineral development.

Bishop Vital Grandin and Father Albert Lacombe, leading Catholic missionaries, acted as intermediaries in these negotiations. They encouraged First Nations to approve the Treaty, urged Métis to opt for *Indian Act* status, and demanded assurances that parents would have the right to have their children educated in schools of the religion of their choice. In this context, both the Catholic missionaries and the government Treaty commissioners envisioned a system in which the only choices open to parents would be between various Christian denominations. When it came to education, the Treaty committed the federal government to "pay the salaries of such teachers to instruct the children of said Indians as to Her Majesty's Government of Canada may seem advisable."[14]

Roman Catholic Bishop Gabriel Breynat lobbied to have further Treaties negotiated in the North.[15] It was not until 1921, following the Norman Wells oil discovery, that Treaty 11 was signed, extending Treaty provisions down the Mackenzie River basin. Once again the government decision to enter into a Treaty was based on its desire to further colonization and economic development. Without a Treaty, the government was uncertain of whether it could dispose of the land under which the oil had been located.[16] Breynat's presence at the Treaty talks played a role in convincing many of the First Nations leaders to overcome their opposition to the Treaty.[17] Like Treaty 8, Treaty 11 provided a commitment "to pay the salaries of teachers to instruct the children of said Indians in such manner as His Majesty's Government may deem advisable."[18]

Having negotiated the Treaties, the federal government demonstrated limited interest in implementing their provisions.[19] In the mid-1930s Breynat helped organize the Oblate Indian and Eskimo Commission to lobby the government for improved Treaty implementation. By then he had concluded that

> the text of the Treaties was too vague and did not contain all of the promises that were verbally made by the representatives of the Crown. Nevertheless, these promises were made, and without them the Indians would never had consented to sign the treaties. It was on the faith of these promises, guaranteed by the bishops and missionaries, that it was possible to persuade the Indians to affix their signature.

In particular, Breynat was distressed by the government's unwillingness to protect Aboriginal fishing and hunting rights.[20]

Responsibility for the provision of services to Aboriginal people was fractured. For example, the 1905 *North-West Territories Act* made no reference to the Inuit, suggesting that they were to be treated like any other Canadians resident in the territories. While they were not seen to have status under the *Indian Act*, Indian Affairs did provide some funding to missionaries and traders who were providing education and relief to Inuit. From 1918 to 1923, this included about $4,000 in educational funding. Finnie sought to have his branch assume responsibility for the Inuit and provide educational services to them. However, in 1924, at the instigation of Duncan Campbell Scott, the deputy minister of Indian affairs, the *Indian Act* was amended to give Indian Affairs responsibility for "Eskimo matters." Within a few years, this responsibility was shifted back to the commissioner of the Northwest Territories, and the provision was dropped from the *Indian Act* in 1930.[21]

The boundaries of Québec were not extended to include Nunavik until 1912.[22] Even after that transfer the provincial government took little responsibility for providing services to the Aboriginal people of the region. During the early years of the Great Depression, the federal government provided relief to the Inuit of Québec, who had been particularly hard hit by the decline in fur prices. It subsequently required the Québec government to cover the cost of relief, arguing that the Inuit were the responsibility of the province. The Québec government made the payment for three years, but then challenged the federal government in court, successfully arguing that Inuit were a federal responsibility. During the four years that the case was being argued, government services remained minimal.[23] In fact, there was little improvement until the 1950s. Aside from the Roman Catholic and Anglican schools at Fort George on James Bay, neither the federal nor the provincial government established formal residential schools in northern Québec until after the Second World War.

Labrador did not join the Canadian confederation until 1949, when Newfoundland became part of Canada. Before then Labrador was governed by the British colonial government of Newfoundland and was, in effect, the colony of a colony. The colonial government in St. John's provided almost no services to the residents of Labrador, be they Aboriginal or non-Aboriginal. Until 1949 any services that were provided were delivered by the Protestant International Grenfell Association and the Moravian Brotherhood.[24]

Given the federal government's lack of interest in entering into Treaties with First Nations in the North or in providing them with services, it is not surprising that residential schooling in the North was, for many years, solely a church initiative.

CHAPTER 2

Laying the groundwork:
Mission schools: 1850 to 1900

The arrival of two Oblate priests at Red River in 1845 marked the beginning of a period of intense Catholic missionary work throughout the Canadian North and West.[1] Oblate missionary Henri Faraud created the church's northern beachhead, establishing a mission at Fort Chipewyan in what is now northern Alberta in 1849 and the St. Joseph's Mission at Fort Resolution in 1856.[2] The Anglicans followed them north. In 1858, Oblate father Henri Grollier learned that James Hunter, a representative of the Anglican Church Missionary Society (CMS) was on a Hudson's Bay Company (HBC) barge headed for Fort Simpson in the Mackenzie region. Hunter intended to drive the Catholic missionaries of the North "into the Arctic sea." To prevent Hunter from seizing the advantage, Grollier sought to travel to Fort Simpson with him. Initially, HBC officials told him he would be taken only to Big Island, where he could minister to the Métis. However, the Roman Catholic boatmen insisted on taking Grollier all the way to Fort Simpson, where he and Hunter devoted considerable energy to undercutting each other.[3]

Throughout the North, the CMS and the Oblates countered one another in this fashion: an Anglican mission at Fort Liard was matched by a Catholic one, with similar pairings occurring at Hay River, Fort Norman, and Fort Wrigley.[4] By the 1890s, the Anglicans acknowledged that, as a result of the Oblates' work, most people in the Athabasca-Mackenzie region were at least nominally Catholic.[5]

The situation was very different farther west, in the Yukon. In the 1860s, two Anglican missionaries, W. W. Kirkby and Robert McDonald, began their mission to the Yukon. When the Oblate Isidore Clut undertook a journey to the region in 1872, he conceded that Kirkby and McDonald had already won over most of the Aboriginal population to Protestantism.[6] William Carpenter Bompas consolidated their work. Born into a Baptist family in England, Bompas converted to the Church of England as a young man. After hearing Rupert's Land Bishop David Anderson speaking at a fundraising meeting in 1865, he volunteered his services to the CMS and was sent to the Canadian North that year.[7] Under Bompas's direction, by the 1880s the Anglicans had ten mission stations in the North that were served by eight clergymen and four teachers.[8] Bompas became bishop of the Yukon in 1891. Just as the Mackenzie River basin was largely Catholic, the Yukon came to be seen as Anglican territory.

From missions to schools

These early missions became the basis for residential schools in the North. Father Henri Faraud was originally opposed to opening a residential school at Fort Providence. He reversed his position when he found out that the wives of Hudson's Bay employees were interested in having their daughters educated by nuns. By 1865, he had set to work on the construction of a school, complete with tiers of bookshelf-like bunk beds. The school's opening awaited the arrival of five Sisters of Charity (Grey Nuns), who trekked much of the way from Red River to Fort Providence in 1867. A few years later, the threat of an Anglican school at Fort Chipewyan led Bishop Isidore Clut to dispatch a small contingent of Sisters of Charity from Fort Providence to Fort Chipewyan, in 1874.[9]

Educational goals were limited. Henri Faraud believed young girls needed little more than knowledge of the Catholic catechism and the ability to read and write.[10] Education was left in the hands of the Sisters of Charity.[11] Religious instruction took the form of ethics, catechism, music, services, and devotions. The hope was that with such an education, the student would not stray from the church after leaving school.[12] It was anticipated that students would return to their home communities, where hunting, trapping, and fishing would remain the primary economic activities.[13]

Life at the schools could be hard. At Fort Providence the Sisters of Charity were initially housed in a storage shed, just over a metre in height. Accommodations remained cramped for them and their students for years. According to a history of the order, by the time there were nine sisters and forty-five children,

> the conditions were no longer tolerable. In the day-time, it was not too hard to find room for all. But at night it was pitiful, though marvelous, to see how the little ones were stowed away in regular lines, some on them on tables or in cupboards, only one corner of the house being reserved for the Sisters themselves.[14]

There were no potatoes, meat, flour, butter, or grease during the school's second year of operation. Not surprisingly, the worry that their children were not being well cared for was a concern for many of the Métis parents.[15] The Oblates came close to closing the Fort Providence school in 1881 because money was so scarce. It was only when the Society for the Propagation of the Faith sent 15,000 francs that the school was saved.[16] At Fort Chipewyan, the Sisters of Charity discovered that the provisions for their first winter at the school consisted of "one sack of flour, one small barrel of sugar, five barrels of wheat, seven or eight of barley, and some potatoes."[17] For years planks suspended on trestles were the only chairs, and the nuns slept on tables and the children on the floor.[18] In 1882, the Sisters of Charity at Fort Providence argued that the students were being made to spend too much time working and not enough in class.[19] The schools had to make do without government funding: in 1875 Faraud had asked for support for his schools at Fort Providence and Fort Chipewyan, but the government declined to provide funding because there was no Treaty with the First Nations people in those regions.[20]

The first permanent Anglican boarding school in what was to become the Northwest Territories grew out of a mission that T. J. Marsh established at Hay River in 1893. He opened a small day school in his residence; with the arrival of seven students from Fort Resolution, it was redefined as a boarding school in July 1895.[21]

Following the negotiation of Treaty 8 in 1899, Indian Affairs began making per capita payments to the Hay River school.[22] It declined to make a similar payment to the Fort Providence school since it lay outside the Treaty 8 boundary.[23] The decision had nothing to do with the education provisions of the Treaty, which made no mention of residential schools. Rather it reflected the department's administrative priorities. Indian Commissioner David Laird supported the decision, saying that schools outside of the Treaty boundaries were "beyond the range of the visits and inspection of the officials of the Department, hence we have little opportunity of ascertaining the precise nature of their work."[24]

Residential schooling in the Yukon got its start in 1891 when Anglican Bishop William Bompas began boarding orphaned children, who attended the mission school he had established in the community of Forty Mile.[25] Because he focused his efforts on Métis children, he received no support from either the government or the Church Missionary Society. By 1896, four of his first six boarding students were Métis. Like others of his contemporaries, he viewed Métis children as a threat to social order if left unschooled—likely to become "the bitterest enemies and most formidable obstacles to our mission"—but having the potential to serve as cultural mediators between settlers and First Nations.[26] The small-scale boarding school closed in 1900 when Bompas moved his mission to Carcross (Caribou Crossing), also in the Yukon Territory,[27] and this eventually became the home of the first government-supported residential school in the territory.[28]

As the nineteenth century ended, certain enduring patterns had been established: a strong Catholic presence in the Mackenzie River basin, Anglican domination in the Yukon, the importance of residential schools in the ongoing competition between Catholics and Protestants, and, with the signing of Treaty 8 in 1899, the beginning of federal funding.

CHAPTER 3

Mission schools of the Northwest Territories: 1900 to 1960

At the start of the twentieth century there were only two residential schools in the North-West Territories: the Catholic Sacred Heart school at Fort Providence and the Anglican school at Hay River. The Catholics would later open St. Joseph's at Fort Resolution in 1903 and Immaculate Conception at Aklavik in 1926.[1] The Anglicans opened a school at Shingle Point, in the Yukon, which was intended for Inuit students from the Northwest Territories, in 1929.[2] The first three schools to open, Fort Providence, Hay River, and Fort Resolution, had been built without government support.[3] The Catholics drew most of their students from the Dene First Nations of the basin of the Mackenzie River, while the Anglicans recruited most successfully from the Inuit and Dene of the Mackenzie Delta. In the mid-1930s the Anglicans closed Shingle Point and Hay River, moving the students and staff to the new All Saints School that opened in Aklavik in 1936 (the Hay River school continued in operation until 1937).[4]

The mission-school era would not come to an end until the 1950s. During that decade the federal government undertook a major expansion of schooling in the North, opening day schools and a series of large and small hostels. As these new forms of residential schooling came into being, the mission-run boarding schools in the Northwest Territories closed: Fort Resolution was the first, ceasing operation in 1957, and the last one, Fort Providence, did not close until 1960.[5]

The northern mission schools were often great distances, sometimes hundreds or even thousands of kilometres, from children's home communities, and transportation was difficult and often dangerous. Children often went years without seeing their parents. Difficulties in transportation also made the northern schools more reliant on local food, which could be scarce.

Children often came to the school because a parent had died or been hospitalized. Once there, they were separated from their siblings, taught a new language and religion, fed strange foods, and given an education that bore little relevance to their culture or their future. Harsh punishments were imposed for behaviours that the children did not view as improper, and much of their time was spent at the drudgery required to support the poorly funded schools. Their surroundings were unfamiliar, and often cramped and dangerous. Students experienced a constant round of illnesses and epidemics; some were subjected to physical and sexual abuse. After a few years, they returned to their home communities, suffering from shame and humiliation.

Enrolment

Enrolment in the mission schools was always limited and most of the students stayed for only a few years, rarely advancing beyond Grade Four (or Standard 4 as it was called at the time).[6] In 1910 there were 148 students attending boarding schools in the Northwest Territories: forty-five at Fort Resolution, sixty-five at Fort Providence, and thirty-eight at Hay River.[7] One government report from 1923 said that the students generally spent between two and five years in the schools "without either holidays or a visit to their home settlement."[8]

As late as 1944 there were only 170 students attending Indian Affairs schools in the western Arctic (55 in the day schools and 115 in the residential schools). At that time there were an estimated 2,450 school-age children in the Northwest Territories.[9] By 1950, for both day and residential schools, Inuit enrolment was 210 and First Nations enrolment was 365 across the Northwest Territories.[10]

Funding

By the 1920s all the mission schools in the Northwest Territories were receiving funding from Indian Affairs if they had First Nations students. The Indian Affairs per capita allocation for the Northwest Territories boarding schools was increased from $165 to $180 in 1929. From its opening in 1926, Aklavik had an allocation of $200 per student.[11] The northern schools were subject to the same cuts in per capita rates that were imposed on the system in general during the Great Depression years of the 1930s. Per capita rates were cut by 10% in 1932 and 5% in 1933.[12] It was not until 1939 that the per capita payments returned to their 1931 levels. The next year, as a wartime cost-saving measure, the maximum number of students the government would fund at each school was reduced by 7.76%.[13] In 1945 the per capita funding for schools at Fort Resolution and Fort Providence was still only $180, and for schools at Aklavik it was $200. In effect, the schools were receiving the same rates that had prevailed more than twenty years earlier.[14]

In the case of non-First Nations students, including Inuit, an application had to be signed by the RCMP, stating that the child was a territorial resident and was "an orphan, destitute or neglected child and not eligible for admission under the *Indian*

Act."[15] Such children were eligible for funding by the Department of the Interior, which had responsibility for education in the territories.

In 1931 the Shingle Point principal asked Ottawa for a definition of "what constitutes a destitute Eskimo child."[16] The issue was of pressing importance because the local RCMP inspector believed most of the children were not destitute and had declined to sign the forms.[17] The federal government agreed to subsidize the Inuit students, but only on a temporary basis.[18] To get around the stalemate, by the end of 1932 the RCMP inspector was striking out the words "destitute or neglected" when signing the application forms of certain students.[19] In 1933 the federal policy was to pay $200 a year for the "maintenance and education of each Eskimo, destitute white or half-breed child."[20] By then, the Department of the Interior was supporting seventy-seven students at five schools: twenty-nine at Shingle Point, twenty-five at Aklavik, three at Fort Providence, four at Hay River, and sixteen at Fort Resolution.[21]

In 1923 the Department of the Interior spent $3,000 a year on education in the Northwest Territories; by 1928 the figure was $3,460.[22] In the face of constant lobbying by O. S. Finnie, director of the federal Northwest Territories and Yukon Branch, by 1931 the government grant for education in the territory was $12,787.50. The money was to be divided among eight day and residential schools.[23] In his history of Inuit administration in Canada, the anthropologist Diamond Jenness praised Finnie for attempting to force the federal government into recognizing its responsibilities to the Inuit for education, health, and welfare. Jenness believed that Canada sought to shuffle these responsibilities "on the traders and missionaries, neither of whom possessed the means to carry them out."[24] However, in a budget-cutting measure, the Northwest Territories and Yukon Branch was dissolved in 1931, Finnie was pensioned off, and most of his staff were dismissed. According to Jenness, Finnie carried with him "recollections he would gladly have forgotten. He knew full well that the schools he had been subsidizing in the Arctic were religious kindergartens that hardly deserved the names of schools."[25] At the same time, the federal government's already limited health care spending, along with that for Arctic patrols, was curtailed. Throughout the 1920s and 1930s the police would be the main instrument and image of the federal government's presence in the North.[26]

Religious rivalry and the war for the Inuit

As it had in the nineteenth century, religious rivalry drove expansion of the system. In 1902, alarmed by the Anglicans' intention to establish a school at Fort Resolution, Bishop Breynat succeeded in winning a commitment from the Sisters of Charity to provide sisters to staff a Catholic school in the community. They arrived in June of 1903. After being initially housed in a storehouse, they moved into a convent by

August, along with five First Nations students.[27] The boarding school opened with these students, whose parents were returning to the land for the winter.[28]

In 1923 the Anglicans made a proposal to the Roman Catholics under which the Anglicans would withdraw from the First Nations settlements along the Mackenzie, while the Catholics would not conduct missionary work among the Inuit.[29] The Catholics rejected these overtures and established not only a hospital but also a boarding school in Aklavik, in what one Oblate described as a war for the Inuit.[30] The Catholics, however, had difficulty recruiting Inuit students for this new school. In early 1926, the principal, Sister McQuillan, had expressed her

> confidence that our Lord will send some Eskimos to complete the decoration. It appears all the protestants here want to put in their children as boarders. Many of them naturally feel sore at our being here, but cannot help admiring our life of sacrifice. Father Superior says he is surprised at their sympathy towards us, it is altogether beyond his expectations as he dreaded the thought of coming among these protestants so bigoted.[31]

Relations became more strained that summer when the Anglican minister prohibited Inuit from visiting the Catholic convent.[32] In 1929, there were only two Inuit children in a school with an enrolment of twenty-eight.[33]

The ongoing interchurch rivalry led a frustrated O. S. Finnie to write in 1928 that "the greatest problem we have is that of creating, if possible, a division of the territory as between the Missionaries of the Church of England and those of the Church of Rome. We are all agreed that better results will be accomplished if these Missionaries work separately rather than both in the same settlements or localities."[34] In response, Minister of the Interior Charles Stewart proposed that the Anglicans cede the First Nations of the Northwest Territories to the Catholics, while the Inuit would be left to the Anglicans. Catholic Bishop Gabriel Breynat responded that while it might seem "friendly" to reach an agreement with the Anglicans, he answered to a higher power and was obliged to observe "the directives imparted to me by our ecclesiastical superior in Rome."[35]

By the late 1920s, Inuit parents were increasingly unwilling to send their children to the Anglican boarding school in distant Hay River for years at a time. In response, the Anglicans promised to build a more northerly school.[36] In 1928 they proposed turning buildings abandoned by a San Francisco trading company and the Hudson's Bay Company at Shingle Point into a residential school. A dozen Inuit children at Hay River would be transferred to the new school in addition to other children in the Shingle Point area.[37] In agreeing to provide financial support to the Shingle Point project, W. W. Cory, the territorial commissioner, noted that the federal government had also concluded that "something should be done in the way of education of the Eskimo children. The white race is now mixing with them freely and the natives must have some measure of education to enable them to better carry on their commercial pursuits with them."[38]

Shingle Point was never intended to be a permanent school. In the mid-1930s the Anglicans closed Shingle Point and Hay River, consolidating their residential school operations in Aklavik. The school they opened there in 1936 could accommodate 100 pupils. Indian Affairs had agreed to support thirty-five pupils while the government of the Northwest Territories was required to support forty-three (most of whom were expected to be Inuit).[39]

Tensions between the Anglican and Catholic principals in Aklavik ebbed and flowed. In 1941 a Mines and Resources employee sought instruction on how to handle a request signed by parents, but submitted by the Anglican bishop, seeking to have a student transferred from the Roman Catholic school in Aklavik to the Anglican school in the same community. The government employee did not know what the policy was for such transfers and feared they would "probably cause friction between the two schools."[40] In this case, an instruction was given not to approve the transfer unless there were extenuating circumstances.[41] A decade later, there were a dozen Anglican students living at the Roman Catholic school in Aklavik. In response to a query from the Anglican Church on this matter, Indian Affairs pointed out that none of these children were 'Indian,' and the department was not paying for their support.[42] In 1956, the Anglican school at Aklavik was so full that an agreement was reached for twenty-eight Anglican children to be lodged and educated at the Roman Catholic school, although they attended church at the Anglican mission.[43]

The curriculum

The educational aims of the mission schools in the North in the twentieth century remained modest. In 1939, Bishop Breynat wrote,

> I confess I do not see need for masters graduates in the north, where we keep the children a short time, just enough to teach them to read and write. Otherwise they become unfitted for the lives they are to lead. The situation is different in the south, and the Indians no longer live for hunting and fishing. I have always insisted that, in the reports of the County [sic] with the Government in Ottawa, we insist on the distinction, which must be maintained between the north and south. We can not and should not be treated the same way.[44]

Anglican Bishop Isaac Stringer took a position that was similar to Breynat's, arguing that in the Northwest Territories, First Nations students should receive just enough schooling to allow them to read and write a letter and to handle the arithmetical calculations that a trader would be required to carry out.[45]

According to its principal, A. J. Vale, the subjects taught at the Hay River school in 1907, its first year in operation, included "reading, writing, arithmetic, composition, grammar, geography, dictation, literature, history and holy scripture in English and native, both in the syllabics and in the Roman characters. The pupils make good progress in their English studies, though of necessity very slow at first, as frequently they come to us not knowing any English."[46] Class hours were "9 to 12 a.m. [sic], and from 1.30 to 3.30 p.m., and in winter from 9.30 to 12 a.m. [sic], and 1.30 to 3.30 p.m., as our daylight is very short."

The school taught no industries but, according to Vale, it aimed

> to teach the boys the outdoor work and occasionally we are able to give them lessons in carpentering, iron repairing, and in building. The girls are taught to be thorough and clean housekeepers, and also to sew, mend and knit. In short, we aim to make each child a clean, thorough, industrious and practically useful person.[47]

An Indian agent's report from Fort Resolution seventeen years later reveals little difference from the earlier Hay River curriculum:

> The girls were being taught the usual household duties of sewing and mending, cooking &c. The boys do the chores and gardening, and are also taught to make snow-shoes, do a small amount of trapping, &c. I saw samples of the work done in the class-room, and as far as I could judge, it was fairly done. Of course these children are not kept in school for very many years, and the highest standing they attain is Grade V.[48]

In 1947, territorial school inspector J. W. McKinnon reported that parents of children at Fort Resolution felt they "were not learning very much by attendance. While such statements are not uncommon wherever a school is functioning, I do feel that a good deal of such criticism could be mitigated by making the instruction in each class more practical." He also described the classrooms as "small and unhealthy." The inspector reported that the school needed a supply of basic readers. By that time there were seventy-eight residential students and forty-seven day students.[49] In that year, McKinnon was also calling for the creation of more day schools, arguing that they had a positive impact on family life.[50]

A 1952 inspection report of the Anglican school in Aklavik noted that the school was "quite short of reading material for the primary grades." There was a film projector for showing National Film Board productions, but the radio was in poor condition and the record player broken. Some rooms were not adequately lit, waste materials in the school dugout constituted "a serious fire hazard," and the playground equipment was limited to four swings.[51]

Catholic demands for Catholic education proved to be a barrier to extending vocational training to Aklavik. Bishop Joseph-Marie Trocellier rejected a 1952 proposal under which students from Immaculate Conception would receive manual training at the public day school in Aklavik. It was not proper, he wrote, for Catholic students to "attend any school from which the religious atmosphere and influence would be absent." While he recognized that the students would be taking vocational as opposed to religious instruction, he felt that they would be denied the "moral aspect of the vocational training, which cannot be inculcated into the minds of the pupils unless they are simultaneously grounded in the religious principles on which Christian ethical and moral standards are based."[52]

The schools were often understaffed. In 1954 at Fort Resolution, four teachers taught 144 students. As an inspector noted, "This is much too heavy an enrollment for four teachers, especially considering the language difficulties of the lower grade children."[53] Three years later, the Anglican school at Aklavik had four teachers and 111 students. One teacher was teaching forty-five students in Grades Two, Three, Four, and Five.[54] In 1952 the salaries for the three teachers at the Anglican school in Aklavik ranged from $80 to $85 a month. Their transportation from the South to Aklavik was paid, and at the end of four years they received six months' holiday with pay. One of the teachers lacked any professional qualifications, and the inspector concluded, "An upward revision of the salary schedule is strongly recommended if the Mission is to obtain experienced and qualified teachers."[55]

But for parents who wished to see their children educated, there were few options other than residential schools. R. A. J. Phillips, who served as the director of northern administration in the Department of Northern Affairs, provided this bleak overview of the schooling available to students in the Canadian North in 1950:

> Eight different authorities operated schools in the North. The Department of Northern Affairs provided only three classrooms. Though it paid grants to other agencies to run classes, the classroom standards were uneven. Some schools operated only four hours a day, four days a week. One teacher in three held no teaching certificate of any kind. Only 117 of the Eskimos got full-time schooling. There was no vocational education of any kind, no adult education, and no teaching for the growing ranks of hospital patients.[56]

Language

In the late nineteenth and early twentieth centuries, French was the language of instruction at the Roman Catholic boarding schools in the Northwest Territories. It could hardly have been otherwise. The vast majority of the eighty-three nuns who worked in the Mackenzie Valley from 1867 to 1919 were of francophone ancestry.[57] The same would be true of the Oblates. Into the 1940s, if they spoke a second language, it was likely to be an Aboriginal one.[58] While the Oblates had been encouraged to learn Aboriginal languages, the Sisters of Charity were neither encouraged nor given the opportunities to become fluent in the languages their students spoke. Not surprisingly, communication between pupils and teachers was difficult: both were struggling to learn a foreign language in a strange and alien context.[59] Northwest Territories school inspector J. W. McKinnon reported that as late as 1946 the classes at Fort Providence were being taught in French and that the students wrote their compositions in French. In 1950 the entire school staff was still made up of French speakers; however, they assured McKinnon that all instruction was now in English.[60] In 1956, the poet Frank Scott travelled down the Mackenzie River with Pierre Trudeau, when the future prime minister was still a relatively unknown lawyer.[61] Scott wrote a poem about their visit to the Fort Providence school:

> The gentle sister in charge,
> A Grey Nun from Montreal,
>
> Welcomed us in French.
> Priests from France, nuns from Quebec,
> Taught Slavies (who still speak Indian)
> Grades I to VIII, in broken English.[62]

The missionaries always recognized that by learning Aboriginal languages and translating religious texts into those languages they were facilitating their ability to make Aboriginal converts. To this end catechism was taught in Dene at Fort Resolution well into the 1920s.[63] Bishop Breynat campaigned, unsuccessfully, in 1935 to be allowed to introduce Aboriginal languages in the schools to ensure that they did not disappear. With more success, he also advocated training students in hunting and fishing.[64] From the students' perspective the schools often appeared to be unrelenting in their hostility to Aboriginal languages. Jane S. Charlie has strong memories of being spanked for speaking her own language while attending the Anglican All Saints School in Aklavik. Because she never learned to speak English well, she felt that other students were able to blame her for their own misdemeanours.[65] When Lillian Elias, an Inuit child, was told not to speak her own language on her arrival at the Aklavik Roman Catholic school, she fought back: "Because they didn't want me to speak it I thought to myself, 'You're not going to keep me from speaking my language,' and so I really picked right back up when I got out of there."[66] For speaking his own language at the Fort Providence school, Samuel Gargan recalled having his head forcibly submerged in a bucket of water. As a result, he said, his ears were constantly running—a problem, he said, that was never treated. "I was subject to physical pain on my hands, fingers repeatedly being whacked with a scissors, my ears were pulled, and knuckle whacked on top of the head, hair was pulled and kicked."[67]

The loss of language skills created real anxieties for the students when they returned to their home communities. Margaret Oldenburg was a researcher who travelled through northern Canada in the 1940s and 1950s, collecting botanical samples for the University of Minnesota.[68] In a 1946 letter to a colleague, she recounted that she had travelled to "Cambridge [Bay] with some girls going home from school at Aklavik and the two older ones wept most of the time because they had not seen their family in so long it was like going to strangers and they couldn't talk Eskimo adequately. Did you know that the children at the Anglican school are forbidden to talk Eskimo?"[69]

Student labour

Parents often felt the students were overworked. In 1952, a federal official reported, "During my last trip around Great Slave Lake in September and October 1951, I was told by at least three different native Indians that during their last two years at Mission Residential School they were employed continuously by the Missions without pay or other remuneration, on work projects such as cleaning hen houses, feeding cattle and maintenance projects in and about Mission establishments, instead of receiving class room instruction."[70] Each fall a barge would arrive in Aklavik loaded with logs for the school furnace. The students would form a long chain leading from the barge to the furnace room and, with the assistance of the school staff, unload the barge.[71]

Samuel Gargan was admitted to the Sacred Heart School in Fort Providence in March 1955. He was six years old and, because of an ankle injury, he had a cast on one leg. Although the cast was eventually removed, he experienced pain in that leg throughout his years at the school. Despite this he was expected to participate in all physical activities. "I would haul, stock pile, load and unload wood, chop urine and human waste from the outside toilet, wash and wax floors and clean up." He was constantly limping but not given any respite. If he complained, "I would be locked up in the boy's closet room."[72]

Proposals for training in the South

In 1925 the anthropologist Diamond Jenness recommended sending single youth between the ages of sixteen and twenty to the Halifax naval college. Jenness believed there were employment opportunities for the Inuit in navigation, mechanics, carpentry, metalwork, first aid, and telegraphy. While Jenness felt that this training "wherever possible, should be given in the north," he also felt that "any training that is of much value can only be given in the south."[73] To his lasting dismay, the project went nowhere.[74]

Some students, however, did go south for education. In 1927 A. L. Fleming, the Anglican archdeacon of the Arctic, was asked by John Ell Oudlanak (also written as

Oudlynnock) if he would take his son from Southampton Island in the Northwest Territories so he could be educated in the South.[75] Fleming noted that Oudlanak spoke very good English; along with his mother, he had travelled extensively with the cartographer and ethnologist George Comer.[76] Fleming consulted about the proposal with one of O. S. Finnie's assistants, who said that, since the Inuit were not wards of the state, there would be no problem with his "trying the experiment." Thinking that a single boy might be lonely, Fleming wrote to Oudlanak to ask that two boys be sent. With the assistance of the Hudson's Bay Company, ten-year-old Benjamin Oudlanak and Samuel Pudlutt of Kimmirut (Lake Harbour) on Baffin Island travelled to Lakefield, Ontario, where they were enrolled in the local school. Oudlanak's father made a financial contribution to his son's education, while Fleming assumed the cost of Pudlutt's schooling. Finnie had never been informed of the initiative and learned about it from the newspapers. He sought details from Fleming. In concluding his response, Fleming wrote, "The idea is not to educate these boys and send them back to the simple primitive Eskimo life, but to send them back for all practical purposes as white men."[77] The experience proved gruelling for the boys: they returned to the North after a year in which they endured influenza, pneumonia, measles, and tonsillitis.[78]

Discipline and abuse

The discipline at the schools was harsh and, for Aboriginal children, unlike anything they had previously experienced. Bill Erasmus's great-aunt attended Fort Providence school after her mother died. She lived with Erasmus when he was a young man and told him of her life at the school. One story that stuck out was the treatment given one student who regularly wet her bed. "They'd get a tub of cold water, either cold water or very, very hot water, and make her sit in it, and they would hold her down, and they could hear the girl screaming and in pain."[79]

Rita Arey's father, Arthur Furlong, attended the Anglican All Saints School in Aklavik. He told her of how he had once placed his younger brother Fred on the swing in the school playground only to find himself surrounded by older boys who wanted to pick on his brother. The two boys defended themselves until a priest broke up the melee. To Furlong's surprise, the priest then made young Fred take off his winter mittens and punch the swing's pole until his knuckles bled. This, he said, would teach him not to fight.[80]

At the Roman Catholic school at Aklavik, the older students were assigned to take care of the younger ones. Since the older students were subject to punishment if their younger charges misbehaved, Lillian Elias said that they "would make sure that we listened to them, even if they had to rough us up."[81] Far less talked about was the physical and sexual abuse. There are no court records of abuse from this period and many of the former students are no longer living. But in a statement to the Truth and Reconciliation Commission of Canada, Samuel Gargan subtly referred to this still largely unexplored issue. "The cries you heard at night was not always because of loneliness or the longing of a parents impress. Nuns knew what was going on, but chose to remain silent on it."[82]

Health and nutrition

Food was often scarce and disease and death common in the northern mission schools. Many former students recalled difficulties in adapting to new foods. Children who were used to eating raw and frozen meat had to make an even more difficult transition. The difficulties in importing southern food and the limitations of farming in the North made the northern schools more dependent on local hunters for supplies than were the schools in the South.

Farming was always chancy, but Hay River, due to its location, fared better than most. It is in the most southerly part of the Northwest Territories, and is known today as "the garden capital of the North." By the time the Hay River school closed in 1936, it had a 1.6-hectare garden capable of producing 400 bushels of potatoes and ninety bushels of other vegetables.[83] But in 1911 conditions were different. The school had two cows, one bull, three calves, and a horse, although the horse wandered off and never returned.[84] In 1929 Bishop A. L. Fleming asked the federal government to provide the Shingle Point school with a supply of pemmican (dried meat and berries). Although the church was sending its own food supplies from the South, Fleming thought that pemmican "would be much better for the students, and be more like their regular native diet."[85] Due to a shortage of hay, two farm animals had to be slaughtered in 1932.[86]

A failed hunt could bring about a crisis. The February 5, 1910, entry in the Fort Providence school journal reports, "We are rationing bread, one piece three times a day." [87] {Nous sommes à la ration pour le pain: un morceau 3 fois par jour.} The journal entry for February 18, 1917, reads, "Our hunters return empty handed. No more meat! What are we going to do?" Ten days later, hunters killed 130 caribou.[88] Despite this reprieve, food shortages arose again the following fall. In September the sisters reported that much of the meat from the previous winter had begun to spoil. The garden produced "small and few potatoes," the chickens were killed for lack of feed, and food was being rationed. By October 3, 1917, prayers were being said to St. Joseph for abundant fishing, "as our children are suffering from hunger." Ten days later fishermen brought in 8,000 fish.[89] In November 1927 Bishop Breynat telegraphed an urgent message to Ottawa, reporting that the fall fishery had failed at Fort Resolution, as had the school's potato crop. He was "fearing serious shortness of food for school and staff" and requesting permission to kill moose or buffalo if no caribou appeared by Christmas.[90]

A former Hay River residential school student recalled that in the years following the First World War, he "didn't see jam from the time I got off the boat to the time I got back on to come back down."[91] Another recalled a constant diet of fish: "They would boil it up real good until the meat falls away, the bones and scales all floating around, then mix in flour and serve it up. I won't use flour for my dogs because there's not much good in it."[92] Another former student recalled, "We had meat once a year, on Christmas day. One time they butchered a cow, hung it to bleed, and some boys rushed out when no one was looking and ripped the fat right off it. There was lots of bacon in the store-room, but it wasn't for the kids."[93] The picture painted by these former students is no different from the one that A. J. Vale, Hay River school principal from 1907 to 1927, left in his memoirs. He wrote that, due to high freight costs, "we had to try to live, as much as possible, on country produce." This was largely fish and potatoes. "Many a time we had them three times a day. No eggs, oranges or the like were to be obtained. In fact, for five years at a stretch I did not even see any and only a limited amount of canned food was put up in those days."[94]

An analysis of the Hay River diet of the 1920s undertaken in the 1970s by the anthropologist Shepard Krech concluded that

> protein intake was exceptional; vitamin A, niacin, ascorbic acid and phosphorus were present in abundance; and thiamine and riboflavin levels were adequate. However, calorie and iron intakes were very marginal. Calcium levels were extremely low. A poor fishery year would have resulted in a significant deficit of calories. A poor harvest may have produced iron deficiency and affected calcium and carbohydrate intake.[95]

An ongoing problem in the Northwest Territories in the first half of the twentieth century was the absence of medical examinations before students were admitted to school. In 1916 three children who had been recently transferred from Fort Good Hope to Fort Resolution fell ill shortly after their arrival. They had been admitted without having undergone the required medical inspection on the grounds "that they were orphans and had to be provided for in some way." Two died, leading Indian Affairs official H. J. Bury to recommend "the regulation covering the admission of children to these boarding schools be more rigidly enforced."[96]

In the fall of 1923 a typhoid outbreak at Fort Providence killed five students. The government doctor was not able to visit the school during the outbreak for lack of a boat. Writing in February, Dr. C. Bourget reported that "a few of the convalescents are so badly affected that their complete recovery is problematic." He concluded that the disease had been brought to the school by recently enrolled students, and had spread through defects in the school's drainage.[97]

A student who died at the Hay River school in 1930 had been admitted without a medical examination "owing to a lack of medical services in the north."[98] In 1931 the Shingle Point principal admitted students without a medical examination since the federally designated doctor "had not come to examine the children, although he had been repeatedly asked to so do." According to the principal, in the two-year period that the school had been in operation, the doctor had come only once during the winter—for a one-hour fly-in visit.[99]

The Northwest Territories Council was told in 1939 that it was common practice for missionaries "to bring children in to the schools and later to ask the local doctor to examine them and complete the certificate of health." In an effort to force schools to have students examined before admission, one northern doctor recommended that the government date the start of payment of the per capita from the date of the student's examination.[100]

A tour of the western Arctic in 1944 led Dr. George Wherrett, a prominent public-health physician, to conclude,

> Only in the minority of instances, however, is there a regular examination of all children on admission and no x-ray surveys are carried out. In some schools, immunization and vaccination are practised; in others, not at all. One cannot stress too strongly the importance of all these procedures ... In practically every school visited ... cases of tuberculosis develop during the term, resulting fatally.[101]

Until the end of the mission era, federal officials were not able to exercise meaningful control over the way the schools admitted students. In 1955 L. A. C. O. Hunt, a district administrator in the Northwest Territories, noted that "it would be highly desirable to scrutinize all Applications for Admission to residential schools well in advance of the entry of the child." Instead, he said, government officials were "often faced with these 'fait accompli.'" Hunt was citing a case in which Roman Catholic authorities had flown a young boy from Coppermine to Aklavik and enrolled him in the school, which Hunt believed to be already overcrowded, without government approval.[102]

This lack of inspection meant the schools were prey to regular outbreaks of infectious illness. In 1913 Sister McQuirk, principal of the Fort Providence school, reported that while student health had been improving, "we had to deplore the death of 9 of our younger pupils, this winter, by a malignant attack of influenza, which nothing could check. Their constitutions are so weak that we keep continually dosing them with iron and cod liver oil to keep them in a normal state."[103]

In September 1919, forty-seven students at Fort Providence came down with whooping cough, forcing a cancellation of classes. Poor health at the school continued into October with an outbreak of dysentery. The school journal reported on October 11 that "Samuel took his last breath"; on October 13 that "Caroline died this morning at 2 o'clock"; on October 21–22 that "Charles lost his little Jean"; and on October 29 that "this morning at one o'clock poor Isidore peacefully left for heaven."[104] The following year influenza (referred to in the records as "la grippe") broke out in August. In September typhoid fever was so severe that classes were cancelled. Two more students were dead by the end of the month.[105]

In April 1943 another flu epidemic hit the Fort Providence school. Several sisters and all the students were afflicted, leading to a cancellation of classes.[106] In early December of the next year, three-quarters of the students were struck down with whooping cough.[107] This was followed by an outbreak of mumps, keeping children out of class until the beginning of February 1945.[108] At the beginning of April 1950, twenty-six students at Fort Providence were in bed with measles.[109] Further outbreaks of measles hit the school in October 1952 and the spring of 1957.[110] An outbreak of the Asian influenza epidemic of 1958 left all the children in bed.[111]

At Fort Resolution the situation was similar. The school journal for 1903 to 1942 reports outbreaks of influenza in 1917, 1921, 1930 (twice in one year), 1932, 1933, 1936, 1937, 1940, and 1941; whooping cough in 1920 and 1941; diphtheria in 1923; chicken pox in January 1926, 1936, and 1938; diarrhea in 1926; and measles in 1935.[112] On July 25, 1920, the Fort Resolution school journal bleakly observed, "We are obliged to return to their families several children who have been weakened by illness."[113] Between December 3, 1912, and February 24, 1941, the Fort Resolution school journal recorded fifty-six deaths, including one elder, two former students, and three members of religious orders. There was an average of over two deaths a year during this twenty-year period.[114]

In nearby Hay River, the run of epidemics was similar to Fort Resolution's. There were outbreaks of measles in 1902,[115] diphtheria in 1917,[116] influenza in 1930,[117] chicken pox and influenza in 1935,[118] and influenza again in 1936.[119] A 1906 an outbreak of measles had reduced attendance at Hay River to thirty boarding students and eleven day students, with very irregular attendance, according to the principal.[120] Bishop Isaac Stringer wrote in June 1910, "No deaths have occurred in the school during the last two years—up to March 1910 which is the date of the latest news received."[121] In later years, the school had a very heavy death toll. At least thirty-two deaths were reported between 1917 and 1937; ten of these occurred in 1930.[122] The situation was sufficiently dire that Duncan Campbell Scott threatened to close the school.[123]

In 1936 Shingle Point teacher Mabel Jones wrote of how Mabel Martin fell ill on December 11, 1935, and died a month and a half later:

> My heart just aches for her parents Laura and Martin in Aklavik. They had
> given her into my keeping two years and a half ago when I was leaving A. [likely
> Aklavik] for the School and I was so looking forward to their joy at seeing her so
> well and so big this summer when the school moved. She was not a strong child
> and for that reason has seemed nearer to me than any of the others. Seldom
> was she out of my mind and heart day or night. I had hoped she had outgrown

her weakness after her recovery last winter after hemorrhage. But God will otherwise, and despite all that could be done, her heart weakened and finally stopped, tired out. I feel so lonely without her.

Jones comforted herself with the thought that "we must ever remember that our real work here is to prepare these children to answer gladly the voice of Jesus when He calls."[124]

Children were subject to accidental death as well. On August 24, 1939, Joseph Sakaluk, a ten-year-old Inuit boy attending the Roman Catholic school in Aklavik, slipped away and sought to join a group of older boys who had been allowed to go for a walk. He was not warmly dressed, the weather was wet, the terrain full of muskeg. He never caught up with the boys. When he was discovered missing, the Mounted Police organized a search. In the afternoon of the following day, his body was found in a thick willow grove—one the searchers had passed by on several occasions. He had died of a combination of exhaustion and exposure.[125]

Building conditions

Health and safety were closely linked to building conditions. In some cases, the schools were simply too crowded. Mabel Jones gave this description of life in the Shingle Point school in 1933:

> Our school is more crowded than ever this year. I have twenty girls in the space which last year seemed overfull with eighteen. But they are such nice children that now I would be sorry to part with any one of them. Now that Walter will not be with us again, the boys' house will contain the same as last year, namely sixteen when Moses returns. This however is one too many for present accommodations and an extra bunk is to be provided this year. You know of course that the children sleep two in a bed and I have three girls in one at present, and in the boys' House the same situation will obtain when the sixteen are there.[126]

A 1911 inspection of the Hay River school concluded that the first two floors of the school building were "not all that might be desired" since the "ceilings of the first two stories are low, the lighting is insufficient and ventilation poor." The third floor was seen as having "extremely good" lighting and ventilation and higher ceilings.[127] A new school was built in 1917,[128] but by 1924 it was in a state of collapse since the sediment deposit it was built on was caving in. Walls were bulging out, the floors were no longer level, doors and windows no longer fit their frames, and the chimneys were on the verge of falling down.[129] To address these issues, a wing of the school was removed, renovated, and reopened as a federal hospital, a short distance from the school.[130] By 1934 it was recognized that the Hay River school was overcrowded, hard to supply with food or medical attention, and lacking a good water supply. These problems led Indian Affairs to support the relocation of the school to a larger facility in Aklavik, about a thousand kilometres farther north.[131]

The Roman Catholic school at Aklavik was short forty desks in 1931.[132] Two years later the same school was so lacking in supplies and basic furnishings that twenty-eight students were sleeping on the floor.[133] In response to the principal's request, the government authorized the purchase of two dozen additional beds.[134]

Clean water and proper sanitation were critical to maintaining student health. An engineer's report on the Fort Resolution school in 1938 concluded that the water from Great Slave Lake "used in the school for all purposes without any boiling" was dangerous due to the possibility of the lake's being polluted. The open-pit privies were "in bad conditions, poorly lighted, unscreened, with dirty seats and floors. Many flies were noted in the vicinity."[135] In 1945 the Indian agent J. H. Riopel judged the toilets at Fort Resolution to be "unfit and unsanitary."[136]

By the 1940s the school buildings were all in need of repair. The Fort Resolution school was described in 1947 as "outdated, dilapidated, and a potential fire hazard."[137] Six years later a new report concluded that the schools at Fort Resolution and Fort Providence were "substandard with respect to size, shape, lighting, and ventilation."[138] A report the following year described Fort Resolution as "badly out of date and ... in fact, a fire hazard."[139]

Fires

There were close brushes with fire at the Anglican Hay River school: the henhouse burned down in 1907,[140] the laundry caught fire in 1931, the roof in 1935.[141] In August 1943, fire destroyed the boys' wash house at the Fort Providence school.[142] The Fort Resolution school was nearly destroyed by fire when the plant that produced the acetylene gas used to light the school exploded in early 1936.[143] Although there were no fatalities, two people were badly burned.[144] Fires broke out at Fort Resolution in 1923, 1929, and 1933. In these cases there was no loss of life. However, in 1924 sparks from a garbage fire set the dress of a girl named Yvette Walters on fire. She later died from the burns.[145]

Parental resistance: "The children are living in hell"

Aboriginal parents in the North were not necessarily opposed to their children attending school, but they were not happy about being separated from them for years at a time. They also came to question the benefit of the schooling the children received in mission schools. Mounted Police Inspector S. T. Wood noted in 1922 that Inuit children sent to the Hay River school were obliged to stay for "periods of four to five years. Owing to the great distance, the parents cannot see their children during the period, and are generally adverse [sic] to sending their children to the school." To overcome this problem, the Inuit offered to build a school and pay for a teacher if the school were located on the coast.[146] In response to one such proposal, Branch Director O. S. Finnie recommended establishing a government school in an Inuit community. The Northwest Territories Council, however, preferred to leave all schooling initiatives in church hands.[147]

For its part, Indian Affairs viewed the northern mission schools essentially as homes for orphans and neglected children. In 1921 Indian Affairs Secretary J. D. McLean gave this instruction to the Fort Simpson Indian agent, T. W. Harris: "Impress upon all the Indians in your agency the necessity of sending children, especially orphan and neglected children, to school." He added that Harris should tell parents that the compulsory attendance provisions adopted the previous year were now in force. This was in fact a bluff, since in his next line McLean admitted that "the Department does not desire to enforce these in outlying districts"—which meant the North.[148] Throughout the first half of the twentieth century, there were always far more school-age Aboriginal children in the northern region than there were places for them in school.

In some cases, parents took their children from the school against the wishes of the principal. In 1913, when a mother removed her daughter from the Fort Resolution school, the Mounted Police were called in and the mother surrendered the girl to the school.[149]

Students believed that if their parents interceded, their treatment at school might improve. Bill Erasmus's father was a student at Fort Resolution. He disliked the school and wanted to return home. He judged the school's disciplinary process to be cruel and unwarranted, and the food "very bad." According to the stories he told his son:

> In the fall time of the year the fish run, and they would gather these fish by the thousands, and we call them stick fish, where, where you put a stick through, through the fish, and then you hang 'em, and you can dry them, and then you preserve, they're preserved, so then you use them in the wintertime. And what has happened is if they didn't preserve them right, or if they didn't catch them right, or stockpile them, they would rot, and some of those fish were rotting, but they would still feed them to the kids, and they were forced to eat that. And he'd say they couldn't leave the table unless they ate it, and sometimes they, they'd have to stay there, you know, if someone was stubborn, or just couldn't force it down, they would make them stay all day, or however long it took to eat it.

When Erasmus's father could stand it no longer, he wrote a letter to his father asking to be brought home. Staff monitored students' mail, so he gave the letter to a friend in the local community to mail for him. Within a few months the treatment he received improved, leading him to conclude that his father had threatened to take him out of school. When the school year ended, his father came by boat to retrieve him. According to Bill Erasmus, "It was just like getting out of jail. He said, 'I never looked back. I got out of there, and that was it.'"[150]

In 1937 the Mounted Police reported that Treaty members at Fort Resolution were refusing to accept their annual payments, to protest school conditions. According to Acting Sergeant G. T. Makinson:

> The Chief complained about the R.C. Mission School, they say that the Indian children when they go to school have to work too hard. Sometimes they work sawing wood from morning until night and that a large number get sick and die. When they go to school we have them well clothed, and when they come back to us they have hardly any clothes on and are half starved. When they are at school it is like the children are living in hell, that is why we sometimes have to take our children away.[151]

In 1941 only forty-five students were enrolled in the Fort Providence Roman Catholic school, which had an authorized attendance of 100.[152] The following year the RCMP conducted a survey of school attendance in the Mackenzie District. It found that in Fort Smith and Hay River, 50% of school-age children, mostly boys, were not attending school. While the government was now making greater use of the compulsory attendance provisions of the *Indian Act*, the police acknowledged that the "Indians have devised various means of defeating the regulations."[153] Another RCMP report from that year questioned whether the force should be acting as truant officers.[154]

In 1945, when lobbying for federal support for a proposed Anglican day school at Fort McPherson, the Anglican missionary A. S. Dewdney wrote that a number of families were prepared to settle at Fort McPherson if there were a local school. These families were not willing, however, "to send their children to a residential school."[155] Their objection was not to school, but to boarding schools.

Parental opposition remained strong into the 1950s. Indian Affairs Superintendent I. F. Kirby reported in 1951 that mission schools were "very reluctant to let the school children go home for the summer holidays for fear they will not come back and if they do they may have to pay for the transportation." As a result, parents were unwilling to send their children to school. Kirby thought it was bad for parents and children not to send them home, and recommended that Indian Affairs "transport school children to and from school where they live in isolated points."[156]

In another report from that year, L. G. P. Waller, regional inspector of schools for Indian Affairs, noted, "The children who are enrolled are those available when the boat or aeroplane arrives to pick them up." Recruitment, he said, was being thwarted by the sort of parent who "withholds children who should go to school." He reported that "few if any Indian children have had continuous schooling from the age of 7 to 15 years with the result that scarcely one has passed beyond the Grade III level and many have remained at the Grade I level." Waller proposed harsh measures: the government should be taking

> all the children of school age from a designated area and retaining them at school—summer holidays excepted—until they have reached leaving age. The implementation of this policy will take time and may not be immediately successful, but it will help the parent to organize his thinking on the purpose of the school and will be the means of getting the educational results we want.

Having blamed the parents for the schools' recruitment problems, Waller commented that the school at Fort Resolution was "woefully inadequate. All of the four classrooms are substandard with respect to size, shape, lighting and ventilation."[157] By the end of the 1950s, attendance was being much more strictly enforced, to the point where overcrowding put the children at risk. By 1957, the Fort Resolution and Fort Providence schools were viewed as being so crowded that, in the opinion of a government inspector, "any additional children will produce crowding to the point of being a fire hazard."[158]

Runaways

Because the northern schools were so distant from children's home communities, running away was less common than in the South, but it did take place. For example, two young girls ran away from Fort Providence in March 1902. They were found and returned later the same day. A month later, one of the girls made a second unsuccessful attempt to escape. In the school journal, one of the nuns wrote that, while the girl appeared repentant, it was doubtful that she was sincere.[159] The following year a boy ran away from Fort Resolution on the first day of school. According to the school chronicle,

> Sister Honorine proceeded with the first article in the program of education in the North, the bathing of the children who arrive filthy teeming with vermin. It was a difficult task because bathing was unknown to them. Having cleaned one, Sister Honorine left him for a moment to fetch a clean shirt and pants. On her return, the little savage was gone, the forest called him too strongly. Fortunately, a brother had seen him and brought him back.[160]

In the summer of 1922, James Laferty attempted to return to his parents, who lived two days' journey from Fort Resolution. Several search parties failed to locate him. However, according to the school journal, "our little rascal arrived in the dormitory, alone, at 3 a.m., very weary and wet and went to bed without a word."[161] Three brothers, ages five to nine, ran away from the Fort Providence school in 1942. The boys were attempting to return to their home, unaware of the great distance they would have to travel. The Mounted Police found them and returned them to the school, charging Mines and Resources (the department with responsibility for the Indian Affairs Branch) $9.20 in costs.[162]

The student memoirs discussed in the following chapter provide a glimpse of what the children were running away from.

Aboriginal schoolchildren outside the Fort Providence school in the Northwest Territories, around 1920.
Library and Archives Canada, F. H. Kitto, Canada, Department of Indian and Northern Affairs, PA-101548.

Students at the Fort Resolution, Northwest Territories, school, around 1928. In 1913, when a mother removed her daughter from the Fort Resolution school, the North-West Mounted Police were called in and the mother surrendered the girl to the school.
Library and Archives Canada, J. F. Moran, Department of Indian and Northern Affairs, PA-102519.

On July 25, 1920, the Fort Resolution, Northwest Territories, school journal bleakly observed, "We are obliged to return to their families several children who have been weakened by illness."

Canada, Department of Interior, Library and Archives Canada, PA-042133.

The Roman Catholic school and hospital in Aklavik, Northwest Territories.

Northwest Territories Archives, N-1979-050-0042.

Residents and nuns from the Roman Catholic school at Aklavik, Northwest Territories, going for a picnic on a barge with a tugboat.
Northwest Territories Archives, N-1979-051-1191.

Inuit children often stayed at the Anglican school at Aklavik in the Northwest Territories year-round because their homes were too distant from the school.
Indian and Northern Affairs, Library and Archives Canada, Meikle, PA-101771.

Students arriving at the Anglican school at Aklavik, Northwest Territories.
General Synod Archives, Anglican Church of Canada, P9901-416.

The Anglican school in Aklavik, Northwest Territories. In 1957, the school at Aklavik had four teachers and 111 students. One teacher was teaching forty-five students in Grades Two, Three, Four, and Five.
General Synod Archives, Anglican Church of Canada, P7538-854

The Hay River school in the Northwest Territories. In his memoirs, long-serving Hay River school principal A. J. Vale wrote that at the school, no "eggs, oranges or the like were to be obtained. In fact, for five years at a stretch I did not even see any and only a limited amount of canned food was put up in those days."

General Synod Archives, Anglican Church of Canada, P75-103-S8-260.

A classroom in the Hay River, Northwest Territories, school. A Department of Mines and National Resources memorandum on education in the Northwest Territories concluded that in 1939 the standard of education in the territories was "not generally as high as in the Indian schools throughout the Provinces."

General Synod Archives, Anglican Church of Canada, P7538-136.

Bishop Isaac Stringer and students at the Dawson hostel in the Yukon Territories.
Yukon Archives, 82-332, #28.

The recreation room of the Carcross school in the Yukon Territories.
General Synod Archives, Anglican Church of Canada, P7561-110.

The Chooutla school in Carcross, Yukon Territories. School discipline was strict. In 1940, Principal H. C. Grant warned that students who stole from the school "would be laid across the classroom desk in the presence of the whole school, clad only in their night attire, and strapped on a different part of their anatomy than their hands."

General Synod Archives, Anglican Church of Canada, P7538-621.

Métis students at the Anglican hostel in Whitehorse in the Yukon Territories.
General Synod Archives, Anglican Church of Canada, P7561-219.

The Whitehorse Baptist residence in the Yukon Territories. For much of its history, the school was located in abandoned military buildings.
Yukon Archives, 80-45 #19.

CHAPTER 4

Student Life at the Mission Schools

O ne of the best sources of information on life in the mission boarding schools is the accounts written by former students. This chapter provides summaries of four such memoirs. It concludes with a summary of the testimony that was presented to the Truth and Reconciliation Commission of Canada by one former mission school student.

Alice French (Masak)

> When the doors to the school closed behind my father and me, I felt free, free at last. In school I was Alice, an Inuit girl being educated. Now, going down the steps with my father, I felt like one who had been lost, having been so long away from home, going back to a way of life I had almost forgotten.[1]

In 1937, when the Inuit girl Masak was seven years old, her mother, Sanggiak, was hospitalized with tuberculosis. Her father, Anisalouk, a trapper in the Mackenzie Delta, placed her and her younger brother, Aynounik, in the Anglican All Saints residential school in Aklavik. At the school she ceased to be Masak and became Alice— she would not hear her real name again until she returned home. When, at dinnertime on the first day of school, she saw her brother looking lost and lonesome, she walked over to comfort him, only to be ordered back into line. During the years they spent at the school, they rarely spoke, shouting out to one another only at mealtime in the segregated dining hall or in the schoolyard and playground.[2]

From the first day, life at the school was strange and invasive: on arrival students had their hair washed with coal oil to remove any vermin.[3] The day started at seven o'clock. Breakfast was monotonous: every morning porridge, molasses, bread and jam, tea.[4] For their health there were regular doses of cod liver oil.[5]

Masak enjoyed learning, but was confused by the strange animals that populated the nursery rhymes: what were sheep, cows, and pigs? What was one to make of dishes running away with spoons?[6] Students were worked hard at the school. As well as shifts in the kitchen and the student and staff dining rooms, Masak had regular shifts in the laundry, working both the washing machine and the wringer.[7]

Among her more pleasant memories were sledding down hills on pieces of frozen cardboard, berry-picking expeditions down the Mackenzie River on the school barge, raiding the principal's garden patch, and listening to other students tell scary stories in the dormitory after lights out. Some of these pleasures were risky—those caught raiding the garden were given a spanking while late-night storytellers had to stand in the corner.[8]

All the supplies from the South had to be brought in by boat down the Mackenzie River, which was frozen for much of the year. The first boat of the year brought a shipment of long-anticipated fruit and vegetables.[9] Given the short shipping season, the school depended on parents to supply the school with meat and fish.[10] Masak and the other students were provided muskrat traps. They were allowed to keep the money they raised from selling the furs, and the meat was roasted at the school.[11]

Shortly after Masak was admitted to the school, her mother died.[12] When her father remarried, he took her out of the school. In her opinion she had been well treated, but she still felt that "going down the school steps for the last time was the happiest moment of my life. I wanted to sing as we rounded the corner and lost sight of the school."[13] Missing the closeness of her family, she said her years in the school had been a period of tremendous loneliness.[14] The return to her family not only brought years of loneliness to an end, it also restored her privacy. While she had little more than a bed with curtains that could be drawn around it, she took pleasure in the private space that awaited her at her family's small house: "How good it felt to have my own bedroom after many years of living in a dormitory. I could pull the curtains around me and yet have the comfort of knowing that my family was close by."[15]

After taking her out of school, her father bought her new clothes: "No more long woolen underwear, itchy black stockings and baggy peach-coloured bloomers." Everything that reminded her of school was left behind.[16] But just as she was beginning to enjoy her freedom, she was confronted with a question about the legacy of her school experience. While leaving Aklavik, the family encountered a friend of her father's, who posed a series of troubling questions. "What," he wanted to know, "has school ever taught you except the English language, even to the point where you cannot even talk in your own tongue. Can you scrape and sew hides for clothing? Do you know how to skin the furs that are brought home? What kind of wife will you be since you must learn all these things which go into homemaking before you get married?"[17]

Despite the fact that she had been surrounded by other Inuit children, she had lost her ability to speak her own language: "We were not allowed to speak it anywhere, be it inside the school or on the school grounds and if we were caught we were punished. So, we learned to become ashamed of it and that divided us from our families."[18] Loss of language was not the only barrier the schools had created between her and her family: she could not drive a team of dogs, could not cut wood, and was squeamish about trapping. "After the first month at home, my self-confidence suffered a lot. I felt that if I had not been away from home all those things would have been taught to me during the course of growing up."[19]

Despite such experiences, Inuit families recognized the value of education. In Masak's recollection, families might send one child to boarding school "because we needed someone to be able to translate what the white man was saying about the price of fur when he was trading with us, or what the doctor said when one of us was ill."[20] When she was sixteen, Masak took a test to see if she could continue her education. She was accepted but before she could leave, her stepmother was diagnosed with tuberculosis and hospitalized. While she was disappointed at not being able to continue her education, she decided to stay with her father to look after her brother and her half-brothers and sisters.[21] In the 1950s she had come to believe her children's future depended on their receiving a good education: "I knew that I would do anything so my children would have the education I so badly wanted and did not have."[22]

Anthony Thrasher

Anthony Thrasher was born into an Inuit family in Paulatuk, Northwest Territories, in 1937. His mother died when he was four, and his father remarried and moved to Tuktoyaktuk, where he worked on *Our Lady of Lourdes*, a boat the Roman Catholics used to transport goods between missions. Anthony's older brothers had all attended Immaculate Conception, the Roman Catholic boarding school in Aklavik. When Anthony turned six, it was his turn to go.[23] "My father packed a few things for me and we walked down to the dock together to wait for the mission schooner to come in and take me to school. I remember waving to him from the railing as *The Immaculata* pulled out into the bay and headed south towards Aklavik. I was crying. I didn't want to leave him. My dad wasn't home that much, but when he was, I was always with him, watching him work, listening to his stories."[24]

When he arrived in Aklavik, the crewmen deposited him at the school. He saw the grey-habited nuns, heard their voices mix with the wind, and turned and ran. But he had no place to go. He was caught, grabbed by his hood and dragged into the school, scrubbed, checked for vermin, and put to bed.[25]

The nuns inspired a variety of emotions. For instance, there was Sister Alice Rae, "who I loved as much as my real mother." He thought Sister Bessant was nice, but "Sister Soka used a rule on our hands and Sister Gilbert was hell-on-wheels for pulling ears, brushing our mouth with lye soap and whipping us with a watch chain. I never understood how she could be so mean, and yet be so very kind at the same time."[26]

Like most of the Inuit students, Thrasher was not used to cooked food. He and the others boys used to sneak into the kitchen to steal frozen meat.[27] When the principal, Sister Kristoff, discovered their love of raw frozen meat, she would provide it to the boys on occasion. "They sometimes served us raw whitefish eggs, too. I'd come away from those meals licking my fingers, with my mouth watering for more."[28] Sometimes he was able to get a taste of country food by doing his own hunting. During a school picnic he trapped a whisky-jack. "I made a little fire, and burned the feathers off the big blue bird, then let it freeze, and ate it when it was frozen hard. It tasted like caribou liver." [29]

Even stranger than the cooked food the school served were the strict rules governing the separation of the sexes. "We were told not to play with girls, because that would also be a sin. I thought that was strange, because I had played with girls before I came to school. Now they were telling me I shouldn't touch them."[30] Once, the male and female students were caught in the school basement—which served as a root cellar—throwing potatoes at one another. They were accused of sinning, and one nun lined the boys up, read out the names of the girls they had been playing with, announced, "This is what I think of them," and spit on the ground.[31]

On another occasion, after being accused of sinning with girls in the basement (something he neither owned up to nor denied), Thrasher was strapped to a bed and whipped with a three-foot silver watch chain. "My back was bleeding but something else burned more. Shame. I was branded in my brain. The silver chain has never left my mind. Even to this day you can see the scars on my back."[32] Punishments were often humiliating: two boys caught swearing had their heads shaved and were paraded in front of the other students in dresses.[33]

There were also conflicts between the Inuit and First Nations students. The First Nations students would call the Inuit 'Muktuk huskies' (muktuk being a meal of whale skin and blubber), while the Inuit referred to the First Nations students as 'tomahawk grabbers.' "Although we were good friends with the Indians, we fought them at the same time. I think we must have been young versions of the old-timers."[34] Religion was another source of conflict. It was not uncommon for boys from Immaculate Conception to get into fights with boys from the local Anglican boarding school. "They picked on me because I was a Roman Catholic and because I was a damn Eskimo,"[35] Thrasher recalled.

Thrasher claimed that, while he was not much of a student, he was a "powerhouse for work," spending much of his time at school cutting and hauling wood or emptying the toilets, which were in a giant outhouse at the end of the playground.[36] He took little pleasure or interest in schooling, saying that while he liked to read, he could never even learn to spell "arithmetic." What he wanted to be was a trapper. "About all I enjoyed was the chance to tend my trapline with the other boys in the bushes across town after classes in the afternoon. We would go there and make an open fire, cooking our own meals and making strong black tea. Later we would take our catches of musk-rats and rabbits down to the basement and skin them."[37] When Thrasher was twelve, his father had a stroke while hauling in the anchor on *Our Lady of Lourdes* that left him half paralyzed. Thrasher was discharged from school to allow him to help support his family.

Alice Blondin-Perrin

Alice Blondin-Perrin entered the Roman Catholic residential school at Fort Resolution in the Northwest Territories at the age of four. "I was a little girl who spoke only Slavey, as my parents did. Because of that language barrier, I was hurt many times. I was pushed, slapped, yelled at and more."[38] She had grown up in a family that lived, in her words, in "the traditional Dene way, hunting, trapping, gathering, and fishing, living off the land, surviving the harshest seasons the north had to offer, as Dene have done for thousands of years."[39] Her father was skilled at making snowshoes.[40] She had warm memories of time spent on her mother's lap while she was being carefully groomed.[41] All this changed in 1952 when, at the end of a two-day plane journey from Cameron Bay, she arrived at Fort Resolution.

> At the mission entrance, there was a parlour with frosted windows all around. Three strangers met us, dressed very strangely. One was a priest. The other two were Grey Nuns. The priest was dressed in a black cassock, the nuns in dark tan habits with a stiff, black, heart-shaped lace around their faces, and black material covering their heads. They looked alien to me. I was scared, even though they smiled. They talked to us in a strange language.[42]

Alice and her sister Muriel had arrived wearing homemade clothing on which their mother had embroidered floral designs. The girls valued the garments for their warmth and the love that had gone into their creation. They never saw them again.[43] The rough washing the girls received on arrival left them in tears.[44] She and her sister were the only students at the school who spoke their northern Great Bear dialect of the Dene language, referred to by non-natives as Slavey. And while education was supposed to be in English, most often the nuns issued their orders in French. Alice said she rarely knew what she was being told, but could usually tell from a nun's tone of voice and body language that she had done something wrong.[45]

Her brother Joseph was also at the school, but because of the strict sex segregation, she was never able to communicate with him, having to satisfy her desire for a family connection by waving whenever she caught sight of him.[46] Like many residential school students, she was taught to be ashamed of her body and received limited education about the changes it would go through. "As girls, we were all to be very modest in the way we washed our bodies. We were not to look at other girls while they washed, and we were under tight scrutiny by the nuns in charge; we did not want to get into trouble."[47] When a supervisor found Alice sleeping on her side with her hands clutched between her legs, she woke the child up, demanded to know what she was doing, and insisted that she get down on her knees and pray.[48]

Even though many caribou—a traditional and favoured food source for most of the students—came near Fort Resolution, she could not recall ever eating it during all her years at the school. At times there was wood bison in the stews and she recalled enjoying it. "We ate porridge, homemade beans, and toast for breakfast every day." The only change in the diet came at Easter when they were served boiled eggs. Alice hated eggs, but came to love beans and toast.[49] When students were not in class they were usually working—either cleaning or sewing. It was difficult and tedious work. Her mistakes were subject to regular criticism, and it took her years to be able to darn properly.[50] While she bridled under the discipline that the supervisors imposed, she enjoyed much of the classroom work. However, "all the books were about white people and I used to wonder why I was brown. Of course I did not dare ask why I was different from the people in the textbooks. The characters in them all had white skin like the Grey Nuns, lived in pretty houses with white picket fences, and had a pet living with them."[51]

Other positive memories included Christmas celebrations, winter picnics, and visits to Mission Island. But these were overshadowed by the routine, the harsh discipline, and the lack of love. "There was absolutely no nurturing from the Grey Nun supervisors. There was no loving touch, only fear in my heart when they were around me."[52] In 1958 she was one of the first students to transfer from Fort Resolution to Breynat Hall, the new government-built, church-run residence in Fort Smith. The move, which brought many changes to her life, also marked the end of the mission era in northern Canadian residential schooling.

Albert Canadien

In 1952, the RCMP came to Albert Canadien's father's camp in the Northwest Territories and told him that Albert, who was born in 1945, would have to attend the Fort Providence school that fall.[53] Albert was determined to be brave when he was dropped off at school, but when his mother let go of his hand and a nun guided him into the parlour, the reality of his situation sank in. "I started crying and tried to hang onto the door frame as the Sisters pulled me away. Trying her best to soothe me, my mother kept promising she would come back and visit us soon." He spent the day with the other new boys; some were silent, others tearful, others sobbed. They were taken upstairs to the dormitory where an older boy helped them to their beds. They were told to prepare for a bath and put their clothes under their beds. Their home clothing was replaced with denim overalls.[54]

Communication was a problem from the outset because most of the new students spoke only their Dene language.[55] Once students had learned a little English, they were forbidden to speak Dene. "The Sisters who supervised us at that time spoke only French; they didn't speak English that well. As a consequence, we learned broken English from them."[56] While there were prayers in Slavey, Albert said that the priests did not pronounce the language well and "some words and phrases used in various prayers didn't make too much sense."[57]

School was strictly regimented: far different from his home life where children learned by watching and listening.[58] "The Sister's way of teaching was to pound it into you until you learned it."[59] Like young Masak in Aklavik, Albert was mystified by nursery rhymes such as "Old MacDonald," "Little Bo Peep," and "Three Blind Mice."[60] Religion was given a predominant place in the classroom, to the point that in his memoir, Canadien concluded, "I think actual education came second."[61] In particular, he realized that he had never been encouraged to question or challenge anything.[62] The boys would be asked to donate a portion of the money that their parents left with them to fund missionary work: "You never said no to a priest or to a Sister."[63]

Discipline was strict and at times humiliating: bed-wetters were stripped and made to stand in the bathtub with their wet clothes draped around their shoulders.[64] Albert recalled that when one boy acted up while playing a game similar to Simon Says, a sister grabbed him, dragged him across the floor, and kicked him. It looked as if she might kick him again, but the father superior walked in. After being told what had happened, he shook his head and left the room.[65] The boys would shine the floors with mitts on their feet, pretending they were skating. Once, while doing this, he bumped into another boy. For this misdemeanour one of the sisters hit him on the top of his hand with her keys, opening up a small cut.[66] Albert was just one of the former students who could recall being punished for whistling, which, he was told, might summon up the devil.[67]

Loneliness and lack of affection were endemic. "Sometimes I would put my head under the blankets and cry softly. I didn't want the other boys to hear me, and I especially did not want the Sisters to hear me, for fear they would think I was crying for nothing."[68] Albert was at school when his mother died of tuberculosis. A sister took him into the chapel. "Gently, she put her arm around me and held me. I looked up at her and saw tears in her eyes and I began to cry. It was the first and only time that a nun had shown any kind of sympathy to me."[69]

There was plenty of work for the students to do: Albert remembered hauling wood and working in the mission fields. "The planting took place just before we went home for the summer holidays, and the harvesting took place after we returned to the residential school in the fall. I guess you could say we were cheap labour for the mission."[70]

There were a few happy memories from Fort Providence: using donated skis on an improvised ski run by the barn, playing hockey with homemade sticks according to rules that one nun remembered from her childhood, and the movies and records that arrived at the school once it began to employ lay teachers.[71] The lay teachers also introduced Scouting at the school, purchasing uniforms for the boys with their own money. "We made bone rings for the scarves we wore with uniforms. Our Boy Scout activities were a lot of fun, and a big change from the usual routine of the residential school."[72]

The boys were also allowed to set snares and traps for rabbits. "Once Tom, Fred and I skinned a rabbit that wasn't completely frozen and cooked it over a fire we had made along the riverbank on the other side of the Mission Island. That way, no one from the residential school or the mission could see the smoke from our fire. Cooking a rabbit over the fire was nothing new to us. It sure tasted good and it was just like being back home in the bush."[73]

Angus Lennie

Angus Lennie is the son of Ernistine and Johnnie Lennie, a Métis man who worked as a trapper, carpenter, and riverboat pilot on the Mackenzie River. He recalled his childhood as happy and felt he and his siblings were well taken care of. However, for reasons he did not understand, he and his brothers and sisters were placed in the Aklavik Roman Catholic school. "From a child's eyes this was a strange environment. A huge sister met us at the door and this began my journey into Residential Schools. Walking through those doors began the split of our once happy connected family."

The boys and girls were separated, and then "our clothes were taken from us. What little money we had was taken away from us. The first thing after taking our clothes, they all gave us brush cuts and put white powder on us for lice. They gave me coveralls and a number." Then he was taken to a dormitory full of children he did not know, all crying for their homes and parents.

Failing to eat the strange food, making too much noise, or not listening could lead to a student being required to stand on a bench in the corner—a punishment that students found humiliating. Angus felt that he and his fellow students were under constant surveillance. "I learned to live in fear. Fear! To be quiet, listen and follow direction. Soon I was taught 'not to think for myself' just 'listen + do' and things would be fine." All the children longed to go home; some tried to make their way back to their families, only to be returned by the RCMP. Parental visits were eagerly anticipated—all too infrequent and short.[74]

CHAPTER 5

Education for what purpose?

Until 1946, when J. W. McKinnon was appointed territorial school inspector, none of the schools in the Northwest Territories were subject to regular, professional inspection; however, a variety of government officials did provide ongoing commentary on them. Following a journey through northern Alberta and the Mackenzie region of the Northwest Territories in 1908, federal Treaty inspector H. A. Conroy wrote, "As for the schools, in my opinion they are doing good work at a very small cost of the government. It would be difficult to see how a better or cheaper policy in regard to schools could be worked out than the one in vogue."[1] Federal official F. H. Kitto wrote of the northern boarding schools in 1920, "The children are given valuable instruction in various manual arts. The girls receive training in sewing, fancy-work, cooking and general housework. The boys are instructed in building, agriculture and various other subjects. All children are taught the English language. In the senior grades of the R.C. Schools French is also taught."[2]

Again and again, however, a number of critics questioned the value of the education being provided in the schools in the Northwest Territories. A recurrent question was "For what are children being educated?" Linked to this question was whether residential schooling was making it more difficult for former students to succeed in their home communities. Both questions gave rise to a third question: "Should residential schooling be abandoned or radically modified?" If the answer to the first question was "to be Christian hunters and trappers," there was fierce disagreement over the answer to the second, as church leaders, northerners—both Aboriginal and non-Aboriginal—and government officials became increasingly skeptical about the value of boarding schools.

In the 1940s and 1950s, a number of studies and surveys of northern education led to more questioning of the benefits of residential schooling. These studies also identified community opposition to the system. Nevertheless, the policy debate was resolved, largely for economic reasons, in favour of continued residential schooling.

The debate on the effectiveness of the schools dates back to the turn of the century. In a 1900 report on education in Treaty 8 territory, Indian Affairs officer J. A. Macrae wrote that since the First Nations people had not established "collective settlement," day schools were "out of the question," leading him to conclude, "Boarding schools, therefore, must be used if education is to be attempted." Macrae wrote that it was important that schooling be introduced not just for the benefit of the First Nations but "in order that crime not spring up and peaceful conditions be disturbed."[3] For others, the key benefit of a boarding school was that it separated the parents from the children. In 1906, Hay River principal A. J. Vale said that the students were "disposed to be more teachable and less difficult to manage than an equal number of white children when they are entirely removed from all intercourse with their relatives."[4]

Other, more cautionary opinions were soon being voiced. As early as 1913, federal official H. B. Bury worried that the schools were not fitting the children for either integration or their traditional lifestyle.[5] Four years later, Bury stated that if the purpose of the schooling at Fort Providence and Fort Resolution was to allow students to "take their place with every other Canadian citizen," the period of education was too short. However, if the goal was simply to provide enough education to "fear God, honor the King, and respect the laws of the country," the schooling was probably overly long. To ensure that students would be able to make their living as their parents had, the leaving age should be lowered from fifteen to twelve. As it was, he thought that young people who did not attend school made better hunters and trappers than graduates. He wrote that a former student was more likely to become a "loafer" and a "burden" than someone who had not gone to school.[6] This identification of residential schooling as an actual barrier to success was to be made repeatedly in coming years.

Even F. H. Kitto balanced his positive assessments of the schools with this observation:

> That the results of their schooling is frequently of a transient benefit only is no
> fault of the school but rather unfortunate circumstances which allows them
> to return to their mother tribes. Hence they are discouraged by their squalid
> surroundings and usually revert to their former low standard of living. Could
> they be provided with means of earning their livelihood under better conditions
> many would no doubt prove worthy citizens.[7]

Anglican Archdeacon A. L. Fleming questioned the benefit of residential schooling in the North as early as 1928:

> The boarding school would serve to make him a less successful hunter, because
> from the age of (say) nine the boy would be taken to a boarding school, and for
> the greater part of the year would be living an artificial civilized life. The general
> result of this would be that when he was finished with school, say between the
> ages of 14 and 16, he would have failed to develop as the Eskimo boys usually do
> develop, into a successful hunter.[8]

O. S. Finnie seconded this opinion, writing that any educational work carried out by the Department of the Interior among Inuit should not be "through established Boarding Schools." He preferred to support missionaries who would travel with the Inuit, and "teach them whenever the opportunity occurs."[9]

In 1934 the federal government physician Dr. J. A. Urquhart prepared a report titled "The Education of Eskimo and Destitute Orphan White Children," which argued for a limited, low-cost approach to education in the North. Urquhart recommended that the boys leave school at the age of twelve, since they were "not going to be absorbed into industry." He thought academic training "should be limited very much to the original 'Three R's', and manual training, carried out as much as possible with the idea of making the schools more industrial than they are at the present." By twelve, he thought, boys should be "back home with their fathers, and learning to trap by travelling with them on the trapping line and actually under the father's supervision." The girls should be kept until they were fifteen and had learned to "sew, cook, and perform the ordinary duties of a housewife." Urquhart believed that the only way the children could "throw off" tuberculosis infection was through "a regular regime with regard to work, play, and sleep, and also must have regular meals of good, plain food, and this is only possible in a residential school. The value of this latter fact, can, I think, scarcely be overestimated."[10] Urquhart's views were given considerable weight and presented to a meeting of the Northwest Territories Council in October 1934.[11] In the end, the council decided to address the school-leaving age issue on a case-by-case basis. According to the council minutes, Harold McGill, head of the Indian Affairs Branch, said, "If boys in purely hunting and trapping districts were kept in school to 16 years of age or longer, the result was that they knew nothing about the only vocation left open to them." He also felt that "there was a natural tendency on the part of the Missions to retain children as long as possible." Therefore the question of whether a student was ready for dismissal was one that needed to "be broached in a careful manner."[12]

A. E. Porsild of the Dominion Lands Administration prepared a sharp indictment of the mission schools in 1934. When boys left the schools, they had "not been taught how to hunt and trap or how to travel and, as a future provider for a family are vastly inferior to the youths that have not been to school." In opposing mission schools, he pointed out that the state had taken over responsibility for educating Inuit in Alaska and Greenland, while in Sweden and Norway, the state provided education to the Sami (the Lapps). In all cases, he said, day schools and the use of itinerant teachers had been found to be preferable to residential schools. He also thought that the state schools had enjoyed more success than Canada's mission schools.[13]

Diamond Jenness, who by 1934 was working for the federal government, was at odds with those who thought the only future for Aboriginal people lay in a return to hunting and trapping. He recommended that young Inuit boys be sent to Churchill, Manitoba. There, they would be placed under the authority of the port's chief engineer and trained in carpentry, motor mechanics, navigation, and telegraphy. Government hospitals in the North would be required to train at least one Inuit girl a year in nursing. He estimated the annual cost of this program as $3,400. His proposal linked a healthy and growing Inuit population to Canada's strategic interests, noting that the Inuit were in decline—having fallen from at least 24,100 at "contact" (a date he did not define) to 7,103 in 1929. If the trend continued, the Inuit would leave Victoria Island, King William Island, Boothia Peninsula, and possibly the east end of Baffin Island. If this were to happen, Canada would "lose her strongest claim to sovereignty over the northern archipelago, a sovereignty that may be extremely valuable in the year to come for air communication" (emphasis in original). His notion was that the Inuit could be used to assert Canadian sovereignty in their own lands. As Jenness noted, "No Europeans will willingly colonize Baffin Island, the northern shores of Hudson Bay, or the Arctic coast from Melville Peninsula westward."[14]

Mary McCabe taught in the Mackenzie Valley during the 1920s and 1930s, where she had the opportunity to observe that "when Mission school pupils return home their lot is not always an easy one as they are expected to return to their old way of living—cutting wood, tanning skins, packing water, driving dogs, etc., and many other things they do not learn at school. They must begin again; it takes time and they sometimes are open to ridicule by their ignorant people."[15]

In addition to the exceptionally long distances northern children had to travel to go to residential schools, officials were also aware of the substandard education northern children were receiving. A Mines and Resources memorandum on education in the Northwest Territories, written in 1939, concluded that the standard of education was "not generally as high as in the Indian schools throughout the Provinces." The mission boarding schools were not subject to any requirement to employ "teachers having provincial qualifications." Nor was there any regular inspection of the schools. It was, however, thought that the "small attendance of pupils in many cases would hardly justify the employment of professional teachers." The memorandum also concluded that the school system did not meet the needs of the growing non-Aboriginal population.[16] In short, the system was not preparing students for a return to their traditional ways of life, nor was it preparing them for anything else.

In 1942 the quality of education came under both internal and external attack. In that year O. S. Finnie's son, Richard Finnie, published *Canada Moves North*, a book that was based on his work as a writer, photographer, and filmmaker in the North.[17] Finnie drew attention to the government's neglect of the North, concluding, "No serious attempt is being made by the Northwest Territories Administration to study the problems of the Indians and Eskimos. In fact, there is no specialist on the Ottawa staff to keep in intimate touch with them."[18] Because the government was unwilling to invest in education, "the Anglican and Catholic churches continue to operate their schools and hospitals with financial assistance from the Government. They compete with each other not only to save souls but to increase revenue."[19] In such an atmosphere, religious instruction and prayers dominated the curriculum.

> Practically everything else they are taught in the schools that may be useful to them they could learn better from their own people while living normal out-of-door lives. The 'domestic arts' which the girls are taught are either those things they would automatically learn if they were at home—such as sewing—or are things which will be useless to them later—such as baking cakes and pies. The 'manual training' of the boys may range from tending fish nets and cutting wood for the mission to painting in water colors and weaving mats in raffia.[20]

From these schools, the children "return to their families unfitted for the lives they must lead."[21]

An RCMP official also voiced the opinion that the former students of residential schools were no better off than those young people who had not gone to school. In response, Indian Affairs education official R. A. Hoey asked the school principals to provide him with a summary of their course of study and quality of education.[22] At Fort Resolution, Sister S. Lapointe rejected the insinuation in the police report that "indifferent ability to reading, writing, etc. on the part of our pupils is due to the course of study or the inefficiency of the teachers." She pointed out that the white students who attended the school did well when they were sent out of the territory to study at higher grades. Aboriginal students, she wrote, often entered school at a late age and had to "learn, what is to them, a foreign language," before they could proceed with their studies. Many students were twelve or thirteen when they entered boarding school in the North and, according to Lapointe, few aside from orphans stayed more than three or four years. "One can readily understand, therefore, how these pupils in a very short time forget the elementary lessons learned by them during their brief sojourn in school." Turning to Hoey's request for information, she said that "reading, writing, arithmetic, and personal hygiene are really the only subjects taught," although senior students might get a little history and geography. Little could be done, she wrote, in the way of providing practical training when the students spent such a short time in the schools. The girls might be taught to sew, mend, cook, and clean, but it was "difficult, if not impossible, to organize manual training for boys."[23]

Sister E. Kristoff, principal of the Roman Catholic school at Aklavik, wrote:

> Our course of study is really confined to reading, writing, and arithmetic, as is judged best by the officials of the Department at Ottawa. Geography and History are on the programme merely as reading lessons, short essays in composition and memory training for a few more advanced pupils who remain their five years in the school. We also give half an hour a day for teaching religion and half an hour three days a week for vocal music.

She took issue with the RCMP criticism:

Not being dependent on education for earning his living, it is only natural that the Indian boy appreciates less its benefit, but however, in most cases, after having spent his five years in the school, he can keep his own accounts and write letters better than many white trappers of this country who have had more schooling outside than the Indian boy receives in this country.[24]

H. S. Shepherd, the principal of the Anglican school at Aklavik, responded that the "greater part of the time spent in the classroom is devoted" to teaching reading, writing and arithmetic. "Most of the children who attend our school stay only for three years, and in most cases I do not encourage them to remain longer."[25]

As a part of the Canadian Social Science Research Council's 1944 study of the Canadian Arctic, Manitoba school inspector Andrew Moore examined the educational facilities in the western Arctic. Limited by his having travelled through the region in the summer, when the schools were not in session, Moore's report depended heavily on what he was told as opposed to what he observed. He said that many of the people he encountered said:

1) that the Indian boys when they return to their native bands after four or five years of such schooling are not nearly as competent as trappers or in general in their natural environment as boys who never left the bands; and

2) that the boys who attended the white man's school are neither good Indians nor good whites. Some old-timers claimed that the most unscrupulous and unreliable among the Indians were those boys who had attended the white man's schools.[26]

The churches' response to these charges was that while the graduates might not initially be as skilled at trapping as those who did not go to school, within a few years they were more efficient trappers.[27] The missionaries claimed that some students did not return to their bands but enjoyed success elsewhere as trappers, guides, boat crewmen, and interpreters. Finally, they said that those who did not turn out well got all the publicity.[28]

Moore visited all four residential schools along the Mackenzie, noting that the buildings were superior to the average rural or small-town school. The premises were cleaner and better repaired than many Prairie schools and the heating and sanitation were equal to those of Prairie schools. The libraries and reading material were well below Prairie standards, as was the general standard of instruction. There were only two fully qualified teachers in the Northwest Territories residential schools, both at the Anglican school in Aklavik. The educational level of the rest of the teachers was between Grade Eight and Grade Ten.[29] He noted that the "living conditions and the general environment in the North West Territories do not tend to attract the best type of teachers unless they are fired by missionary or religious zeal and of these there is an insufficient supply even at present under church auspices."[30]

The search for alternatives

At the time of Andrew Moore's investigation, the *Northwest Territories Act* provided for the establishment of a department of education and school boards in the territory but none had been established. The first public school in the Northwest Territories opened in Fort Smith in 1939 and was followed by one in Yellowknife in 1941.[31] At the start of the Second World War, there were 5,000 people living in the Yukon and 9,000 in the Northwest Territories. The war temporarily brought 40,000 people north. When they left, there were new highways and many abandoned military buildings.[32] The United States military had a strong presence in the Canadian North during this period. Many American officers and civilians were shocked by the degree of poverty and poor health among the Aboriginal population. Their repeated and increasingly public questioning as to why the Inuit in particular had not been protected from exploitation and provided with education and health care became a diplomatic embarrassment, to the extent that the Canadian government lodged a complaint with the United States military attaché.[33]

Stung by the criticism, by the mid-1940s federal officials were casting about for northern educational strategies. In the spring of 1944, R. A. Gibson, the deputy commissioner of the Northwest Territories, distributed a British Colonial Office pamphlet titled "Mass Education in African Society" to senior department officials, noting that "there are some ideas in this that should be considered when we are studying our education problem in the Northwest Territories."[34] One official, W. F. Lothian, politely noted that while the conditions in Africa and the territories were dissimilar, there were a few ideas that might be applicable.[35] P. D. Baird of the Northwest Territories and Yukon Affairs Bureau was less polite, declaring that "African society is quite incomparable with Eskimo society." More tellingly, he noted that on the "vast subcommittee" that had prepared the Colonial Office pamphlet, "there is not a single African." Since Canadian Inuit education policy was being drafted under exactly the same conditions, he closed his letter by maintaining, "We must get Eskimo counsel on Eskimo affairs and the sooner the better."[36] His call for Inuit participation in the planning of northern education went unheeded.

Residential schooling: "An easy and relatively inexpensive way out"

The first major federal government educational initiative in the Northwest Territories was the appointment of an inspector of schools for the Mackenzie District in 1946. The following year the Education Section was created as part of the Mines and Resources Department's Development Services Branch.[37] In June 1947 the Northwest Territories

Council, which was still run out of Ottawa and made up of southerners, established a Special Education Committee made up of Northwest Territories Commissioner Hugh Keenleyside, Deputy Commissioner Roy Gibson, and R. A. Hoey from Indian Affairs.[38] The committee oversaw a general expansion of northern schools. From 1948 to 1954, a combined total of twenty-five day schools and hospitals were established in the Northwest Territories and northern Québec. Included in this number were nine Indian Affairs schools.[39]

The committee commissioned a series of studies on education—few of which favoured residential schooling. Andrew Moore's 1944 report called for the development of what he described as a middle-of-the-way curriculum, "one which is not too academic and which includes suitable occupational courses and activities together with adequate instruction in health and hygiene," and that innovative ways be found to take "suitable white man's education" to the community.[40] This would include using schools as community centres where health, education, and welfare services could be provided; having a teacher and nurse who could accompany Inuit families on their summer hunts inland; and establishing a travelling school barge to operate on Great Slave Lake, serving both children and adults.[41] He also advocated compulsory attendance and a requirement that all teachers have, as a minimum, first-class professional certificates and a year of special training, and be hired as civil servants.[42]

Two years after Moore carried out his survey of the western Arctic, J. G. Wright, of the Bureau of Northwest Territories and Yukon Affairs, prepared a report on education in the eastern Arctic. The only residential schools in the eastern Arctic were the two schools at Fort George on the eastern coast of James Bay. In preparing the report, he consulted with the Roman Catholic Father François-Xavier Fafard about education on the west coast of Hudson Bay. Fafard informed him that most of the families in the Chesterfield region were Roman Catholic. While Fafard favoured the establishment of religious schools, Wright reported that the priest was also satisfied with the work being done by day schools in that region (two at Eskimo Point, two at Baker Lake, one at Mistake Bay, and one at Chesterfield) and did "not seem to be enthusiastic about starting a residential school."

There is no evidence in Wright's report that he consulted with any Aboriginal people. The missionaries he spoke with advocated church schools, while the lay people tended to favour government schools. In either case, he reported, "practically all agree that any education given should be provided in the north and that it would be a grave mistake to transport native children any distance from their homes for education since they rapidly become unfitted for the native way of life."

The consensus on the education of the Inuit was, Wright concluded, that it should "equip him to meet changing conditions in the north but should not make him discontented." This would involve teaching English, arithmetic, hygiene, and the use of technology. Pride of race should be fostered and folklore encouraged. These, he noted, "were rapidly disappearing under missionary instruction."[43]

In 1948, S. J. Bailey surveyed residents of the eastern Arctic to determine their views in regard to future educational initiatives. He reported that at Chesterfield Inlet the local school was providing only one hour of classes during the summer. "In discussing this problem, everyone agrees that the establishment of a residential school is NOT the answer as these children must remain with their parents during the winter months." Bailey reported that the "residents" seemed to favour the establishment of a day school that would operate in the summer. Any teachers hired would be sent north with no other duties for nine months than "to learn to speak the Eskimo language." It would appear the residents Bailey referred to were non-Aboriginal. The idea arose out of a "lengthy discussion" with a local physician and a Mounted Police officer, and gained the support of "Fathers [priests] from other settlements who were listening to the discussion."[44]

A similar study, conducted two years later in the western Arctic, confirmed Bailey's belief that the Inuit wanted education, but in a way that allowed families to remain together—and on the land—during the winters. On this trip he consulted with Inuit. He said they were anxious that their children be provided with some educational opportunity—if only to prevent them from being exploited by traders. Bailey wrote that everyone with whom he spoke agreed that "it should not be our educational policy to train the Eskimo children into being 'white men.' Rather they should be helped to live their own lives more successfully, which should result in better health, more prosperity, and greater happiness for them." It was recognized that the schooling provided at the mission schools was having the opposite effect. "Time and again, reference was made to children returning from the Aklavik schools, unable to speak the Eskimo language, accustomed to the soft life of the institution, unacquainted with even the most fundamental knowledge necessary for life in the igloo." Bailey also rejected a cornerstone of Canadian Aboriginal education policy: the separation of parents and children. He had been told "repeatedly throughout the trip that an Eskimo child's main education should be that training that best fits him for the life that he must eventually lead, and this can only be given to him by his parents." He said it was the parents who taught the children to build shelters, work with animals, hunt and trap, make clothing, cook and care for a home. Because Inuit families did not live at any settlement for lengthy periods, schools would have to be residential and operate from Easter to the fall.[45]

The Anglicans were also open to the idea of turning their northern residential school at Aklavik into a hostel and sending the students to a federal day school. Henry Cook, of the Missionary Society of the Church of England, wrote that such a move might create some problems in the hostel, saying it would "hasten assimilation of the native children into the Canadian scheme of things."[46] In the end the government would opt for just such an assimilationist approach in the North.

In 1952 the federal government established the Sub-Committee on Eskimo Education, chaired by J. G. Wright, chief of northern administration in Northern Affairs. The other committee members were Henry G. Cook of the Anglican Church, Father G. Laviolette from the Catholic Indian Welfare and Training Commission, R. F. Davey from Indian Affairs, Dr. H. A. Proctor from Indian Health Services, and E. N. Grantham. Despite the fact that eight years had passed since P. D. Baird had called for Inuit input in the creation of Inuit policy, there were no Inuit members on the committee. At its first meeting in the fall of 1952, it recommended that serious consideration be given to the establishment of tent hostels at Coppermine and Chesterfield Inlet. The committee also felt that "instruction should be in English. The use of the Eskimo language should not be discouraged but the use of Roman characters in writing should be encouraged."[47]

E. M. Hinds, a teacher at Port Harrison, opposed the summer school idea, telling the committee that, after a long winter, the children would far prefer to spend their summers playing outdoors than sitting in class. Instead, she advocated a system of travelling teachers who would live with the Inuit during the winters. On the question of language, she wrote that "subjects dealing with Eskimo culture should be taught in the Eskimo language, just as in Lappland subjects dealing with Lapp history and culture are taught in the Lapp language." She added, "If we are genuine in our desire to help the Eskimo we must respect his right to use and retain his own language." Educators, she felt, had a "duty to keep alive the Eskimo culture."[48]

By the spring of 1953, the Roman Catholics had decided to proceed with a more traditional residential school at Chesterfield Inlet.[49] Bishop Marc Lacroix argued that the proposed school year for the camps was too short, that the children would be difficult to control during the long days of the Arctic summer, and it would be expensive to return children to their homes in August. He favoured keeping the students in the schools from Easter to Christmas. He also wanted to replace government teachers with nuns, thus relieving the government of the need to build a teacherage. In an internal memorandum, Wright observed that accepting the Catholic proposal would "be an easy and relatively inexpensive way out."[50]

The federal government's December 1954 *Education in Canada's Northland* report drew attention to two major difficulties in expanding educational opportunity in the Northwest Territories: cost, which was dictated by the low population density and remoteness of the North; and the fact that largely nomadic Aboriginal people accounted for two-thirds of the population. The report concluded, "The residential school is perhaps the most effective way of giving children from primitive environments, experience in education along the lines of civilization leading to vocational training to fit them for occupations in the white man's economy." The report recognized that the sort of education provided in such institutions could make it difficult for students to return to life in their home communities. To help overcome this, the school year was going to be adjusted to leave children "free to travel with their parents during the hunting and trapping seasons."[51] In short, while this report acknowledged the drawbacks of residential schooling, it laid the groundwork for the expansion of such schools in the latter half of the 1950s. As a result, residential schooling would play a major role in the post-1950 education system in the Northwest Territories, even as the role of the churches declined. Although study after study had concluded residential school was inappropriate, the number of schools was increased, largely because, for the government, residential schools were "an easy and relatively inexpensive way out" of meeting its educational obligations to Aboriginal people in the North.

CHAPTER 6

The mission era in the Yukon

One of the reasons that the federal government did not include the Yukon First Nations in any Treaty-making process is that it did not believe that the territory was likely to undergo permanent non-Aboriginal settlement. Certainly when the gold rush collapsed, the population of the Yukon went into a rapid decline. Although the Yukon had an elected territorial council and a member of Parliament by 1908, real political power lay with the federal government.[1] Throughout the first half of the twentieth century, the federal commitment to the territory dwindled. The number of judges was reduced, civil servants were laid off, and jobs consolidated. In 1932 George Jeckell, the territorial comptroller, was appointed territorial commissioner. At the time he was also serving as the head of public works, the mayor of Dawson, the income tax inspector, and the registrar of land titles. He continued as a virtual one-man government until 1947.[2]

The Klondike gold rush led to the establishment of the first school in the Yukon in 1898. No system of school districts developed in the first half of the twentieth century, and by the start of the Second World War, the only public schools were in Dawson City, Mayo, and Whitehorse. The school buildings in Whitehorse were replaced in 1950 and expanded in 1954. By that year there were also schools in Swift River, Brook's Brook, Haines Junction, Kluane Lake, and Elsa Camp. Added to these were Roman Catholic private schools in Dawson and Whitehorse.[3] These schools were largely closed to Aboriginal people. For example, in the 1940s Clara Tyzya and her husband moved from Old Crow to Dawson City to give their children a chance to attend school. On arrival they discovered that their children "were not accepted in the Dawson City schools." As a result they moved to Carcross, where they found work in the Anglican residential school that their children attended.[4]

The Anglican Church took on responsibility for much of the education provided to Aboriginal people in the Yukon before the Second World War, often establishing day schools at church missions. The number of schools fluctuated wildly: in 1916 the Anglicans were operating nine such schools; fifteen years later, only two were in operation. They were dependent on government funding and the availability of missionaries and teachers, all scarce commodities. The fact that most Aboriginal people did not spend the entire year in a single location meant that in many cases the schools operated for only a few months at a time, often in the summer. Government inspectors were not impressed. A 1907 report suggested the schools were useless, while a report from 1926 questioned the value of supporting such schools. For their part, the missionaries came to pin their educational hopes on residential schools.[5]

The Anglicans, under Bishop William C. Bompas, opened a short-lived boarding school at Forty Mile Mission in the Yukon in 1891. It closed when Bompas moved his base of operation to Carcross (Caribou Crossing) in 1900, where he soon had established a boarding school that would serve as the forerunner to the Carcross residential school.[6] In 1923, the Anglicans opened a residence for Métis students attending school in Dawson City. When that hostel closed in the early 1950s, they opened a similar one in Whitehorse. The Anglicans did not face any competition during the first half of the twentieth century until a Baptist missionary opened a school in Whitehorse in 1947. During that time, residential school enrolment in the Yukon was never more than 150 students at any one time—and was often less. In the 1950s the federal government expanded residential schooling in Yukon, while allowing the residences and many of the schools to remain under church control. Furthermore, unlike those in the Northwest Territories, the old mission schools were not closed. A new Roman Catholic school was built at Lower Post on the Yukon–British Columbia border in 1951; the Carcross school was expanded in 1954. In the Yukon the mission school era continued, in diminished form, into the 1970s.

The Carcross school

In 1903 Bishop Bompas requested that the federal government fund a proposed residential school in Carcross. The request was rejected, but Bompas opened a boarding school that year, operating it out of two log shacks.[7] When Bompas died in 1906, the Reverend John Hawksley was made school principal, and the new bishop, Isaac Stringer, kept up the pressure for federal support.[8]

As in the Northwest Territories, the government was reluctant to extend residential schooling—or any form of schooling—to the Yukon. The notes of a 1909 Anglican meeting with Indian Affairs Minister Frank Oliver report him as saying, "I will not undertake in a general way to educate the Indians of the Yukon. In my judgment they can, if left as Indians, earn a better living."[9] Despite this rather forthright statement, in the spring of 1908, Indian Affairs instructed A. W. Vowell, the British Columbia Indian superintendent, and A. E. Green, the Indian Affairs inspector of the schools for that province, to investigate the need for a boarding school at Carcross.[10] They concluded that "the Boarding Schools are under the conditions prevailing, the most suitable for the education of the Indians." That education should, they felt, include "reading, writing, and arithmetic, with instruction as to housekeeping, sanitary measures and, it may be carpentry." To go beyond this "would be rather to unfit them for their condition in life."[11] By the end of the year government officials and church representatives were corresponding over plans for the school.[12]

The school at Carcross, which was named the Chooutla School, opened in 1911. It received a per capita grant of $200 and had an enrolment of thirty.[13] Angela Sidney was one of the first students to attend the school.

> When we first went over to that Chooutla school, all those kids got off the cars, horse teams—we all started running around the Chooutla school first. Oh, boy, lots of fun! We thought it was a good place we're going to stay. But that's the time we found out we couldn't even talk to our brothers! We got punished if we did. And we weren't supposed to talk Indian, Tlingit. There were three of us: my cousin Sophie and my sister Dora and me. Daisy [Jim] she never went back to school again; one year was good enough for her! She never went back. She told them about the school, I guess, and her father and mother didn't want to take her back anyway.[14]

Getting and keeping the students would be an ongoing problem. In 1912, E. E. Stockton, an inspector with the federal auditor general's office, reported that when he visited the Carcross school, parents complained that "the pupils had not been receiving sufficient nourishment, and from that cause, they were developing tubercular troubles." Stockton concluded the complaints were "well founded" since the students had not been receiving "the nourishment to which they were entitled." Although the school had a cow and hens, it was selling most of the eggs and milk they produced because, according to the principal, E. D. Evans, the "children did not care for either milk or eggs." Stockton investigated and concluded, "The children were given to understand that they could not have these things and that they must say that they did not care for them." He instructed the principal to stop selling the school's eggs and milk. He noted that the local First Nations people had been "taking their children away from the school," forcing the administration to recruit from distant communities. If the school did not improve, parents would stop sending their children to the school, he warned.[15]

Angela Sidney's father was one of those parents.

> Even then, we didn't stay there for very long, because my father took us out of school when I was ten. That was because my sister died there, so my father blamed the school because they didn't get help soon enough. He took me and Johnny out of school—Johnny was in the fourth grade then, and I was in the first. I was just going to pass that spring![16]

In the early years, medical services in the Yukon were limited. Anglican Bishop Isaac Stringer recommended that the federal government station two doctors in the territory. One at Whitehorse would have responsibility for visiting the Carcross school "in events of such serious nature that the person making the request would do so even if he were compelled to pay the full expense of the visit himself."[17] In September 1913 it was reported that "little Eunice," who had been in the Whitehorse Hospital since the previous February, had died.[18] In late 1915 Ada Roberts, a Carcross student, fell ill and was taken to the Whitehorse hospital. She died there in early January 1916.[19] There was one student death at the school in 1927.[20] In 1929, the Carcross school experienced influenza and septic pneumonia epidemics, the latter resulting in the deaths of two more students.[21]

The death of a child could turn an entire community against the school. Clara Tizya, who grew up in Rampart House near Old Crow in the northwest corner of the territory, recalled:

> In the early 1920's a girl had died at Carcross Indian Residential School and when they sent the body back, there were many rumours about the children receiving bad treatment and this scared the parents or gave them an excuse for not sending their children to school. And so for the next 25 years, no children were sent out to the Carcross Indian Residential School.[22]

In 1945 parents from Old Crow were still boycotting the school and petitioning the government for a day school.[23]

In 1931 one Carcross student died of tuberculosis in the Whitehorse hospital, while another boy, suffering from the same illness, was discharged from the school. In reporting on these events to Ottawa, John Hawksley, former principal and now Indian superintendent, pointed out that the doctor on contract to Indian Affairs had certified them both as being fit to attend the school. "It would appear that the medical examination was not as thorough as it should have been. May I suggest that the Doctors in the Department's employ should be advised to be more careful in the medical examination of prospective pupils. Admission of unfit children causes trouble and expense both to the school authorities and the Department."[24]

In 1932 the Carcross school was hit by what was termed "a mild epidemic" of influenza.[25] A July 1936 inspection of the Carcross school reported that there had been a measles epidemic at the school that spring but all the students had recovered. The inspector said that students all appeared to be "happy and contented," and the school to be "clean and sanitary, the food supplied the children is good and all well dressed."[26]

Former students had a different assessment of the food they were served. According to one,

> They starved us up there! We got one egg a year—at Easter. The rest of the time we got dog-food mush [corn meal] and skim milk. Them in the staff dining

room, though, they got bacon and eggs every day. We never saw fruit from one Christmas to the next, but they sure had it. Why some of those kids just starved to death. One year there was six of 'em right there at the school ... starved to death.[27]

The following timetable from 1913 gives some sense of the routine of the school:

6:00 The ringing of the "getting up" bell
6:30: Morning chores
7:15 Breakfast, followed by morning prayers and more chores
9:00 Junior students go to class
12:15 Dinner followed by playtime
2:00 Senior students go to class/junior students vocational training
5:30 Supper
6:00 Playtime
7:00 Evening prayers followed by lights out[28]

Staff turnover was an ongoing problem. In 1929, the principal and the teacher, the head matron, and the kitchen matron resigned. Despite this, the Carcross school could boast of the fact that two students had passed their high school entrance examination. The school inspector noted that the students were "brought up chiefly on a meat diet" and did not "thrive on a largely farinaceous [starch-rich] diet." So while he thought the school meals were wholesome, he recommended that students be served "a larger quantity of native meat."[29]

But problems soon arose again. In response to complaints from parents about the school, Indian Superintendent Hawksley travelled to Carcross in early 1931. Hawksley prefaced his report with a typical example of the colonial mind at work, reminding his superiors that "reports and rumours carried by Indians are not always reliable. Some have really wonderful imaginations and can relate a very feasible story based on the very slimmest of facts." He did acknowledge that under the previous principal the school had undergone a decline in "cleanliness, discipline, deportment of the pupils, and care of the institution generally." But he had high hopes for the new principal, H. C. M. Grant. While Hawksley thought the students were well clothed, he did admit some problems in relation to diet. He believed there was enough food, but said, "The diet is not varied enough and the pupils tire of the sameness of the meals." Furthermore, he thought the "supervision of the pupils was not all that it should have been partly due to the school being understaffed and partly to the laxity of the late Principal who certainly did not understand the nature and characteristics of the Indians."[30]

The enforcement of game regulations made it difficult for the principal to purchase moose meat in 1935. In the past the school had been allowed to purchase moose meat from any Aboriginal hunter, whether or not he had a commercial licence. By 1935, First Nations people were not being allowed to sell moose meat unless they had a $25 commercial licence. This, as an Anglican missionary representative noted, was more than "any of the Indians can afford to pay."[31]

Hawksley's confidence in the new principal, H. C. M. Grant, may have been misplaced. Eight years later Grant was put to the test by an outbreak of theft and a devastating fire. Food was stolen, as were the personal belongings of staff and school property. In addition, some students had stolen items from local residents. He responded to the thefts in 1939 with harsh discipline. The principal strapped the "culprits" and issued a warning that in the future those guilty of theft "would be laid across the classroom desk in the presence of the whole school, clad only in their night attire, and strapped on a different part of their anatomy than their hands." When the thefts continued, one boy was punished in this manner. According to the principal, "So severe was this strapping that the child had to be held down by the Head Matron and the Farm Instructor." To the principal's surprise, this did not stop the ongoing thefts. He then threatened to shave the head of any transgressor. Within days he put the threat into effect. The measure brought thieving to a halt but angered parents.[32] The fact that Grant could report this harsh punishment to Indian Affairs in 1940, forty-five years after Indian Affairs Deputy Minister Hayter Reed had ordered that "children are not to be whipped by anyone save the Principal, and even when such a course is necessary, great discretion should be used and they should not be struck on the head, or punished so severely that bodily harm might ensue," is a sign of how unregulated corporal punishment was in residential schools.[33]

In April 1939 the school building and the workshop were destroyed by fire, obliging the church to rent a number of local buildings to use as dormitories and classrooms.[34] Grant was not able to maintain the buildings in appropriate condition—in large measure due to poor funding. In September 1942, Yukon Medical Health Officer Dr. Frederick Burns declared the Carcross school buildings "unfit for use as a residential school." He called on the government to arrange suitable alternatives by October 31, 1942. Burns thought the dormitory space needed to be doubled or the enrolment cut in half.[35] He was also concerned over the number of epidemics at the school, including a recent outbreak of measles that had left one child dead. He noted it was not possible to recruit "skilled nursing personnel" under "the present living conditions."[36] The Anglican Church recognized that conditions at the school fell short "of what we would desire," but they had to be endured during the "stress and strain of war conditions."[37] In 1944 the Anglicans decided to build a temporary school without government assistance.[38] While the building was meant to be a stopgap, it was not until 1954 that Indian Affairs replaced it.[39]

The influx of servicemen brought north by the Second World War also created problems for the Carcross school. In December 1942 two American soldiers were found in bed with two students in the girls' dormitory. They were arrested and tried by court martial.[40]

By 1946 staff members were complaining about the conditions in the temporary facility. After visiting the school, H. A. Alderwood, the acting superintendent of the Anglican Indian School Administration, wrote that it was "in a very poor condition and the standard prevailing is probably the lowest of any in our care." He noted that Principal Grant was about to undertake a medical leave and was no longer able to administer the school properly. Alderwood concluded that "the lady workers were living in intolerable conditions, but the principal did not appear to see anything wrong." As a result, three of the four were resigning.[41] Another tragedy struck in 1953, when a student, Bertha Jimmy, died of leukemia.[42]

Principal Grant may have had shortcomings, but the history of the Carcross school reveals a deeper pattern over the years. A series of problems would accumulate—parents withdrawing their children, staff members quitting in even higher numbers than usual, truancy increases, and intensifying health problems. The principal would be identified as the problem, and great expectations would be placed upon his replacement, typically a younger man with a stronger sense of discipline and drive. Within a decade the deeper problems would reappear, with the solution being to once again replace the principal.

The Anglicans put their hopes in a new principal and a new school that was constructed in 1954. Shortly after the new Carcross school opened, it suffered a serious fire in the boiler room.[43] In 1956 the new principal, C. T. Stanger, was seeking to transfer out a boy who, while often "polite, well mannered, pleasant, kind and is generally a good pupil," had bullied smaller boys, stolen from other students and the school, and been convicted of truancy. During the five years the boy had been at the school, the principal said, he had tried everything: "At first I strapped him for infractions of the rules after he failed to respond to loss of privileges [sic]. Later I encouraged him to keep busy. When he had been in trouble he lost privileges [sic] but was given useful things to do to use his energies. Lately he has been punished for bad conduct, being treated with kindness only. Still no success."

The last, unsuccessful measure to shame him into improving his behaviour had been to move him into the junior dormitory.[44] A week later the boy took off in sub-zero weather with little clothing. He was found and returned to the school. A few days later he was transferred to the Whitehorse Indian Day School. According to the Indian superintendent, M. G. Jutras, "The fact that he has relatives at this school helped considerably in his adjustment."[45]

Former students whose own children were attending the school in the late 1950s did not feel that the school had improved since their student days. One told the anthropologist Richard King about his conflict with the principal:

> They didn't feed them kids so good, you know, and I used to take my girl an orange now and then or something special, and he didn't like that. He was all the time finding out things she done and punishing her for it. Then one day he really

beat her up and she ran away and came on down here. I went and told him she wasn't coming back and I was going to see the agent about how he was running things. But he apologized and said "Let's forget about the whole thing." So I did. But she never went back there no more.

In order to get his child into the local school, this father decided to take enfranchisement, giving up his status under the *Indian Act*.[46]

With its harsh climate, running away from the Carcross school was dangerous, but not unknown. On a Sunday morning in July 1932, two boys walked away from the school playground. The next morning they turned up at a railway station house fifty-two kilometres from the school. When they overheard plans being made to send them back to school, they disappeared again. The Mounted Police tracked them down eight kilometres outside of Whitehorse and arranged their return.[47] In the summer of 1947, two boys attempted to raft down the Pelly River to Dawson City. After three days they were located on the Yukon River. One of the boys had run away in the past and was expelled. The other was returned to the school.[48]

After running away from the Carcross residential school on three separate occasions, a female student was punished in 1959 by having her hair cut short. When the matter was raised by Yukon Member of Parliament Erik Nielsen, the Indian superintendent explained that the girl's hair "was not cut any shorter than it normally is when the children are admitted to the school." The superintendent reported that after speaking to the girl, the only reason he could determine for her running away was the fact that "her mother would prefer having Ruth at home, to baby-sit, and help about the house."[49]

In 1960 the government built a large Protestant residence in Whitehorse, and the older students were transferred there. Carcross became the main boarding school for First Nations students in Grades One to Three.

There was always uncertainty as to what the Carcross school was training students for. It made little sense to train Aboriginal children to farm north of the sixtieth parallel. Nor were there factories or workshops in which the students might work if they had the training. The compromise was to provide students with training that was thought to be of use to them in their home communities. Along with general carpentry, Carcross students were given lessons in hunting and fishing. As in the South, the girls were prepared for domestic work.[50] Earlier in the century, the school had produced a typeset school newsletter.[51] One former student worked as a typesetter in Whitehorse for many years while another found employment as a junior bookkeeper with a railway.[52] Another young man, though, was just as successful in a traditional career. With his father's encouragement, he quit the school and learned to hunt and fish, making a thriving living providing game to the railway, the school, and miners.[53] From the beginning, there were worries that former students would not be able to fit into their home societies. Eight years after the school opened, an Aboriginal woman from Moosehide complained to Bishop Stringer that "when they have been too long at school they won't have anything to do with us; they want to be with white people; they grow away from us."[54] In 1934 an Anglican missionary worried that the students were "potential outcasts of their own people and are not quite up to the standards of the white intellect. In other words, they are 'betwixt and between'—a condition of pitiful helplessness."[55]

One solution was to try to keep the students on as employees of the school. In 1918 Stringer was seeking Indian Affairs approval—and funding—to keep an orphan on as a labourer once he finished school and was about to turn eighteen.[56] Duncan Campbell Scott turned down the request for additional funding, saying that the government had spent $3,000 on the boy over thirteen years. If the school wanted to hire him, it would have to pay his salary out of its own budget.[57] In 1933, the Carcross principal was hoping that James Tyzya, a student from Old Crow who was going to graduate that year, would agree to work for the school as a labourer. When he turned the job down, Hawksley expressed his disappointment, saying that Tyzya was a decent lad who had benefited from his training—all of which he would lose if he returned to the "somewhat lazy life of the Old Crow Indians."[58] When Tyzya relented and agreed to stay on, Hawksley instructed the principal that if Tyzya changed his mind again, he should be told that "he will have to either pay his own fare back to Old Crow or try to get work locally."[59] In 1935 Tyzya was still on the school staff list as a labourer.[60]

The Whitehorse Baptist School

In the 1940s the possibility of employment on construction projects drew many Aboriginal people to Whitehorse,[61] where parents discovered that neither of the community's two day schools would accept Aboriginal students, creating what was seen as a growing social crisis.[62] In September 1946, the Reverend H. J. Lee, a Baptist minister and former Mounted Police officer, responded by establishing an Indian day school in the Baptist mission he had opened in Whitehorse earlier that year.[63] Lee's initiative won him considerable local support. The Whitehorse public health nurse, the Kiwanis Club, the Men's Council, and the local First Nations leader Jim Boss endorsed the school.[64] For its part, Indian Affairs was reluctant to support the project without clearance from the Anglican Church.[65] The Anglican bishop of the Yukon informed Indian Affairs that he thought the proposed school "would be of great advantage to the Indians." It was a decision the Anglicans were to come to regret.[66]

The school opened in January 1947, and by March Indian Affairs had agreed to pay for supplies and a teacher.[67] Lee eventually moved the school from his mission to an abandoned hut leased from the War Assets Corporation.[68] He then purchased a second military surplus building for use as a dormitory. The Indian Affairs assessment of the school was that it was a "very creditable effort and enjoys much local good-will."[69] In August 1947, Lee asked Indian Affairs to support boarding twenty children in the school.[70] Most of the boarding students were to come from the community of Champagne, which had no regular day school.[71] Indian Affairs, sensitive to Anglican claims to be the dominant church in the Yukon, refused to recognize the school as an official residential school. It did, however, continue to pay for supplies and, by late 1947, was paying for two teachers.[72]

By the fall of 1947, there were over forty boarders at the school, including at least a dozen non-status children.[73] As the Indian agent R. J. Meek noted, "It is possible that some of these would have the right to attend the local white school, but it is not denied that the children are not welcome there"—a convoluted way of acknowledging that the students in question were Métis and therefore were not welcome in the territory's public schools.[74] In the face of the unwillingness of Indian Affairs to subsidize these students, the Yukon Territorial Council agreed to pay $1.10 a day for each non-status child boarding at the school.[75] In September 1948, Indian Affairs agreed to provide a daily payment of ninety-five cents for every status child, fifteen cents less than the territorial government was paying for every non-status child boarding at the school. At the same time, Indian Affairs continued to maintain that the school was not "an Indian residential school."[76]

Aside from the two teachers, the school depended on the work of a volunteer director, plus a mechanic, cook, boys' supervisor, girls' supervisor, and laundress. The local Indian agent's assessment stressed that, while Lee was a Baptist, the school was run as an interdenominational institution, not a Baptist mission, and that the teachers were fully qualified.[77] In an effort to stimulate production of crafts for the tourist market, the school purchased a loom. The intent was to give lessons to both children and adults.[78] In 1949 the territorial government gave surplus tools and supplies to the school to be used in a vocational training program. Indian Affairs agreed to pay half the cost of renovating the workshop.[79] A teacher from the territorial school provided manual training for an hour and three-quarters, three times a week.[80]

Concerns about the medical screening of children arose when ten-year-old Donald Miller died in February 1951 of tubercular meningitis. The death led Indian Affairs official Philip Phelan to ask if "every possible precaution is being taken to insure that only medically fit children are being admitted to the hostel?" His suspicions had been raised by the fact that the school admission forms were being signed by a nurse, as opposed to a doctor.[81] Meek explained that the only civilian doctor in Whitehorse was not always available to examine new students. The doctor, however, had given his consent to having the school nurse, in whom he had confidence, carry out the examinations. Following Miller's death, every child at the school was given an X-ray examination.[82]

By 1950 the shortcomings of the wartime surplus buildings that Lee had acquired were becoming apparent. Lee described his school as a "serious fire hazard" and petitioned the federal government for a new building, to be run under his auspices.[83] At the same time, Indian Affairs was considering moving the Carcross school to Whitehorse. It rejected Lee's proposal, expressing concern about the fact that Lee did not have the support of a "church body."[84] In partial response to this complaint, the school was then incorporated as the Indian Baptist Mission School.[85] The question as to whether the school was a one-man show was put to the test in 1952, when Lee died following a car accident. His widow and later his brother, Earl Lee, continued to provide direction for the organization, which retained local support.[86] But neither of them could get the government to replace the increasingly dilapidated buildings. By 1954 Indian Affairs official R. F. Davey had concluded that the Baptist hostel building huts had "fallen into such disrepair that they should be abandoned."[87] At the time, the school was providing both schooling and hostel facilities to 140 First Nations and 25 "non-Indian" students.[88] Even though both the territorial government and Indian Affairs recognized the need to provide more and safer classrooms and accommodation for Aboriginal students in the Whitehorse area, nothing was done.[89]

Few students have left a record of their stay at the school. One reminiscence suggests that while Indian Affairs was not prepared to recognize the Baptist mission as an "Indian residential school," students would have found life in the school much the same as in any other northern school. Daukaly, also known as Hammond Dick, was raised in Ross River, Yukon, and in 1954 was recruited to the Whitehorse Baptist Mission School.

> We were hauled away in covered army trucks as our parents watched. It was a sad occasion. The kids were piled into the back of these trucks and taken down the South Canol Road to Whitehorse. They would pick up more students along the way and many times it was cold and there was no heat in the back of these trucks and there was no way to keep out the choking dust. My older cousins tell me that I cried half the way to Whitehorse.

At the school Daukaly "met students from far and wide. We interacted like any school age kids. We made friends, we made enemies, we made foes. We learned how to steal from the kitchen and from cellars because we were not fed enough." To keep the school heated in the winter, he and other students hauled wood from the woodpile to the school. When he was caught making a fort with wood from the woodpile, a supervisor struck him on the head with a length of firewood. For speaking his traditional language, he was sent to the principal's office. "We would be asked to roll up our sleeves and he would strap us hard as he could. We would end up with red welts all the way up our lower part of the arm."[90]

By 1954 some Anglican parents were refusing to send their children to Carcross, preferring to see them enrolled in the Whitehorse Baptist School, because they "could then visit their children whenever they come to Whitehorse." The local Indian superintendent noted that, because Carcross was "over fifty miles from Whitehorse and transportation is difficult," he found "some understanding in their action."[91] Nevertheless, the federal government sought to shift students from the Whitehorse school, which now was boarding 140 students, to the newly rebuilt Carcross school. In March 1955 the Whitehorse Baptist Indian School successfully blocked a federal government transfer of forty-four students to Carcross.[92] This was only a temporary victory. In June the government cut the school's pupilage (the number of students it would support in each school) from 140 to 80 because "of the serious fire hazard existing in the Whitehorse Indian School owing to its rambling nature and the highly inflammable materials used in its construction."[93] Lee protested the move, complaining that government officials were "endeavouring to discourage the Indian people from sending their children to our school."[94] The day after Lee wrote his letter, L. R. Shields, of the Southern Yukon Children's Aid Society, informed the Yukon superintendent of child welfare that she was not "pleased with the sanitary conditions and cleanliness at the Indian Mission School." On a recent visit she discovered that "some of the children have impetigo and diarrhoea and now one of the worker's [sic] in the orphanage has contracted infectious hepatitis."[95]

The student transfer went ahead. According to a report by an Anglican missionary society superintendent, the students who transferred from the Whitehorse Baptist school to the Carcross Anglican school were finding it "hard to adjust to the relative freedom of Chooutla. Apparently they are very strict at Lee's School—few games, no free time, etc."[96]

By this point, there was general agreement that there needed to be an expansion in educational services provided to Aboriginal people in the Yukon. The government, the Anglicans, the Catholics, and the Baptists all wanted to see new schools and residences built in Whitehorse. The Catholics wanted, and were eventually given, control over their own residence, Coudert Hall. The Anglicans wanted similar control over the Protestant residence. But as Henry Cook, the head of the Anglican Indian School Administration, noted in a letter to the bishop of the Yukon, the government could not build the Anglicans a school in Whitehorse to "replace a school begun by another group when the need was so urgent. Our church slipped badly a few years ago in allowing conditions to exist which made it possible for Lee to get a foothold."[97]

Reluctantly, the Anglicans accepted a government proposal to build a non-denominational Protestant hostel. They recognized that if they failed to accept the offer, the government would be obliged to build the Baptists a residence.[98] As for the Baptists, in 1959 Earl Lee accepted the position as the supervising principal of the new Whitehorse Hostel.[99] In 1960 the Anglican Henry Cook complained to Indian Affairs that the officials of the Baptist Mission in Whitehorse were not exhibiting "the spirit of co-operation I.A.B. [Indian Affairs Branch] expects as regards the placing of Indian pupils in the Yukon."[100] But neither were the Anglicans. At one point, the Anglican bishop indicated:

> We are NOT willing to co-operate with the 'Baptists' UNLESS there is no other way of maintaining contact with our native children whom we have been caring for over a long period of time. One of the difficulties of any co-operation with the 'Baptists' is that they are not, so far as I know, members of any Baptist Federation nor are they members of the Canadian or World Council of Churches. They are simply a sect.[101]

While the Anglicans did not win this battle, they did succeed in having the federal government agree to have all Protestant students in Grades One to Three educated at the Carcross school. This prompted the Baptists to keep their Whitehorse school and residence in operation for younger students.[102] However, Indian Affairs refused to provide funding for this initiative.[103] It would appear that the conflict between the Anglicans and the Baptists undermined Lee's tenure as head of Yukon Hall, as the new Whitehorse non-denominational residence was called. Four months after it opened, the federal government had to appoint a new officer-in-charge. It chose a man who was neither Baptist nor Anglican: Ivan Robson was the former principal of the Presbyterian school in Kenora, Ontario.[104] By 1962 Lee was working for Indian Affairs in British Columbia.[105]

The opening of the hostels in Whitehorse marked the beginning of the end of the missionary period in the Yukon. Students from the Yukon continued to attend Carcross school until 1969, and the Catholic Lower Post, British Columbia, school until 1975.[106] (The post-1960 history of those schools is covered in the next section of this volume.) However, from the 1960s onward it was governments, first federal and then territorial, rather than churches that determined the future of residential schooling in the Yukon.

The missionary period in northern residential school history stretched back to the 1850s. It was characterized from the beginning to the end by fierce inter-denominational conflict. Because governments had been reluctant to provide any sort of educational services to Aboriginal people in the North, the impact of the missionary schools was restricted. They were largely limited to the Mackenzie Valley and portions of the Yukon Territory. The overriding goal of the schools was the conversion and religious education of the students: little consistency or clarity existed as to any other educational goals. Indeed, concerns were often raised that young people who had *not* gone to school but had been raised by their families were better prepared for life in the North. As in southern schools, discipline was harsh and the diet limited, and living conditions were often precarious. By the 1950s, the federal government had decided to replace the mission schools—most of which were in serious disrepair—with a series of government-run hostels and day schools. The missionary era would give way to a new administrative regime in coming years.

Bureaucrats replace missionaries: Residential schooling in the North after 1950

Introduction

Before the 1950s there was little in the way of formal education for Aboriginal people in any part of the Canadian North. What did exist had been created by missionaries. Small residential schools operated in Carcross and Whitehorse in the Yukon, in three communities in the Mackenzie River Valley in the western Northwest Territories, and in small communities along the shore of Labrador. These mission schools had long histories: the Catholic school in Fort Providence was founded in 1867, and the Moravians' educational activity in Labrador dated back to the late eighteenth century.

In the 1950s, in the wake of significant oil and mineral finds in the Northwest Territories, the federal government sought to assert its political authority over the Canadian North. A significant element in this assertion was the establishment of a series of student hostels and associated day schools. These changes marked the end of the mission period of residential schooling in the North, and the dawn of an age of governmental control.

The federal government chose to employ this residential school model in the North at the same time that it was committed to closing its southern residential schools. By this time, the government was also well aware of the many problems associated with residential schooling. The student experience of residential schooling in the North resembled that of Aboriginal students in all other parts of the country. Students were separated, often by great distances, from family, language, community, and culture. The education they received failed to prepare them to succeed either in the wage economy or in a return to life on the land. The students were not adequately supervised, were placed at risk at a vulnerable point in their lives, were subject to bullying, and, most seriously, were easy targets for sexual predators.

The pace and impact of this change varied across the North. In areas such as the Yukon and the Mackenzie Valley region of the western Northwest Territories, there was considerable continuity between the new policies and the old. New institutions were being constructed, but while they were owned by the government, church officials retained responsibility for the day-to-day management of the facilities. Most of the children who went to these schools were likely to be the children of parents who had attended residential school themselves.[1]

The situation was very different in the eastern Arctic and northern Québec (contemporary Nunavut and Nunavik). In these regions, the introduction of residential schooling was part of a series of dramatic and traumatic changes. This was in the homeland of most of Canada's Inuit population. The hostel and school system was imposed on them with no consultation, by people who did not speak their language. Few parents had any experience of schools, and the residences were often located thousands of kilometres from their homes. They had no opportunity to see where their children would be living or to keep in contact with them once they left. The building of a series of small hostels in communities in the eastern Arctic and northern Québec hastened the process by which the Inuit shifted from a world of close to one thousand migratory communities to inhabiting fewer than one hundred year-round settlements. Government planners had expected that families would place their children in the hostels and still spend part of the year on the land themselves. Instead, families settled in communities year-round to be near their children. Other government policies, particularly those related to family allowances, housing, and health care, accelerated this process.[2]

For the Inuit students who were sent out of their home regions, almost every aspect of life was different and strange—and all too often traumatic. At the same time, the region was dealing with the impact of a widespread tuberculosis epidemic. A third of the Inuit population is thought to have been infected with tuberculosis in the 1950s. A common form of treatment was removal to sanatoria in southern Canada: in 1956 the largest concentration of Inuit people in the entire country was the 332 Inuit in the Mountain Sanatorium in Hamilton, Ontario. In that year over 1,500 Inuit were undergoing often lengthy treatment for tuberculosis.[3] In Labrador (contemporary Nunatsiavut) the federal government sought to avoid responsibility for Aboriginal people. As a result, it did not extend the hostel and day school model in this region. The Newfoundland government also neglected the region. As a result, the missionary era of residential schooling continued into the 1970s in Labrador.

There are two distinct periods to the era of governmental control in most of northern Canada. Before 1969, the federal government oversaw the educational system for Aboriginal people in the Yukon, the Northwest Territories, and Arctic Québec. It was then that the hostel and day school system was established. During this period, the Yukon and the Northwest Territories were governed by southerners who had been appointed by the federal government. In 1969 much of the responsibility for Aboriginal education was transferred to the territorial governments. In northern Québec during the 1970s, responsibility for education was transferred to an Aboriginal school board as a result of the 1975 James Bay Agreement. Local control of education in communities with large Aboriginal populations contributed to the eventual demise of residential schooling in the post-1969 era.

CHAPTER 7

The federal government rethinks its northern policy

Two factors distinguish the federal government's residential school policy for Inuit and northern First Nations people from earlier residential school policies in the South. The first was the relatively late start and rapid implementation of these schools. It was not until 1955 that the federal government took the lead in developing an extensive residential school program in the North. Before this time the federal government had limited itself to providing some financial aid to church-run residential schools. In the 1950s there were eight such church-run schools: four along the Mackenzie River in the Northwest Territories, one in Carcross and two in Whitehorse in the Yukon, and one in Lower Post in northern British Columbia. The second distinguishing feature of this policy was the dramatic increase in the number of Inuit children in residential institutions. As late as 1949, only 111 Inuit were receiving full-time schooling in the North. Twelve were attending a federal day school in Kuujjuaq (Fort Chimo) in northern Québec, eight were at the Anglican residential school at Fort George, Québec, and ninety-one were at the two residential schools in Aklavik, Northwest Territories.[1]

Before the 1940s northern Canada remained relatively unimportant to the federal government's principal goal of expanding and protecting the Canadian state. While Hudson's Bay Company personnel, Anglican and Catholic missionaries, and a few interested scientists and explorers had visited and lived in the North since the late nineteenth century, the government's main representatives in the North before the Second World War were members of the Royal Canadian Mounted Police (RCMP).[2] The government had no concrete policy about how the vast region north of the sixtieth parallel (from the Yukon to northern Québec) should be governed and administered. This lack of policy meant that unlike Aboriginal peoples in most of Canada, northern Aboriginal peoples received little attention and assistance from Ottawa before the 1940s.[3] In the 1930s the federal government refused to accept any responsibility for the welfare of Inuit in Québec, arguing that since they were not "Indians," they were a provincial responsibility. In 1939 the Supreme Court of Canada resolved this issue in favour of Québec, ruling that Inuit were "Indians" and that therefore, under the *British*

North America Act, their well-being throughout the country was a responsibility of the federal government.[4]

The combination of the Second World War and the Cold War changed Canada's role in the North. Following the attack on Pearl Harbor in 1941, the American military created a system of airfields connecting Edmonton to Alaska. This was followed by the construction of the Alaska Highway between northern British Columbia and Alaska, via the Yukon Territory. Completed in two years, this road, like the fur trade routes of the nineteenth century, brought both new opportunities and new stresses, including disease, to northern Aboriginal populations.[5] The American military also had a presence in the eastern Arctic. During the early 1940s, American forces built and maintained airfields or weather stations at a variety of northern locations including Kuujjuaq, Iqaluit (Frobisher Bay), Churchill, and Coral Harbour (on Southampton Island). The Canadian military had limited involvement in or control over these American projects.[6] The United States also funded the construction of the Canadian Oil Pipeline (commonly referred to as the Canol Pipeline). After tremendous cost overruns the pipeline was closed in 1945, thirteen months after it opened. Its legacy was a scarred and littered landscape.[7] In line with its pre-war northern policy, the Canadian government seemed uninterested in regulating American intrusion into the North. The American presence continued after the end of the war. As the tensions of the Cold War increased, the Americans, with Canadian help, repositioned their defence systems in the North. Instead of bolstering defences in the western Arctic, military strategists turned their attention to defending southern Canada and the United States from air attacks originating in the Soviet Union via the North Pole. Between 1945 and the 1950s, the American and Canadian militaries built a series of weather stations and air defence stations in the North. More significantly, beginning in 1955, three lines of radar stations were constructed, the Distant Early Warning system being the most significant. Known as the DEW Line, and stretching from Alaska across northern Canada to Greenland, those radar stations became sites of contact between the Inuit and the relatively isolated military personnel.[8]

The increased military presence in the North pushed the Canadian government to recognize its responsibility to the Inuit. As a federal government report observed in 1955, the war brought the problems of the northern peoples more "forcefully to the attention of the Government and of the country as a whole."[9] These concerns for the Inuit, along with Canada's growing concern for military defence and its interest in the natural resources of the North, led to a wave of postwar government activity. The symbolic start of this new era of bureaucratic control was Prime Minister Louis St. Laurent's announcement in 1953 that his government would create, for the first time, a government department, Northern Affairs and National Resources, under the direction of Jean Lesage. The department was charged with creating a coherent and consciously centralized policy to modernize the North and its people.

Politically the North was, in essence, an internal Canadian colony. In the Northwest Territories, for example, executive power was vested in a southern-based commissioner appointed by Ottawa who, between 1921 and 1963, was the deputy minister of the federal department that administered federally owned natural resources. Over the years these were the departments of the Interior (1921 to 1936), Mines and Resources (1936 to 1945), Resources and Development (1945 to 1953), and Northern Affairs and National Resources (1953 to 1966). The commissioner was a powerful departmental official and the territorial staff were his direct subordinates. The commissioner presided over the Council of the Northwest Territories.

Until 1951 the council members were all federal government appointees, drawn from the upper ranks of the federal civil service. Their meetings were held in Ottawa. In 1951 the government allowed for the election of three councillors from constituencies in the Mackenzie River Valley. The government continued to appoint the remaining five council members. Further elective seats were added in 1966, including the first members for Inuit constituencies. Administrative and legislative functions were slowly being transferred from Ottawa to the North: in the western Arctic, a small administrative office in Fort Smith (1921) and a town council in Yellowknife (1940) added a thin layer of local government, and eventually the seat of government moved from Ottawa to Yellowknife in 1967, although the head of government of the Northwest Territories was still an appointed commissioner, with his deputy commissioner, and two assistant commissioners, both former RCMP officers. The year 1975 was the last in which appointed members sat in the Legislative Assembly. However, the appointed commissioner still held on to the key executive functions of the territory— government, finance, and personnel—until the mid-1980s. These gradual changes followed the move of the government from Ottawa to Yellowknife in 1967. Even today the Northwest Territories is still in the transition phase of assuming control from the federal government of its own non-renewable resources. Nunavut still does not have full authority over its natural resources.

The Yukon was also governed for many decades by an appointed commissioner and a council that contained a mix of appointed and elected members. The equivalent of a territorial cabinet was established in 1969, but the majority of members were appointed members of the council. It was not until 1979, when the Yukon introduced political parties into its territorial governance model (replacing the no-party consensus system that still exists in the Northwest Territories and Nunavut), that the commissioner's role was transformed into one similar to that of a provincial lieutenant-governor, and the first majority party in the legislature was granted authority to form the territorial cabinet.[10]

A new policy for the Northwest Territories

The change in policy for the North, particularly for the Northwest Territories, was heralded in a series of articles between the spring of 1953 and the spring of 1955 in the *Beaver*, a magazine published by the Hudson's Bay Company. Because the government presence in the eastern Arctic, the homeland of most of Canada's Inuit, had been limited up to that point, these articles highlighted the differing opinions about the degree to which Inuit should undergo cultural change.[11] Featuring work by anthropologists, missionaries, and fur traders, and concluding with an article by Jean Lesage himself, the series presented case studies on "the dilemma confronting western man in his dealings with primitive peoples," each of which was designed to "contribute to the discussion at present taking place in this country involving the fast moving developments in Canada's own northland."[12] The series reveals that there was significant tension among these writers about the fate of "primitive" peoples, and the Inuit in particular, in the face of the expanding frontier of modernity. Although all contributors agreed that "primitive" peoples, as they were then described, inevitably changed during their interactions with modern societies and economies, and that this change was generally a positive development, there was considerable disagreement about the degree to which such groups could or should be allowed to retain their cultural practices and their cultural identity.

In general the anthropologists writing in the series, including Margaret Mead in an article on the South Pacific, argued that the integration of "primitive people" into modern society needed to be rapid and complete. For Mead and others like her, the "primitive culture" and identification with that culture should and would be completely absorbed by the "dominant" modern culture, through intermarriage, government education schemes, or participation in the modern economy.[13]

Donald Marsh, the Anglican Bishop of the Arctic, explained that what the government needed to do in the North was create a system of education that would "provide the Eskimos with an education whereby they may be prepared to meet the white man's ways, and at the same time be able to live in [a] native fashion."[14]

In the last article in the series, Jean Lesage attempted to balance the need to modernize the North with the value of protecting Inuit culture. Lesage had spent the summer of 1954 visiting the North, assessing the desirability of extending education to the Inuit and First Nations in the region and the possible ways of doing so.[15]

There were three central themes in Lesage's article. First, it was for the benefit of both the Inuit and the Canadian nation that the North and the Inuit become integrated into modern Canada. "The objective of Government policy is relatively easy to define," he wrote; "it is to give the Eskimos the same rights, privileges, opportunities, and responsibilities as all other Canadians; in short, to enable them to share fully the national life of Canada."[16] He dismissed the "sentimentalists" who argued that the "Eskimo be left alone lest he be spoiled."[17] Modernity could not be stopped: "It is pointless to consider whether the Eskimo was happier before the white man came, for the white man has come and time cannot be reversed."[18] Given the inevitability of these changes, Lesage argued, it was the government's responsibility to help the Inuit "climb the ladder of civilization."[19] This project to modernize the Inuit and the North would not be a one-way process. Canada too, he argued, would reap the rewards of bringing modernity to the North: the re-educated Inuit would be a major asset to Canada's northern expansion. "The development of these lands," he explained, required "the assistance of their oldest residents."[20]

Second, modernizing the Inuit did not mean cultural assimilation. Lesage sought to modernize the Inuit while letting them retain their cultural identity and their cultural practices as Inuit. He argued that Inuit families should be told that adopting new technologies and sending their children to school would not "mean the loss of the identity of the Eskimos' culture."[21] Lesage even argued that the delivery of these changes should rely, to some degree, on consultations with the Inuit themselves and, following the example of Greenland and Alaska, should place some decision-making powers in the hands of Inuit leaders.[22] The overall thrust of Lesage's proposal was to bring the Inuit into a modern Canada, while keeping their cultural identity intact: "The Eskimos do not have to be made over into white men," Lesage explained.[23]

Third, the article explained, the government would use three main vehicles, education, health care, and a "sound economy," to integrate the North and the Inuit into Canadian modernity.[24] In real terms this meant setting up and staffing southern-style hospitals in the North, creating new economic opportunities that would supplement what he saw as a dangerous dependence on the trade of white fox fur, and erecting schools.[25] In discussing schooling, Lesage was somewhat vague on his exact goals. He wrote that there should be government schools near established populations; however, most importantly, he dismissed boarding or residential-style schools as inappropriate. "Boarding schools," he wrote, "entail long separation both from parents and from the traditional ways of life, and can result in a student returning home ill fitted for the life he must lead."[26] Instead of residential schooling, Lesage suggested the government might experiment with the use of "itinerant instruction," featuring a teacher moving from camp to camp, supplemented by some kind of instruction using radios.[27]

The 1955 annual report of the Department of Northern Affairs and National Resources repeated many of the observations and arguments from Lesage's *Beaver* article.[28] Like the article, the report emphasized the need to modernize how the Inuit economy operated; it explained the moral and economic imperative for Canada to act in the North (the government must "transform Canada's Eskimo from a financial liability to a national asset"); and it emphasized that any changes brought to the Inuit should allow them to retain their cultural identity ("some of these new means need not significantly affect their traditional way of life").[29] The only major difference between the report and the article was over the policy for education. Unlike the magazine article, the government report explained that "hostels" must be used to deliver education in the North.

Echoing Lesage's phrase in the *Beaver*, the report recognized that "residential schools entail long separation from parents and the traditional ways of life, and can result in a student's returning home ill-fitted for that life."[30] However, in the very next paragraph, the report explained that the government had already approved a policy of using day schools and residential hostels in the North.

> The government early in 1955 approved an extensive program for the construction of schools and hostels to provide better education ... for children in the Northwest Territories. This program is designed to prepare native children—both Indian and Eskimo—to meet the changing conditions of the times and to enable them, through knowledge and training, to take advantage of new employment opportunities. Since their nomadic or semi-nomadic lives make it impossible to provide continuity in their education except at centres where residential facilities are provided, the new program includes the provision of hostels. These schools and hostels will be constructed over a six-year period and will be located mainly in the Mackenzie Valley, where the need for them is most urgent. Provision will be made for construction of day schools and hostels at Fort McPherson, Fort Smith, Fort Simpson and Aklavik ... and at Frobisher Bay.[31]

There would be two main types of schools: "day schools," teaching general education, and "vocational training schools," to teach trades.

> The schools will be attended by the Indian and Eskimo children resident in the hostels as well as by the children, of whatever race, whose homes are in the settlements. It is most important that segregation of race in education be avoided. The mingling of all children—whether Indian, Eskimo, part-blood or white—in common schools in their formation will have important social and psychological advantages in the north.

Aboriginal and non-Aboriginal students might have been allowed to mix, but Protestant and Catholic students were to be kept separate from one another in this system. Under pressure from the churches, the government agreed to require that Catholic students be taught by Catholic teachers and Protestant students be taught by Protestant teachers. At Fort Smith, where most of the students were Catholic, it was agreed that from the outset all teachers up to Grade Nine, as well as the principal, should be Catholic. At Inuvik and Fort Simpson, the schools had two separate wings, one Catholic, one Protestant.[32] Even though the teachers were federal government employees, complex rules were developed under which principals were to be of the same religion as the majority of students in a school. In large schools, vice-principals were appointed who were of the religion of the minority student group. Specialist teachers, such as science, vocational arts, or home economics teachers, were to be of the religion of the majority of students. If all the students in a class were Roman Catholic, the teacher could be a member of a religious order, wear the clothing appropriate to the order, and display religious pictures and emblems in the classroom. Catholic schoolbooks could be used where Protestant students were in the minority.[33]

Each of these schools was to have a hostel or boarding residence, built by the government but operated by the churches. Initially the residence at Yellowknife would be the exception. It was to be government-run and non-denominational.[34] The federal government had already begun to assume some responsibility for Inuit education. In 1949 it opened a school in Kuujjuaq, Québec. The following year it opened schools in the Northwest Territories in Tuktoyaktuk, Kugluktuk (Coppermine), Coral Harbour, and Kimmirut (Lake Harbour), and in Inukjuak (Port Harrison), Québec.[35] In 1955 Oblate Missionaries opened Turquetil Hall, a residence at Chesterfield Inlet on the western coast of Hudson Bay. The children attended a federal day school that was administered by the Sisters of Charity (Grey Nuns).[36]

Responsibility for the education of northern First Nations children was transferred in April 1955 from the Indian Affairs Branch to Northern Affairs and National Resources. It was argued that "this centralized direction and control will result in a uniform and more effectively planned educational system. The Indian Affairs Branch will continue to administer its educational facilities for Indian children in the Yukon Territory."[37] The most immediate result was the transfer of responsibility for the residential schools in the Northwest Territories from Indian Affairs to Northern Affairs.[38]

In coming years, the Indian Affairs Branch played a more direct role in the supervision of residential schooling in the Yukon, while Northern Affairs directed schooling in the Northwest Territories. In 1955 Indian Affairs was a branch of the Department of Citizenship and Immigration, while Northern Affairs was a branch of the Department of Northern Affairs and National Resources. With the creation of the Department of Indian Affairs and Northern Development in 1966, the two branches were brought together in a single department.[39]

By 1958 much of the new education system was starting to take shape. That year the government reported:

> School accommodation at Fort Smith was increased to 20 classrooms by the opening of a new 14-classroom federal school. A 200-pupil hostel was also opened. Federal school facilities at Fort McPherson were expanded from 3 to 6 classrooms and a new 100-pupil hostel was opened. The Hay River federal school was expanded to 9 classrooms. A new federal High and Vocational school with a staff of 15, and a 100-student hostel were opened at Yellowknife and the vocational training program previously conducted at Leduc, Alberta, was transferred there. The federal schools at Fort Simpson, Inuvik and Tuktoyaktuk were expanded from 2 to 3 classrooms. The school at Fort Good Hope was expanded from 1 to 2 classrooms. The school at Old Crow, Yukon Territory,

was taken over as a new federal school by special arrangement with the Indian Affairs Branch.[40]

The construction of two residences in Inuvik was part of a larger Northern Affairs attempt to create a planned community in the North with southern urban amenities. Aklavik, in the Mackenzie River Delta, had been a federal government administrative centre for the region. But it was flood-prone. As a result, a new community, Inuvik, was to be constructed fifty-five kilometres to the east. There was little consultation with local residents, many of whom declined to relocate to the new community. Inuvik itself developed into a physically segregated community. The above-ground "utilidor" system, which carried water and waste in insulated steel tubes, did not, for example, reach the northwestern portion of the community, where most of the Aboriginal families lived.[41]

A more piecemeal approach was reported in the eastern Arctic, where non-Aboriginal populations were smaller, the hunting and trapping economy (boosted by government transfers) was still sustaining a largely dispersed population, and putting up new buildings was challenging because of costly ocean shipping and a short construction season. According to the same 1958 report:

> In the Arctic region one-classroom federal schools were opened at Arctic Bay, Eskimo Village near Rankin Inlet, Resolute, and Spence Bay in the Northwest Territories, and at Povungnetuk [sic] in the province of Quebec. At Rankin Inlet the one-classroom mine school was replaced by a new 2-classroom federal school. The federal school at Baker Lake was enlarged to 2 classrooms. The staff of the 4-classroom school at Frobisher Bay was increased to 6. A new 2-classroom school was opened at Cambridge Bay. The school at Great Whale River was enlarged from 2 to 4 classrooms. Construction proceeded on new schools at Payne Bay and Fort Chimo in Quebec and at Eskimo Point in the Northwest Territories.[42]

These developments brought dramatic changes to people's lives, particularly in the eastern Arctic. Whereas in 1949 there were 111 Inuit children receiving full-time schooling in the North, by February 1959 the number had risen to 1,165.[43]

In 1965 the federal government was planning a further expansion of the hostel system. There were plans for the construction of 200-bed facilities in both Iqaluktuuttiaq (Cambridge Bay) and Behchoko (Fort Rae), and for 100-bed facilities in Igloolik and Pangnirtung. In addition, the government planned for a sixty-bed facility at Fort Good Hope, a forty-four-bed facility at Deline (Fort Franklin), a forty-bed facility at Uluqsaqtuua (Holman Island), and a thirty-six-bed facility at Mittimatalik (Pond Inlet).[44] None of these facilities, however, were ever constructed.

Although it spoke of day schools, hostels, and vocational training centres, the 1955 policy initiated by Lesage would lead to the creation of two distinct types of residential schooling, the "large hostel" or "hall," and the "small hostel." According to the federal government the small hostel was for "8 to twelve children of elementary school age, normally supervised by an Eskimo or Indian couple." The large hostel was to have "usually 100 or more beds, associated with large elementary or elementary-secondary schools, administered by a staff employed either by the contracting Church authorities or by the Federal Government on a continuing basis."[45]

In practice, the large hostels came to be dominated by students in higher secondary grades and in vocational programs, while the small "family-type" residences were almost all out of use by 1970. In 1967–68, Indian Affairs and Northern Development's annual report noted that the department's architectural services branch had designed "for construction at various locations" a "new standard 12-pupil hostel."[46]

As the new hostels and day schools opened, the old residential schools closed. Fort Resolution closed in 1957.[47] The two residential schools in Aklavik closed in 1959 when the Inuvik hostels opened.[48] The Fort Providence school, which had opened in 1867, closed in 1960.[49] By 1963 seven new hostels had been constructed in the western Arctic with a combined capacity of approximately 1,100.[50] The Anglicans were to administer Stringer Hall in Inuvik, Fleming Hall in Fort McPherson, and Bompas Hall in Fort Simpson. The Roman Catholics were to administer Grollier Hall in Inuvik, Lapointe Hall in Fort Simpson, and Breynat Hall in Fort Smith.[51] In addition, Turquetil Hall on Hudson Bay had a capacity of seventy students.[52] In 1964 the Churchill Vocational Centre opened with an initial capacity of 160.[53] By 1969 the boarding system in the Northwest Territories would accommodate 1,331 students.[54]

This was a significant departure from what senior bureaucrats had envisioned. Hugh Keenleyside, who became the deputy minister of Mines and Resources and commissioner of the Northwest Territories in 1947, had wished to see northern education delivered on a non-denominational basis. Church pressure on the governing Liberal Party had led to the compromise that was developed.[55]

Some federal officials, such as W. E. Winter, the superintendent of schools for the Mackenzie Region, saw the church involvement as a betrayal of principle and took a strong stand. In 1957 he wrote a lengthy letter to his superiors outlining his objections. He started out by arguing that hostels should be "a last educational resort and be intended only for children who are so neglected or isolated that schooling would otherwise be impossible." Those hostels that were established should, in his opinion, be operated by the government "and no religious distinction shown whatsoever in their operation." His preferences, though, were for the establishment of government-run secular day schools wherever possible. For those children who lived in truly isolated conditions, he recommended that, rather than sending the children to hostels, the government should hire itinerant teachers. This would allow children to "live with their parents and still be taught." He went on to oppose the decision to hire only Catholic teachers at Fort Smith, recommending that the churches be "divorced from all aspects of the organization and administration of this school." He was also opposed to the policy of establishing separate Protestant and Anglican wings for the schools in Fort Simpson and Inuvik (at the time his letter was written, Inuvik was referred to simply as East Three, indicating its location on that branch of the Mackenzie River Delta). The concluding lines of his letter were harsh. He believed that the churches "must no longer retain their crippling and demoralizing influence on the educational program of the North." If Northern Affairs did not proceed on the basis of the approach he outlined, Winter said, he could not continue in his position.[56] When the government did not change its policy, Winter resigned.[57]

The Yukon

Similar education policies were implemented in the Yukon. The territory was distinctive in the North for having a non-Aboriginal majority population, in large part because of the Klondike gold rush of the 1890s and later the wartime opening of the Alaska Highway, which connected Yukon with the South. With approximately half the territory's population living in Whitehorse, services were concentrated there, especially after it replaced Dawson City as the capital in 1953. While Aboriginal people accounted for between 25% and 30% of the territorial population, the percentage was much higher in the outlying communities and remains so today.[58]

As late as 1945 there were only six schools and fourteen teachers in the territory. They taught fewer than 450 students. During the 1940s there were two residential schools: the Anglican school at Carcross and the Baptist day school and residence in Whitehorse. In 1951, a Roman Catholic residential school opened in Lower Post, British Columbia, located on the Yukon–British Columbia border. It drew students from both northern British Columbia and the Yukon.[59]

Before 1948 the territorial government left responsibility for students with status under the *Indian Act* to Indian Affairs. Aside from the residential schools, the Anglican Church operated day schools for First Nations students in Old Crow, Moosehide, and Mayo. Similar Roman Catholic day schools operated in Snag, Burwash Landing, Carmacks, and Ross River. By 1957 First Nations students accounted for only 79 of the 1,754 students attending territorially supported schools.

In 1956, an internal Northern Affairs and National Resources memorandum on education in the Yukon noted that Indian Affairs was considering constructing a hostel in a new subdivision in Whitehorse to replace the Baptist residential school. Northern Affairs official F. E. Cunningham recommended, "The children who are to be housed in this hostel should attend either the Whitehorse Public School, or the Whitehorse Roman Catholic School. We think it of the utmost importance that there be no segregation in classrooms of Indian and non-Indian children." The memorandum further proposed that "during the next five years education in grades 9 through 12 should be provided only at Whitehorse."[60] That same year Catholic Bishop J. L. Coudert lobbied Ottawa for support in establishing a Roman Catholic hostel in Whitehorse. It was felt that students leaving the Lower Post school, which went only to Grade Eight, lacked the training they needed "to compete with their white neighbours." While living in the proposed Catholic hostel in Whitehorse, they could study at "the vocational training schools, which the government of the Yukon proposes to establish."[61]

The major change came in 1960 with the opening of two hostels in Whitehorse. Students from these hostels attended public and private (Roman Catholic) schools in Whitehorse. The Yukon Hostel housed Protestant First Nations students, while the Whitehorse Hostel (later Coudert Hall) housed Catholic First Nations students. The initial enrolment at the Yukon Hostel was 86; by the 1965–66 school year it was 109. The initial enrolment at the Whitehorse Hostel was forty-five; by the 1965–66 school year it was sixty-seven.

The opening of the two hostels in Whitehorse was coupled with the closing of the Baptist school and residence in that community. However, the Carcross and Lower Post schools remained in operation. In the 1965–66 school year, the Carcross school had 110 students in Grades One to Four, while the Lower Post school had 152 pupils in Grades One to Six. After graduating from these schools, students were transferred to either Watson Lake or Whitehorse. With the opening of new territorial-run day schools, G. R. Cameron, the commissioner for the Yukon, thought that it was only a matter of time before the Carcross school closed. The expansion of the number of territorial day schools had already led to the closure of the church-run day schools in the territory, and by 1965 there were 489 First Nations students attending territorial-run day schools (176 students would have been living in the two Whitehorse residences).[62]

While the hostels in the Northwest Territories were operated under the authority of Northern Affairs and the department stressed that they were open to all school-aged children in the territories, the Yukon hostels were under the authority of Indian Affairs and admission was more restricted. In 1961 Indian Affairs informed the Yukon Department of Welfare that it would accept up to six to ten non-Indian students, providing either the territory or Northern Affairs subsidized the spaces.[63]

By 1960 the system that had been proposed in 1955 was in place. It would be administered by the federal government for the following nine years. At the end of that period, the federal government transferred responsibility for First Nations education in the Yukon to the Yukon territorial government and responsibility for the hostels in the Northwest Territories to the Northwest Territories government. The transfer to territorial control lead to the gradual dismantling of the hostel system in the North. Most of the small hostels were no longer in operation by the 1970s. The large hostels, however, remained in place.

CHAPTER 8

The federal day schools

Large and small hostels were built near federal day schools. They were funded by the federal government, and operated in concert with the day schools. In each community, the hostel and the school were intended to form a two-part complex or campus that provided what one observer called a "total educational experience" comprising classroom learning and residence life.[1] In this model, the classroom learning would provide the theoretical lessons about modernity and life in Canada, and the hostel would make these lessons concrete. As one government-appointed expert observed of the hostel-school relationship in 1965, "A good hostel environment ... can complement the social teachings of the school and give reality to what in the school can be mere theoretical exercise [sic] in idealism."[2]

The federal day schools were a key part of the hostel program. For the most part, the federal schools emphasized two central elements: English-language training, and the values, skills, and knowledge embedded in the curriculum of southern Canadian schools. Thus, for students sitting in these classrooms, the school day was quite literally marked by exposure to the language and images of elsewhere.

Curriculum

In his 1947 presentation to the Special Joint Committee of Parliament studying the *Indian Act*, J. W. McKinnon, who had been appointed inspector of schools for the Northwest Territories in 1946, said:

> Ultimately we must have our own curriculum for the schools in the Northwest Territories. Since this area has problems that are particularly its own, we cannot meet the educational needs of its residents by adhering to curricula prepared for entirely different localities and transplanted there. So far as the Indian children are concerned, they must be educated for better living, taught how to save money, how to follow clean health habits, how to make better homes, and how to secure their livelihood other than by fishing and hunting. The aim must be to make the Indian self-supporting with an adequate standard of living.[3]

Despite this early recognition of the need for a northern curriculum, the schools continued to use southern curricula. Throughout the 1950s and 1960s there was no centralized push from officials in Ottawa to adapt curriculum in a thorough manner. While Jean Lesage and his successors continued to promise the creation of a more appropriate northern curriculum, through the period from 1955 to the 1970s, Inuit and other northern students were almost exclusively taught a curriculum developed for southern schools, and using southern materials. Between 1958 and 1965, every annual report of the Department of Northern Affairs and National Resources promised that a "special curriculum" was being "developed" for the North but explained that in the short term the department would continue to use a southern curriculum, taught in English in its northern schools.[4]

In the early 1960s, the American anthropologist Richard King taught at the Carcross, Yukon, school for a year as part of a research project. In the book that he wrote based on this experience, he noted that neither the British Columbia *Programme of Studies for Elementary Schools* nor the Yukon *Manual for Teachers* contained "any reference to Indian children or Indian schools." No teacher at the school had received any special training in how to teach Aboriginal children.[5] Record keeping was minimal.

> None of the prescribed diagnostic or achievement tests had been given to the children at any level. Indeed, the information on students' permanent record cards was scanty and confusing. Many children had completed grades with satisfactory marks, but had then been overlooked and required to repeat that grade the following year. Other children had been at the school one or two years before any card was made or any record kept of their attendance. Still others had unexplained gaps of a year in their record cards.[6]

The only record that existed for one girl, who had been in the school for eight years, was "one sheet of grade scores."[7]

Staff turnover in the schools was very high. At the Carcross school in the year that King taught, there were five teachers; only one had been at the school for more than one year.[8] Teachers had little training as to what to expect when they came north. Ivan Mouat, a long-time education official in the Northwest Territories, wrote in 1970:

> Teacher turnover is a problem in the Arctic District. Rarely a teacher stays more than two years in a settlement and many stay only one year. There have been cases where a teacher refused to leave the aircraft when it reached the isolated centre; the local school did not open until a replacement had been recruited. Some, who have not been able to endure the isolation, have had to be removed. The policy now is to send in two teachers to a new school whether the enrolment warrants it or not.[9]

Students were taught the Alberta curriculum in the Mackenzie District, the Manitoba curriculum in the Keewatin District, the Ontario curriculum in the eastern

Arctic, and the Québec Protestant curriculum in Arctic Québec (Nunavik).[10] As late as 1987, the educational consultant Roger LeFrancois told a territorial commission studying First Nations education, "The British Columbia curriculum is administered in Yukon. The orientation of the curriculum is largely urban, middle class and caucasian." Where more versatile materials and programs had been developed, they were mostly being made available in larger centres, not in those where First Nations people formed a large part of the population.[11]

The schoolbooks that the students read usually featured issues and examples more appropriate to living in a southern, urban setting. Ann Meldrum, a school principal in Kangirsuk (Payne Bay), Québec, reported in 1960 that "the only books and workbooks, in any quantity, are the Dick and Jane series."[12] Compounding this southern approach and content was the emphasis teachers placed on the connection to the British Commonwealth and monarch, and to the Canadian nation. For Inuit children, many of whom had grown up in remote camps or locations along the Distant Early Warning (DEW) Line, the focus on foreign knowledge and concepts of nationhood in the classroom was clearly out of step with their experience and background.

While Northern Affairs did little to develop a northern curriculum, it did focus on the provision of vocational training. Schools at Yellowknife and Churchill were given a special mandate to fill this need, with the former offering vocational training to Inuit and First Nations people from the western Arctic, and Churchill serving Inuit in the East and in northern Québec.[13] Among the vocational training available at Akaitcho Hall in Yellowknife were courses in building construction, full-time mechanics, heavy-duty equipment operation, home economics, and trades required for employment with the Northern Canada Power Commission Project.[14]

According to the Northern Affairs annual report for 1966–67 at the Churchill Vocational School:

> The senior boys built and completely finished a five-room house during the year, including the electrical, plumbing and heating installations. All the pupils spend one-half of their time studying the academic subjects related to their prevocational training. The laboratories for the girls' program are located in the classroom wing. The girls' program includes typing, office practice, food preparation, child care, dress-making, beauty culture and home management courses. In order to provide realistic work experience, arrangements were made through the co-operation of the Manitoba Hospital Commission and the CNIB Catering Services to have all the senior girls given on-the-job training as hospital ward aides and as food services assistants.[15]

At Inuvik, with two residences that had a total capacity of 500, vocational training was limited to home economics for girls and shop-work for boys.[16]

Attendance

Even the school year was out of step with life in the North. From 1960 the Northern Affairs policy was to vary the school year if there was agreement from local leaders, the principal, and the area administrator. As the director of the Northern Administration Branch noted, "Many of our smaller schools and some of our medium sized ones suffer seriously from poor attendance in May and June because of children accompanying parents on hunting and fishing trips for periods of up to two to three months." In Deline (Fort Franklin), in an attempt to address the issue, the school was closed in 1960 from mid-May or early June to early August. It also closed from November 4 to January 2. By 1963 it was operating on a traditional school schedule: according to the principal, it was no longer the case that entire families went on the spring hunt, while in the fall fewer boys were accompanying their fathers trapping.

However, the director wrote, it was very difficult to get families to bring their children to school immediately upon their return to the community at the end of the spring hunt. "They regard the summer months as a period of freedom and many have made it quite clear that they do not wish their children to attend school in August." It was also very hard to conduct classes during periods of near twenty-four hours of daylight, when "communities are active on a twenty-four hour basis." One year two teachers at Uluqsaqtuua (Holman Island) travelled with families on the spring hunt. At Chesterfield Inlet the holidays were from May 15 to August 15 to allow students to get home before the spring breakup.[17]

Language of instruction

English was the language of education. In 1965, in response to Catholic criticism of the prominence that English played in Inuit education, senior Northern Affairs official R. A. J. Phillips explained, "We have far too few teachers with a command of the Eskimo language to make it possible to teach the language, and we still must wait several years before there is a body of Eskimos who have had sufficient education to pursue teaching careers." It was also argued that denial of knowledge of one of the country's national languages would relegate coming generations of Inuit to second-class citizenship.[18]

In 1959 E. W. Lyall, a Hudson's Bay Company official at Taloyoak (Spence Bay) in the Northwest Territories, wrote to Northern Affairs official J. V. Jacobson on behalf of parents attending school in Inuvik.

> I believe the regulations at the School in Inuvik is that none of the children are allowed to talk, read, or write in their own language; this I think is shocking, in the first place it would be an awful crime if the Eskimo lost their very fine art of

writing, in the Second place the parents of these children would always like to hear from their Son or daughter, how will they be able to do this if they forget how to write or read in Eskimo?

I for one think there should be something done about this, as you know in 1953 I sent three of my children to the Anglican School in Aklavik. When they came home none of them could speak Eskimo at all. Two years ago I sent another of my boys to Aklavik to School he had a wonderful command of the Eskimo language and could write it fluently his mother who speaks only in Eskimo made him promise to keep writing her every chance he got, for a year he was writing her all the time, you can imagine how pleased she was in getting a letter which she could understand, but last winter he wrote her a letter in Eskimo so badly written she could not make head or tail of half the letter, on the end of his letter he wrote, "I am forgetting how to write in Eskimo now as we are only taught English." She was heart broken.

Lyall recommended that the children be provided with "a couple of lessons a week" in their own language and be required to send a letter home once a week. While it was "a very good idea of teaching the Eskimo the ways of the White man," he asked, "What is going to become of the ones who have to go back to their own land and make a living of it?"[19]

A Northern Affairs official responded that he could "well understand that the teachers at Inuvik in their attempt to familiarize the Eskimo pupils with the English language are discouraging them from speaking Eskimo at the school." He added that he disapproved of any school policy that prevented them from communicating with their parents in their own language at home. It was recommended that someone be hired to provide students with "training in the use of the Eskimo language and to ensure that they write regular letters to their home in the Eskimo language."[20] Some schools made modest efforts at providing some education in Aboriginal languages. At Chesterfield Inlet in 1959, Northern Affairs gave approval for the hiring of Rosalie Iguptak to teach syllabics at Turquetil Hall one hour a day, five days a week.[21]

Some teachers did try to adapt the English-language southern curriculum for their Inuit students. For example, a teacher at the federal day school at Taloyoak helped her students create a booklet of stories written by students about their community, and a teacher in Arctic Bay wrote and sang songs about the local landscape.[22] Even in this adapted form, however, English was the dominant language, while the form of the songs and the stories remained Euro-Canadian: songs were sung in English and accompanied by guitar, and local stories were written in English and bound in books.[23]

In 1967 the Oblate missionary J. M. Rouselière wrote that a recent visit to the North had done nothing to

dispel my impression that no place is envisaged in the schools for the Eskimo language, even if Mackenzie teachers have just received instructions to encourage native assistants to speak Eskimo to beginners. Last winter in a Pelly Bay school, I myself heard an Eskimo assistant, a young woman, tell children who were talking together: 'Don't speak Eskimo here!' ... and this was not in class time.[24]

In 1967, R. A. J. Phillips, the former director of the Northern Administration Branch, defended the schools' language policies against charges of "cultural genocide." Northern Affairs, he wrote, regarded itself as "the most effective protector of the Eskimo cultural tradition. It is prepared to use the local language in the lower grades, but as a matter both of principle and practicality it is heavily committed to English. It is a matter of principle because a liberal education can be achieved only by the use of a major language."[25]

Although many students who attended hostels said that they were allowed to speak Aboriginal languages in the hostels, there was a report in 1963 that one student from Snare Lake had had her mouth taped shut for speaking Dogrib at Grollier Hall.[26]

Margaret Leishman, who lived in both Lapointe Hall and Grollier Hall, had strong memories of students being punished for speaking Aboriginal languages.

> I excelled in school so that I didn't have to bother with them, you know, and I saw a lot of my schoolmates getting ... Whenever we spoke Slavey language, we did that all the time anyways, but when we were caught, you know, they were punished for speaking their language, because we need to communicate with each other. Because in our tradition, that's how we communicate to meet our needs and there, you didn't ... you were not allowed to do that. So that was really, really hard for us, and I saw a lot of my friends being punished, you know, especially by the Sisters where they take a stick or ruler and they just hit them over the head and things like that. Again, I saw a lot of ... I saw a lot of things in the residential school and my sisters and my brothers did too, you know.[27]

In 1964, Northern Affairs reviewed its language policy for the hostels. Up until that point the policy had been "to encourage and promote the use of English in pupil residences and in as many out-of-school situations as possible." The policy document noted that "native languages are still widely used in residences" and that children are encouraged to write their parents, usually making use of their "native language." While there was no plan to ban Aboriginal languages in the residences, the policy decision was to "continue our present policy of encouraging a wider use of English outside of the classroom rather than planning a program for wider use of the native languages." There was, however, an expectation that in coming years, Aboriginal languages would be taught in the schools.[28]

R. G. Williamson, a member of the Northwest Territories Legislative Assembly, raised concerns about the lack of Inuit language training at the Churchill Vocational Centre (cvc) in 1970. He said he had been told that an Inuit language program conducted by Roger Briggs, an Anglican minister, for forty minutes a week for six weeks the previous year was not being offered in the current school year.[29] The matter was referred to Ralph Ritcey, who at that point was the superintendent of vocational education for Northern Affairs. According to Ritcey, Briggs had conducted classes at the CVC in the 1968–69 school year for a brief period. Furthermore, attendance had been voluntary. In the face of Williamson's criticism, Ritcey said Northern Affairs was prepared to allow Briggs to offer the classes again—so long as they were held in the evening and attendance remained voluntary.[30] Northern Affairs official Ivan Mouat observed that Ritcey's answer was not likely to satisfy Williamson.[31] In April 1970, the Northwest Territories director of education, B. C. Gillie, announced that an "Eskimo Language Reading Program would be initiated" at the CVC the following September.[32] Although it was not possible to meet that deadline, S. T. Mallon of the Eskimo Language School in Rankin Inlet was hired to develop an Inuit program for the CVC in 1971.[33] A former CVC student was hired to teach Inuktitut; Jose Kusugak went on to become a manager for the Canadian Broadcasting Corporation and president of the national Inuit Tapiriit Kanatami. Eva Aariak, a future premier of Nunavut, was one of Kusugak's language students. She recalled Kusugak

> always connected with his class through jokes, puzzles, or some other activity entirely unrelated to the lesson at hand. He taught us the new standardized ICI (Inuit Cultural Institute) writing system and I credit Jose as one of the key individuals who inspired my love of Inuit language and culture.[34]

Partly in response to Aboriginal organizations, the Northwest Territories government did make room in its curriculum for students to learn and practise traditional hunting and land skills. Although these reforms were modest, they were enough to incite complaints from the federal government that officials in the Northwest Territories were allowing "training for a life of leisure" in their schools.[35]

Staff

In 1974 Bryan Pearson, member of the Legislative Assembly for Iqaluit (Frobisher Bay), proposed, somewhat facetiously, that the education system in the North could be improved by firing half the teachers at once and replacing them with people from the communities. This prompted an editorial comment by the Inuit cartoonist and writer Alootook Ipellie:

> I think this would be one of the grandest miracles the North could ever experience, if it were to happen ... I would support Mr. Pearson's statement, if he could give the department of education in the NWT more time to convert the Inuit to positions of full-time teachers ... I am sure Mr. Pearson is a lot smarter than his statement would suggest.

After reflecting on the importance of Inuit teachers as role models, and also on the need to ensure that Inuit really wanted those jobs, Ipellie went on:

> If the majority of the teachers in the North were Inuit, Inuit children would relate to them and react to them in a more positive way. Instead of thinking that they could never become better than their white teachers, Inuit children would start to think that, if an Inuk could do that, they could do it too. This would also help to create a better relationship between the young and the old, not only in the schools but in the whole community. There is no doubt that there would be many other benefits resulting from this venture.[36]

Parents often felt alienated from the school staff and administrators. Inuit parents in Cambridge Bay took their concerns about the poor relations between the school and the community to local welfare officials and a missionary rather than to school officials in 1970. They felt the school was not sufficiently challenging, that discipline was too lax, and that the staff members took insufficient interest in either the students or the community. N. J. Macpherson, the superintendent of education, instructed the staff members to review the list of complaints and "take steps to improve any phase of the school operation that is in need of such improvement."[37]

In 1979 two members of the Legislative Assembly, Ipeelee Kilabuk and Piita Irniq (a former residential school student), stressed that the maintenance of Inuit culture required Inuit teachers. This would require hiring Inuit and Dene, preferably Elders, as full-time teachers in selected communities. Deputy Commissioner John Parker replied that quite clearly the administration might have to respond by cutting other programs or laying off other teachers.[38]

The operation of the schools was marked by conflicts over the religious faith of staff members. In 1966, for example, the Anglicans complained about a Northern Affairs decision to hire a non-Protestant, in this case a member of the Baha'i faith, to teach at Qamani'tuaq (Baker Lake). Northern Affairs official C. M. Bolger responded:

> It is the Department's policy to employ only Roman Catholic teachers in those classrooms which have a majority of Roman Catholic children enrolled. Roman Catholic principals are employed in those schools where the majority of the total enrolment is of that faith. Teachers of religious denominations other than Roman Catholic are employed in classrooms where the majority of the children enrolled are Protestant. Similarly, principals adhering to faiths other than Roman Catholic are hired for schools where the majority of the total enrolment is Protestant.[39]

This failed to satisfy Anglican Bishop Donald Marsh, who wrote, "Many years ago, when we discussed the question of the religious affiliations of teachers and principals, it was agreed upon and understood that teachers must be first of all Anglican, and if sufficient Anglicans did not offer for service in the Arctic then those accepted must be of the major religious denominations in Canada." It was his expectation that such individuals would be Protestant. Members of the Baha'i faith, he said, were not Christian and should not be considered Protestant. Since "the Eskimo people are almost entirely Anglican," he argued that their teachers should be so as well. Non-Anglicans, particularly non-Christians, might "introduce their own peculiar beliefs into their teaching in school, or open up rival Sunday Schools which create as you can imagine, uncertainty and distress in the minds of the pupils, their parents and the clergy concerned."[40] Without acknowledging it, he was of course describing exactly the same process that Anglican missionaries had followed when they set about converting Inuit and other Aboriginal people away from their own spiritual practices.

For its part, the Catholic hierarchy remained suspicious of and hostile toward Northern Affairs. In 1961, Father André Renaud, director general of the Oblate Indian and Eskimo Commission, said senior administrators were not only secular Protestants but often openly anti-Catholic. In the case of education, he said, "Thanks to the virtual elimination of Catholics from top posts, the education section of the northern affairs department is a veritable Orangeman's paradise."[41]

Educational outcomes

Overall, educational outcomes were disappointing in both the Yukon and the Northwest Territories. The Roman Catholic hostel in Whitehorse (later named Coudert Hall) opened its doors in the fall of 1961. The following year, the residence's principal, the Reverend Eugene Cullinane, wrote a disheartening assessment of the attempt to integrate the students into the Whitehorse school system. After three months of school it had become apparent that most of the students, who were enrolled in Grades Eight through Twelve, were failing. "The deteriorating academic situation presented a very grave threat to the very stability and life in our new hostel, causing us much concern. By mid-year the great majority of our students were in a state of pronounced frustration from their inability to cope with the academic program." An emergency tutoring program was put in place and many of the students were placed one grade back. This led to some improvements among the younger students. The older ones, however, were "full of misery, discontent[,] hostility"; many asked to be allowed to return home and others simply ran away. When they turned sixteen, fourteen students left. One was taken home by her parents "in a state of near collapse from nervous tension." Of the forty-five students who had started at the school, he expected only eighteen would return the following year. Sixty per cent of his enrolment had dropped out.

Cullinane then went on to assess the impact of the previous twenty years of educational work. Despite what he termed "the honest and sincere efforts" of the government and the churches, "a candid and unbiased appraisal of results thus far achieved reveals comparative failure." The lot of First Nations people in the Yukon during that period, he wrote, has not improved; "it has worsened."

The schools had left their students unprepared for life. "Reared in a well ordered severely disciplined residential school from the age of 6 to 16, they know no other way of life—neither that of their ancestors nor that of the White Man, and they have no skill or trade to make it possible for them to earn a living in either. They hang suspended somewhere between these two worlds in a void that is filled with little else than emotional turbulence."

To prepare for the coming year, Cullinane directed his staff to spend the summer "living in the Indian villages so as to get to know the natives better," while during the school year, staff members were to take correspondence courses in cultural anthropology.

As for the education offered, he said that it was apparent that "only a small percentage of our Indian youth of both sexes is capable at present of being integrated into the White Man's schools, colleges and professional training." A larger group, but still a minority, should be given vocational training. But the majority should be given a trade school education: a hands-on apprenticeship with "a minimum of academic education of any kind." Finally, "a specially designed curriculum and environment should be provided for the great majority of our Yukon Indian girls to indoctrinate them in the age-old arts and science which pertain to the establishment and care of a home and to develop in them that emotional stability and maturity so necessary for a successful marriage and a stable home." Cullinane judged the school's failure to be particularly severe in the case of women: "Physically and sexually mature, but emotionally still very young children, they will be exploited, victimized, desecrated and demoralized by the depraved, psychotic, predatory type of White Man that the Yukon always seems to attract. This is integration at its worst."[42]

In another assessment from that period, Cullinane wrote that he expected the dropout rate for sixteen-year-olds would be 100% despite the fact that "weak and emotionally insecure teachers" had been replaced by "more stable and effective ones." Integration, which he viewed as being implemented at a revolutionary pace, was to blame. Moving students from "an almost totally Yukon-Indian environment (of the village and residential school), based de facto on a segregationist policy, and then suddenly after 13 or 14 years plunging him into a White Man's world and schools in an attempt at integration—this violates all elemental biological and physical laws." It was his opinion that "current procedures actually induce in our students personality disorientation and neurotic illness leading to alcoholism and so called juvenile delinquency."[43]

A very similar message had been sent the year before in 1961 by W. E. Grant, the Indian superintendent for the Yukon Agency, to the assistant Indian commissioner in British Columbia, pointing out that in "places where children are living at home and attending a local day school they gradually pick up sufficient training from the parents to at least know how to trap, hunt, and fish. Children who spend seven or eight years in Residential School and who do not progress beyond Grade 6, are indeed 'lost' when they return to the Reserve at sixteen." He recommended that the teachers at residential schools be asked to identify those students who they did not believe would reach high school. They would be given a minimum of classroom training. Instead they would spend their days on carpentry, mechanics, electrical work, plumbing, and trapping or housekeeping, home nursing, waiting on tables, handicrafts, and sewing.[44]

In 1963, D. W. Hepburn, the former principal of the federal school in Inuvik, published an article with the ominous headline "Northern Education: Façade for Failure." He argued that the education being provided in the new federal schools was "hopelessly inadequate. The reasons for this failure are clear: the aims of education set forth by the Department are thoroughly confused, the curriculum is inappropriate, and many current practices of the system are not only ill-conceived but actually harmful."[45]

Department officials contended the schools were designed to allow students "to become efficient in [English], without losing their own cultural and linguistic tradition." But, Hepburn wrote, "no provision whatever is made in the curriculum to encourage retention of native language, culture or skills." Although 60% of the students at the Inuvik school were in the first three grades, few teachers had any background in primary education and "almost none has any special training in native education, and will receive none from the Department."[46] In the process, the schools were producing individuals who "lack not only the skills required for most permanent wage employment but also those necessary for the traditional economy."[47]

Former students in their statements to the TRC have confirmed the accuracy of Hepburn's prediction that students would lack the skills needed to follow a traditional lifestyle. Petah Inukpuk, who went to one of the hostels in Inuvik, explained that before going to school he had been a nomadic hunter, who, even at the age of five, had his own dog team and was able to hunt seal.[48] He spoke proudly of these years. Going to the hostel and school at Inuvik ended this lifestyle, creating a gap between himself and his own past, and between himself and his parents. As he stated, after finishing school "I began from scratch as if I had no knowledge whatsoever of anything."[49] More than anything else, the experience of residential schooling was this experience of being forced—in a very short period of time—to separate from one way of living and become rapidly acculturated through the hostel into another.[50]

In 1970, after the hostel system had been in operation for a decade, the number of Northwest Territories students in high schools was just 1,800, even though high school at the time included Grades Seven and Eight. Just over a third of these (644) were in the highest grades, Ten to Twelve. In the eastern Arctic just fourteen students were enrolled in Grades Nine to Twelve.[51] A 1971 review of Grollier Hall (Inuvik) enrolment statistics concluded that of the fifty senior boys who enrolled in the school each year, three would be expelled, nine would leave of their own choice, and thirty-eight would complete the year. Of them, about twenty-four would return the following year.[52] In later years, there were some positive signs: in the second semester of the 1986–87 school year, the pass rate for students at Akaitcho Hall (Yellowknife) was 88%.[53] For the first semester of the following year, it was 78%.[54] Other results were less heartening: in 1990–91 thirty-eight students from the Kitikmeot region (formerly known as the central Arctic) dropped out of Akaitcho Hall.[55] There were 12,000 students enrolled in Northwest Territories schools in 1980, but only 192 graduated in that year.[56] In 1988, Aboriginal students accounted for 70% of high school enrolment in the Northwest Territories but only 31% of graduates.[57]

Many students could not identify with the content of the classroom materials. For instance, Lillian Elias remembers, "When I looked at Dick and Jane I thought Dick and Jane were in heaven when I saw all the green grass. That's how much I knew about Dick and Jane."[58] However, others felt being in the classroom was a rewarding experience. Paul Quassa commented that the Chesterfield Inlet school, although extremely strict, was successful: "Looking at the way the education system was set up, it really worked. We were taught well."[59] Piita Irniq agreed: "The education system that we got was top notch at Chesterfield Inlet," despite the abuses that he and many other students reported from their time at that facility.[60] Eddie Dillon, who attended Sir Alexander Mackenzie School while living at Stringer Hall in Inuvik, was thankful for the education he received in the 1960s. In his testimony to the TRC, he made a point of thanking both his parents and the "government of Canada" for giving him a chance to get an education—something he would not have had in his own settlement.[61]

In her 1994 report on abuse at the Joseph Bernier School and Turquetil Hall at Chesterfield Inlet, conducted on behalf of the Northwest Territories government, the Yellowknife lawyer Katherine Peterson wrote:

> One could make a strong case for the generalized statement that the existence of the residential school in and of itself constituted an abusive experience for the students in that they were removed from familiar settings and placed in an environment which was frightening and detached from their family and culture.[62]

Specifically, she wrote of the way students were ridiculed for inappropriate use of English or an inability to complete school work; "over zealous discipline"; the arbitrary isolation of siblings of the opposite sex; the underemphasis of Inuit culture and an overemphasis on "western culture and its superiority"; and the separation of young children from their traditional supports and family connections.[63] She singled out cultural assimilation for specific comment:

> Education about, enhancement of and value accorded to the Inuit culture did not form any significant part of the former students' experiences at the Chesterfield Inlet school. Rather, the emphasis appeared to be one of promoting the

english [sic] language, western culture and [tenets] of tl
As a result of this, Inuit children were not only robbed, ...
least, of a sense of value of their culture, they also lost y...
ence that culture in their own community settings. In a...
of family and connection with the land is so prominent...
students experienced such a sense of detachment and l...

Peterson noted that some former students did speak po...
at the school. One, for example, said that he would not have learned to read or write
in syllabics had he not attended the school. Others said the school prepared them for
positions of responsibility in their communities. The overall assessment, however, was
that their time at the school had alienated them from those communities, broken their
links to their culture, and diminished their capacity to serve as effective parents.[65]

In their statements some former students also spoke positively of the benefit of
learning English.[66] Former students also remembered the excitement of learning
about the wider world outside the Arctic. Students who attended the Churchill school
spoke about how they were taught by open-minded teachers who were willing to
expose them to the social and political changes taking place across the world in the
1960s.[67] John Amagoalik wrote that at the Churchill Vocational Centre "we had excellent teachers. To this day we still talk about them ... They treated us as ordinary people.
We had never experienced this sort of attitude before and it was, in a way, liberating to
be with new teachers that treated you as their equal."[68] David Simailak, who attended
the Duke of Edinburgh School in Churchill, spoke of how his time at residential school
gave him a series of new opportunities. He fondly remembers excelling at math and
spelling competitions, and travelling to Montreal for Expo 67.[69]

For some other students, the classroom was enjoyable for another reason altogether. For children who were bullied or who suffered physical or sexual abuse in the
hostels, the classroom was a safe haven. Marjorie Ovayuak, who was bullied by older
girls at Stringer Hall, saw the classes at the school as her sanctuary: "I was mocked; I
was teased; I was picked on ... The hostel was so bad but when I went to school, I was
happy ... As long as I was away from Stringer Hall...."[70]

Not all northern students studied in the North. In the late 1950s, the federal government sent fifty-one young Inuit to Leduc, Alberta, for training for jobs on the DEW
Line.[71] In the 1960s the federal government launched the "experimental Eskimo" program, hand-picking some promising young people to live a middle-class existence
and attend school in places as diverse as Petite Riviere, in Lunenburg County, Nova
Scotia; Winnipeg; and Ottawa.[72] The experiment was meant both to further the young
people's education and to show skeptics that Inuit students were academically, at
least, equal to their non-Inuit contemporaries. Like others who followed them, some
were able to thrive both socially and academically, and they acknowledged the benefits of their participation in the program. Because of their immersion in white society,

e students returned home they proved to be indispensable in helping to the gap between the people of their home communities and government orities.[73] Many went on to play leading roles in campaigns for Inuit rights and recognition. Peter Ittinuar, who attended high school in Ottawa for two years, became the first Inuk member of Parliament.[74] Despite his success, Ittinuar felt that for many the program had mixed results. In his autobiography, Ittinuar wrote that fellow student Zebedee Nungak from Puvirnituq always remarked that "he has never regretted the experience, but he has also never recovered from it."[75]

CHAPTER 9

The large hostels

Despite the fact that in 1955, Northern Affairs and National Resources Minister Jean Lesage had written that boarding schools were inappropriate for northern Canada, by 1961 the federal government's system of large hostels was fully established throughout the North. The hostels replicated the problems that had characterized the residential school system in southern Canada. They were large, regimented institutions, run by missionaries whose primary concern was winning and keeping religious converts. They employed a curriculum that was culturally and geographically inappropriate. While a number of schools developed admirable reputations, most students did not do well academically. Sexual abuse was a serious problem in a number of these institutions. The abuse was coupled with a failure on the part of the government and the residence administrations to properly investigate and prosecute it. Institutional interests were placed before those of the children.

Most of the students who lived in the two Yukon hostels, located in Whitehorse, came from First Nations families. In the Northwest Territories, seven large hostels were located in five communities in the western Arctic: Yellowknife, Fort McPherson, Fort Smith, Fort Simpson, and Inuvik. (Grandin College, also located in Fort Smith, was not part of the federally organized large hostel system and will be discussed separately.) These communities are either on the Mackenzie River and its delta or on the lakes and rivers that flow into the Mackenzie. First Nations, Métis, and Inuit students could be found in all the hostels in the western Arctic. Until 1964, when the Churchill Vocational Centre opened, there was only one hostel in the eastern Arctic: Turquetil Hall at Chesterfield Inlet, on the western shore of Hudson Bay. The limited number of hostels in the East meant that many Inuit children were enrolled in schools and hostels in the western Arctic, particularly those in Inuvik (the most northerly of the communities with hostels in the West) and Yellowknife (which provided students with access to a variety of vocational education programs.) In 1970, for example, Stringer Hall in Inuvik was home to 185 Inuit students who came from places as distant as Iqaluktuuttiaq (Cambridge Bay), Taloyoak (Spence Bay), and Gjoa Haven.[1] Yellowknife drew students from across the entire Arctic, including in

1970 from Iqaluktuuttiaq, Kugluktuk (Coppermine), Inuvik, Iqaluit (Frobisher Bay), Bathurst Inlet, and even Arctic Québec.[2] In one year the Churchill Vocational Centre housed students from Qamani'tuaq (Baker Lake), Chesterfield Inlet, Coral Harbour, Arviat (Eskimo Point), Igloolik, Kangiqliniq (Rankin Inlet), Naujaat (Repulse Bay), Whale Cove, Qikiqtarjuaq (Broughton Island), Kinngait (Cape Dorset), Iqaluit, Grise Fiord, Pangnirtung, Mittimatalik (Pond Inlet), and Resolute Bay, all still part of the Northwest Territories at that time, before the creation of Nunavut in 1999. Students also came from Ivuyivik (Port Harrison), Quaqtaq, Kangirsuk (Payne Bay), and Sugluk in northern Québec.[3] The distances some of these students travelled are staggering. Inuvik is more than 1,500 kilometres from Taloyoak, while Iqaluit and Yellowknife are over 2,200 kilometres apart.[4]

The residences were often large institutions. Grollier and Stringer Halls in Inuvik, for example, were built to house 250 students each.[5] Initially Akaitcho Hall in Yellowknife was intended to accommodate 100 students, while the Anglican Bompas Hall in Fort Simpson had an initial capacity of 50 and the Catholic Lapointe Hall in the same community had a capacity of 150. The initial staff complement for Akaitcho Hall was ten: a superintendent, a matron, an assistant matron, a cook, an assistant cook, a laundress, a caretaker, a choreman, and two dormitory supervisors (one male, one female). Lapointe Hall, with fifty more students, was allotted three more staff members.[6] By the late 1960s at Stringer Hall, for instance, there were two distinct groups of employees. The first included four non-Aboriginal supervisors of the boys' and girls' dormitories (one each for senior and junior boys and girls) and a number of Aboriginal assistants to help with the youngest children. The second group, including the nurse and the kitchen and dining room staff managed by the hostel matron, worked in the areas outside the dorms. Most of the hostel staff, except for the dormitory assistants and sometimes some of the kitchen and dining room staff, were not from the North and spoke only English. While the matron and her staff were tasked with supervising the dining hall, the supervisors were in charge of the dormitories.[7]

By the early 1960s, it was not uncommon for Stringer Hall in Inuvik to have an enrolment that exceeded its capacity. In 1963, for example, it housed 277 students, at a time when the building had a capacity of 250. At the same time, Grollier Hall in the same community had seventy-five empty beds. However, the excess children in Stringer Hall could not be moved into Grollier Hall because they were identified as Anglicans, and Grollier Hall was operated by Catholics.[8] In 1964 Stringer Hall was housing 300 students with no immediate relief in sight.[9] Not surprisingly a 1965 review of the hostels observed that "the existence of separate and distinct hostels alongside of schools following separate and distinct extra-curriculum programs can only lead to unnecessary and unwarranted duplication."[10] A 1967 medical inspection of Turquetil Hall in Chesterfield Inlet concluded the facility was "grossly overcrowded."[11]

Privacy was limited in many residences, particularly in the early years when the students in most residences slept in dormitories in which the beds were "arranged army-style for fifty or sixty in one room."[12] Residents in hostels at Yellowknife and Churchill enjoyed significantly more privacy and comfort. There, the relatively modern residence buildings featured smaller, four-person rooms.[13]

Recruitment and resistance

In 1960, the federal government had seven criteria for selecting students to attend northern hostels and residential schools:

- They had to live in an area "reasonably adjacent" to the institution.
- They had to have undergone a medical examination and an X-ray.
- They had to have reached the age of six by December 31 of the year of admittance.
- Priority would be given to those who had attended in the previous year.
- They had to be of the religious faith of the authority operating the institution.
- They had to lack access to a day school or other school facilities.
- Enrolment could not exceed the approved registration for the school.[14]

Initially Northern Affairs recommended that before being admitted to the hostels, "Indian children be examined by a doctor and Eskimo children by a nurse." While this likely reflected the fact that there were few doctors in the eastern Arctic, it did lead one government official to comment that he could not understand "why a doctor is required for Indian children and nurse for Eskimos."[15]

In selecting the first students for the Inuvik residences, Northern Affairs relied in 1959 on preliminary surveys carried out by missionaries, Hudson's Bay Company employees, teachers, and Mounted Police officers. Students were flown to collection points in small planes. From these locations they were flown in larger planes to Inuvik.[16]

Norman Burgess was in charge of arranging many of these early airlifts. His descriptions of the way in which a girl was collected from her family in a remote area east of Herschel Island is harrowing. The family was on a boat in the water when the plane

> landed down beside them right out in the middle of nowhere and took the little
> girl, screaming and kicking, put her in the aircraft—the mother crying, the father
> crying, the kid crying, all part of the game in those days—and flew her into
> Inuvik and put her in the hostel. It was pretty nerve-wracking and I don't think
> I could get to where I agreed with it, but nonetheless, there wasn't that much
> choice.[17]

Some children, such as Eric Anautalik, had never seen an airplane before.[18] While this may have added a degree of excitement to the journey, several former students remembered the air journeys to, and later from, the hostels as uncomfortable and unsafe.[19] Beatrice Bernhardt stated that as a six-year-old she was given neither food nor water during her flight from the Kugluktuk area to Inuvik.[20] Paul Quassa, who was also about six years old when he was sent from Igloolik to Chesterfield Inlet, remembered there were no seats or safety precautions taken on the plane: "We just sat on the floor of the plane." He also remembers children having to urinate in the plane. "I remember there was no washroom, but because we were children we had to go." Like many other journeys to and from the hostel, Quassa's first plane journey made several stops along the way, collecting more children at Naujaat and Kangiqliniq: "We just landed along the way. Then we'd lift off and go."[21]

"Eyewitness Says: Kidnap Children to Fill School"

The hostels opened to a flurry of negative publicity. In September 1959, the *Winnipeg Free Press* reporter Erik Watt's article on school recruitment ran under the headline "Eyewitness Says: Kidnap Children to Fill School." According to Watt, a resident of Old Crow, Yukon, had told him that children had been, in essence, kidnapped to "fill and thereby justify a super-school that no one in the north wanted except the government and the Anglican Church." According to Watt, the children from Old Crow had been taken to the new Anglican hostel in Fort McPherson. The article drew attention to the distance children had to travel, parents' opposition to being separated from their children, and the religious segregation that was central to the system. An anonymous Mounted Police officer was quoted as saying, "Neither church wants its converts tainted by any contact with the other. It's a fine way to teach them to become citizens."[22]

The allegations of kidnapping did not go away. In the early 1960s, Citizenship and Immigration Minister Richard Bell said, "Much publicity has been given to the claim that the Government has been dragging babes from their mothers' arms and placing them in hostels (all in the name of education). The absurdity of such claims is pointed out by the fact that all pupils in hostels must be of school age, at least aged 6 and that the consent of the parent or legal guardian is a requirement for admission."[23]

Consent forms were indeed usually obtained from parents, but at times pressure was applied to get that consent. In 1963 Northern Affairs official W. G. Booth travelled through the Northwest Territories with the Treaty payment party to recruit students for the Inuvik hostels. In one community, parents insisted that, rather than send their children away, they wanted a day school in their community. "At first, it did not seem as though any children would be going to the hostel," he wrote. However, with the help of the Mounted Police officer, who was there as a part of the Treaty payment party, and the government translator, he succeeded in "getting the signatures of the parents of some six children."[24]

In a 1977 article in *Inuit Today*, Armand Tagoona explained the pressures that were placed on parents to win their consent. He recalled being taken by the settlement manager to act as interpreter for a couple whose daughter was on a list to be sent to the Churchill Vocational Centre. The parents objected to her going, as she had reached marriageable age. The official told Tagoona to explain to them, "'If you don't let your daughter go, I don't want to see any of you in my office at any time. Even if you no longer have any food, you will not be given welfare ...' The mother and father looked at each other as if in agreement, then the mother said, 'Okay, let her go.'"[25]

Norman Attungala recalled that it was a Department of Indian Affairs official who told him to send his son to school.[26] At other times, Survivors have explained, their parents sent them to the schools because the government threatened to withhold family allowance payments if children were not sent away.[27] In many cases children were simply taken to school without any "prior consultation" with parents or the children themselves. In some extreme cases physical force was used. Eric Anautalik explains the trauma that he felt as a three-and-a-half-year-old being picked up by an RCMP officer and, in his words, "brought into the modern age."[28] As he remembers, "I was in shock, I mean I was taken, literally, I was snatched by the policeman from my mother's arms ... In that single day, my whole life changed."[29]

Mary Charlie from Ross River in the Yukon recalled being rounded up and taken to the Lower Post school in northern British Columbia.

> I remember when I went to school I was out in the bush about 14 miles from here and we were living out there and there was a big truck that came and got everybody. I remember one girl, my friend, her name was Agnes ... She didn't want to go to school so she run half around the lake and it's a pretty big lake to run around, but they caught her anyway and we went into that big truck. And we never sat down, there was no bench or anything in that big wood truck or whatever but there was no seats in there to sit down, or had any water or anything to eat all day while we run around, pick up kids, and it was dusty and dirty and we didn't even—I didn't even know where I was going.[30]

Angus Lennie, who attended residential school in Alkavik and Inuvik, said his life changed forever when he first entered residential school.

> I recall walking as a small boy up to this big building with some clothing. Nobody explained to me what was happening at this point. I remember my parents dropping me off with my brothers and one sister and from a child's eyes, this was really a strange environment. So, each Sister ... met us at the door and this began my journey into residential schools. A journey I will never forget. Walking through those doors, began the split of our once happy, connected family. Once the doors were shut, that's when it began my nightmare. Our parents were no longer there to be—to protect us. My sister was taken to the other side, from then

we had no contact, with no more playing, sharing stories, and this is the point I really believe in my life that our once happy family began to break apart.[31]

The experience was painful for the parents. Towkie Karpik recalled that a federal government representative came to Pangnirtung to recruit children for the hostels.

> When he came to get the children he was so aggressive and intimidating. I had no choice but to let him take them. I had no choice but to say yes, even though I didn't want them to go. Who would want that? No one had ever taken our small children from us before. When they took them all of the mothers began to grieve as if our children had died. Believe me it's the most terrible thing in the world to have someone take your children away and there was no way to stop it. The White man was so intimidating and he came to take our children, our innocent children that we had every expectation of raising ourselves. We thought they would stay with us until they were grown. It was so horrible to be left behind by our children because we weren't meant to be separated from their children when they were small. They were meant to stay with us.[32]

Apphia Agalakti Siqpaapik Awa raised her children in the Baffin Island area. Two of her boys went to the Churchill school.

> We couldn't communicate with them because there were no phones, and since we were in the camp, we didn't get any letters from them. We didn't hear from them for a long, long time. We didn't know how they were down there. I remember being so worried about them. Finally Simon wrote a letter that someone brought to us at the camp. He wrote that he was very homesick and that he wanted his parents to talk to the teachers and ask them to let him come home. He wrote that he was scared of the Indians in the school. He was just a little boy. I wrote back and told him that he had to be patient and wait for the time to come home. I wrote to him that he had to wait until springtime.[33]

Almost as difficult as the separation was the return to the home community after months or years of schooling. Peggy Tologanak illustrates how these broken relationships manifested themselves the moment that children returned to their communities for the summer holidays. Some of the younger children, she explains, had literally forgotten who their parents were: "I remember when we'd land in Cambridge [for the holidays] we'd all be brought to the school and the parents would come up and pick us up. There was a lot of kids that were crying cause they didn't know who their parents were. They forgot about them." Older students, although remembering their parents, resented returning to their parents' home: "Some ... kids didn't want to go with their parents, they said, They're so dirty, and they're so stinking,' ... and they would be crying and had to be forced to be taken home."[34]

The schools were quite conscious of the implications of the changes that they were introducing into northern communities. A handbook prepared for the Churchill Vocational Centre advised:

> There must be able acceptance on the part of both the parent and the child that the learning of English and its associated acculturation is a very necessary factor in this further education. The child, when he returns home, will certainly not be the same individual who went to school. He will have a different outlook and might not readily accept what he finds upon his return.[35]

Once they arrived at the hostel, children were put through a series of procedures to register, wash, and reclothe them. Many Survivors still remember the number they were given on arrival, and several remember the experience of having their own hand-made clothing taken from them. Norman Yakeleya recalled that he was given number 297 when he went to Grollier Hall.

> I was six years old when I got my number.... You had an older boy look after you and they give you a black marking pen and they put a number on your—you got to put all on your clothes, your socks, long johns, shorts, pants, shirt, boots, and they put your number on you, put your number on your clothes and they didn't say, "Norman," they said your number and you got to put your hands up and say, "Here." So, they weren't given a name. You were given a number and that's how you identify yourself. And I thought about this in the bush again. What kind of society does that to people?[36]

Peggy Tologanak from Iqaluktuuttiaq explained how every year her mother pains-takingly made her and her siblings new sets of clothing to wear to school, and how, on arrival, these homemade clothes were confiscated by authorities at Stringer Hall and replaced with manufactured clothing from southern Canada.[37] When the nuns at the Lower Post school took her clothes, Marjorie Jack asked, "Well, what are you going to do with my clothes? My mom just made me coats, my mom was a seamstress. My mom made me these clothes, why are you taking them?" They said, "Well, we all have to wear the same things here and we'll distribute your clothes to you."[38]

In more extreme cases, students witnessed authorities burning the clothes their parents had given them.[39] Along with removing these "old" clothes, students were forced to shower and have their hair checked for lice; if necessary, they were forced to have their hair washed with a powerful cleaning agent.[40] Helen Naedzo Squirrel had a strong memory of how humiliating and frightening she found this process: "Our clothes were taken away from us. They assembled us all in a line and told us to go into the shower stalls. They washed our hair and washed whatever—they thought we had lice and whatever. After that they cut our hair."[41] As Piita Irniq remembered of his first days at Turquetil Hall, this whole process of cleaning and reclothing had an unsettling effect on him and other children: it was as if "we had overnight become White men and White women."[42] For Anna Kasudluak, the changes ushered in by the new clothing were quite literally difficult to bear: it felt "very heavy to be under a new wardrobe."[43]

From the official perspective, the students' home clothing was in need of replace-ment. Remembering the arrival of students at the Churchill residence in 1964, the superintendent of vocational schooling in the Northwest Territories, Ralph Ritcey, said, "Less than ten had clothing you would use in a regular school." This teacher explained how he and other staff, assuming they were improving the health of the students, spent the first few days of the school year washing and reclothing the students; some teachers, he noted, "spent twelve to fourteen hours a day washing people and cutting hair, delousing them, burning clothes and refitting them with new clothes."[44] By 1963 the hostels were allotted forty-eight dollars a year for clothing. Parents from Snare Lake in the Northwest Territories complained that year that the students had not been allowed to return home in the hostel clothing, but were sent home in the clothing they came in, "which was pretty well worn out."[45]

Regimentation: "We went to a total alien place"

Once washed and dressed, the students were initiated into their daily routine. At the same time the school system was forcing them to conform to a new—and very foreign—type of schedule, it failed to make the children feel loved or cared for.[46] Veronica Dewar, a resident at Churchill in the 1960s, explained how her time at residential school, although a success in terms of her experience in the classroom, was marred by a hostel lifestyle that was highly regimented and unable to offer the love and caring she had enjoyed from her parents in Coral Harbour. It "seems like we walked into the army," she remembered of her first days at the Churchill hostel; it felt "totally cold, and totally different environment than our parents' homes and we went to a total alien place."[47] Eva Lapage recalled having mixed emotions about her time at the Churchill school.

> It was bunch of Inuit from everywhere that were in that residential school. So that's where I was and there was no way of communicating. And it was exciting, it was fun, but I was very homesick.... Because I was the oldest of the family and they loved me. My parents loved me so much. I was kind of spoiled one, you know, I just cried and I'd get what I want. So I had that and all of a sudden it was cut off.

She said she felt well treated while she was at the school. However, she felt that the school was run in a highly disciplined fashion.

> It was army base, that old building and it had many wings and was long way to go to cafeteria and we would have to line up and we were wearing uniform and we all look alike.[48]

Tables 9.1 and 9.2 outline daily schedules at Akaitcho Hall and Stringer Hall.

Table 9.1.   Daily schedule, Akaitcho Hall, 1958

6:30:	Students on Breakfast detail rise, wash and report to chef by 7 a.m.
7:00:	All students rise
7:30 – 8:00:	Breakfast
8:00 – 8:25:	Work details
8:30 – 11:30:	Classes
11:45–12:30:	Lunch
12:30 – 1:00:	Free period (smoking, recreation room)
1:00 – 3:00:	Classes
3:30 – 5:00:	Free period (students are free to visit town for shopping etc.)
5:00 – 5:30:	Dinner
5:30 – 6:00:	Free period (smoking, recreation room)
6:00 – 7:30:	Study period
7:30 – 9:30	Free period (recreation room, gym etc.)
9:30:	To dorm for quiet hour
10:30:	Lights out

Source: TRC, NRA, Library and Archives Canada, RG85, volume 708, file 630/105-7, part 3, High School Facilities – Yellowknife [Public and Separate School], 1958–1959, A. J. Boxer to J. M. Black, 9 December 1958. [AHU-000005-0000]

Table 9.2   Daily schedule, Stringer Hall, c. 1966-67

6:45 – 7:30	Rise, dress and wash
7:30 – 8:00	Breakfast
8:00 – 8:45	Clean up dorms, dining room and halls, set up tables etc. Prepare for school.
8:45 – 12:00	Attend school
12:00 – 1:00	Return for lunch. After lunch clean dining room, set tables etc.
1:00 – 4:00	Attend school
4:00 – 5:30	Play in the hostel, gymnasium and dorms. Play cards (gamble), play guitars.
5:30 – 6:00	Dinner
6:00 – 6:30	Clean dining room, wash dishes, etc.
7:00 – 9:00	Study period in dining room
7:00 – 7:30	Junior boys and girls prepare for bed
9:00 – 9:30	Snack in the dorm for the younger students, lunch in the dining room for the older students
9:30 – 9:45	13–14 year old students prepare for bed
9:45 – 10:00	14–15 year old students prepare for bed
10:00 – 10:30	All other students prepare for bed
11:00	All lights are turned off

Source: Clifton, *Inuvik Study*, 57.

At the Churchill residence, students rose at 7:00 on weekday mornings, had hour-long meal periods at 7:30, 12:15, and 5:30, and had an evening snack at 8:30. They left for school at 8:45 a.m., returned to the residence for lunch, and went back to school until 4:00. Their recreation periods were from 4:00 to 5:15, and again from 7:30 to 9:00. The period from 6:30 to 7:30 was set aside for studying, and lights were supposed to be out by 9:30. Chores were limited to a daily making of beds and tidying and cleaning of washrooms and weekly washing and waxing of dormitory floors.[49]

Because the hostels organized dormitory life along lines of age and gender, most siblings slept, ate, and attended schools separately. The tight regulation of male-female interactions, in particular, meant that even if they lived in the same Hall, brothers were rarely able to talk to or visit their sisters and vice versa. Peggy Tologanak, at Stringer Hall in the 1960s, vividly remembers the experience of being separated from her eight siblings at Stringer. "From the moment you walk in until you go home you're not allowed to see your family members, you can't sit with them, you can't hardly talk with them."[50] Christmas at the hostel was a rare moment for Peggy to reconnect with her siblings. "The only time we get together as a family [at the hostel] was on Christmas day," remembered Peggy.

> We'd all get to get up in the morning and run and go see our brothers and our sisters. [We'd ask about] how they were, and then, they would always allow the kids to go into the dining room on Christmas day ... from biggest families to smallest. And every year that I was there, the Tologanaks were always first to be called 'cause we always had the biggest family. And then we get to sit with our brothers and sisters on Christmas day. And we'd sort of catch up because we weren't allowed to mingle [during the rest of the school year].[51]

Veronica Dewar explained how being at the hostel robbed her of the opportunity to receive love and caring from her parents: "There was never love around us or caring for us for a very long time." While the medical services at the hostel may have been superior to what she could have accessed at Coral Harbour, she explained that she could "never even receive hugs" she needed from her parents when she got sick or hurt.[52] Without the provision of affection, the hostel, despite its modern medicine and well-meaning routines and activities, was unable to properly care for her and her classmates.

In some instances, encountering the physical layout of the hostel and even the landscape around the hostel was an alienating and unsettling experience. Piita Irniq, accustomed to living in a relatively small family group in the restricted space of an iglu, remembered that noise and especially the size of the open-style dormitory at Turquetil Hall were a "culture shock" for him.[53] Likewise, for children raised in the eastern Arctic and sent to schools at Inuvik, Chesterfield Inlet, and Churchill, the physical landscape—most notably the trees—compounded the sense that they were in a foreign place where not just the language and culture of the hostel were new, but so too was the very land on which it was built. One Survivor from Nunavut remembers that soon after her arrival at Churchill, she wanted someone to cut down all the trees "so I could see far enough."[54]

Friendship and bullying

Cut off from family, students turned to each other for support. In notes that he took when he worked at Stringer Hall as supervisor in the mid-1960s, Rodney Clifton observed, "Often when a meal is over and the students are returning to their dorm, they put their arms around one another as they walk down the halls," and once in the dormitories, some of the younger boys would "often sleep together or lay in each others [sic] beds and tell stories."[55] According to Clifton, older boys would similarly talk late into the night: "The grade 11 and 12 students almost [n]ever slept together but they often would lay in each others [sic] beds and talk till late at night. They would relate stories of their ancestors, sexual experiences, hunting experiences and daily news."[56] Some students clearly felt very positive about the friendships they developed at the hostels. Many remembered meeting many good people at the hostels, among both the staff and the student body.[57] "I didn't fit in Grollier Hall," remembers Beatrice Bernhardt, "except when we had fun with each other and when we were allowed to just be together at playtime."[58] A former resident at Stringer Hall, Eddie Dillon, reflected on the role of friendship this way: "I do regret not being able to communicate with my family through those years [at the hostel] ... but the students we end up going to school with in Stringer Hall, that's the extended families we have. We share that."[59]

Rather than support each other, some students engaged in bullying. Inuit, Inuvialuit (Inuit of the western Arctic), and First Nations girls were all targets of bullying by members of the other groups, and sometimes by members of their own groups. Beatrice Bernhardt remembers that, more than any of the things the staff did, the "biggest abuse [at the hostel] came from other students." She bitterly remembered how she was called "dumb," "stupid," and "dirty Eskimo" at the hostel. They were "wicked, wicked mean," Beatrice said of the girls who teased her.[60] Girls coming from the central Arctic had similar stories of being tormented by other girls. Peggy Tologanak said that Gwich'in as well as Inuvialuit girls teased her during her time at Stringer Hall. She remembers being called "dirty and stinking."[61] Likewise, Jeannie Evalik, from Iqaluktuuttiaq, was targeted as an outsider when she went to Inuvik. She specifically remembered a staff member calling her a "stupid Eskimo."[62] Other girls felt they were bullied because of a handicap. Marjorie Ovayuak says that while she got along with most of the other children at Stringer Hall, she was teased because she suffered from hearing loss in one ear.[63]

Judi Kochon recalled how a group of older girls at Grollier Hall bullied a younger girl into stealing candy for them.

> That whole time that she was gone, like I felt so bad, you know like, I knew I couldn't do anything but I felt so bad for her because I knew what she would go through if she got caught. But she came back with the candies and that, but just it took so long for her to come back so it was just like, for me it was just an agony just waiting for her to come back and that nothing would happen to her.[64]

Students often had trouble adjusting to hostel life. In reporting on the discharge of five "problem students" in Akaitcho Hall's first semester, administrator A. J. Boxer recommended "greater care be exercised in selecting students for the hostel. It is entirely improper to place delinquent and immoral people among wholesome, developing teenagers."[65] In approving a student's request to be allowed to return from Yellowknife to his home community, Sir John Franklin School principal N. J. Macpherson said he felt that "a more careful selection would prevent this recurring problem of students finding themselves unwilling or unable to adjust to life here."[66] In writing about the difficulties that students had in adjusting to hostel life, a child care worker at the Ukkivik hostel in Iqaluit noted in the early 1970s that for many students, the residence housed

> more people than exist in their entire home community. Most have never been among so many people of their own age before. The new environment requires adjustment. There are no grandparents or parents to answer to. There are no babies and small children to care for. The boys cannot go out hunting. Even the traditional visiting become hazardous in Frobisher Bay where alcohol is passed out freely and girls are continuously accosted by drunks.[67]

Food

It is apparent that the food in the hostels, when compared with the diets served in the mission residential schools of the 1950s, represented a significant improvement in both quality and quantity. Alice Blondin-Perrin, who had attended the St. Joseph's Catholic residential school in Fort Resolution, transferred to Breynat Hall when it opened in Fort Smith. In her memoirs, she recalled that food improved dramatically. At Breynat Hall students were served "hot lunches of soup, stew, shepherd's pie, bread, and milk. The stew was made from various meats, always prepared well and always tasty. The dinners were always delicious, with mashed potatoes, meat, meatloaf, or fish, and vegetables. I could now eat cooked carrots, beets, turnips, and peas which I used to hate the taste of, but now loved."[68]

A 1965 review of the hostels in the Northwest Territories concluded, "The food received by the residents is excellent in both quantity and quality." Students were being fed in keeping with the Canada Food Guide and "the administrators have used their collective imaginations and skills to give the children more than the minima called for by the guide." The supply of milk, fruit, vegetables, cereal, bread, ice cream and butter was judged ample.[69] But while quantity and quality had improved, it was, as Blondin-Perrin's comments reveal, a southern diet. It was not one that students adjusted to easily. In the early 1970s, a child care worker at the Iqaluit hostel wrote that, while the food was adequate by southern standards,

> the Eskimo diet is not the white man's diet. Ham hocks and sauerkraut do not appeal to the students the way seal, char and caribou do. As a result much of the food is going into garbage cans instead into stomachs. The difference is being made up in soft drinks and chocolate bars.[70]

After initially tolerating some traditional foods, the government had in fact banned country food from the residences. In 1961 students at Turquetil Hall were being fed two meals of raw fish and two meals of raw beef a week. The meat was not traditional northern caribou but rather beef that came from a Winnipeg packing plant; the fish was caught locally. The residence principal, René Bélair, was a strong supporter of the practice. He said that none of the children had become ill as a result of eating raw food. "Do not forget that they are eskimos and not white: They like it and it is good for them. This is one thing that you will never be able to stop, is to stop an eskimo from eating raw meat. It is just like ice cream to us."[71] Medical advice provided to Indian Affairs concluded that such a diet was a threat to the health of the children since the meat could be "infested with worms that can cause illness, incapacity, and in some cases death." R. A. Bishop of Northern Affairs informed Bélair that he believed the school had no choice but to accept the medical advice not to serve children raw meat even though the decision would not be popular with the students.[72] As result, the practice of serving raw meat and fish was halted at the school in the summer of 1962.[73]

In 1961 the students at the Anglican Stringer Hall in Inuvik were being fed frozen raw whitefish once a month and raw reindeer meat about once a month as well. Residence administrator Leonard Holman said that discontinuing the serving of raw foods, which he said was provided as a "special treat," would not cause any problems.[74] In a separate note, Holman questioned whether raw, frozen food was as dangerous as federal government officials claimed, pointing out that "it was men from the same Department who advised and recommended that we include these items as a 'special' in our diet and that they would be perfectly safe." He also relayed the following story:

> Over a year ago in the midst of the Measle epidemic, one little Eskimo lad from a very primitive section was really very sick and was showing no sign whatsoever of recovery. Just lay there with a high fever not even wanting to drink. We have on our staff an Eskimo lady, Mrs. Annie Anderson, who comes from the Coppermine area and knows their dialect, so whenever there is sickness

she leaves her sewing and goes in to help the Nurse, and talks away to them in their own language, which we have found to be very beneficial. He called and asked her to PLEASE get him a piece of frozen caribou. None was available so she slipped downstairs and came back with a little piece of frozen Reindeer. He fairly grabbed it out of her hand, pushed it into his mouth and lay there sucking and chewing on it. This was the turning point on the road to recovery. Just a little taste of 'home' from one of his own, who knew and understood.[75]

By the end of the first decade of operation, the diets were almost completely southern in nature. In 1970 this was a typical daily menu at Stringer Hall:

Breakfast puffed wheat, toast, jam, milk
Lunch grilled cheese sandwiches, canned tomatoes, plums, milk
Dinner roast beef, gravy, mashed potatoes, peas, ice cream, cookies (home made), milk.[76]

In the 1990s there were attempts to reintroduce traditional food. In 1990 Anglican pastor Tom Gavac reported that at Akaitcho Hall "many students wish that more traditional, customary foods were served—namely caribou and fish." When he inquired into the possibility of serving such food, he was told that such meat could not be served unless it was government inspected, a process that was deemed to be too costly. Gavac said it was "almost inconceivable to me that youth who normally consume caribou and fish (often every day in the home community) cannot have such items at least once weekly."[77]

Many students had a great deal of difficulty adapting to the southern diet. The food at Turquetil Hall was remembered as very repetitive and poor: breakfast was always porridge, and lunch was some combination of sandwich, soup, and tea.[78] Without any real choice, however, the children were forced to adhere to this institutionalized food.

Health care

In 1960 the Indian and Northern Health Services of the federal health department recommended that there be a registered nurse for every hostel with a capacity of 200 students or more. For isolated hostels, it was recommended that there be a nurse available even if the enrolment was less than 200. Fulfilling this recommendation required the hiring of nurses in Inuvik and Fort Smith. It was thought that the matron at Turquetil Hall would be able to provide adequate nursing care as long as she was an "alert motherly person who is highly reliable" and had "a knowledge of home nursing and first aid."[79]

In the hostels with more than 100 residents, it appears that students had access to a level of medical care far superior to what had been available in the older residential schools. The first matron at Akaitcho Hall was a registered nurse. From the outset the local schools arranged for the X-raying of students and eye tests. A local doctor was able to extract teeth, but it was felt that the services of a dentist were urgently needed.[80] At the Churchill Vocational Centre a sick parade (to which students who were feeling ill could report) was held each morning, the hostel matron was a registered nurse, and a public health nurse was available three half-days a week. The hospital was about 200 metres from the school, and appointments with doctors and dentists were arranged whenever necessary.[81]

The initial plan was for the Anglican hostel at Fort Simpson to be covered by periodic visits from an Indian and Northern Health Services nurse, while the Roman Catholic hostel could be covered by the staff of the outpatient department of the local Roman Catholic hospital.[82] In operation the system was far from ideal. When a boy with tuberculosis was admitted to Bompas Hall in Fort Simpson in December 1963, the administrator, Ben Sales, protested. He pointed out that the boy was supposed to receive large doses of medicine each day for seven months. Sales wrote, "We have no professional nurse on our staff to be responsible for this medication."[83]

Contagious illnesses spread quickly in large dormitories. Initially infecting four students, a 1959 outbreak of the measles affected seventy students at the two Inuvik residences.[84] The following year there were twenty cases of a "mild epidemic" of influenza among the children at the same residences.[85] Another urgent report went out in 1961 stating that there were 106 cases of influenza in the hostels.[86] Ninety-three students came down with influenza in Fort Simpson in 1963.[87] Three years later an influenza epidemic hit both Fleming Hall in Fort McPherson and Bompas Hall in Fort Simpson, leading to the cancellation of an Easter Festival at Fort Simpson.[88] First aid and medication were available from infirmaries in each of the Whitehorse hostel buildings in 1971, but neither infirmary had beds, making it impossible to separate children with infectious illnesses from the rest of the student body.[89] Despite these problems, a 1965 assessment of the Northwest Territories hostels concluded that the hostels all had "excellent infirmaries for boys and for girls."[90]

Policies on the reporting of illnesses to home communities appear either to have been non-existent at first, or to have not been properly communicated to staff. When a girl from Qamani'tuaq was hospitalized with suspected appendicitis in the fall of 1964, the residence administration did not inform the girl's family. Students, however, sent letters to the community that led her mother to believe that the girl had been hospitalized because of injuries received in a playground altercation. As can be imagined, this caused the mother considerable anxiety. In apologizing for the delay, the Keewatin regional superintendent of schools wrote, "Procedures for reporting hospital admittances to me have now been established and you can be assured that such reports will be forwarded to home settlements in the future."[91]

The parents of a boy from the Kangiqliniq (Rankin Inlet) region discovered that their son had been hospitalized with pneumonia in late 1978 only when another student phoned his family with the news. This apparently was only the latest in a string of failures to communicate such news. Melinda Tatty, the vice-chair of the Rankin Inlet Community Education Committee, said that in the past students had been hospitalized, treated for broken bones, and even undergone surgery without their parents being notified. "A phone call informing the parents of a sick or injured student right away and a follow up phone call on the student's progress and eventual recovery for a serious illness is not too much to ask."[92]

Over time the buildings began to deteriorate, creating health and safety hazards. An inspector judged the sanitation system at the school in Deline (Fort Franklin) "inadequate and unsanitary" in 1965. Waste from the school was pumped into a ditch that drained into Great Bear Lake at a point just 200 metres from the intake that supplied the school with water.[93] Conditions in a temporary classroom structure in Inuvik in that year were so serious that an inspector contemplated closing the building. The girls' lavatory consisted of buckets with plastic liners and lacked a working fan, while the barrel from which students got drinking water was rusty and coated on the bottom with a deposit of yellow sludge.[94] There were also problems at the school in Fort Simpson. There, students were still using two "small and very inadequate" buildings that, according to an Anglican Church official, had been "condemned as unfit for use." The smaller of the two—a one-room, poorly ventilated unit used to instruct twenty-three children — had both an oil stove and a badly leaking oil tank. It also lacked drinking water and a toilet, forcing children outdoors to use the other building's facilities.[95] A call for their replacement would not be heeded until 1970.[96]

By the early 1970s there were growing concerns about the condition of Fleming Hall in Fort McPherson. A 1973 inspection described the residence as being "in poor condition, and ill-kept, cleanliness having been ignored in some areas." For example:

- The first floor "stairways and fire exits were dirty, some contained broken glass and food and garbage on the floors."
- The games rooms had "dirty walls, floors and ceilings.... A torn mattress with exposed springs was being used for tumbling."
- The girls' washroom had "two of 6 water closets not functioning" and "five of the 6 stall doors broken off hinges," and "toilet paper was lying on the floor" due to a lack of dispensers.[97] In 1975 federal Public Works officials concluded that "much of the plumbing is very close to rotten as [are] some parts of the electrical system."[98]

An improvement on the mission schools

Students who were transferred from the old mission residential schools tended to have positive assessments of the new hostels. In her memoirs, Alice Blondin-Perrin, who had attended the Fort Resolution school, wrote of Breynat Hall in Fort Smith:

> Everything looked huge and new, compared to the old St. Joseph's Mission. The most beautiful Christmas tree stood in the little girls' play area. It was nicely decorated with colourful lights, in the freshly painted new residence. There was only Father Mokwa and I as he personally toured me around until we reached the dormitory. A Grey Nun was there. They showed me the brand new beds, much bigger than the cots we had in Fort Resolution, with brand new sheets, spongy pillows, and bedspreads. It all looked so clean and attractive to sleep in. We had our own lockers to store our personal things.[99]

Albert Canadien had gone to the Fort Providence residential school as a young boy. He attended Grade 10 in Yellowknife, while living in Akaitcho Hall.

> Instead of the large dormitories that I was accustomed to, we were assigned four to a room. There were two sets of bunks, closets and dressers, and desks by the window for doing homework. There, I lived and went to school with Inuit, Métis, white, and even Chinese students. This was quite a change for me from the residential school days. Living at the hostel at that time proved to be a good experience for me in later life. It taught me to get along with and respect people from other cultures, to treat them like you would anyone else.[100]

Canadien appreciated the fact that the students were no longer under close supervision. "We had freedom, based on an individual honour system. This was a great improvement from the residential school system."[101]

After his time in the Coppermine tent hostel, Richard Kaiyogan said life at Akaitcho Hall was "like staying in a Four Seasons Hotel."[102] Florence Barnaby did not care for the year that she spent at Grollier Hall, the Roman Catholic residence in Inuvik. She did, however, enjoy her time at Akaitcho Hall.

> It was good there because everybody was mixed up. It just ... they didn't separate the Catholic, the Anglican, and the Protestant. And we—I came home for summer, and then go back again to Akaitcho Hall. And I liked Akaitcho Hall because we have dances every Friday night, you know, and it was good. We eat with the boys. It was, no, "You can't, you have to sit by yourself, or boys this side." It wasn't like that.[103]

Willy Carpenter went to a mission school at Aklavik and then to the hostels and day schools at Inuvik and Yellowknife. He said that life in the mission school was "the hardest part of my life; I was very young and just like—I was treated like an animal. I was treated like an animal. They even fed us like animals." Stringer Hall in Inuvik was, he said, "totally different from Aklavik. And from Stringer Hall I went to Akaitcho Hall; that one was just like living in a hotel, you know."[104]

Steve Lafferty stayed only a short time at Breynat Hall and was sent home because he was too lonesome. When he later went to Lapointe Hall, he said, "I liked it because we played lots of hockey, and then there, too, they gave me a job.... I liked to work, they knew I liked to work, so I used to work in the kitchen a lot." He also liked the fact that the boys were allowed to go out on the land to snare rabbits. Many lifelong friendships were developed at the school. What he recalled about Akaitcho Hall was the fact that it was "totally free."[105]

Other students who had no experience of the old residential schools had positive assessments of Akaitcho Hall. Brenda Jancke and Bernice Lyall, who both went to Akaitcho Hall in the 1980s, shared several positive memories of their school experience. Brenda Jancke remarked that although she recognizes that many Inuit have lost their ties to traditional knowledge, she "didn't really have a bad experience at all" at school, and was able to retain her traditional knowledge thanks to her father who had never been away to school.[106] Bernice Lyall praised many aspects of her time at Akaitcho Hall when she was seventeen: "We had a great time," she stated. She especially remembered the sports—volleyball and hockey—and the excellent staff at the school: they had the "best teachers, best educators," she remembered.[107]

Aboriginal children often received a hostile reception in the public schools. Leda Jules said the transfer from the isolated residential school at Lower Post to Coudert Hall in Whitehorse came as a shock. "I never knew white people before until I went to the Coudert Residence in Whitehorse where we still stayed in a residential school but we went to a public school next door, Christ The King High, that's where I first encountered racism." When a boy in the school called her a 'squaw,' she fought back. "I remember Sister Agnes used to hit us with yard sticks trying to break us apart, I was a real scrapper back then too, but I wasn't going to... I wasn't that little obedient, little kid that came out of Lower Post anymore, you know?"

The role of the churches in hostel life

Even though the hostels in the Northwest Territories and the Yukon had been paid for and usually designed by the federal government, missionaries continued to play a major role in residential schooling. Most of the hostels, for example, were operated, at least initially, by either the Anglican or Roman Catholic church. The continued influence of the churches was reflected in the hostel names. Initially the federal government wished to name the schools after northern explorers and the hostels after First Nations or Aboriginal figures. This was the model that was followed in Yellowknife, where the school was named for Sir John Franklin and the hostel for the Dene Chief

Akaitcho, who served as a guide to Franklin.[108] The Roman Catholics preferred that the hostels they administered be given names that would indicate that the hostel was under church management.[109] As a result the church-administered hostels were named after Catholic or Anglican missionaries. At Chesterfield Inlet, Turquetil Hall (named after an Oblate missionary, Arsène Turquetil) was built alongside Joseph Bernier School (named for the leader of twelve Canadian government expeditions to the Polar Seas). In Inuvik, children lived at Grollier Hall and Stringer Hall, named respectively after a Catholic missionary, Father P. Grollier, and an Anglican missionary, Isaac Stringer. They attended Sir Alexander Mackenzie federal school (named for the fur trader whose travels took him down the Mackenzie River to the Arctic Ocean).[110] In the Yukon the Protestant hostel was simply Yukon Hall, but the Catholic residence was Coudert Hall, after Bishop Jean L. Coudert.[111] It was only in 1971, with the opening of the Ukkivik hostel in Iqaluit, that the practice of incorporating Aboriginal names and languages in the naming of hostels was revived.[112]

While the Churchill school and residence were meant to be non-denominational, both the Anglican and Catholic churches still expected to play a role in their operation. Anglican Bishop Donald Marsh was alarmed to discover that five Anglican boys from the communities of Igloolik and Foxe Basin had been housed in the Roman Catholic dormitory at Chesterfield Inlet, as a stopover en route to school in Churchill. Housing the boys in "that environment" did not give Marsh confidence that "they are being looked after as Anglican children."[113] In 1964 Roman Catholic church officials complained that not enough was being done to ensure that Catholic students were not living in dormitories that were supervised by non-Catholics.[114] The residence had arranged to house Catholic boys in separate rooms from the non-Catholic boys. However, in the opinion of Father R. Haramburu, this was not sufficient.[115]

Even at such non-denominational hostels as the Churchill Vocational Centre, students were expected to attend chapel on Sunday. In 1970 Catholic and Anglican officials, alarmed by a drop in the number of students attending local church services at Churchill, asked that the school implement an existing government policy of giving assignments to students who did not attend church. Such assignments, they said, were to be seen not as punishment, but "as a means to make clear that the time for church services is not to be used as they like."[116] The actual policy stated that children who did not attend church could be assigned other duties such as supervised study or "some light duty."[117] For his part, the school principal, F. Dunford, resisted the measure, since in his opinion such assignments "would be a punitive or retributive act."[118]

In 1969, the government provided the following assessment of the policy of church management of the schools. Church management, it was argued, had provided:

1) Superior care in the terms of personalized concern and human understanding have been provided by a group of dedicated people that could not be duplicated;

2) The cost of operation has been less than could be achieved under government control; and

3) Although hostels for persons of a particular belief have a divisive effect in a community, religious bias has been kept to a minimum and appears to be growing less rather than more over the years.[119]

Given the ongoing sexual abuse at a number of church-run residences, it is hard to accept that church-run hostels provided "superior care." The assertion that religious bias had been kept to a minimum is debatable: the statements of former students make it clear that Catholic students were taught to be suspicious of Protestants and vice versa. Undeniably, though, the churches did save the government money over the years, drawing on the cheap labour that came with many of their religious orders, and thus operating the hostels for many years for less than it would have cost the government to run them.

Extracurricular activities

Compared with the mission schools, the hostels, with their gymnasiums and skating rinks, provided students with an improved range of extracurricular activities. The federal government provided $10 per student per year to help pay for extracurricular activities—an amount Anglican Church representative Henry Cook judged to be ridiculously small in 1959.[120] According to one observer at Inuvik in the 1960s, the sports teams were almost exclusively made up of Aboriginal students.[121] Grollier Hall was equipped with a swimming pool, a covered arena, and a variety of gymnasium equipment that had been purchased through Roman Catholic fundraising efforts.[122] When the Oblates ended their involvement with the management of the residence in 1987, they sought to donate the facilities to the Northwest Territories government.[123] Following a series of ski clinics in 1965 and 1966, Grollier Hall was also the centre of the Territorial Experimental Ski Training (TEST).[124]

From the outset Akaitcho Hall had a student council that was responsible for writing a column in the local newspaper, organizing dances, and representing student issues. It was funded by revenue from a soft-drink machine.[125] Athletic recreation included skating, hockey, and basketball.[126] There were also square dancing, hot-rod, science, rifle, fine arts, radio, and newspaper clubs.[127] Among the sports activities available at the Churchill residence were skating, hockey, broomball, bowling, and basketball. Students could also take part in amateur radio and chess clubs, gymnastics and square dancing groups, choir, Boy Scouts, and Cadets. As well, there were Friday night dances and Saturday afternoon and evening movies at a movie theatre in the residence.[128] At Turquetil Hall in 1957, recreational evenings were held at the day school and the hostel, giving children a chance to engage in such activities as board games, singing, listening to music, bingo, and ping-pong.[129] Northern Affairs official J. V. Jacobson applauded the establishment of a Boy Scout troop at Turquetil Hall in 1959, saying that it "should help a great deal to round out the education being given the boys of this community."[130] In 1963 the Cubs at Fleming Hall were looking forward to a weekend of camping at the beginning of May. Earlier that year a large caribou herd had passed through the region, making it possible "for many of the older boys in the school to go with their parents for a short hunt, and have the thrill of shooting their first caribou."[131]

Some students had positive memories of the new opportunities and experiences that were part of hostel life. At the Churchill hostel, Paul Quassa enjoyed movie nights, listening to *Hockey Night in Canada*, ice skating, and playing basketball against teams of non-Aboriginal boys from northern Manitoba: "We were very short as Inuit, and the *qallunaat* [non-Inuit/White people] were very tall! [But] we beat them all."[132] David Simailik remembers playing in a rock band, and several others remember the good friends they made in the dormitories.[133]

Alex Alikashuak had positive memories of the amenities available at the Churchill centre.

> Our school, it used to be, like, an army camp, so it already had everything....
> Our dormitories used to be the old army barracks, and all these dormitories
> were connected by a long utilidor system, that connected to what we call the
> recreation hall. Then you go further down, it was connected to a theatre, like a
> full size theatre, like the ones they got today, we had one of those. And then at
> the end, you had a main floor and a second floor that were, like, convenience
> stores. Like, you know, we had a little coffee shop there. We had a little this, we
> had a little of that.... We were very, very well, well equipped. I don't know how to
> put it. We had everything. Like, we had, like a gym, where people could go and
> play basketball, volleyball, or whatever they do in the gym.[134]

Betsy Annahatak had similar memories. She went from Kangirsuk, in northern Québec, to the Churchill Vocational Centre, when she was in her early teens. "I had fun. I thought I had fun. I went to school, it was exciting. We had recreation activities, volleyball, basketball, movies, all these exciting activities. And at the time I thought, 'It's ok, it's good, it's fun, we're young.'"[135]

An early concern was the fact that few students had any spending money. Akaitcho Hall administrator A. J. Boxer said the lack of spending money had "been contributory to some troublesome petty thievery in the dorms where no locker facilities are provided." To combat the problem, he put in a request for locks that students could install on their dressers.[136] In 1965 Northern Affairs authorized the provision of a dollar-a-week allowance to be given to hostel residents age fifteen and over who had "no other source of money."[137]

Fewer resources were available for non-sports-related activities. In a 1965 review of the hostels, University of British Columbia education professor Joseph Katz observed that the fact that most hostels were equipped with adequate playground and athletic facilities meant that "other types of programs are lost sight of." He recommended the introduction of more "music, painting and sculpture, weaving, knitting, beadwork, sewing and similar activities."[138]

While the students enjoyed their participation in these games, sports, and clubs, from the Northern Affairs perspective all such extracurricular activities were valued for their assimilative benefit. A policy document from 1964 observed that Northern Affairs encouraged "Scouts and Guides, Cadets, hobby clubs, film showings, inter-schools competitions, field days, as some of the activities which offer these students opportunities for acculturation experiences beyond those given in school."[139]

At the beginning of January 1977, an inspection of Lapointe Hall identified the need for more staff training and direction for sports and recreation programs.[140] It does not appear that these recommendations were acted upon. When four students from the residence appeared in court in Fort Simpson in late 1977 on charges of theft from a private home, the local magistrate asked for a Mounted Police investigation into conditions at the residence. In reporting to the territorial commissioner on the development, Brian Lewis, the Northwest Territories director of education, wrote, "I expect considerable repercussions over this issue since we cannot expect a positive report."[141] The report highlighted the limited number of recreational activities available to students. "Nearly every student mentioned that lack of activities was their major drawback to hostel life. The students claimed that they were bored sitting around the hostel with nothing to do."[142]

Disciplinary regulations and practice

There appears to have been no overall Northern Affairs policy on the rules covering student behaviour or regulations to govern discipline in the residences. As a result each institution established its own policies. Corporal punishment was not banned in the Yukon until 1990. The Northwest Territories government banned the practice in 1995.[143] In reporting on the establishment of Akaitcho Hall in 1958, the resident administrator, A. J. Boxer, wrote, "We have granted wide freedom to students on town leave. A large percentage have not abused this privilege: and for those who have, we have made progress in establishing satisfactory preventative measures through prolonged detention periods; and in serious cases, indefinite detention—unless supervised—has been imposed."[144]

In 1962 a number of girls announced that discipline was so severe at Akaitcho Hall that they planned not to return to the residence. According to an investigation carried out by the regional superintendent of schools, a number of girls felt the girls' head supervisor was overly strict. Staff members felt that the supervisor was both hard-working and dedicated, and noted that her strictness was a product of her "devotion to the girls in her care, for whom she feels great responsibility." It was also said that many students willingly went to her for advice and counselling. However, it was also thought that she had a tendency to pick on certain students and remind them of their past misdemeanours and, as a result, "created an air of tension in the dormitory."[145]

At Stringer Hall in the late 1960s, privileges could be withdrawn from an individual or a group, such as a whole dormitory. Failing that, corporal punishment was used, albeit rarely. In these circumstances, it was left to the hostel administrator to carry out the punishment, although there were instances when supervisors would slap or hit children without the sanction of the administrator.[146] These forms of punishment, especially corporal punishment, were resented by students who had grown up in a culture where children were rarely struck. As one supervisor observed, the "white people in the hostel impose an alien form of control which is harsh and severe to the children."[147]

Residences that took in younger students appear to have employed harsher disciplinary practices. In the Yukon, the Carcross school operated in the manner of a traditional residential school institution. Discipline was strict, and the church staff exercised considerable control over the facility. Of his year as a teacher at the Carcross school in the early 1960s, Richard King wrote:

> Punishments are usually more severe than one cares to encounter. Beatings can be endured, but beatings are infrequent. The most frequent punishments are removal of privileges, confinements, or isolation—all of which involve serious damage to one's image with others, as well as to his own ego. It is therefore often necessary for children to lie when discovered in any behaviour that was not specifically directed.

Because children would not reveal who among them had broken any specific rule, administrators imposed group punishments. "Once the entire boys' dormitory was put to bed immediately after dinner for a month—including movie nights—because they had not remained silent after lights out, and nobody would reveal who had been telling stories in the dark."[148] In 1964, a teacher at Carcross, I. M. McCoy, complained to Indian Affairs about the way some of the other staff members at the school were treating students. She pointed in particular to one who hit young children on the head with a rolled-up newspaper if they got out of line during the bathroom parade. McCoy felt persecuted by other teachers when she stood up for her students and left for a position with a public school.[149]

It appears that at the remote Chesterfield Inlet school and residence, conditions also resembled those of a more traditional, punitive residential school. In her 1994 report on physical and sexual abuse at the Joseph Bernier school and Turquetil Hall residence in Chesterfield Inlet, the lawyer Katherine Peterson wrote:

> From the detailed investigations conducted by the RCMP, there have arisen 115 allegations of physical abuse. Some of the allegations of assault take the form of overzealous discipline such as strapping or striking of students with rulers, yard sticks or spanking. These forms of discipline at times exceeded reasonable measures. In addition to this, there were allegations of physical assault which resulted in injuries to the students. One teacher in particular, who was not a member of the Roman Catholic Institution, was well known for his harsh and overzealous discipline. Experiences related to me included students being thrown against classroom walls, a student being picked up physically from her seat by her ears. Shortly thereafter she suffered bleeding and discharge from her ears although it is difficult now to establish whether this was as a result of this action. Students reported being struck repeatedly about the face, back, shoulders, back of the head and buttocks. One child recalled being removed from her seat by her hair. In addition, my review of statements provided to the RCMP indicates one allegation of physical assault involving a child being placed in an automated bread mixer and left in that machinery for an extended period of time. Bruising and lacerations resulted from this. A further statement has been obtained by the RCMP respecting a student being thrown through a classroom window.[150]

In some cases it was felt that the administrators had failed to impose or maintain order. In 1966 a federal government official concluded that conditions at Yukon Hall in Whitehorse were so out of control that the school administrator needed to be dismissed. Among the examples he gave of lack of discipline at the school were "comments by students and about the Administrator, older students reporting in under the influence of alcohol, older students in possession of alcohol in the Hostel, deliberate baiting of the Administrator by the pupils as they walked down the halls." Staff complained that the hostel administrator laid down rigid rules but did not enforce them when staff identified violations of the rules. In one case no disciplinary action was taken after a student struck the principal. The unnamed author of the report recommended that "the administration of the Hostel be turned over to a church group," preferably the Anglicans.[151]

The residence administrators had to determine which behaviours to ban and which to accept. Because so many students smoked, the Catholic hostel in Whitehorse established a smoking lounge. This was seen as being preferable to students smoking in the dormitories, where it would create a fire hazard. Students who brought alcohol into the hostel were at risk of expulsion.[152]

The haphazard nature of rule making came to national attention in March 1969 when Ron Haggart, a columnist with the Toronto *Telegram*, described the rules governing Akaitcho Hall as examples of "apartheid and paternalism." At meals students were to confine their conversation to their own table, girls were not to wear slacks or jeans to the cafeteria, and soap and toothpaste would be issued only "on production of remains of previous issue." Students required permission to leave the residence. On Sundays, they could not leave unless they had first attended church service because "religious teaching and practice has ever been a significant part of life in Canada's north." Student also needed permission to bring guests into the hostel: they were to be "limited to one guest per month." Students who brought cars to the hostel were obliged to turn their keys over to the administration since they were not allowed to drive their vehicles while in residence.[153] In defending the rules, the best that Indian Affairs Minister and future prime minister Jean Chrétien could say was that "over half" of the approximately 180 residents were eighteen or younger. He also rejected implications that the rules were racist by pointing out that seventy of the residents were non-Aboriginal.[154]

Within a month of Haggart's column appearing, a student council was established at Akaitcho Hall and the rules were subjected to a review.[155] In private correspondence, Stuart M. Hodgson, the commissioner of the Northwest Territories, blamed the controversy on Steve Iveson, a member of the Company of Young Canadians (a federal government community-development agency), who had been in contact with a number of dissatisfied hostel residents. Hodgson added that unfortunately it had been necessary to discharge two of these students from the residence.[156] They had been involved in a verbal confrontation with residence officials when they attempted to read out a statement critical of the Akaitcho Hall administration in the school lunchroom. The girls, who were judged to be capable students, were discharged, but a decision was made to provide funding to allow them to board at a private residence and finish their schooling.[157]

When he reviewed the new rules, Chrétien congratulated Hodgson for removing "questionable items" from the previous rules. He did observe that a proposed rule prohibiting students from consuming alcoholic beverages "anywhere and anytime" during the period that they were living at the residence "trespassed the personal rights of students who are over the age of 21." He suggested that the rules simply ban the use of alcoholic beverages in the hostel.[158] The finalized list of regulations was only five pages long (the previous rules had been twenty-seven pages) and contained none of the provisions that Haggart had ridiculed.[159] The new rules were not always applied consistently. In the 1980s supervisors who had grounded a student for violating a residence rule might discover that an earlier supervisor had, without consultation, lifted the measure. As the residence administrator noted, this practice was rendering "the discipline procedure ineffectual."[160]

When asked for a copy of Stringer Hall's residence guidelines in 1969, administrator Leonard Holman said there were no written rules. However, from his letter it is apparent that there was a set of expectations about student behaviour. Students were expected to be on time for meals, could chew gum anywhere but in the chapel and the dining room, and could smoke if they were sixteen or over (fifteen-year-olds could smoke if they had a note of permission from their parents). They could invite friends for meals and to spend the weekend at the hostel, and in turn could eat meals or spend weekends with friends—providing notice was given in advance. Older students could stay out late one night a week—but were expected to be back by midnight. Holman was proud of the fact that the majority of students respected this rule.[161] For example, on a Friday night in 1967, 104 students from Stringer Hall signed themselves out to attend movies or a local basketball game. Of this number, all but one student returned at the end of the evening: the one who did not return had decided to spend the night at an aunt's house.[162] Holman told students who had reached the legal drinking age that while they were legally entitled to frequent beer parlours, he preferred that they did not.[163]

Within months of a new residence administrator being appointed in 1974, Stringer Hall students submitted a petition calling for the dismissal of the assistant administrator. According to the petition, the official had assaulted students who lived in the residence and blackmailed them into doing things they did not wish to do.[164] Although a number of the students later signed a document saying that they wished to withdraw the petition, it is clear there were problems at the residence.[165] According to an investigation carried out by a Northwest Territories government inspector, staff members felt that the new administrator did not support staff on disciplinary matters, was absent from the residence on too many occasions, and "condoned drinking and other antisocial behaviour among the students." For his part, the new administrator felt that some staff members expected him "to run the residence like a 'prison.'" The inspector concluded that there was a "lack of communication and mutual respect amongst the staff."[166]

In the late 1980s, Grollier Hall had a student court that imposed penalties such as grounding and chores for violations of school rules.[167] As part of the court process, students had to fill out a form explaining what they had done, why they had done it, and what they were going to do about it.[168]

Gary Black, the assistant superintendent of education for the Northwest Territories, wrote after visiting Lapointe Hall in 1973 that the residence could "at best ... be described as tolerable. Only very extensive renovations would make it any more than tolerable." Black said there were numerous staff problems that he attributed to the authoritarian nature of the residence administrator. According to Black, "People outside the hostel, with some justification, see it as an island surrounded by heavily armed walls. Many integrating activities between hostel and town students which took place in previous years have disappeared."[169]

This comparison of the residence to a prison or a fortress was drawn not by a critic of the system but by one of its senior officials. The fact that he placed considerable responsibility for the problems in the residence on the administrator draws attention to the central importance of staffing for the success or failure of the residences. The following year the residence was taken over by the Koe Go Cho Society, a Dene organization in Fort Simpson.[170]

Supervision

Issues of discipline were complicated by the fact that the hostels were understaffed, supervisory jobs were poorly defined (in fact, often undefined), and hostel employees often had neither the background nor the training needed for the work they were doing. Low wages exacerbated all these problems.

A 1965 review of the hostels in the Northwest Territories identified problems in the staff-to-student ratios. At the Roman Catholic Breynat Hall in Fort Smith, there were seventeen supervisors, responsible for 145 students. There were only three male staff members to supervise sixty-three boys. At Stringer Hall in Inuvik, twenty-three staff members were responsible for 290 students. In September 1965, at the beginning of the Churchill Vocational Centre's second year of operation, one of the staff members took her concerns over staffing levels to Anglican Bishop Donald Marsh. She wrote, "There are not enough staff members employed so that staff members can have definite time off. Everyone suffers when people are expected to work without a break. Personally, if relief supervision doesn't appear in the near future, a replacement will be needed for me."[171]

A 1965 Indian Affairs report on conditions at Yukon Hall in Whitehorse observed:

> There appeared to be only one male and one female supervisor on duty with little attention being given to the organization of any program except the study situation, which was being supervised by Miss Loan. A spirit of friendliness and spontaneity, which is evident among many of our youngsters of high school age, appeared to be totally lacking at the Yukon Hostel.[172]

Six years later a review of Yukon Hall, which had just been merged with Coudert Hall, identified a number of problems with the child care service at the residence. Because the chief child care worker was also responsible for the direct supervision of a group of students, there was minimal "direct supervision of child care workers." Nor was there any formal orientation program for new child care workers. As a result, "many child care workers were uncertain as to their exact duties and responsibilities." The student-to-staff ratio was also very high: in one dormitory building, it was sixty-five to two.[173]

In January 1976 a father said that he was concerned about the safety of his son, who was living in Fleming Hall at Fort McPherson. L. Donavon said that on a visit to the hostel he saw a locked escape door, garbage piled up in front of the kitchen's escape door, insufficient water supply, and "children left alone on weekends with no supervisory staff or the staff drunk."[174]

An RCMP investigation into conditions at the hostel at Fort Simpson in 1977 concluded that the facility was understaffed. At any time the supervisor-to-student ratio was one to twenty when, in the opinion of the investigating officer, it should have been one to eight or one to ten. Frustrated staff would "yell, swear and actually strike the students." He noted that the supervisors acted as "house mothers," waking students in the morning, ensuring they had sufficient clothing, and putting them to bed at night. "Furthermore, they administer the discipline when required." While there was a list of rules for the hostel, there were no policies or directives regarding the method or type of discipline to be used: "The decision is left up to the supervisor."[175]

Dormitory supervisors were largely untrained. As the author of the 1965 report, Joseph Katz, observed, "Those hostel personnel directly involved in giving social, academic, spiritual and group guidance are as much in need of specialized training as are chefs and the like."[176] The fact that the student records at the hostel were judged to be "rudimentary" and "ineffective as guides to other supervisors or other interested personnel" is just another reflection of the need for better training.[177] In his notes from the mid-1960s, former supervisor Rodney Clifton observed that few of his colleagues at Stringer Hall were properly trained to work in the North. They had undergone little or nothing in the way of cross-cultural education, knew little about the North or the people who lived there, and did not understand the role of the hostel itself. Nor was any training available to help them address this shortcoming.[178] In his opinion many hostel employees were guided by a generally racist assumption that students' misbehaviour was the result of their not caring about anything.[179]

An investigation into conditions at the Churchill Vocational Centre concluded that the supervisors had not been provided with written job descriptions before they were hired: "It would appear that each Supervisor has a different understanding of his conditions of employment and they all are unanimous in agreeing that the actual conditions they are experiencing are somewhat different than those described when they were hired." The problem was compounded by the fact that there still did not appear to be written job descriptions. As a result, the Northern Affairs employee conducting the investigation recommended "no time be lost in reducing their conditions of employment to writing."

In addition, the residence administrator was locked in a power struggle with the school principal and the residence matron (who was the wife of a regional Northern Affairs official). Residence staff members found themselves in the middle of these conflicts.[180] By October 1965 five supervisors had resigned, although eventually the resignations were withdrawn.[181] Staff problems would recur: in November of 1971 it was reported that staff "morale was so low it was affecting the students."[182] Five staff members resigned in August 1972.[183]

In December 1974 students from the hostel went to the home of the chair of the Fort McPherson Settlement Council, John Simon, to complain that the hostel administrator was drinking and verbally abusing students. Simon visited the residence and discovered that the administrator was scolding a number of children and had been drinking. It was recognized that there was a "real lack of supervision at the hostel," since "liquor, beer and glue can be smuggled into the dorms and not detected by the staff."[184] In 1974 the Northwest Territories government was considering closing Fleming Hall because of low enrolment. Students would be either placed in local homes or sent to Inuvik.[185] The hostel was closed at the end of the 1975–76 school year.[186]

The understaffing of the schools led to a lack of supervision that could have tragic consequences. On June 11, 1972, two boys who were living at Stringer Hall in Inuvik left the residence for a walk. Robert Toasi and David Kasoni found a canoe in Boot Lake, on the edge of the community. Using boards as paddles, they set out in the canoe, travelling through a channel to another lake. When they attempted their return journey, they tipped the canoe. David was able to swim to shore but Robert Toasi, who was fifteen years old, drowned. His body was found the following evening. An inquest returned a verdict of accidental drowning.[187]

Heavy workload and low wages led to constant turnover. The resignation of two supervisors at Akaitcho Hall in 1966 prompted K. W. Hawkins, the administrator for the Mackenzie District, to observe, "During the past two years we have been plagued with a steady turnover of supervisory staff at Akaitcho Hall and for long periods have operated without adequate staff." Given the wages that were being offered, it was "almost impossible to recruit and hold people with only minimal qualifications, let alone those who are as qualified as we feel they should be." Hawkins feared that "we may shortly face a situation where it will be impossible to operate Akaitcho Hall at all."[188]

Despite such concerns, wages remained low. In 1973 Evelyn Nind wrote a letter to the Northwest Territories government and compared two government job advertisements that ran on the same day: one for a dormitory supervisor at Akaitcho Hall and one for a personal secretary for the deputy commissioner of the Northwest Territories. The pay range for the supervisor was $6,632 to $8,034; for the secretary, it was $7,513 to $9,055. She asked, "Can we assume from these two advertisements that in the Government's opinion a secretary is worth more than a person charged with the responsibility of guiding and counseling our youth into maturity?"[189]

Because staff were poorly supervised, conflict with students became inevitable. In 1987 members of the Kitikmeot Regional Education Committee (KREC) in the central Arctic visited Yellowknife to meet with students going to school there from their region.

Mel Pardy, a Northwest Territories education official who was part of the KREC delegation, reported that the students described the Akaitcho supervisors as "uncaring and ... expressing little, if any, genuine concern for the welfare of the individual student."

> Only a couple of supervisors were perceived as genuinely caring for the students' welfare, the majority of the supervisors perceived as being there only to enforce the rules. Supervisors viewed as "probation officers," who are "looking over our shoulder every minute," and "just waiting to catch us doing something wrong" only serves to illustrate the level of student paranoia.[190]

There were two dominant disciplinary issues in the northern hostels. One was the problem of students running away. The second was relatively new to residential schooling: alcohol—and later drug—use and abuse.

Runaways

The hostels in Whitehorse had an ongoing problem with runaways. By the beginning of October 1960, F. Barnes, the acting administrator of Yukon Hall, the Protestant hostel in Whitehorse, reported a disturbing number of runaways.

The problem was complicated since many of the children had been admitted without signed admission slips. His description of the four main causes of truancy provides a glimpse into the life of the institution.

> (a) Relaxation of Discipline and absence of Locked doors—We have treated the children leniently and kindly and they probably attribute it to "softness." This I understand they are not used to but I believe it will "pay off" in the long run. We have given them much more freedom than they are used to and they are taking advantage of it. However, I would like to see it given a fair trial even though we do lose some older children by it. Mr. Grant feels that every child who runs away should be brought back and punished but I have been dubious about corporal punishment since I don't even have the admission slips yet to know which children have been signed over to us.

> (b) Lack of understanding on the part of the parents and children alike as to the need and value of an education. It seems to me that the various religious groups have been after the parents to send their children to their particular school until the parents feel it is a privilege for them to send their children anywhere. Hence if the children don't like it here the parents will just keep them at home etc. The children complain bitterly at having to make their beds and sweep the floors which should "all be done for them" according to one father I encountered.

(c) Self-consciousness—Many older children were brought in who are only in Grades 5 or 6 and they feel so out of place with white kiddies 3 and 4 years younger that I can hardly blame them for giving up.

(d) Homesickness—This can be a real illness and many are homesick and frightened. The surroundings and faces are strange and the first or second night the fire alarm went off frightening everyone. No one knows why it did and it still does on occasion but not at night any more thank goodness.[191]

Shortly after Barnes wrote this note, a number of girls ran away from the residence. The school official sent to retrieve them "met with opposition on the part of parents toward the children returning." The father of one of the children complained that a beating from the principal had left his daughter with a swollen hand. Barnes did not accept the allegation, saying, "No child has yet been given corporal punishment this fall." Barnes sought permission from Indian Affairs to have the RCMP bring back those who were refusing to return to school.[192]

Coudert Hall, the Roman Catholic hostel in Whitehorse, adopted a policy of simply discharging runaway students who were sixteen years of age or older. When discharging two such runaways in 1961, hostel principal E. A. Cullinane noted that the girls had "responded admirably to the loving care and firm discipline administered here." But while they had put considerable effort into their studies, they had been frustrated by the "academic-type education which has been imposed upon them." It was, he wrote, "very sad indeed that we do not have available for them a more realistic and practical curriculum designed to develop their feminine qualities and provide them with the specialized training which they need in order to become good wives and good mothers."

Cullinane was not sure how to punish runaways who were under the age of sixteen, since he felt strapping them "only makes matters worse, intensifying their resentment and hostility towards authority."[193] His successor Marcel Piché reported in 1965 that he had strapped three girls for "their conduct during the Sourdough week-end" in Yellowknife. On a previous weekend, they had run off and, according to Piché, engaged in bad behaviour.[194]

In 1964 two fifteen-year-old girls and two fourteen-year-old girls were returned to their home communities after running away from Coudert Hall and spending the weekend in town. The administrator was reported to be relieved that the older girls were gone since they had been "troublesome in the hostel."[195] In 1967 the Coudert Hall principal issued instructions that a fourteen-year-old girl who had run away for the third time be returned to her parents once she was located.[196]

Many of the children in the Northwest Territories were from isolated settlements, thousands of kilometres from the school residences. In 1967 one student from Stringer Hall in Inuvik bought a ticket for a flight to his home community, packed his belongings, and left without telling either his friends or the school administrators that he was leaving. At his request his mother had sent him the money for the ticket home.[197] In February 1968 the Mounted Police were called in after three girls, aged thirteen to fifteen, took off from Stringer Hall with only "several blankets ... plus a bit of food off the evening snack cart." The father of one of the girls had recently said he would take her out of school if she did not behave. They were located two days later in a private house in Inuvik.[198]

The most successful and safest way to turn truant was to simply refuse to be returned to school after a visit home. In 1985, for example, thirty-four students did not return to Akaitcho Hall from spring break.[199] Each Easter, Peggy Tologanak's parents would visit the Inuvik hostel and take her and her siblings, by plane, to Reindeer Station to visit relatives. At the end of the visit, Peggy, along with other children, would try to avoid returning to the hostel. "When the plane would come and pick us up, those of us from the hostel, we used to hide because we didn't want to go back. But they'd search for us, and search for us in the hills, and then they'd take us back to the hostel."[200]

Two boys under the age of ten attempted to run away from Stringer Hall on four separate occasions in 1972. They were either brought back or returned each time.[201] On June 23, 1972, three boys, Lawrence Jack Elanik, Bernard Andreason, and Dennis Dick, ran away from Stringer Hall.[202] Andreason was found alive a few kilometres from Tuktoyaktuk. He had walked approximately 150 kilometres and lost almost fourteen kilograms. His feet were badly swollen. Elanik's body was located, but the search for Dick was called off. Stringer Hall principal L. Holman reported:

> Everything that could possibly be done, was done, to try and locate these boys
> before it was too late. The R.C.M.P., the Regional Director's Office & Staff, owners
> of private aircraft, the various Air Services, Helicopter Operator's[sic], private
> citizens and the men of the Armed Forces at Inuvik, did a valiant job.[203]

Rather than running away, other students employed more passive strategies to resist and cope with life at the hostel. One coping mechanism was for students to "shut down" their emotions. Lavinia Brown explains that being at the hostel made her block out everything she should have known and experienced as a child: "We were shut down," she says.[204] Richard King, who taught at the Carcross school in the early 1960s, observed, "By the time the children are in their third year at school, they simply prefer routine as the simplest way of coping with life. The spark of learning for learning's sake is gone, replaced by a programmatic gamesmanship. Decisions are detestable events unless one directly benefits from them."[205]

Alcohol and drugs

In the early winter of 1992, a student living at Akaitcho Hall died of exposure, apparently after becoming inebriated at a weekend party.[206] His death underscored the fact that the consumption of alcohol—by both hostel staff and students—was an ongoing problem at the northern residences from the day they opened until they closed. Shortly after Akaitcho Hall opened, the residence administrator began dismissing students for drunkenness.[207] The residence adopted a policy under which students would be dismissed after their second alcohol-related incident.[208]

The Akaitcho Hall policy initially had not only banned alcohol from the residence but prohibited residents from consuming alcohol even off the property. Since the legal drinking age at that time was twenty-one, the ban on alcohol consumption was largely in keeping with territorial legislation. This changed in 1970, when the drinking age in both the Northwest Territories and the Yukon was lowered to nineteen.[209] This exacerbated what was already a serious problem for the hostels.

At Akaitcho Hall staff members were not allowed to drink while on duty or while they were in the hostel. However, a note by the administrator of Akaitcho Hall in 1965 suggests these rules were sometimes broken. The administrator reminded staff members that they should not drink while on duty and that he was "not prepared to accept that inebriation or semi-inebriation is a proper state for staff members ... on duty or off duty."[210] At the same hostel in 1971, a boys' supervisor resigned over his "drinking problem." Discussing the resignation, the hostel administrator commented that it was a good thing, since the supervisor's drinking had "been causing concern and anxiety."[211] At Stringer Hall, drinking among the staff was also a problem. According to Rodney Clifton, some of his colleagues "drink quite heavily," and drinking caused some staff to be "late for work or turn up slightly inebriated."[212] Controlling this staff drinking was a constant problem for administrators and other teachers. At Stringer Hall, staff were not often disciplined for drinking. One assistant was fired and then quickly rehired.[213]

Student consumption of alcohol was not only illegal, it could end in violence. In 1971 four students from Akaitcho Hall (two aged seventeen, two aged eighteen) spent an evening at a cabin owned by the hostel. They were drinking, and one of them had borrowed a handgun from another student at the school. For reasons that were not clear, he shot and wounded the other three.[214] A Grade Ten student was discharged from Akaitcho Hall after she attacked and beat another female resident while inebriated. The victim required four stitches to close the wounds on her head.[215] In 1986 a mother from Deline complained that a woman in Inuvik was hosting drinking parties for students from Grollier Hall. She said her son had attended one of these parties and was subsequently accused of assaulting a person he met there.[216]

Discharge from a residence carried serious consequences. Students who had been dismissed from a residence on two occasions were no longer eligible for financial support from the Northwest Territories residential boarding program.[217]

From the beginning the rules were applied with discretion. In 1959, two girls, one sixteen, one twenty, attended a house party in Yellowknife, after saying they were going to church. When one of them returned to the residence in a state of inebriation, the Mounted Police were dispatched to the house. The other girl was located and returned to the hostel. Although the residence rules of the day prohibited residents from consuming alcohol in any location, the decision was made to discharge the twenty-year-old, who was judged to be a bad influence, and to allow the sixteen-year-old to remain.[218] In 1966 the district superintendent of schools for the Mackenzie District of the Northwest Territories complained that the Akaitcho Hall administrator had not been sufficiently strict in dealing with a "recent drinking episode involving a number of girls from Akaitcho Hall." He also thought that some of the girls involved should not be allowed to return to the residence for the next school year.[219] In June 1972 the administrator of Akaitcho Hall recommended against admitting at least thirty former students in the coming school year. In most cases, the reason was their problems with alcohol.[220]

Many students were discharged and later refused readmission to hostels because of their involvement with alcohol. In 1966 approximately twenty of the older students at Grollier Hall were going into town in the evenings and coming back drunk, occasionally bringing alcohol back into the hostel with them. On the tenth occasion that one twenty-year-old returned drunk in a three-month period, the head of Grollier Hall sought the permission of the superintendent of schools in Inuvik to evict the student.[221] In 1967, Stringer Hall administrator Leonard Holman recommended the discharge of three students from Stringer Hall for belligerence, disobedience, and under-age drinking.[222] The following year eleven students were discharged from the hostel for "drinking and intoxication, obnoxious, insolent and rude behaviour, disobedience and refusal to comply with hostel regulations, and foul language, lack of respect for the school, hostel and staff."[223]

In 1976 Piita Irniq (then known as Peter Ernerk), a former residential school student who had become a member of the territorial council, intervened on behalf of a boy from his constituency who had been expelled from Akaitcho Hall for fighting. Irniq, who felt that the boy was a "good student," said he was concerned about the case because he was "very aware of the kinds of things that can go on while away from home." He asked that the boy be given one more chance. "What will happen when he [returns] to Rankin Inlet after being expelled? The rest of society will forget about him and he will never be able to get a proper job anywhere."[224] In this case Irniq's effort appears to have been unsuccessful: the June 1977 quarterly return lists the boy as having been expelled in December 1976.[225]

By the 1980s Akaitcho Hall would place a student with an alcohol-related violation on probation and send a letter of notification to the student's parents.[226] A student might not be actually expelled until the fourth violation of the rule.[227]

Students who had violated the rules about alcohol at Grollier Hall were required to sign contracts with the administration. One such contract obliged the student to join the Grollier Hall Drummers and live by the Drummers' Code of Ethics, to sign up for two sports programs, to participate in six support group meetings, and to stop "'hanging around' with his girlfriend in the main hallway of Grollier Hall."[228] Into the 1990s Grollier Hall administrators were regularly sending parents letters alerting them to the fact that their children had violated the hostel's alcohol and drug policies.[229]

At the beginning of 1980 the Akaitcho Hall administrator had identified a new problem: drug use. He estimated that it had "reached such proportion that some immediate action must be planned and taken." Until that point, he said, the school had addressed the use of drugs—which he said included marijuana, hashish, and LSD—by "counseling, advising, etc." He wanted the RCMP to conduct a thorough investigation, including a search of the residence.[230] Police officials said they had made only two drug seizures at the school, neither of which resulted in the laying of charges. Nor did they appear to be interested in carrying out a search of the dormitory. They did agree to co-operate with the administration in addressing the issue.[231] In the spring of 1982, three boys were caught smoking marijuana in the washroom, and a new administrator concluded that "drinking and drugs in the residence continues to be a serious problem with no apparent effective method of control."[232]

Parents were both fearful of what might happen to their children when they were in residence and anxious about the conditions that prevailed in the institutions. They saw alcohol abuse as a sign of larger problems. In 1982 some parents from Kangiqliniq were distressed to discover that their child was being sent home from Akaitcho Hall. The parents felt that they had not been made aware that their child had become a discipline problem. In another situation, the hostel administrator had declined to take action when an inebriated boy had panicked and left the hostel late at night improperly dressed. Rather than look for him, the supervisor was reported to have said the boy would sober up and return. Three boys who did not share the supervisor's confidence decided to conduct a search on their own and stayed out until past midnight. In light of these concerns, the Akaitcho Hall Parents' Committee of the Keewatin Region called on the administration to dismiss the supervisor in question.[233] Parents from several Keewatin Region communities followed up on their concerns by travelling to Yellowknife to visit Akaitcho Hall. They produced a detailed twenty-one-page report on their assessment of the residence. One of their first observations was that the student body was fractured into small groups and had little sense of cohesiveness. They also concluded it was necessary to hire "bilingual counsellors who can communicate in both Inuktitut and English." In addition, "too much unorganized time is available for the children. It became very apparent early in our meetings that alleged drug and alcohol abuse was an end result of social situations and not underlying causes as we had initially felt." The students also said that some staff members were thrusting their personal religious values on the students. The problem, the parents thought, lay with the lack of constructive direction being given to the staff.[234]

Despite changes in approach, the problem remained. In 1987 the punishment for a group of boys who were inebriated when they returned to Akaitcho Hall included confinement to the dormitory for a week, writing an essay on the issue, a meeting with a student counsellor, and being placed on probation.[235] Three years later, five staff members drew up a proposed alcohol and drug treatment plan for Akaitcho Hall. It included the steps to be taken on the initial detection of drug and alcohol use (loss of privileges, letter to parents, requirement to attend counselling sessions). In the case of a second incident within three months, the student was to make a commitment not to use drugs or alcohol for sixty days and to participate in an individual assessment session and three educational sessions. After a third occurrence, a team of staff and outside professionals (and, if possible, a family member) would prepare a specific plan for the student.[236] To the frustration of at least one member of the group, it appears that the plan was not implemented.[237]

When asked to comment on Akaitcho Hall's drug and alcohol policy in 1991, Jim Martin of the Dogrib Divisional Board of Education said that he felt the matter should be dealt with not as a discipline issue but as a health issue. "The expelling of an untreated student with an alcohol and drug problem back to their communities does not benefit the student, their family, the community or the Northwest Territories. In the short term it helps the dorm supervisors."[238]

A March 1992 report on the Akaitcho Hall girls' dormitory observed, "Alcohol abuse seriously threatens our youth. So far this year, we have not been able to get on top of the problem. It is time we made a few changes and we must have a firm bottom line."[239]

Staff struggled to find appropriate policies to deal with drinking into the 1990s: some feared that students were being dismissed too quickly, while others spoke of how the institution seemed to be focused on getting "the residents through difficult times one month at a time." The fact that students ranged in age from fifteen to twenty-two created problems. V. J. Feltham, the head of the boys' dormitory, wrote, "It is difficult enough to deal with 15/17 year olds without having the role models of 20 year olds who tend to find pleasure in drink."[240]

The situation was no different in the Yukon hostels. In Whitehorse the problems were related to the difficulties and risks that students faced when they were away from the residence. In 1966 M. Brodhead, the acting assistant regional school superintendent for Indian Affairs in the Yukon, painted a bleak picture of the situation at Yukon Hall, the Protestant hostel in Whitehorse. He wrote:

> The degree of social disorganization in the community of Whitehorse is appalling. This disorganization is evident in the numerous discipline problems manifesting themselves amongst the students in residence at the Yukon Hall. Alcohol, truancy, and sexual promiscuity are adding new dimensions to our problems of educating these children.

He hoped to improve the situation by dividing the student body into groups, each under the director of a supervisor. The groups would be given the responsibility of determining how their free time would be spent.[241] The following year, three girls were sent back to their home communities from Yukon Hall for under-age drinking in Whitehorse.[242]

The large hostels did not introduce alcohol or drugs to the North. But they did remove young people from parental and community supervision during their adolescence. Students who attended the large hostels found themselves in communities with few recreational opportunities and, in some cases, reputations for hard living. The availability of alcohol and drugs, particularly after 1970, placed the students at high risk for substance abuse, a risk that the school and hostel administrators were never able to effectively control.

"A particularly evil place"

Many of the problems described above were interrelated. Parental resistance, overworked and undertrained staff, lack of supervision, and the traumas of being separated from home and family were never isolated phenomena. These factors interacted and compounded one another at the two large hostels in Churchill and Iqaluit. The Churchill Vocational Centre was actually located in Fort Churchill, where the federal government had transferred a portion of a military base to Northern Affairs.[243] According to Ralph Ritcey, a Northern Affairs education official, the Anglican and Roman Catholic churches initially opposed sending students to the Churchill school when it opened in 1964. Anglican Bishop Donald Marsh pointed out that the school had originally been planned for Qamani'tuaq or Iqaluit and was being located in Churchill only because of the presence of "a series of empty buildings."[244] He thought that it would be difficult to get parents to send their children to Churchill. "I do not think there is any doubt whatsoever that the Eskimo people are anxious to have their children educated but they are not anxious to lose their children or lose touch with them. However, their greatest fear is Churchill itself."[245] They did not wish to lose their children to the rough life they associated with a military base and a port.

To encourage recruitment, E. A. Côté, deputy minister of Northern Affairs, toured the North and made a promise that any student who completed three years of training at the Churchill school would be eligible for "further training or education in Southern

Canada, if they so desired."[246] By July 1964 Côté could write, "There has been a good response from the Roman Catholics in the Keewatin but less enthusiasm from the Anglicans from that region ... Almost all the available Roman Catholics in the Keewatin have already been enrolled." Altogether the deputy minister expected 160 students: 100 Anglicans and 60 Catholics. The six supervisory positions would be distributed in a similar ratio.[247]

Despite the initial success, as Bishop Marsh had noted, many parents were reluctant to send their children to Churchill—and once they did, they found it hard to get them back. When a parent in northern Québec tried to get his son back from Churchill in March 1965, the local Northern Affairs official in Ivuyivik was informed, "We are concerned with how the sending home from Churchill of one student in May would affect the others. Make no promises to the parents now."[248]

By the end of 1966, the federal government felt it necessary to develop a public relations strategy to address the Churchill school's negative reputation among Inuit parents.[249] According to a CBC radio news report, parents' concern over alleged drinking and sexual misconduct at the school had led them to refuse to send their children to the school and to withdraw students who were already in attendance.[250] There had been complaints about drinking parties at some of the employee dormitories at Fort Churchill, and Northern Affairs had to admit that Fort Churchill was "a large camp with a great many single people living in it." While it was possible for Northern Affairs to exercise control over its own employees, "this is not possible with respect to other departments." As a result every effort was being made to separate students from "adult social activities elsewhere in the Fort."[251]

The entire debate was replayed when the Churchill school was replaced by a new school in Iqaluit. The Ukkivik residence did not open until 1971, although it had been proposed in the late 1960s. The hostel and high school that was opened in Iqaluit was constructed in the face of significant parental opposition. The federal government's primary reason for deciding to build a high school and residence in Iqaluit was to address the concerns of parents who did not wish to send their children to the more distant facility in Churchill. The government also considered the "infeasibility of building smaller high schools scattered in other areas of the region." It was pointed out that Iqaluit had "25% percent of the native population in the region." According to government official W. W. Buell, there were concerns that Iqaluit "is not a good place morally or socially for this school. It must be noted here that most people who plead this point are doing so without actual knowledge or understanding and rely on hearsay."[252]

Yet those beliefs were deeply held by many parents. In November 1968, seventy Igloolik residents turned out to a community meeting to discuss the proposed Iqaluit school. They opposed sending their children to Iqaluit and sent a petition to that effect to a number of politicians, including Martin O'Connell, an Ontario member of

Parliament. In raising the issue on their behalf, O'Connell noted that while the parents did not oppose the idea of sending their children away to a centralized high school, they viewed Iqaluit "as a particularly evil place." In a letter to Northern Development Minister Jean Chrétien, O'Connell said, "I am given to understand that these views are shared by other communities in the area."[253]

Despite this, a large federal school, the Gordon Robertson Educational Centre (GREC), and the Ukkivik residence were both in operation by 1971. Shortly after the school opened, the principal of the federal day school, C. D. King, complained about the lack of discipline at the residence. He had concluded that there were

> students running about all night and some staying at undesirable places, male and female students seen in dark corners of the residence necking and petting, students being in the warehouse, boxes of shaving lotion bottles found under the residence, boys visiting girls' rooms, female students practising prostitution, etc., etc.

King said he could not blame parents for not wishing to send their children to Iqaluit: "I would not want my own children living at our residences at present."[254]

Following a visit to the new Ukkivik residence, Northwest Territories education official N. J. Macpherson expressed his concern over reports that "certain residents live in fear because of the drinking and fighting that goes on in the Frobisher Bay Pupil Residence." He informed the residence director that he and his staff could not "modify the behaviour of a pupil who terrorizes other pupils," and that the pupil would have to be expelled.[255]

As the school year was drawing to a close, Principal King requested an investigation into reports that "female students are frightened to live in the residence," that one student "has threatened students" and another student had "threatened and beaten male students," that two male students "have visited female students' rooms," and that a third male student invited female students into his room where he offered them alcohol.[256]

In June 1972, at the end of the residence's first year of operation, administrator Rod McKenzie resigned to take a job with the Manitoba government.[257] His successor James Earle lasted only a few months before he quit in November 1972. In his letter of resignation he wrote, "I find it impossible to carry on as administrator," adding that his reasons for leaving were numerous, but he did not wish to "point fingers in any directions and create hard feelings in many areas."[258] A review concluded that among the reasons for his resignation was an incident in which a supervisor had been attacked by a resident. Dissension among the staff had also led two supervisors to resign, and two other supervisors had been sent out during the term for what was termed "psychiatric treatment."[259]

That fall a group of students signed a letter outlining their frustrations with hostel life.

> We speak but no one seems to listen. We can't have confidential conversations with our supervisors because everything we say is recorded in a report book that any of the staff could read. So we keep everything to ourselves and our tensions cause us to damage the building or fight with one another because of frustrations that can't be communicated. Many of the students try to retreat into the past because the past seemed happy, and reject the future because it seems unhappy and confused.[260]

A child care worker who resigned from the residence the following year wrote a lengthy report outlining the frustrations encountered while working in the facility. The worker felt that students were not properly clothed, and that vision and hearing problems were not adequately addressed.

> There are also problems with students having need for psychiatric treatment or, at least, far more extensive counselling than can be received anywhere on Baffin Island. The residence is not equipped to deal with these individuals and although, in some instances, staff has recommended further treatment or consideration, the present policy is to send the individuals back to the settlement where they won't cause "us" any more trouble. Considering that most of their problems are provably rooted in the Eskimo-white man identity struggle, it would seem much more logical to treat these students rather than to let their problem grow and erupt in the settlement.[261]

Mary Olibuk Tatty was sent to Akaitcho Hall in Yellowknife because of the Iqaluit residence's poor reputation.

> Back in the '80s, my late mother had a choice of sending me to a place called Frobisher Bay one time, now it's Iqaluit, or Yellowknife. I didn't know where my mother was gonna send me, but then a couple older ladies that were ahead of me that went to Ukkivik came home pregnant, so my mom sent me the other way. So, I was happy she did, because, you know, ... I wanted my mom to trust me if she's the one pushing me to finish grade 12. Out of her 16 kids, I wanted her to be proud of me.[262]

It would appear the parental concerns about the Churchill and Iqaluit communities were well founded, yet the federal government failed to recognize the legitimacy of the concerns or to take steps to effectively eliminate the problems. Nor were Churchill and Iqaluit the only dangerous communities. In 1959 a Yellowknife man was convicted of seducing a student in residence at Akaitcho Hall. He was also convicted of supplying alcohol to a minor. He received a one-year sentence. The students involved in the incident were expelled from the residence and returned to their home communities.[263]

A sixteen-year-old student from Arviat living at Akaitcho Hall was raped by a young man she met in a Yellowknife restaurant in November 1971.[264] That same year a female student from Stringer Hall was raped by four young men whom she met in an Inuvik coffee shop.[265] School life may have also presented a threat to the students' mental health. In December 1977 a student from Iqaluktuuttiaq living at Akaitcho Hall attempted suicide. When he was released from hospital, he was returned to his home community.[266]

Another parental concern was that their children might become pregnant while at residential school. When this happened, the usual response was to expel the students. In 1962, a student left the Roman Catholic hostel in Whitehorse after becoming pregnant.[267] In 1968, another student did not return to school after the Christmas holiday because she was pregnant.[268] In the face of these pressures, the hostels could offer little in the way of support. By the 1989–90 school year, Akaitcho Hall had a chaplain who was providing counselling; in November and December 1989, he saw nine students about alcohol or substance abuse, three students about loneliness and adjustment to dormitory life, five students with relationship issues, and two students who were dealing with grief.[269]

Abuse

Two of the hostels in the Northwest Territories became notorious for the extended history of sexual abuse of students that took place while they were in operation: Grollier Hall in Inuvik and Turquetil Hall in Chesterfield Inlet, both Catholic residences. Four of the Grollier Hall staff were convicted of abusing students. Two of the convictions took place while the men were staff members or shortly after their resignations. In both cases, neither the school nor government authorities conducted a sufficient investigation. As a result, many years later, both of these men were convicted of additional assaults that had been committed while they worked at Grollier Hall. For a twenty-year period from 1959 to 1979, there was at least one sexual predator on staff at Grollier Hall at all times.[270]

The allegations of sexual assault at Turquetil Hall, which operated for a much shorter period and closed in 1969, were not raised until the 1990s. The matter was investigated by the RCMP, which eventually recommended against the laying of charges. In her report on the hostel, Katherine Peterson concluded that "serious incidents of sexual assault did in fact occur at the Chesterfield Inlet school during its years of operation."[271]

In the early 1960s, two men working and living at Fleming Hall, the Anglican hostel in Fort McPherson, were convicted on charges stemming from inappropriate relations with minors.[272]

In 1971 the federal government became aware that an employee of the Catholic Coudert Hall in Whitehorse was sexually assaulting students. Rather than bringing the matter to the attention of the police and offering assistance to the family, the government simply dismissed the man. He was not prosecuted—or convicted—for these activities for another nineteen years.[273] In 1993 a former employee of both Grollier Hall and Lower Post school in British Columbia—which was attended by students from the Yukon—was convicted of having sexually assaulted students at Lower Post in the late 1950s.[274]

Convictions present only a partial picture. Not all students were believed when they brought forward claims of abuse. It is, however, clear that the sexual abuse of students was much more prevalent than the number of convictions suggests. For example, as of September 14, 2014, 1,383 residents of the Northwest Territories had made claims that were admitted under the Independent Assessment Process for compensation for injury arising from sexual abuse while in residences and schools. Similar claims from 344 Nunavut residents and 438 Yukon residents had been admitted. Inuit from northern Québec also attended schools in the North; they would be included in the total of 1,776 claims for compensation admitted from Québec residents.[275] (An admitted claim is an application made by anyone eligible for compensation under the Indian Residential Schools Settlement Agreement. Because the adjudication process is ongoing, it is not yet possible to determine how many of these claims have been compensated.)

Former students spoke about their experiences of abuse at these schools and hostels in both public and private statement-gathering events organized by the TRC. Paul Voudrach spoke about being abused by a staff member at Grollier Hall in the 1960s. "Before my 8th birthday," he said, "I was taken from my bed with my mouth covered.... I don't remember going into the room, his room. But that morning [after] ... I can remember clearly the time it happened.... I got up at 6:30, because the nun always came out at seven with her clapper to wake everybody up. I had to go back to my bed before that happened. And on my way out I was asked to take some candy because that was where the candies were when we were allowed to buy them before the Sunday movie night. I said, "No I'm not going to take 'em." And I said, "I have to get back to my bed before the nun wakes up."[276]

Girls were also abused. When speaking at the Inuvik TRC public panel, Beatrice Bernhardt said that she'd been abused at Grollier Hall in "that little stairway, in the little playroom."[277] Veronica Dewar, who lived at Churchill in the 1960s, explained how she was sexually harassed by teachers. One time, she remembers, a male teacher approached her, and "he was drunk [and] trying to touch my skin." On another occasion, "in the bathroom, our supervisor tried to take a picture of me totally naked when I was taking a bath. These are not good. And they're not proper [actions]."[278] Margaret Bouvier spoke of abuse that occurred after she was called into a priest's office at

Lapointe Hall. "I know I didn't do anything wrong. And till this very day, I don't even know [what he said]. He put me on his lap and lifted up my dress and stuck his finger in me. You know when I think about that, like, what are you supposed to do? You were supposed to trust them. I wanted my mom and my dad. I wanted my dad so badly. I tried running away; I got caught. They told me they were gonna tie me up if I tried to run again. And I couldn't talk about anything. I was so scared."[279]

The abuse left the victims feeling confused. They had been taught to respect the church, school, and government authorities at the hostel, and to trust them as people charged with caring for them; however, being abused by these same people was difficult for the children to understand. Paul Voudrach described his abuser as someone "who was supposed to be a trusted man."[280] Dewar was just as confused as to why a man would start touching her: "Those [actions] are all totally foreign to me [as a teenage girl], especially when you don't know them and ... they're not related and they're trying to do sexual advances to you."[281]

Coupled with this confusion was a fear of telling anyone about the abuse. Because of either shame or fear of reprisals, few victims of abuse told other hostel staff, their own siblings, or even their parents about their abuse. Andre Tautu, a victim of abuse at Chesterfield Inlet, was, like Voudrach, a young boy when he was abused by male staff. Tautu explains how the pervasive power of the priests and the Catholic Church made him and other children too afraid to tell anyone, even their own parents, about the abuse. Throughout his life, Tautu was unable to explain to his mother, who was deeply Catholic, what had happened at the school to make him stop going to classes.[282] Elijah Nashook explains how he refused to return to Churchill after his first year of school because he could not face seeing his abuser at the school every day: leaving the hostel was "my mechanism to survive," he explains.[283] For people like Voudrach, Tautu, and Nashook, the fear of disclosure would continue long after they left school and their abusers had died. In his TRC testimony shortly before his own death, Andre Tautu explained that, even as his mother lay on her deathbed, fear and/or shame kept him from telling her about the sexual abuse, and that it was not until the early 1990s that he started to talk about it. Paul Voudrach and Veronica Dewar made a first disclosure about their abuse only at the TRC hearings in 2011. As Voudrach said in his statement, "I carried it [around] ..., that sexual abuse and assault, for forty-nine years."[284]

Jimmie Itulu recalled enjoying his first year at the hostel in Iqaluit, but at some point during his second year at school, he was abused by the dormitory supervisor. "If we were really sick, we had to stay in [at the dormitory] and we had supervisors at the residence," he explained. On one of these sick days, Itulu was abused.

> I was in my room. And our supervisor went into the room to see how I am. And [he] stated: "I'll make you feel better. Go on your stomach and [I] will massage your back." [And he] start massaging my back. And told me to turn around and lie on my back, and I started getting suspicious at that point. I've never seen

somebody being massaged from the front. And it was at that point that he started abusing me.[285]

Eric Idlaut said he was abused by his roommate at Ukkivik, an older male who also happened to be related to him. "It turns out that every time I would go to sleep that he would molest me, because our rooms are locked and nobody is going to enter our room. We are totally alone in our room."[286]

Some students found the whole experience abusive. Agnes Chief attended Lower Post school and lived in both Coudert Hall and Yukon Hall in Whitehorse. She described her life in these institutions as little more than "Hell on earth."

> I call it the 'hate factory' where you learn to distrust everybody because there
> are some kids in there who are always willing to make points at the expense of
> other people. I saw little girls in the recreation room standing on tables with dirty
> panties over their head because they can't articulate, they can't speak. They're
> not allowed to speak in their own language and they can't speak in English. And
> I remember seeing little boys being put in dresses because they dare to say hi to
> their sisters.[287]

The ongoing abuse of students at these institutions represents a complete failure on the part of the government and churches to properly screen and supervise employees. When problems were identified, neither the police, nor the church, nor the government conducted thorough investigations. As a result, the extent of abuse was not properly identified and victims were not provided with the support that they required. Instead, the seriousness of the violations appears to have been downplayed. Having convinced—and forced—parents to send their children to residences and having made promises about the quality of the care that would be provided, the federal government failed to ensure the children of the North were safe from abuse. The state had failed to uphold its basic duty to the children and parents of northern Canada.

Grandin College and the Churchill Vocational Centre

In 1960 the Roman Catholic Oblate order opened Grandin Home in Fort Smith, then the capital of the Northwest Territories. This facility differed in a number of ways from the other hostels that had been built in the western Arctic. The federal government, for example, had paid for the construction of the other seven hostels. It operated one of them directly and entered into contracts with religious organizations to operate the other six. Grandin Home, however, was a Catholic initiative. It was originally intended to serve as a seminary for the training of boys, age twelve and up, for the priesthood. They hoped to recruit at least twenty students in the first year.[288]

Four years later a new building, renamed Grandin College, opened with a capacity for forty students. In announcing the expansion, Oblate Paul Piché explained that he was convinced

> the future of the North rests on those native people of the North who are bound to remain in the country, and who through higher education will be prepared for leadership in taking over community responsibilities in their own portion of the country. In order to reach this goal, means must be sought to provide these students with every suitable way of completing their high school studies with more than just fair or merely passing marks.

In seeking federal funding for the residence, Piché argued that the establishment of the college was a complement to the hostel system, providing an atmosphere and training that was not available in hostels for those students who showed leadership potential.

> In the present hostels, this group of students would be continually mixed with others of less talent, working toward undetermined goals, or even none in particular, having varied interests, sometimes far removed from obtaining good grades in class, and frequently as not, little inclined to make any noticeable effort to improve academically.

As envisioned, Grandin College was to have an enrolment of thirty-five boys who were taking courses at the Grades Nine to Twelve level at the local day school. Since the residence was no longer focused on preparing students for the priesthood, it could also take in female students. The female students, Piché said, would be housed in the Grandin Home since the existing Catholic-run residences in Fort Smith (Breynat Hall) and Fort Simpson (Lapointe Hall) were "very inadequate for girls desiring to pursue high school studies."[289]

Grandin College's first rector, Father Jean Pochat-Cotilloux, is generally credited with both the school's change in direction and its success. In an interview given in retirement, he said, "It's okay to train priests. I'm not against it, but there are more urgent needs. You have to build a nation first." Basing his approach on the work of the Catholic social philosopher Jacques Maritain, he focused on leadership development. As he recalled, his message to the students was, "They won't give you power, you have to take it. You are the leaders of tomorrow. Run for election. Take whatever you can. Be greedy ... or you'll bow, shuffle and be on welfare all your life."[290]

In 1965 there were fifty-four students at Grandin College. At that time the Oblates were planning to offer university entrance courses. The students continued to attend the Fort Smith local day school. However, there were two "degree-holding" priests to provide them with academic support. The college had a gymnasium, a band, and a glee club. The Oblates hoped to develop a core group of students who would serve as community leaders throughout the North. As Maurice Beauregard told the press in 1965, "From Grandin, youngsters should be able to organize recreation in a small community."[291]

Rosa Van Camp was one of the first girls to enrol in Grandin College in 1964.

> I was the youngest in the girls' residence. Academic expectations were high, and this was physically evident within the building. Every student had a desk in his/her room, a library was available in both the girls' and boys' residences, and supervisors were available day and evening as tutors or counsellors. Study hours and chores became the norm for all of us. Gradually music and band lessons, sport activities and camping trips were included in our schedule. These enabled the students to participate in activities together and develop lasting bonds of friendship.[292]

In addition, "Slavey, Chip and Dogrib were spoken at Grandin College. We were never punished for it, unlike the practice in some of the residences in the past."[293] Another former student, Barney Masuzumi, said that at Grandin he was told that if any staff member laid a hand on him, he could have him charged with abuse.[294]

In a school newsletter from 1981, a number of students contributed their assessment of what the school had done for them. One girl wrote that when she first came to Grandin College, she was "very selfish, cheeky and bad-tempered." After three years she was "a totally different person, a bit cheeky but in a good way." A second student wrote that the school had given him "the needed confidence in myself in order to pursue and accomplish the goals I have set for myself." A third wrote, "At Grandin, Education comes first." While students could participate in school sports teams, "if you are behind in your school work, you are forced to quit your sports."[295]

Initially Northern Affairs officials opposed providing any funding to Grandin College. It was argued that it would undermine existing schools and residences and lead to needless duplication.[296] The Oblate request for funding also raised questions as to whether decisions over education should be made by the federal government or the territorial government. In the ensuing debate, the deputy minister of Northern Affairs, E. A. Côté, favoured funding Grandin College since the federal government had a responsibility for First Nations and Inuit education.[297] It was not until the spring of 1966 that the federal government formally offered to provide Grandin College with funding.[298] Rather than funding it with the same method as it used for the other hostels in the Northwest Territories, Northern Affairs agreed to provide the college with a boarding allowance.[299] As late as November 1967, the funds had yet to start flowing to the college.[300]

Under Pochat-Cotilloux's leadership, Grandin College developed a reputation as a "leadership factory." Ethel Blondin-Andrew, the first Aboriginal woman appointed to the federal cabinet, said she was "saved" by Grandin College, where she "learned that discipline, including physical fitness, was essential."[301] Antoine Mountain transferred to Grandin College in 1965 after he had "had just about all I could take of Grollier

Hall, having pretty well shut down emotionally." There, he said, the students "were expected to perform at the very top of our abilities, and not only academically, but also in other activities, sports, the horrid Bishop's Orchestral Band, which I avoided like the bubonic plague." While a student, Mountain joined the arts club and, along with a local art teacher, Violet Shawanda, "went on drawing field trips to local exotic locales like the Pelican Rapids."[302] Among the future northern Dene and Métis leaders who passed through Grandin College in the 1960s were Nick Sibbeston, Stephen Kakfwi, John T'seleie, James Wah-shee, and Michael Miltenburger.[303] Pochat-Cotilloux was credited with emphasizing leadership training at the school. For this he was fondly remembered by many former students. In 2005 forty to fifty former students gathered to celebrate Pochat-Cotilloux's eightieth birthday. Melody McLeod recounted how "each individual was encouraged to cultivate their own interests and abilities." The school was set apart, she felt, by the fact that students were never discouraged from speaking their own minds or speaking in their own language.[304]

Pochat-Cotilloux left Grandin College and Fort Smith in 1970 to return to missionary work in Behchoko (Fort Rae), near Yellowknife.[305] His departure from Grandin appears to have led to an internal rethinking of the college's role. An unsigned review conducted by a staff member at the end of the 1972–73 school year noted that of the forty students who had started that year, only twenty-seven were left. The author felt that the boys were "not really that serious about education," while the "girls' spirit has been at 'a low' this year. The older girls were involved with boys from town and by the same token their interest was divided." In addition the boys' and girls' supervisors had left in the middle of the year.

The author of the assessment had been with the college since late 1969. In reviewing the school's history, he noted that in 1964 there had been a shift from educating boys for the priesthood to educating leaders. The question, he asked, was, "Did we form Christian Leaders?" It was his opinion when he arrived at the college that it had hit a new low. Enrolment had grown too large, not enough attention was being paid to who was being let into the school, and the "staff had been of low or inferior quality." He questioned whether, without significant change, the school could become the "center for Christian education" that it was intended to be.[306]

Such concerns continued: in 1983 the school administrator wrote that he had serious reservations about the residence's ability to "give an opportunity to some Catholic teenagers to complete their High School studies with a Catholic input." His major objection lay in the fact that the students attended the local public school. "It is rather impossible for a Priest at Grandin to undo what the Public School is doing and at the same time give a positive Catholic Education." It might, he wrote, be preferable to close the school and relocate the Grandin College students to Yellowknife, where they could attend a Catholic day school.[307]

In 1985 the Mackenzie-Fort Smith Diocese decided to close Grandin College. Bishop Paul Piché wrote that the goal of "bringing about a generation of men and women who would contribute to society at large as well as to the Church" had been partially achieved since many former students had gone on to play leadership roles in northern society. However, it was felt that "Christian Family Formation should now take precedence over specifically Youth Formation."[308]

Grandin College's impact was pervasive. When he was education minister for the Northwest Territories in 1990, Stephen Kakfwi proposed the establishment of a northern residential school with a focus on academics and leadership training. Drawing from his own experiences at Grandin College, Kakfwi told the media that such institutions can create "a community where young people go to challenge themselves and are pushed to do well. You can see tremendous growth in self-confidence and belief in themselves."[309]

Grandin College was not the only institution to play a significant role in forming Aboriginal leadership in the North. Paul Quassa notes that the Churchill Vocational Centre in the late 1960s was a home for many future Inuit politicians from both Nunavut and Nunavik, including himself, Sheila Watt-Cloutier, Piita Irniq, John Amagoalik, and James Arvaluk. He explained that, along with these other future leaders, he was exposed to a much wider world than any of them would have otherwise known had they stayed in their camps or settlements. Quassa talked of how he learned about land claims in Alaska, the working of the Canadian Parliament, and the general atmosphere of social movements in the late 1960s.[310] Likewise, John Amagoalik has said, "We [at Churchill] were inspired by outside forces, by individuals like Martin Luther King Jr., John F. Kennedy, and Pierre Trudeau."[311] Amagoalik and Quassa agree that the combination of these outside forces and the fact that Churchill was home to Inuit from across the Arctic were crucial reasons why many of the students from Churchill became so involved in politics. For both men, Churchill in the late 1960s was where they, and other future Inuit leaders, developed the urge to create change in the Arctic: "We spent a lot of time [at Churchill] discussing how we were going to change the Arctic," said Amagoalik.[312] Paul Quassa likewise remembers that it was at Churchill "where a lot of us started developing a rebellious way of thinking. Probably we [thought we] were old enough to stand up to *qallunaat*."[313] In the 1980s, many of the graduates of Churchill and Grandin played central roles in the creation of the new territory of Nunavut.

Some former students formed positive relations with federal education officials as well. Ralph Ritcey, who headed vocational training for Northern Affairs in the 1950s, was fondly remembered by Piita Irniq, who delivered the eulogy at Ritcey's funeral in 2003. Irniq described Ritcey as a man who "cared greatly about the future of Inuit, defended their rights and played a big part in eventually dismantling colonialism in the Arctic."[314]

Eddie Dillon made similar observations about his former classmates from Stringer Hall. As he said at the beginning of his statement to the TRC, the legacy of residential schooling is also about the many people who left the schools and became important leaders in the North. In listing some of these people who attended Stringer Hall, Eddie Dillon stated that he was "proud" to have gone to Stringer Hall, and proud of his many classmates who went on to be important leaders in northern politics.[315]

As the federal minister of Northern Affairs and National Resources, Jean Lesage initiated a major expansion of residential schooling in northern Canada.

Into the 1950s, the government depended on missionaries to provide education and medical services in the Canadian North.
Library and Archives Canada, Wilfred Doucette, National Film Board fonds, PA-189152.

Turquetil Hall, the Roman Catholic residence in what was then Chesterfield Inlet, Northwest Territories, and is now Igluligaarjuk,
Nunavut. A 1994 report concluded that "serious incidents of sexual assault did in fact occur" at the school and residence.
Diocese of Churchill-Hudson Bay, CHB 07 02909.

Students and staff at the Anglican Coppermine, Northwest Territories, tent hostel in 1958.
Library and Archives Canada, Joseph Vincent Jacobson and family fonds, e004923640.

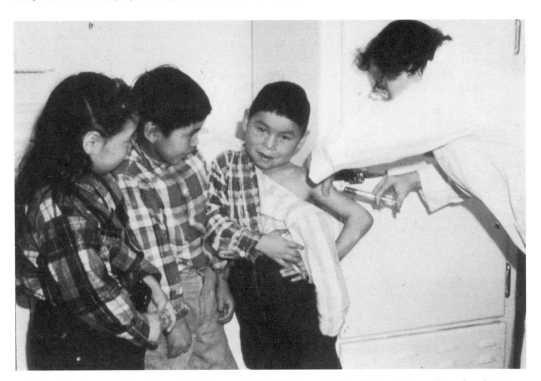

Public health nurse Peggy Ross giving an injection to an Inuit child at a vaccination clinic in what was then referred to as "Fort Chimo" and is now Kuujjuaq, Québec. In the 1940s, Fort Chimo was one of the few communities in northern Québec with a school.
Library and Archives Canada, Department of National Health and Welfare fonds, e002504588.

A government day school, residence, and nursing station in what was then referred to as "Cape Dorset" in the Northwest Territories and is now Kinngait, Nunavut.

Library and Archives Canada, Alexander Stevenson, Department of Indian Affairs and Northern Development fonds, e008128820.

The Fort Simpson, Northwest Territories, residence and day school. The school at Fort Simpson also had separate Catholic and Protestant wings.

Dechâtelets Archives, Oblates of Mary Immaculate collection.

Staff and students at Breynat Hall, the Roman Catholic residence in Fort Smith, Northwest Territories.
Dechâtelets Archives, Oblates of Mary Immaculate collection.

Akaitcho Hall in Yellowknife. Initially, Akaitcho Hall was the only large hostel that was not administered by a church organization in the Northwest Territories.

Public Works and Services, Northwest Territories Archives, G-1979-023-2149.

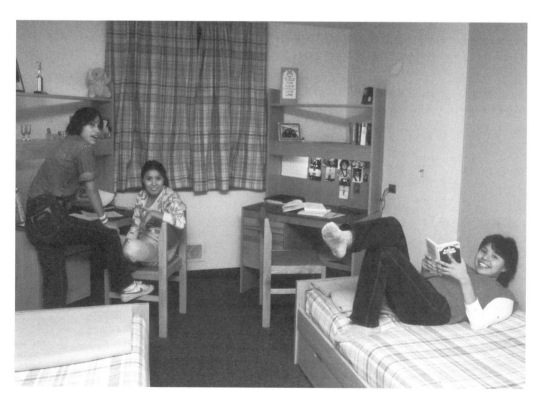

Students in the Akaitcho Hall dormitory in Yellowknife, Northwest Territories. Students who had transferred from older mission residential schools often spoke favourably of the conditions in Akaitcho Hall.

Public Works and Services, Northwest Territories Archives, G-1995-001-1605.

Breynat Hall in Fort Smith, Northwest Territories.
Public Works and Services, Northwest Territories Archives, G-1995-001-1876.

Extracurricular activities loomed large in life at the Roman Catholic Grandin College in Fort Smith, Northwest Territories.
Deschâtelets Archives, Oblates of Mary Immaculate collection.

The dining hall at Stringer Hall, the Anglican residence in Inuvik, Northwest Territories, 1970.

Public Works and Services, Northwest Territories Archives, Wilkinson, N-1979-051-0400S.

The exterior of Sir Alexander Mackenzie School in Inuvik, Northwest Territories, April 1970. The school had two separate wings: one Catholic, one Protestant.

Public Works and Services, Northwest Territories Archives, Wilkinson/N-1979-051: 0409S.

Grollier Hall, the Roman Catholic residence in Inuvik, Northwest Territories. Four Grollier Hall staff members were convicted for sexually abusing students at the school.
Public Works and Services, Northwest Territories Archives, James Jerome fonds, N-1987-017-2240.

Inuit students at the Fort Churchill, Manitoba, school in 1964.
Avataq Cultural Institute Photographs Collection, Ida Watt Collection, NUN-IWT-23.

Fleming Hall residence and day school at Fort McPherson, Northwest Territories. In the early 1960s, two men working and living at Fleming Hall, the Anglican hostel in Fort McPherson, were convicted on charges stemming from inappropriate relations with minors.
General Synod Archives, Anglican Church of Canada, P8454-66.

Bompas Hall, the Anglican residence in Fort Simpson, Northwest Territories. When a boy with tuberculosis was admitted to Bompas Hall in December 1963, the administrator, Ben Sales, protested. He pointed out that the boy was supposed to receive large doses of medicine on a daily basis for seven months. Sales wrote, "We have no professional nurse on our staff to be responsible for this medication."
General Synod Archives, Anglican Church of Canada, P7530-87.

The Roman Catholic school in Lower Post, on the Yukon–British Columbia border, opened in 1951. It drew students from both northern British Columbia and the Yukon.

Deschâtelets Archives, Oblates of Mary Immaculate collection.

Staff and students at the Lower Post school in northern British Columbia.

Deschâtelets Archives, Oblates of Mary Immaculate collection.

Yukon Hall, the Protestant residence in Whitehorse, Yukon.
Yukon Archives, Edward Bullen fonds, 82-354 #25.

Coudert Hall, the Roman Catholic residence in Whitehorse, Yukon.
Yukon Archives, Edward Bullen fonds, 82-354 #26.

The day school at Pangnirtung, Northwest Territories (now part of Nunavut).
University of Saskatchewan Archives, Institute for Northern Studies fonds, slide 15.

Moravian church and mission school, Makkovik, Labrador, 1926.
L. T. Burwash, Canada, Department of Indian and Northern Affairs, Library and Archives Canada, PA-099500.

Children moving into the new International Grenfell Association orphanage in Labrador, 1922.
The Rooms Provincial Archives Division, International Grenfell Association photograph collection, VA 94-40.7.

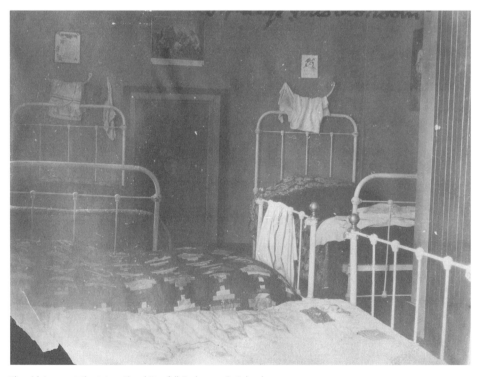

The girls' room at the International Grenfell Orphanage in Labrador.
The Rooms Provincial Archives Division, International Grenfell Association photograph collection, VA 118-62.5.

CHAPTER 10

The small hostels

The program of small hostels was intended to offer Inuit families a less disruptive kind of boarding experience than the large hostels. By 1960 the federal government had come close to establishing school facilities in all Northwest Territories and Nunavik (Arctic Québec) communities with large enough school-age populations to justify a day school. However, approximately 1,100 children were without access to schools. Their parents lived in small camps and spent much of the year on the land, hunting and fishing. Some of these children were already being boarded in homes in communities with day schools. Where local boarding facilities were either not available or inadequate, the plan was to board the children in "small family type hostels" in communities with day schools. According to one 1960 planning document,

> As far as possible these hostels are to [simulate] family units with the normal home atmosphere. Standards are to be as close as possible to those prevailing in the area and supervision, including cooking, laundry, and so on is to be carried out under contract by an older Eskimo couple or widow who might otherwise require some form of Government assistance. Local food resources are to be utilized to the greatest extent possible.

Payment to these "hostel parents," as they came to be called, was to "be kept to an absolute minimum."

Rather than having the government fly the children to the community, the expectation was that parents would bring them to the hostel. "In so doing they will see where their children are going to live and become acquainted with their supervisor, thus satisfying themselves as to the child's care and safety."[1] Children were to come from an area within a radius of eighty kilometres from the hostel. Half of the students admitted were to be male, half female, with priority given to students between the ages of six and ten. Priority was to be given to those who would otherwise be unable to attend school. Medical examinations were a prerequisite to admission. Finally, "the consent of one or both parents must be obtained before admission." Child welfare cases could also be placed in the hostels with the permission of the Northern Affairs superintendent of schools. Food rations were to be provided at the rate of "half an adult ration for each child." An additional $200 was provided for every eight students for "fresh food."[2]

In many ways, these small hostels were a more permanent version of the "tent hostel" experiment run by the Anglican Church at Coppermine in the 1950s. In 1952 the federal Sub-Committee on Eskimo Education had recommended that consideration be given to establishing summer tent hostels at Coppermine and Chesterfield Inlet to work in conjunction with the federal schools in those locations. The Coppermine hostel would be Anglican and have an enrolment of fifty, and the Chesterfield Inlet school would be Catholic. However, the Catholics, after an initial experiment with the tent hostel model, decided instead to establish a permanent hostel.[3]

The Anglicans pursued the tent hostel approach more vigorously. Bishop Donald Marsh proposed that children be left at this temporary hostel in the spring until August, "when their parents leave for their winter camps." The hostel would consist of canvas tents fitted over wooden walls and floors. Under these conditions, Marsh believed, the children could "retain as much of their native life as is possible and as is moreover desirable."[4]

Starting in 1955, students were housed four to a tent, and the school ran for six months a year. The number of students in residence ranged from thirty to forty-five in any given year.[5] The tents were heated by kerosene and propane stoves.[6] Difficulties in recruiting locally meant that students came from more distant communities including Uluqsaqtuua (Holman Island) and Read Island.[7]

There were ongoing complaints about the quality of the federal government supplies: the tents were drafty, the heaters created a fire hazard, and Bishop Marsh termed the staff housing to be inadequate.[8] In 1956 Marsh reported, "The children are sleeping in the Dining Room Tent as the wooden doors which were promised for the sleeping tents were not put on. As a result the tents fill with snow in a wind and the oil stoves keep going out because of the cold."[9] The tent hostel's closing in 1959 coincided with the opening of the large Anglican-run hostel in Inuvik.[10]

There were at least fourteen small hostels in the Northwest Territories and four in Québec (hostels also operated at Fort George and Mistassini, Québec, in the 1970s, but they were not part of the original program and did not operate in the same fashion). The majority of the hostels drew their students from Inuit communities.[11]

The hostels were built by southern construction crews, who were often working on a tight timeline. At Qamani'tuaq (Baker Lake), construction of the hostel was completed only three days before the first students arrived, leaving little time for the training of hostel staff.[12] The quality of the hostels varied from community to community. Principal Ann Emmett said that in the fall of 1965, the hostels in Igloolik looked like "slum dwellings.... The roofs had leaked badly, encrusting here and there the ceilings and some of the walls with a white, salt-like deposit."[13] David Davies, the principal at Mittimatalik (Pond Inlet), was proud of the hostel in his community, writing, "These beautiful buildings each have three four-bed dormitories, a playroom, a large dining room, a well equipped kitchen and two bathrooms."[14] P. B. Gorlick, the regional superintendent of welfare, reported in 1965 that Dr. J. P. Harvey was "quite disturbed" to discover that the hostels in Arviat (Eskimo Point) lacked bathtubs or shower stalls. Harvey said that "proper bathroom facilities are essential for the health of the children maintained in these small hostels."[15]

Maintenance was an ongoing problem. In 1970 the water lines for the bathtubs and one of the showers at one hostel at Iqaluktuuttiaq (Cambridge Bay) froze. Since they were made of plastic, it was not possible to use heat to thaw them. Nor was there any construction blueprint to show where the lines ran under the floor. At the same hostel, lack of fittings made it difficult to pump out sewage tanks. The fact that the hostels had been built without porches left them vulnerable to cold weather and strong winds. According to Principal F. S. Ellis, "During a storm two weeks ago the north door of Annie's hostel blew off taking one boy with it."[16]

The administration of the hostels could be chaotic. Northern Affairs had prepared a manual describing the training that hostel mothers were to be given. Although the manual was supposedly sent out in late 1960, school staff in Qamani'tuaq and Kuujjuaraapik (Great Whale River) said in 1962 that they had never seen it.[17]

The first hostels were constructed to house eight students, but by 1970 Northern Affairs indicated they were capable of housing twelve students. In addition to these twelve students, the hostel parents' children also lived in the hostels, usually in a single 3-by-3.6-metre room.[18]

From the outset there were concerns that rather than allowing parents to continue to live on the land while their children attended school, the small hostels might actually lead more Inuit to settle in communities year-round. In 1957, a Northern Affairs official recommended a cautious approach to the establishment of a hostel in Qamani'tuaq, stating, "We should seek to avoid placing in the traditional communities institutions which contribute to congregation and which may work to the detriment of hunting and trapping on the land. Baker Lake is one of the traditional communities."[19]

Karl Kristensen, a local teacher, opposed boarding students at the hostel in Kimmirut (Lake Harbour) on Baffin Island. It was, he wrote, "better to bring the school environment directly into their camps (homes) where the children can share both their every day, native environment and the school environment than to alienate the children from their native environment in order to bring them into a school environment (which we are doing to an extent when we bring them into hostels)." He feared that parents would migrate into Kimmirut to be with their children. This would put great pressure on the local hunting, trapping, and fishing resources and create an "unnecessary welfare problem." The Inuit of the Kimmirut area were, he wrote, "a very proud, self-supporting group of people. It would be unwise and unfortunate to do something new which would tend to change this very desirable situation."[20] A Mounted Police report from Mittimatalik in 1965 warned:

> The only foreseen problem in the immediate future ... will be the mass migration from the camps to the settlements. This has been quite noticeable this year in Pond Inlet.... This is brought about mainly by the parents wishing to be close to their children, when they leave the camps to attend school in the settlement. Because of the close knit Eskimo family, this will continue to be a problem, and in the future, I would imagine a very great one. This past year a whole camp moved into the settlement, the only reason given, to be close to their children attending school.[21]

According to the guidebook for the operation of the hostels, the small hostels were to "serve as an intermediate stage between the native home and the modern home of the white man to which it is hoped the indigent child will readily adjust."[22] A 1960 memorandum on the planning and operation of the small hostels noted that while there should be incentive for the students to speak English,

> we do feel it would be a good thing to allow children to speak their native tongue in the hostel when they so desire. The Hostel may indeed be a vital part of the learning process but it should also be a symbol of security for the child, providing a familiar atmosphere, and we all know how much more at home we feel when we can communicate in our own language.[23]

In practice, school staff found it difficult to operate an institution that was meant to serve as an "intermediate stage." In describing his "philosophy of education" for the Qamani'tuaq school, Principal Ivan Mouat wrote in 1962 that "Eskimo children are Canadian children first, then Eskimos. Canadian children go to school every day, they get there on time. We cannot spend hours out of the classroom for a hike or a game." That, he said, was the line that he had taken at the school that year.[24]

In 1965 Orland Larson, principal at Qikiqtarjuaq (Broughton Island), wrote, "We consider the teaching of English as a second language as the <u>key</u> issue in the northern curriculum." He said that he and another teacher had made considerable use of puppets in language lessons and had "written innumerable stories based on local happenings and myths and favorite children's stories as supplementary reading material." Larson was emphatic about the need to develop a northern-oriented curriculum, stating, "It is not enough to ape the southern curriculum with a few adaptions."[25]

The decision to have the hostels operated by local Inuit rather than a white supervisor from the South was an important departure from past practice. According to the hostel guidebook, hostel parents were "to provide adequate meals, to see that the children's bedding and clothing are clean and in good repair, to ensure that the hostel is kept clean and orderly, and to supervise and discipline the children as a wise and judicious parent would do."[26]

The local federal day school principal was responsible for the hiring of the hostel staff. The principal was also instructed to "keep himself constantly aware of hostel operations and seek the co-operation of other community officials should problems occur." Initially a hostel instructor, "perhaps the wife of a Government employee," was to provide hostel parents with two weeks of instruction before the opening of the hostel. After that she was to inspect the hostel on a weekly basis.[27]

In his 1962 report, Qamani'tuaq principal Mouat wrote that the hostel mothers had done "an admirable job under trying conditions. They have no water pressure system, no hot water system, and no dryer yet they are expected to do all the washing for 8 children in addition to the extra chores around the hostel."[28] The following year Mouat wrote that while the work of one of the hostel mothers had "not been outstanding," too much had been expected "of a neophyte" and he expected that she would improve with experience. The problems he had identified the year before remained unresolved.

> They are expected to do all the washing of clothes, bed linen etc., for eight or more children, yet the equipment provided is most inadequate. They have no running water, no piped hot water, no water system, and no clothes dryer.[29]

M. P. Walsh, the principal of the Arviat school, raised concerns in 1960 about the government interest in hiring widows to serve as hostel mothers.

> We should provide for training of the older boys in the skills of their own culture and should therefore set these hostels up with a 'house father' who can take them hunting, etc. and so provide training for the Eskimo way of life. If it is our intention to try to simulate the natural home environment and to allow these hostels to be operated as Eskimo homes we must face the fact that we plan to have them eat some Eskimo food. This must come from somewhere, and the best way is through the presence of a husband and 'father' in the home.[30]

Not all hirings were successful. At Kangirsuk (Payne Bay), a house mother was fired after three months because, according to the principal, Ann Meldrum, "she was unkind to the children, even her own relatives—which is unusual,—and as a result we had two bed wetters." When the house mother was replaced by her sister, the atmosphere was reported to have improved "one hundred fold."[31] In 1963, Igloolik principal Ann Emmett reported that one hostel father, who was "mentally ill, with a tendency for violence," was evacuated on an emergency flight.[32] In 1967 there were complaints from parents in Sanikiluaq (Belcher Islands) that their children were not pleased with the hostel mothers or the general conditions of the hostels at the Kuujjuaraapik hostel in Québec. It was recommended that photographs of the residence, along with information "concerning the pupil activities, the quality of the food and supervision," be presented to the parents so as to reassure them that their children were being properly cared for.[33]

While the hostel parents were supposed to be raising the children in a setting that reflected community practices, they were closely monitored by local school staff. In northern Québec, for instance, house parents were sent on a six-week course that taught them what was expected in housekeeping, cooking, and child care. These courses also included English-language training.[34] In discussing the hostels at Mittimatalik in 1967, Principal David Davies wrote, "Suitable Eskimo couples are paid to run the hostels under the supervision of the School Principal, though my wife really looks after the hostels." While local food was meant to be an important part of the diet, Davies reported, "Advice is given to the hostel mothers on the preparation of food and on the best system of household management."[35]

A 1976 inspection of the hostels at Iqaluktuuttiaq concluded that in one hostel, "all the children appear to be getting tender, loving care." The meals were described as "well prepared and tasty." While operations at the other hostel needed improvement, the inspector felt that the hostel parents "both love kids and in my opinion are giving tender, loving care to their charges."[36] In 1989 Iqaluktuuttiaq principal Dawn Wilson gave a very positive assessment of one set of hostel parents. He noted "country foods are available at all times," adding that the "hostel father hunts and fishes for the family." In addition, the students were encouraged to make use of the kitchen for making bannock. In general, the meals were considered "well balanced and nutritious." The hostel residents were always clean and well groomed and their clothing was well cared for. It was felt the hostel parents encouraged the students in both their studies and their recreational activities, scheduling study time and organizing dances and video nights for them.[37]

While there was an expectation that hostel parents would ensure a supply of local fish and meat, the hostels were supplied with canned food.[38] In addition, food was purchased from local hunters. In 1968 the principal at Kuujjuaraapik was purchasing seal meat, ptarmigan, and geese from local Inuit and First Nations people for use in the hostels. At Igloolik the hostel parents supplied the bulk of the fish consumed, while at Mittimatalik local fish were being "used sparingly due to high price."[39]

Initially Northern Affairs expected parents to provide clothing to the children who went to the small hostels.[40] In 1963 W. C. Devitt, district superintendent of schools, reported that the pupils attending the small hostels usually had "only the bare necessities of clothing, often reaching the situation where when clothes are washed clean clothing is not available." Rather than supply them with clothes, he recommended that commercial dryers be installed in all hostels to make it possible to wash and dry clothes at night when the children were sleeping.[41] Igloolik principal Ann Emmett reported in 1963 that many children arrived at the hostel "in filth and rags."[42] The following year, when the parents of children in the Igloolik hostel came to the community to trade, the principal asked them to purchase any needed clothing for their children. Those who were on relief were given material from which to make the clothes.[43]

In 1965 the policy governing clothing at the large hostels was extended to the small hostels. Under this policy, clothing was to be provided to children entering small hostels. A. Stevenson, the administrator of the Arctic, wrote that supply was to be "based clearly on need and we must be careful to make a realistic assessment of how much responsibility we can take over from the parents for clothing their children." Principals were authorized to spend up to $60 per student on clothing (compared with $100 per student at the Churchill school, which was attended by older students).[44] While there was an effort to purchase parkas manufactured in the North, funding restrictions led to a decision to import parkas from southern Canada in 1968.[45] It is not clear how well communicated these policies were. For example, in 1970, Iqaluktuuttiaq principal F. S. Ellis was asking if there was a clothing allowance for children whose parents could not afford to buy clothes for their children.[46]

Recruiting students and keeping them in the hostels was an ongoing problem. In 1961 C. M. Bolger, the administrator of the Arctic, wrote, "We are doing everything possible to recruit suitable teenage pupils to fill at least two" of the three hostels in Kuujjuaraapik. To this end, applications had been sent to all the communities in Nunavik.[47] Recruiting efforts may have been coercive since the following year, a Northern Affairs memorandum stressed the need for field staff to obtain signed parental approval for the recruitment of children from Sanikiluaq to Kuujjuaraapik.[48]

By the fall of 1963, Northern Affairs had recognized that it was faced with a serious problem ensuring hostel occupancy. In November all three hostels at Qikiqtarjuaq were empty. In August all the school teachers had resigned, necessitating a reduction in enrolment and a decision not to take any students into the hostel. At Kinngait (Cape Dorset) only one of the three hostels was in use. At Kangirsuk, there were two hostels with no occupants. The one hostel at Arctic Bay was being used as a temporary classroom. Pangnirtung had three hostels, but since the local school had only two teachers, no more than one hostel was needed. At Arviat there were three hostels, only two of which were occupied. The third was being used as office space. At Sanikiluaq, Kuujjuaraapik, Kangirsuk, Qamani'tuaq, and Igloolik, all the constructed hostels were occupied.[49]

The issues at Kinngait illustrate some of the problems that were experienced in recruiting and keeping students in the hostels. In 1963 three of the eleven students initially admitted were discharged because their parents "felt the hostel staff was unsuitable." In one case a father withdrew his son because he was being bullied. Another took his son out because he was homesick. In the third case a girl was withdrawn by her father because she was not happy with the treatment she received from other girls. Principal Brian Lewis concluded that the hostel father disliked his job intensely. Lewis wrote that community members had no confidence in the hostel father "as a supervisor of young boys." The principal let parents withdraw their children because he felt that the hostel system had been imposed on the community. To prevent people from taking their children would, he felt, "cause irreparable damage." He thought that it had been a mistake to try to fill all the hostels at once. "It would have been far better to try one hostel, and find some suitable people to live in it and to run it."[50]

While the original plan had been to recruit only from camps that were within eighty kilometres of the settlement, the fact that the Kinngait hostels were half empty led to a recommendation from Northern Affairs official B. Shasstein that "children should be brought in from more distant camps, in fact from any place where they can be found."[51] By 1967 one hostel had been put to use as a classroom, and federal officials were planning to convert the remaining hostels to classrooms.[52]

W. Berry, Northern Affairs area administrator, took a hard line at Mittimatalik. In 1964 he refused to allow two sets of parents to remove their children from the hostel there. He said that in previous years he had been able to fill the two hostels in Mittimatalik through persuasion. But, he wrote, "the parents of the children still in the camps, and who will be required to send their children to school when the new 12 pupil hostels are built next year, are unconvinced of the benefits of schooling and dread the prospect of separation from their children. They are unaware that their little backwater world is inevitably changing, and wish only that their children be good hunters and sewers. They cannot be, or have no desire to be persuaded otherwise."

Berry recommended that the government should "invoke the full provisions of the school ordinance which provides penalties for truancy." If not, it should cancel the construction of the hostel. He asked, "Are we to adhere to the ordinance, or will the unsophisticated and backward parents be the arbiters of our policy?"[53]

Many of the hostels were never occupied. By 1965 there were three hostels in Qikiqtarjuaq, far more than were needed. As a result, students lived in two of the buildings, while the third hostel was used for a variety of purposes, including adult education. Principal Orland Larson wrote in 1965 that since there were not enough students to fill even two hostels,

> it was decided to let all the school children in the settlement experience hostel living. Each week six new students go to live in the hostel for six days. Using a rotation basis it means that every school child can live in the hostels once every three weeks. Not only does this use up hostel rations [of which there was a surplus] it provides the children with well-balanced meals, adequate sleep and a chance to wash and bathe. Everyone goes home on the weekends to help their parents. Most of the permanent residents come from a nearby camp. We believe we have been able to eliminate any feelings of prejudice towards a few who might be in the hostels all the time.[54]

While many hostels sat empty, others were consistently overcrowded. In 1964 there were twenty-seven children living in the Igloolik hostels, which had been built to accommodate eighteen.[55] Because of the fire risk created by this overcrowding, there was a ban on visitors, including visiting parents, spending the night in hostels.[56] The following year, the Igloolik and Pangnirtung schools had to turn away students because of lack of space in their hostels.[57]

Most of the hostels had very short lifespans. A tent hostel was operated along-side a seasonal school for twenty-four students at Kangiqsualujjuaq (George River), Québec, in the summer of 1960.[58] The Kangirsuk hostels were closed in February 1962 and all seven remaining students sent home.[59] By the following year, all the families that had been using the hostel had settled in Kangirsuk.[60] Federal officials hoped to fill the hostels with students from Koartak, but, according to a Northern Affairs official, in the fall of 1964 Koartak parents refused to even consider sending their children to Kangirsuk.[61] The Sanikiluaq hostel opened in October 1963 with six student board-ers.[62] In the winter of 1964, the families of the children at the school decided to stay in the community for the winter. As a result, the students left the hostel and returned to their parents' homes. Federal officials were able to convince the boys to return to the hostel. At the time, an official wrote, "The whole concept of the hostel operation is now well-known to the local people, and understood. In forthcoming years this will serve good purpose."[63] This was an overly optimistic assessment. In September 1964, after one year of operation, there were only two students living in the hostel.[64] By November 1964, the Sanikiluaq hostel was empty.[65] In 1968 four children from South Camp were being boarded with local communities so they could attend school in Sanikiluaq. Three of the children were reported to be living in "overcrowded and unhealthy con-ditions." However, the fourth was boarding with the government interpreter, who was being allowed to rent the six-bed hostel building, which would otherwise have been unoccupied.[66]

Health services were limited. In 1962 Qamani'tuaq principal Ivan Mouat was crit-ical of the federal health department's slowness in providing treatment to persons diagnosed with tuberculosis.

> There was a boy in my class (he has still not left the settlement) who is a suspect-ed TB case. If he has TB, then he should be sent immediately for treatment. As it is, he has been left almost three months in a crowded house. Looking at this from a purely personal point of view, I object to being needlessly exposed to active TB germs in a crowded classroom. Taking the larger view, I certainly must protest the needless endangering of a whole class.[67]

The following year Mouat wrote, "Ever since I arrived here, evidence of visual defects have been observed. In spite of many memos on the subject no child has received an eye examination."[68] A 1962 influenza epidemic in Inukjuak (Port Harrison), Québec, so overtaxed local medical facilities that six children were cared for in one of the hos-tels.[69] In 1967 there was an outbreak of meningitis in the Arctic, particularly in the Keewatin region. Two children died in Repulse Bay, two at Arviat, one at Rankin Inlet, and one at Qamani'tuaq. One of the teachers at Arviat was diagnosed with meningitis.

He recovered, but the illness was judged to have "a demoralizing effect upon other married staff with children in that community." While it was not clear at that time whether the meningitis was related to tuberculosis, the disease continued to be a serious problem in the communities. Arviat was hit by an outbreak of tuberculosis in the spring of 1963. The June class lists show that thirty-three of eighty-four students were in the Clearwater, Manitoba, sanatorium.[70] Consideration was given that year to transforming hostels in Kinngait into facilities for sick children from that region.[71] In 1964 fourteen Inuit children who had been treated at the hospital in Moose Factory, Ontario, were transferred to the Moose Factory school.[72] Between September 1966 and March 1967, twenty-five people had to be evacuated from the community of Arviat for treatment. An additional fifty people had tested positive for tuberculosis. There had been a serious epidemic of the disease in the community just four years earlier.[73]

Some former students recall life in the small hostels as harsh and even abusive. One former student spoke of being sexually assaulted by the hostel father.[74] Although not abused in the same way, Carolyne Nivixie explained how her hostel parents failed to provide proper care for children at a hostel in northern Québec. In Nivixie's opinion, her hostel parents used their position to benefit their own family. For instance, instead of using the food supplies to feed hostel children, she remembered, her hostel parents sent away portions of the food rations to relatives in a nearby camp, leaving the hostel children without adequate supplies for their meals.[75] Lack of food, and control of food, seemed to be a problem remembered by other Survivors of small hostels. Eric Anautalik remembered having to rely on local families for food after the hostel's supplies ran out.[76]

Many Survivors remember feeling like "double outsiders" at the small hostels: not only were they outsiders to the hostel environment, they were also outsiders to the local community around the hostels and at the day schools. Several former students said they were bullied by local children and local hostel parents. Sarah Peryouar remembered that she was made to feel different: "We were treated differently because of who our parents were and who we were."[77] Although not a resident of a small hostel, Jimmy Itulu noticed how the children at the hostel in his settlement of Kimmirut were punished more severely by the teachers than were local children.[78] Likewise, Annie Agligoetok, who was abused by her hostel parents, was also bullied by local children from Iqaluktuuttiaq during her years in the hostel there. She told of how her brand new parka, given to her by the hostel staff when she arrived at Iqaluktuuttiaq, was torn and ripped by other children after weeks of bullying.

> I use to be afraid to go out for recess … because kids would bully me. I use to be afraid to go home just from school to the hostel 'cause kids … want to pick on me for no reason, I don't know—I was just a different person from another community maybe…. They did that for one week…. It really bothered me…. My brand new parka, it was torn from those kids that were bullying me. I went home with

my parka torn and I got scolding for that. I was grounded for three days just for my parka being torn, and it wasn't my fault—it was the kids that were bullying me.[79]

Dora Fraser said that at hostels in the eastern Arctic, students were sometimes tied to their chairs as punishment. She also said that in some cases, the people who were supposed to be supervising the hostels were absent. When that happened, "some of the older kids used to take advantage of the younger ones for sexual purposes." When a woman from her home community became the hostel mother, she thought conditions would improve. "She was the worst. She shamed us, like, shamed us to death. We were nothing to her. We were bad. We're very negative. She was a very negative person." She also recalled the teasing that children were subjected to.

> We were in this strange land. We were terribly teased 'cause of our language. We had different dialect. We were called seal meat eaters, doggies, islanders. "You smell like seal." That was our, my first experience, but as this time goes on ... We are islanders, we eat seafood, food, country food, but as soon as we got into this hostel, it changed.[80]

While envisioned as a way to create a less dislocating and alienating experience than the large hostels, in many ways these small hostels may have made it harder to build friendships with other children, and just as hard to retain contact with their own families. Inuktitut was allowed and, theoretically, a connection with Inuit culture was supported; however, without family or the opportunity to build friendships, the small hostel could well have been a more isolating and lonely experience than the larger hostels. Sarah Peryouar, for one, believed "more damage" was done to her at the small hostel in Qamani'tuaq than during her time at the large hostel at Churchill.[81]

Over time parents moved into the settlements, eliminating the need for such residences. In February 1969 the principal of the once crowded Igloolik hostel wrote, "As most of the outlying camps have now been abandoned and the families concerned being now housed within the settlement, only a small number of children now make use of the hostels. At this moment six children are in residence."[82] By July of that year it was reported to have closed.[83] Most of the hostels in the eastern Arctic and Nunavik were closed by the end of the 1971. There was slight expansion of the system in 1985 when Kivalliq Hall opened in Rankin Inlet. It had an initial enrolment of thirty-two students—making it larger than most small hostels, but smaller than the large hostels.[84] It closed in the mid-1990s.[85] In the early 1990s the Samuel Angnetsiak hostel opened in Mittimatalik.[86] It appears to have operated until at least 1995.[87] Small hostels also continued to operate in the western and central Arctic. The eight-bed Fort Franklin hostel in what is now Deline opened in 1967. Demand declined rapidly in the coming years. It was not used at all during the 1972–73 school year, and had been used only slightly in the previous year. At that point it was recommended that it be converted to an adult education centre. A similar recommendation was made in regard to a twelve-bed hostel at Tulita (Fort Norman).[88] In 1980, there were four small hostels in the western Arctic, in Iqaluktuuttiaq, Fort Liard, Fort Good Hope, and Fort McPherson.[89] The number was down to two by 1985–86: the Iqaluktuuttiaq and Fort Good Hope hostels.[90] The Iqaluktuuttiaq hostel continued to operate into the mid-1990s.[91]

The large and small hostel system had been designed by the federal government to impose its authority in the North and to bring the benefits of modernity to its residents. It was intended to replace the church-run mission school system. There is no doubt that the physical facilities represented a dramatic improvement over the old mission schools. The expansion of the number of day schools also made it possible for a significant number of children to receive schooling in their community. The system, however, was imposed with no meaningful consultation, taught a largely irrelevant curriculum, undermined family, community, and cultural bonds, and placed students at risk. In many ways it was simply an extension rather than a replacement of the southern residential school model, complete with extensive church involvement. Although the federal government and the churches reduced their responsibility for the administration of the schools in the years after 1969, the student experiences described above remained much the same before and after the transfer of responsibility. While the experience remained similar, the number of students undergoing that experience declined significantly, as the territorial governments moved, over time, to bring the hostel system to an end.

CHAPTER 11

Territorial administration: 1969 to 1997

The year 1969 was pivotal for residential schooling in the North. That year saw the closing of one school (Carcross in the Yukon) and one residence (Turquetil Hall in Chesterfield Inlet, Northwest Territories), the transfer of responsibility for First Nations education to the Yukon Territory, and the transfer of management authority for hostels in the Northwest Territories to the territorial government. It also marked the peak of the system of large hostels. In the Northwest Territories, for example, there were nine large hostels in 1969; by the beginning of 1976, only four were in operation: Grollier Hall in Inuvik, Ukkivik in Iqaluit (Frobisher Bay), Akaitcho Hall in Yellowknife, and Lapointe Hall in Fort Simpson.[1] In 1969 there were two residences and two residential schools for First Nations students from the Yukon; by 1976 only one was still in operation.

Dismantling the hostel system in the Northwest Territories

In January 1969, the commissioner of the Northwest Territories opened a session of the legislature with the announcement that on April 1, the territorial government was to take over six of the seven large hostels in the North, the one exception being Turquetil Hall. "The Minister recommends that to begin with the Territorial Government should be prepared to operate pupil residences in exactly the same way as they are now being operated, that is, by agreement with the Anglican and Roman Catholic Churches."[2]

In reality, the churches' involvement would decline in the coming years. Rather than being transferred to the territorial government, the Roman Catholic Turquetil Hall was simply closed in 1969.[3] In total nine residences were transferred. Tables 11.1, 11.2, and 11.3 show that at the time of transfer, the hostels had a total enrolment of 1,289. Forty-four percent of the students were Inuit; thirty-eight percent were First Nations.

Table 11.1   Enrolment, government-owned and -operated pupil residences, March 1969

Location	Inuit	First Nations	Others	Total
Yellowknife, Akaitcho Hall	23	59	59	141
Fort Churchill	230	5	0	235
Total	253	64	59	376

Source: TRC, NRA, Government of Northwest Territories Archives, Akaitcho Hall Reports, 1969–1970, Archival box 9-2, Archival Acc. G1995-004. [AHU-003844-0003]

Table 11.2   Enrolment in government-owned residences operated under contract

Location	Residence	Operated by	Enrolment			
			Inuit	First Nations	Others	Total
Fort McPherson	Fleming Hall	Anglican	0	82	18	100
Fort Simpson	Bompas Hall	Anglican	34	17	17	68
Fort Simpson	Lapointe Hall	Roman Catholic	1	123	20	144
Fort Smith	Breynat Hall	Roman Catholic	0	120	34	154
Inuvik	Grollier Hall	Roman Catholic	83	71	52	206
Inuvik	Stringer Hall	Anglican	155	13	29	197
Chesterfield	Turquetil Hall	Roman Catholic	44	0	0	44
			317	426	170	913

Note: The total enrolment for Stringer Hall is inaccurate in the original source and has been corrected.
Source: TRC, NRA, Government of Northwest Territories Archives, Akaitcho Hall Reports, 1969–1970, Archival box 9-2, Archival Acc. G1995-004. [AHU-003844-0003]

Table 11.3   Enrolment for government-owned and -operated hostels and government-owned and church-operated hostels, 1969

Type	Inuit	First Nations	Others	Total (%)
Government-owned and -operated	253	64	59	376 (29)
Government-owned, church-operated	317	426	170	913 (71)
	570 (44%)	490 (38%)	229 (18%)	1,289

Source: TRC, NRA, Government of Northwest Territories Archives, Akaitcho Hall Reports, 1969–1970, Archival box 9-2, Archival Acc. G1995-004. [AHU-003844-0003]

As Tables 11.4, 11.5, and 11.6 show, in the first five years of territorial operation, the number of large residences in the Northwest Territories declined from nine to seven. Their enrolment dropped by over 50%, going from 1,289 students to 618. At the beginning of 1975, the Anglican Church announced that it would not be renewing its contract to operate Stringer Hall in Inuvik for the coming school year.[4] The residence closed in June of that year.[5] Breynat Hall and Bompas Hall also closed in 1975.[6] This trend continued, and in 1985 only four of the large residences remained open (and one of them, Lapointe Hall, had enrolment that was closer to that of a small hostel). Hostel enrolment was only one-third of what it had been at the time of transfer.

Table 11.4. Enrolment in Northwest Territories large hostels, 1969 to 1985

Location	Residence	Enrolment			
		1969	1974	1979	1985
Yellowknife	Akaitcho Hall	141	145	142	184
Churchill	Churchill Vocational Centre	235	–	–	–
Fort McPherson	Fleming Hall	100	60	–	–
Fort Simpson	Bompas Hall	68	60	–	–
Fort Simpson	Lapointe Hall	144	–	71	12
Fort Smith	Breynat Hall	154	61	–	–
Inuvik	Grollier Hall	206	121	174	134
Inuvik	Stringer Hall	197	91	–	–
Chesterfield	Turquetil Hall	44	–	–	–
Iqaluit	Ukkivik	–	80	97	92
Total		1,289	618	484	422

Note: Total enrolment values have been adjusted to correct calculation errors in the original sources.

Sources: 1969: TRC, NRA, Government of Northwest Territories Archives, Akaitcho Hall Reports, 1969–1970, Archival box 9-2, Archival Acc. G1995-004. [AHU-003844-0003]

1974: TRC, NRA, Government of Northwest Territories Archives, Hostel Enrolment, 1974, Archival box 9-11, Archival Acc. G1995-004, "Enrolment by Residences by age, October 1–December 31, 1974." [RCN-012620-0001]

1979: TRC, NRA, Government of Northwest Territories – Education, Culture and Employment, Residences 1979-80 – Quarterly Returns [Akaitcho Hall, Ukkivik, Lapointe Hall, Grollier Hall, Fort Liard, Cambridge Bay], 09/79–06/80, Transfer No. 0349, box 25-4, "Student Residences Quarterly Returns." [RCN-012634]

1985: TRC, NRA, Government of Northwest Territories – Education, Culture and Employment, Student Residence Enrolment and Semi-Annual Attendance 1985–1986 [Grollier Hall], Transfer No. 1201, box 9-1, "Student Residence Quarterly Return," September 1985; [GHU-000127] "Occupancy Report on Children Placed in Lapointe Hall," 30 September 1985; [LHU-000600-0000] "Student Residence Enrolment," Ukkivik Residence, October 1985; [FBS-000065] "Akaitcho Hall, Student Residence Enrolment, 1985–1986." [AHU-000915]

The reduction in the number of hostels and the number of students living in hostels was accompanied by another trend: the aging of residential school students. In 1950 few teenagers attended school outside of Yellowknife and Aklavik, because there were few opportunities in the smaller communities to go even as far as Grade Six. In 1961, 727 pupils were enrolled in schools in what was described as the Arctic District. Of these, 93% were in Grades One to Three. Only two pupils were above Grade Five, and none above Grade Seven. Typically, boys started school around age nine and dropped out at twelve, when they were old enough to make a serious contribution to hunting for the family.[7] By 1970, the community day schools were producing students who were ready for high schools and vocational schools, and the growing preponderance of day schools over residential schools meant that the youngest children were being educated closer to home. The territorial government claimed to have reversed the pattern of previous decades, and 10% of students in residences in the Northwest Territories hostels were under the age of ten in 1970.[8] By 1977, 63% of the students in the four largest residences in the Northwest Territories were at or above the legal school-leaving age of sixteen.[9] (For details see Tables 11.5 and 11.6.)

By the mid-1970s, a substantial number of the students in the hostels who were under the school-leaving age fell into the "social development" category. These were often young people whose parents had been judged unable to care for them, and many were living in hostels in their home communities. In 1975, social development students accounted for 36% of the children in hostels who were ages twelve or under.[10] Younger children also came from families who spent much of their time on the land. The most dramatic example of this phenomenon was reported in Fort McPherson in 1972, when there were seventy-two students ages twelve and under at the hostel. All were from the Fort McPherson community.[11]

Table 11.5 Age distribution of pupils in residences, all Northwest Territories, 1970

Age	6	7	8	9	10 and up	Total enrolment
Number	3	27	36	48	886	1,000

Source: Director of Education B.C. Gillie, reply given to Legislative Assembly, NWT Hansard (11 February 1971), 503.

Table 11.6. Enrolment in Northwest Territories large hostels by age, June 30, 1977

Age	Grollier Hall Inuvik	Ukkivik Iqaluit	Lapointe Hall Fort Simpson	Akaitcho Hall Yellowknife	Total by age
6	3	-	1	-	4
7	7	-	2	-	9
8	5	-	6	-	11
9	6	-	4	-	10
10	7	-	3	-	10
11	7	-	8	-	15
12	7	-	3	-	10
13	4	-	4	1	9
14	8	-	9	4	21
15	17	8	8	23	56
16	19	19	3	44	85
17	12	21	1	54	88
18 +	6	18	5	63	92
Total by residence	108	66	57	189	420

TRC, NRA, Government of Northwest Territories – Education, Culture and Employment, Residences 1976–77 – Quarterly Returns [Akaitcho Hall, Ukkivik, Lapointe Hall, Grollier Hall, Fort Liard, Chief Jimmy Bruneau], 10/75–07/77, Transfer No. 0349, box 25-1, "Enrolment in Residences by Age," 30 June 1977. [RCN-012415]

The number of hostels also declined throughout the 1970s. In 1974 the Koe Go Cho Society, a Dene organization, took over operation of the Fort Simpson hostels.[12]

In 1985 management of the one remaining residence was provided by the Deh Cho Regional Council and the residence became Deh Cho Hall.[13] The following year, it provided accommodation for thirty-eight students.[14] It closed in 1986, bringing the number of large hostels operating in the Northwest Territories to three.[15]

Projections in the fall of 1993 showed Akaitcho Hall enrolment declining from 159 in the 1992–93 school year to twelve in the 1995–96 school year.[16] In the face of this decline, the territorial government closed Akaitcho Hall at the end of the 1993–94 school year. Students who came to Yellowknife for high school were now boarded in private homes.[17]

The Roman Catholic Church operated Grollier Hall until 1987.[18] The church chose not to renew its contract because it was "running out of religious personnel which would allow us to continue the work."[19] Following the withdrawal of the Roman Catholic Church, the territorial government contracted a local firm, TryAction Management Ltd., to administer Grollier Hall.[20] In the spring of 1990, the Department of Education delegated responsibility for Grollier Hall to the Beaufort Delta Divisional Board of Education.[21] A 1995 projection for Grollier Hall showed enrolment declining from fifty-one in 1994–95 to thirty-two in 1995–96 and fifteen in 1996–97.[22] In the spring of 1996, layoff notices were issued to Ukkivik staff as plans were made to close the facility.[23] Grollier Hall was turned over to Aurora College in the summer of 1997.[24] With that transfer, the era of the large hostels had come to an end.

Dismantling the hostel system in the Yukon

A process similar to that of the Northwest Territories took place in the Yukon. In 1968, Indian Affairs transferred older students from the Carcross school to Yukon Hall in Whitehorse. According to a policy directive, new enrolment at Carcross was to be kept to a minimum.[25] The following year the Carcross school was closed because of decreasing numbers of students and the policy of providing "integrated schooling for Indian children wherever possible."[26] In 1969, Indian Affairs turned the responsibility for the schooling of First Nations students over to the Yukon government. It did, however, retain responsibility for operating the two hostels in Whitehorse and the Lower Post residential school, over the border in British Columbia.[27]

The Yukon government also moved to reduce the number of residences. In the summer of 1970, Keith Johnson, the administrator of the Anglican Yukon Hall, was made administrator of the Catholic Coudert Hall. Starting that fall, students were assigned to one of the two residences on the basis of age, not religion. The smaller Coudert Hall housed children ages six to twelve, while Yukon Hall housed students thirteen and over. In addition, students from Carmacks, who had in the past been sent over

600 kilometres from home to the Lower Post school, were now to be housed in the Whitehorse hostels, 400 kilometres closer to their home community. In announcing the changes, Yukon Commissioner James Smith said that residential complexes were to be phased out in the coming years.[28] By the following year, Coudert Hall and Yukon Hall had been completely amalgamated, leaving the Yukon with only two large residential options: Yukon Hall and Lower Post.[29] The expected enrolment for Yukon Hall for the 1970–71 school year was 150 students, with 135 students expected at Lower Post. The Lower Post principal sought to have half a dozen Grades Eight and Nine students transferred to Yukon Hall for "social reasons." An Indian Affairs official noted that such a move would not be in keeping with the departmental policy of keeping students "in their home community wherever possible."[30] In the face of rising costs and declining enrolment, Lower Post closed at the end of June 1975. It was replaced by three group homes in Yukon communities.[31] Yukon Hall would operate until 1985. According to the Indian Affairs annual report for 1984–85:

> The Chiefs' Advisory Board was the forum for Yukon Indian participation in regional policy formulation and decision making. After discussion with Yukon chiefs, the region decided to close the student residence, Yukon Hall, an institution many Indian people felt was detrimental to their education.[32]

After Yukon Hall closed, a room-and-board subsidy was provided by the Yukon government for students who wished to take grades or courses not available in their home community. Because the subsidy did not cover the total cost of boarding, Indian Affairs provided an additional supplement for First Nations students. As Indian Affairs official B. Zisman observed, "Parents feel the Yukon Government should cover all costs or expand the grades in their community so that students would not have to leave."[33]

The dismantling of the system of large hostels in the North after 1969 can be attributed to several factors. Key were government decisions to increase both the number of day schools in First Nations and Inuit communities and the number of grades taught in these schools (a process known as grade extension). Two other factors were the construction of small group homes for students and an increase in the practice of boarding students in private homes. These policy measures were often adopted in response to growing Aboriginal criticism of the residential school system. In the Northwest Territories, this criticism was often voiced by former residential school students who had become members of the legislature.

Aboriginal criticism of the residences

In the late 1960s, two non-Aboriginal legislators raised concerns about the impact of the large hostels. Gordon Gibson, who was appointed to the Northwest Territories

Council in 1967, was critical of "the policy of the education department in sending children above grade six level from many small centres to larger communities to continue their education." An editorial in a Yellowknife paper lauded Gibson's speech, adding that the hostel system was outdated. "With some 500 teachers in the north, we would say we do have enough teachers for the smaller places and if more are required, then pay them enough money so they will accept the positions in the smaller communities." Rather than developing the North, the hostel system was, in the editorialist's opinion, "destroying the smaller communities."[34] R. G. Williamson, another appointed member of the Northwest Territories Council (which has since evolved into the Northwest Territories Legislative Assembly), was highly critical of the conditions in the Churchill Vocational Centre. In 1967 he wrote:

> Inadequate supervisors have been providing inadequate services. It is an open secret that the youngsters slip out of the Hostel at night with impunity—into a town which is justly notorious as a moral nightmare. The Hostel itself is, by accounts I have received, not a healthy place for young people to spend more than ten months of their lives each year. Potentially good students are not receiving the kind of background they need—and are performing well below their real capacity in some cases. And yet each year, I receive complaints from parents that they have been obliged, against their will, and sometimes with veiled threats to send their children to that institution.[35]

Northern Affairs officials were beginning to re-examine the department's policies. A 1967 memorandum reported: "We are now establishing small schools in communities where formerly they would not have been established, for example Repulse Bay, Hall Beach, and Sachs Harbour. We are also examining the feasibility of retaining in certain local schools pupils beyond Grade VI."[36]

Momentum for change continued to build in the 1970s. By then, a youthful and talented Aboriginal group of leaders, many of them bilingual, were emerging in the North. They included Piita Irniq, Nick Sibbeston, Tagak Curley, James WahShee, Georges Erasmus, John Amagoalik, Nellie Cournoyea, Richard Nerysoo, Jim Antoine, and Stephen Kakfwi. Most of these leaders had attended either residential schools or schools in southern Canada. This new generation took on leadership roles across the territories, in both Aboriginal rights organizations and territorial government, and several eventually attained the office of premier. They had consistent approaches, based on personal experience, an awareness of Aboriginal rights, and a first-hand understanding of the challenges of schooling in territories where economic development was promised, and where Aboriginal languages, hunting, trapping, and other traditional land-based activities remained important to their collective well-being, and essential to their identities.

As a result, Aboriginal people began to shape the debate over northern education. For example, Alain Maktar from Mittimatalik (Pond Inlet) told Northern Affairs officials in Iqaluit in 1968 that "we want the Eskimo's to be taught in Eskimo" and "we want hunting included in this education as well as home economics." He argued for employing Elders in the classroom and summed up, "There are about four things we want them to learn, hunting, building igloo's, in the wintertime and the sewing and the language. If they learn those things they will be able to live in the Arctic."[37]

Delegates from several Inuit regions gathered at Kugluktuk (Coppermine) in 1970, to lay the groundwork for the formalization of the national Inuit organization, the Inuit Tapirisat of Canada (now the Inuit Tapiriit Kanatami). The delegates concluded that the present school systems "fail to provide our children with a meaningful education suited to their environment, fail to preserve our native cultures and fail to provide useful Canadian citizens." They demanded:

- that each community council have a voice in the curriculum content so that native history, culture and skills be included as full credit courses;
- that each community council determine what vacation months during the year will apply to a community. The Southern Canadian standard of July and August is almost universally unsuited to the wishes of Arctic Communities;
- that more schools be provided as rapidly as possible to eliminate the absences from home of ten months per year for our children;
- that instruction in native language dialects in the primary grades be implemented now ... We are decades behind the educational systems of Greenland and Siberia in this regard; that the program to utilize native teachers and teaching aides be greatly expanded immediately.

These points became the standards against which Inuit and other northern peoples would judge their school systems.[38]

A similar critique emerged from representatives of twelve Yukon First Nations, meeting as the Yukon Native Brotherhood in January 1972.[39] The position paper *Education for Yukon Indians* argued that "our children should be educated in public schools, but ... consideration should be given to the special problems, the preservation of the language, and the factual representation of the culture of a group comprising nearly one-third of the Yukon's population." In addition, the chiefs argued that certain vocational and technical courses "must be designed and presented in an Indian setting outside regular educational jurisdiction."[40]

In addressing educational policy, Yukon First Nations grappled with the fact that while they were outnumbered in the territory as a whole, they were a majority in many of its smaller communities. Their needs, they believed, were not being met in either context. They proposed that residential schools (which they referred to as the "hated hostel") be replaced by group homes. These homes would be located "centrally in each village, operated by Indian couples" and would offer short-term accommodation to anyone, especially children and Elders, who needed it to "free parents for the trapline or employment, or to provide warm meals for the young and old who cannot care for themselves."

In 1977 the Council for Yukon Indians published *Together Today for Our Children Tomorrow: A Statement of Grievances and an Approach to Settlement by the Yukon Indian People*, which criticized residential schools for their role in undermining intergenerational relations, destroying First Nations spirituality, and producing a dropout rate approaching 100%. No school in the Yukon taught students—white or First Nations—anything about the culture or achievements of First Nations.[41]

In the *Dene Declaration* of July 19, 1975, the Dene of the Mackenzie Valley issued their own assertion of Aboriginal rights.[42]

Aboriginal legislators were also raising the issue. Nick Sibbeston, a Dene from Fort Simpson and a member of the territorial council for Mackenzie-Liard, had been taken to residential school at age four. In speeches in the Northwest Territories legislature in 1971, he called for

- parental involvement in education;
- Dene control of schools and hostels, exemplified in plans for the new school and Dene-run hostel at Edzo (the Chief Jimmy Bruneau School);
- more schooling in communities so that no children need be taken from home before age twelve or thirteen at the earliest; and
- cultural content in curricula.

He was highly critical of an educational system in which children's "history, language, beliefs, whatever the parents have taught them, are thought to be minor details and excluded in many cases as a nuisance." He treated residential schools as part of a phenomenon of unemployment, lack of training, and "the anguish in adapting to a different society."[43]

In the late 1970s, Stephen Kakfwi, then an official with the Indian Brotherhood of the Northwest Territories (later called the Dene Nation), wrote of the way the schools had separated the generations:

> The elders had much difficulty in relating to the young. Many of the young lost the language, the values and the views which they had learned from their elders. The elders realized that what was happening to their young in school was not exactly what they wanted. The government was literally stealing young people from their families. They realized that, if the situation remained unchanged, they as a people would be destroyed in a relatively short time.[44]

Bob Overvold, of the Métis Association of the Northwest Territories (now the Northwest Territories Métis Nation), drew on the eight years he spent in Anglican, Catholic, and government schools to make a similar point:

> First, traditionally Dene children learned from their parents. In residential schools the adult-child relationship was almost non-existent; most, if not all the

school and residential staff were non-Dene and thus quite alien to the majority of Dene students. Second, because of the style of those institutions, their size, and layout, this meant that many rules and regulations had to be imposed and thus the students were essentially forced to conform.[45]

The Mackenzie Valley Pipeline Inquiry of the mid-1970s provided former students with a forum to discuss their experiences. Justice Thomas Berger's final report included a brief discussion of the residential schooling system in the North and its adherence to the assimilationist program followed in the South. In testimony at Deline (Fort Franklin), Dolphus Shea told of years of pain and humiliation, concluding, "Today, I think back on the hostel life and I feel ferocious."[46]

The Aboriginal critique of boarding schools received a mixed reception from education officials. F. Dunford, the supervising principal of the Churchill Vocational Centre, complained in 1970 about the attitude of an Aboriginal speaker at a conference of northern residence administrators held in Yellowknife. Dunford wrote that the speaker, whom he did not name, "preached the gospel of Indian rights and told us what is wrong with white people." It was not, he felt, a constructive presentation.[47]

The campaign of the Inuit of the eastern Arctic to gain control of education from Yellowknife was filled with statements and manifestos that denounced the past system and called for a culturally inclusive, locally based educational system. Early on, the only eastern Arctic member of the legislature was Bryan Pearson of Iqaluit. While not Aboriginal himself, he made sure the legislature was aware of the desire of his Inuit constituents to see classrooms with Inuit teachers in every community and to see hostels become a thing of the past. Landmark events for the Inuit organizations included a four-part series of articles in *Inuit Today* by Tagak Curley, an early president of the Inuit Tapirisat, titled "Inuit in Our Educational System." In 1981 the Inuit Cultural Institute at Arviat (Eskimo Point) celebrated the International Year of the Child with an anticolonial review of northern education (*Ajurnarmat*). In the same year, the English/Inuktitut government periodical *Inuktitut* published a special issue on Inuit education, with articles on Alaska, Greenland, the Soviet Union, and four projects of current interest in Canada, including Inuktitut teacher-training programs.[48]

Tagak Curley addressed a meeting of Northwest Territories teachers in 1972:

> Most of all, I admire Canadian Inuit for resisting the total assimilation (change) attempted by the dominant Canadian society through their present education policy which you serve. It has been indicated by Inuit that they do not accept this total assimilation which is threatening our values today. It has been said by many Inuit and organizations that there is room in our Canadian society for Inuit to live in harmony (peace) by recognizing their rights through participation. They have the language, they have the traditional economy, and most of all they are the majorities in the settlements in which you will be teaching. We must

seriously explore how to modernize those techniques without harming the values they so respect amongst themselves.[49]

In 1974, when the territorial government sought to rebuild the Iqaluktuuttiaq (Cambridge Bay) hostel, Pearson asked for details, adding: "Whenever I see that term 'pupil residence' I see red. Could we have an explanation of why we need a 16-bed pupil residence in Cambridge Bay?" When told that the previous residence had burned down, Pearson responded, "That is good. Who attends it? Why would we have a 16-bed pupil residence in Cambridge Bay?" The explanation was that the hostel was needed for the children of families that were "living off the land, in particular the people in the Bathurst Inlet."[50]

As this period drew to an end, Aboriginal political leaders became more explicit in their criticisms of the residential school system. One of the first to speak out in the North was Aivilik MLA Piita Irniq. On March 4, 1991, he told the legislature that "too much remains untold by the Government of Canada, and even by the Government of the Northwest Territories. I truly feel that Inuit who were assimilated have a right to know the blunt truth." He spoke of the "failure of a policy of the government, the result of which is the terrible damage to the preservation of our language, culture, values and the alienation of generations of Inuit peoples of the North." He called on the territorial government to take up the cause of the residential schools: "I would urge this government not to stall any further to have the Canadian government state their position on the residential school era so that many of us, former students and parents, can begin to deal with the emotional trauma which follows this era. We need to know what the real story is."[51]

Grade extension and boarding homes

Criticism by Aboriginal people provided a powerful rationale for dismantling the hostel system. It would take the construction of local day schools offering elementary, and later high school, grades (a process referred to as grade extension) and the adoption of various small-scale board options to finally empty the hostels.

Grade extension

The transfer of authority over education to territorial governments led to a reconsideration of earlier policies regarding whether schools could be located in small communities and which grade levels could be offered in those communities. Initially, educational administrators insisted that grade extension was too expensive.[52] A senior educational administrator told a legislative committee in 1971 that for educational reasons he preferred schooling in communities to stop at Grade Six, but strong community pressures had led to a decision to provide up to Grade Eight in many places. It was a trend he expected to continue.[53] The following year Northwest Territories Commissioner Stuart Hodgson said, "We are trying to extend the education system in some of the larger communities ... but it is not always possible to extend it as far as what one might like, and therefore residences have to be used."[54] The pressure for grade extension was irresistible. As Table 11.7 shows, by 1995 even the Baffin Division Board of Education was offering Grade Twelve in six of its fourteen communities, with plans to raise that to ten communities within three years.[55]

Table 11.7 Actual and projected grade extension in Baffin Region communities, 1994–95 to 1999–2000

Community	Achieved			Projected		
	94/95	95/96	96/97	97/98	98/99	99/00
Arctic Bay	11	12	12	12	12	12
Cape Dorset	11	11	11	12	12	12
Clyde River	10	11	12	12	12	12
Grise Fiord	9	10	10	10	10	10
Hall Beach	11	11	12	12	12	12
Igloolik	12	12	12	12	12	12
Iqaluit/Apex	12	12	12	12	12	12
Kimmirut	11	11	11	11	11	11
Nanisivik	9	9	9	9	9	9
Qikiqtarjuaq	10	11	11	12	12	12
Pangnirtung	12	12	12	12	12	12
Pond Inlet	12	12	12	12	12	12
Resolute Bay	9	9	9	9	9	9
Sanikiluaq	11	12	12	12	12	12

Source: TRC, NRA, Government of Northwest Territories – Education, Culture and Employment, Ukkivik – Future Plans [Capital Planning], 1995, Transfer – Nunavut, box 21, untitled consultant's report, 2 February 1995, 6. [FBS-000451]

The impact of school construction and grade extension can be observed more closely by looking at the history of the Chief Jimmy Bruneau school and residence. This community-controlled school and residence opened in the new community of Edzo, near Behchoko (Fort Rae), in 1971. It was intended to be a new sort of residence. At the school's opening ceremony in 1972, Chief Bruneau said, "I have asked for a school to be built on my land and that school will be run by my people and my people will work at that school and children will learn both ways, our way and whiteman's way."[56]

At the start of the 1971–72 school year, the Chief Jimmy Bruneau residence housed thirty-nine pupils.[57] By the following year, the figure had risen to ninety-three.[58] Due to the construction of day schools in other communities, the number of students in the residence declined to forty-five by the next year, and by the start of the 1974–75 year the residence had ceased to operate.[59] The school extended only to Grade Nine. Students who wished to complete further grades usually had to go to Yellowknife; between 1985 and 1990, only six students completed their high school education. To address this problem, the school introduced a Grade Ten program in 1991 (with Grades Eleven and Twelve added in the following years). Ten students graduated in 1994. The following year, the residence reopened, and the school served for a period as a regional high school.[60]

In the Yukon, a significant argument in favour of grade extension was the high dropout rate of what were described as "rural" students studying at the F. H. Collins High School in Whitehorse. In 1978 they had a dropout rate of 49%; the general Whitehorse dropout rate was 25%.[61] Table 11.8 provides an overview of the extension of grades at fifteen schools in the Yukon from 1974 to 1984.

Table 11.8 Changes in school grade offerings in the Yukon, 1974 to 1984

School	Grades offered
Pelly Crossing	Fluctuating Grades 7, 6, 8, with Grade 9 after 1980
Old Crow	Grade 8, 9, or 10, with Grade 10 in 1982 and 1983
Burwash	No school until 1980; Grade 7, 8, or 9 thereafter
Carmacks	Grade 9 in 1974, Grade 10 thereafter
Teslin	Grade 10 most years, Grade 12 1981 to 83
Ross River	Grade 10 throughout
Haines Junction	Grade 10 1974 to 1979, Grade 11 in 1980, Grade 12 1981 to 1984
Carcross	Fluctuating Grade 6 to Grade 9
Watson*	Grade 12 throughout
Mayo	Grade 12 throughout
Dawson	Grade 12 throughout
Elsa	Grades 8 or 7, declining to Grade 6 after 1983
Beaver Creek	Grade 7, 8 or 9, especially Grade 9 after 1981
Kluane	Grade 8 throughout, occasionally ending at 7 or 9
Faro	Grade 12 throughout

* The populations of Watson Lake and Upper Liard, eleven kilometres apart on the Alaska Highway, apparently shared a school and have been combined here.

Source: School data from Sharp, *Yukon Rural Education*, 52.

Boarding homes and home boarding

Grade extension did not solve the problem of children who wished to finish high school but lived in communities so small and isolated that the higher grades would never be available locally. In the Yukon, the federal government, under pressure from First Nations organizations, adopted a group home policy. At its 1972 and 1973 annual conferences, the Yukon Native Brotherhood had approved resolutions calling on Indian Affairs to replace student residences with group homes.[62] Group homes opened in Watson Lake and Ross River in 1975. At Ross River, a married couple were hired to provide care for up to eight children. The couple had to be approved by the Ross River Indian Band before being hired. The hostel was intended to "provide supervision and care in a native community to native children, who would normally be placed in a Student Residence for social or educational reasons."[63]

By 1985, there were three group homes, one in Ross River and two in Watson Lake—one of which was slated for closure in that year.[64] A 1986 review of the problems facing students from small rural communities called for a new small hostel at Haines Junction. According to the review, some high school students from farther west in Burwash, Destruction Bay, and Beaver Creek had taken their secondary schooling in Haines Junction, and "have remained in school for longer, passed more of their courses, and have encountered less strife" than others who went to high school in Whitehorse.[65]

The long-term future of schooling outside the home community was specifically addressed in the Umbrella Final Agreement of 1993, which set the framework for settlement of all First Nations land claims in Yukon. The agreement specifically allows as a "permitted activity for Settlement corporations" the granting of "scholarships and reimbursement of other expenses for juvenile and adult Yukon Indian People to enable them to attend conventional educational institutions within and outside the Yukon."[66]

Until at least 1980, the Northwest Territories government provided a "private-boarding home allowance" in Yellowknife only for those students who were "handicapped" and therefore could not stay in Akaitcho Hall. A former Akaitcho Hall employee recommended that the boarding option be expanded to include other students. She felt this option would help reduce the institution's dropout rate.[67] Such a program was in operation by 1984.[68] The rates for home boarding were increased from $15 a day to $20 a day effective January 1, 1987. Even with the increase, Akaitcho Hall had "difficulty in finding suitable places for students."[69] The government further increased the boarding rates the following year: they ranged from $25 to $40 a day, depending on the region.[70]

By the mid-1990s the Northwest Territories government was giving thought to making greater use of boarding arrangements.[71] A proposal to expand the use of boarding arrangements in Iqaluit identified a number of potential problems. Not only was there a housing shortage, but boarding homes had to be screened to see if they offered students a suitable place to study, sleep, and eat, along with a "caring, firm and supportive environment in which to learn and grow. In spite of screening some homes may not turn out to be suitable." Furthermore, the boarding home operators "may not themselves have sufficient interest in education to assist the students," which would force the board to hire tutors. The study noted that "some home-boarded students in the past have not been properly fed. The home boarding parents have spent the money on other things. At times, the students have been used as babysitters for the family at the expense of their studies."[72] The review concluded that home boarding should be considered only "on an exception basis," when students' parents and the board both agreed.[73] A committee reviewing the future of Akaitcho Hall in 1992 came to similar conclusions, noting cautiously that "home boarding of students can work well if a careful selection of home boarding parents is assured." And this long-term solution was offered: "If student residences are needed, they should be small (15–20 students) and contracted out to a good family who will live in the residences."[74]

Northern education in southern Canada

The policy of sending a limited number of Aboriginal students south to continue their education continued after responsibility for education was transferred to the territories. According to former Northern Affairs official Ralph Ritcey, from 1967 to 1978, the program sent between thirty and forty students a year to Winnipeg and a hundred a year to Ottawa.[75] Students from the western Arctic tended to go to Edmonton, while students from the eastern Arctic typically found themselves in Ottawa or Montreal. Federal involvement was significant, and was delivered in its later years through a Vocational Training Section in Northern Affairs. In 1980 about sixty-five Inuit went south through this program, but only sixteen of those went to high schools; the rest were in vocational programs, with a few in academic upgrading.[76]

These students often boarded with non-Aboriginal families. In 1983 Tagak Curley questioned the government's policy of having Inuit children board with families in southern Canada. As an alternative, Curley called on the government to establish an "Inuit House" in Ottawa.[77] Northern leaders were always alert to the distress and hardship their young people felt, and Inuit-language magazines in particular published special issues, with articles written by young students, to try to prepare their fellow Inuit for the culture shocks ahead.[78] By 1983, the territorial government's official position was that it would not send high school students south.[79]

CHAPTER 12

The residential school experience in Arctic Québec and Labrador

T his volume has so far focused on the residential schools that operated in Yukon and the Northwest Territories (including the portion that later became Nunavut). The residential school experience in Arctic Québec (Nunavik) and Labrador await further research and investigation. The following pages are meant as an outline of a story still to be told.

Arctic Québec: Nunavik residential schools

In 1939 the Supreme Court of Canada ruled that the Inuit people of Canada were a federal, not a provincial, responsibility, even when the Inuit were living in a Canadian province.[1] The only Canadian province at that time with a significant Inuit population was Québec, where they lived along the eastern coast of Hudson Bay and the northern coasts of the Ungava Peninsula. This territory is often referred to as Arctic Québec or Nunavik. From 1939 to the early 1960s, successive Québec governments paid little attention to the Inuit or to northern Québec.[2] Following the federal government's decision to expand schooling in the North in the mid-1950s, four hostels were built in northern Québec. They were located in Kangiqsualujjuaq (George River), Kuujjuaraapik (Great Whale River), Kangirsuk (Payne Bay), and Inukjuak (Port Harrison).[3] The education provided in these schools was in English.[4] When the Churchill Vocational Centre opened, students from Nunavik were also sent there for training. In 1970, for example, a third of the students in the Churchill facility were from Arctic Québec.[5] In addition, a small number of students went to southern Canada for secondary education.[6]

From 1960 on, the Québec government attempted to play a larger role in the delivery of a variety of services in Nunavik. Starting in 1963, the province began funding and operating its own system of day schools for Inuit children throughout Nunavik.[7] Enrolment in the federal schools remained significantly higher than in the provincial schools throughout this period; when parents had a choice, they clearly preferred federal schools, although some Inuit families were known to alternate between the two systems.[8]

The last federal hostel in northern Québec, at Inukjuak, closed in 1971, and the Churchill Vocational Centre closed at the end of the 1972–73 school year.[9] The need to send children out of the region would decline as grade extension was introduced under a new, Inuit-controlled education system.

The 1975 James Bay and Northern Quebec Agreement among the Cree and Inuit of Québec, the federal and provincial governments, and Hydro-Québec brought this system of federal and provincial schools to an end. Under the agreement, all schools in Nunavik were to be controlled by an Inuit-run school board, called the Kativik School Board. (The Cree would have their own school board.[10]) In 1978, the Kativik board assumed control of all Inuit schools in Nunavik. With a locally elected education committee in each community, and a centralized executive committee, the school board system marked a significant departure from the federal and provincial schools. Responsible for over 2,000 Inuit students and 150 teachers in several isolated communities across Nunavik, the board was in charge of designing curriculum to meet the needs of the Inuit communities and of training teachers from the North to deliver the curriculum.[11] The Kativik board established a residential school near Montréal in 1978 but closed it after six months of operation, concluding that there were too many adjustments for the students to make all at once.[12] By the mid-1980s, the board was offering schooling up to Secondary III (Grade Nine) in all communities. Secondary IV and Secondary V (the equivalent of Grades Ten and Eleven) were also offered in some northern communities. The trend was to increase the number of trips home for students outside their home community at the secondary level.[13]

The Labrador schools

The history of residential schooling for Aboriginal people in Labrador differs from that in the rest of the country, primarily because the British colony of Newfoundland, to which Labrador belonged, did not join Canada until 1949.

There were two major groupings of Aboriginal peoples in Labrador. The Inuit lived in the northern part, in what is now called Nunatsiavut.[14] The Innu First Nation lived to the south, hunting caribou in the interior and harvesting fish on the coast.[15] As in the rest of Canada, missionary organizations played a central role in establishing residential schooling in Labrador. The two key organizations were the Moravian Mission and the International Grenfell Association.

The official name of the Moravian Mission is the Unitas Fratrem, or United Brotherhood. One of the earliest Protestant churches it founded was in Moravia, in what is now the Czech Republic. In the early eighteenth century, it established a base in Saxony, in what is now Germany. The Moravians developed a strong missionary tradition, sending missionaries to the Americas, Africa, and Asia. In 1733, the Moravians established a mission in Greenland. In 1752, a missionary expedition to Labrador ended in a conflict with the Inuit that left seven members of the Moravian expedition dead. In 1764, Newfoundland's British colonial governor, Sir Hugh Palliser, endorsed a second Moravian expedition to northern Labrador. After two exploratory journeys, a mission was established in 1771 at Amitok Island, near what is now the community of Nain.[16]

Owing to their experience in Greenland, the Moravians came to Labrador able to speak Inuktitut. Between 1771 and 1905, they established eight missions there. The British had granted the Moravians the right to expel anyone from these extensive mission holdings if they did not obey the mission's rules. As late as the 1940s, private traders needed the Moravians' permission to operate at the missions, and a Moravian trading company handled most trade.[17] As a result, the Moravians were a dominant force in every aspect of mission life in northern Labrador.[18]

The Moravians established boarding schools early on at two of their missions in Labrador. They taught children how to read and write in Inuktitut, using the Roman alphabet. As a result, most Inuit in Labrador were literate in Inuktitut.[19] Inuit cultural practices were suppressed as 'heathen.' So little value did the Moravians attach to these practices that, in their extensive diaries and accounts, they neglected to document or describe them.[20]

The International Grenfell Association was an outgrowth of the work of Dr. Wilfred Grenfell, a British doctor and Protestant evangelist whose work with the Mission to Deep Sea Fishermen in the late nineteenth century brought him to Labrador.[21] He was struck by the desperate living conditions of the approximately 25,000 men, women, and children who migrated to Labrador annually to work the shore fishery and of the permanent settlers who lived there year round.[22] His work among these non-Aboriginal people eventually gained international attention. Grenfell Associations were established in England, the United States, and Canada to raise funds to support his missionary and medical aid work in Labrador.[23] By 1909 he had established a hospital and an orphanage in Labrador.[24] At a time when much missionary work in Canada focused on Aboriginal people or on eastern European immigrants, Grenfell directed his efforts toward people of Anglo-Saxon descent.[25]

The role of boarding schools and orphanages in Labrador was expanded in the wake of the 1918 influenza epidemic. The high death rate, and lack of government support led the Grenfell Mission to raise money for a dormitory school at Muddy River, to house children orphaned by the epidemic.[26] By the mid-1920s, the Grenfell Mission had established four hospitals, two orphanages, and three public schools.[27] The International Grenfell Association, organized to carry on Grenfell's work, was operating three boarding schools by 1935.[28] Many of the teachers in the Grenfell schools were unpaid volunteers, who were expected not only to pay their own trans-portation to Labrador but also to bring their own school supplies.[29]

Starting in the 1950s and up to the 1970s, the Grenfell schools accepted Inuit chil-dren who were attending high school.[30] When Newfoundland and Labrador joined Canada in 1949, education and social services in Labrador were left largely to the missionary organizations.[31] Under a 1954 federal-provincial agreement, the Grenfell Association had responsibility for health in northern Labrador. The services were pro-vided under provincial authority, but the funding came from Ottawa.[32]

The federal government did not extend its network of hostels and federal day schools for Aboriginal people into Labrador in the 1950s. This decision appears to have been due to the fact that the terms of union between Canada and Newfoundland and Labrador made no mention of Aboriginal people.[33] The federal government took the position that Aboriginal people in Newfoundland and Labrador were a provincial responsibility. The federal government would eventually enter into specific agree-ments with the province to provide financial assistance to Aboriginal communities, but the amounts provided were less than what similar communities received in the rest of the country.[34]

The Moravians and the International Grenfell Association continued to operate residential schools.[35] Some of these schools, in Cartwright, Nain, Makkovik, North West River, and St. Anthony, operated into the 1970s.[36]

The experiences of the students who attended the Labrador schools are similar to those of other residential school students. Rose Oliver grew up in Rigolet, Labrador. She told the Truth and Reconciliation Commission of Canada that for her first four-teen years, she lived in "a big happy family with traditional foods, and mom ... was teaching me how to be a Inuit woman; how to clean seal skins and that kind of a thing." When she was fourteen, her father insisted that she go to the boarding school at North West River. Her mother was opposed to the decision. "Every time I left she would cry her heart out. And I would cry too."

At the school, students were not allowed to speak their Inuit language, except in secret: "Only at night time when we had to whisper it." Oliver also missed the foods that she ate at home. She found the rules and regulations oppressive. In particular, there were "a lot of chores to do for a young girl. Make a great big bed for the whole dorm. Wash huge sheets in the morning; and iron them before school started. And it seemed like we had no social life anymore; there was no time spent with us, like, to help us to be young women. The house mothers were cold and they were from England; I don't think they understood our ways." Christmas was a particularly hard time: "It was very lonely in the dormitory. There was ... it wasn't like home. Home was where we had stockings hung up and there was food on the table and there was laughter and Santa Claus came to the school. But here it was just a cold environment."[37]

Rosalie Webber, an Inuit woman, attended a Grenfell Mission school in Cartwright in the 1940s. The children travelled to the school by boat, and she remembered

> all the people, especially the younger ones crying, all of the way; being very seasick. 'Cause this boat was confined and we were used to being in the boat with our dad, in the open boat.

> So when we arrived there, everybody was taken off and deloused; kerosene. Everybody crying and tired and then our hair was cut, our clothes was taken from us and we were given a bibbed, farmer's blue jeans and the lumberjack shirts, two items of underwear and two socks and two shirts ... and gumboots, which was our—what we wore for the rest of our duration there, winter or summer.

Even though her mother worked at the school, she was not allowed to speak with her: "She had one day off, I think every month and a half. No, she had a half a day off, every month and a half, but she wasn't allowed to speak with us. It was very, very traumatic as a child, to go from a homey family environment to a sterile, where you were wakened by a bell, cleaned your teeth by a bell, made your bed by a bell."

Webber found the diet strange and inedible:

> So, and then my first meal there I didn't eat potatoes, well we didn't have potato peels. Well we didn't have potatoes in the islands, you know. We didn't have too much fresh fruit and we ate off the land.

> Because I didn't eat my potatoes then I was refused food and I was sent to my room. And it wasn't my room, it was everybody's room. And for three days I didn't have food. And when my meal time came they presented the potato skins to me again and I'd refuse to eat them, till the third day. And, I guess I must have ate them because I was allowed to go back to classroom, or the dormitory.

It was a limited, regimented life that left her feeling angry and humiliated:

> So you grow up, always hungry. You get up by a bell, you ate by a bell, you sat by a bell, you got up by a bell, you went to school by a bell, you come in from outside by a bell, you had your other meal by a bell and you went to bed by a bell. And when that bell rang there was no communication between anyone; very isolating, very lonely. I was filled with anger that you couldn't express.[38]

Matilda Lampe attended the boarding school in Nain in the 1970s. When she and her younger sister, Doris, were taken to the school, they thought they were only staying overnight. Matilda recalled comforting her sister on the night of their arrival. "I said, 'Doris, we go sleep in boarding school overnight. Mom's going to pick us up tomorrow; must be tomorrow night.' Doris was happy." As was the case at many residential schools, the two girls were left in tears when their long hair was cut on their first day at the school. According to Matilda, Doris was punished for speaking Inuktitut at the school. They stayed at the school for three years.[39]

The treatment they received on arrival left many students feeling humiliated and inferior. Rose Mitsuk attended the North West River school in the 1970s. In her recollection the children were made to feel dirty from the day of their arrival at the school:

> After we went in the dorm and put our clothes away and all that, there was a— one of those parents was a Sister. And she took me and brought me into the bathroom and she washed my hair with lice shampoo. And that made me feel that she must've felt that I was dirty. But I don't know if she did that with the other students. I know that she did it with me and I don't know, it's ... that I'll never forget it. 'Cause I think that I was—I wasn't a dirty person. I think I was a clean person, to me, but that, that thing I'll never forget.[40]

Joanna Michel attended the North West River school.

> As an Innu person I ... I felt I was dirty all the time. There was always something wrong with me because of these constantly, constantly remarks that were made to us; that we were dirty Indians and we were, should be happy that we are in that place; to look after, to look after us; give us better life. I was one confused little girl. I felt like my parents didn't want me; that's why I was in that institution.

On at least one occasion, she got into a fight with the person in charge of the dormitory. "I remember feeling very angry and helpless; there was nothing I could do to protect my little sister. So I jumped on the house mother's back and I started pulling on her hair; started hitting her. 'Why you being so bad to my sister!?'"[41]

Sophie Keelan was born in 1948 and recalled her family's traditional way of life: "We were Inuit people and we were living like nomadic people of the land. Surviving by hunting and fishing on the land and. . . . And we were living in a tent. I was born in a tent, with two midwives. And I was born in northern part of Labrador; it's called Saglek Bay on a very small island." When she was young, her family moved south to the community of Makkovik, where she attended a day school.

> In school we had a hard time because we're Inuit, we're native and these children—they're white and we had to mingle with them. And ... after every time after school, they would wait for us outside, outside the school, and wait for us. Then they start throwing rocks at us, calling us names. We would run, run for our lives, and we even had to make a little road up in the trees. We couldn't go on the road anymore 'cause if we did they gonna run after us. We had to hide, kind of hide and go in the bushes and trees, and the rocks were at us. They were throwing rocks at us.[42]

Many former students also spoke of being bullied. Marjorie Goudie briefly attended the North West River school in the 1960s. As she recalled, "Not real long after we got to North West River me and my sister got beat up by the other children, just because. I didn't want to be there, and I hated being there." When she went home for Christmas, she announced that she was not going back to school. "I didn't even care what my parents was going to say to me because they wanted me to get an education. But I really didn't care because I didn't want to be in that dormitory. So I just stayed home."[43]

Abraham Nochasak attended the Hopedale Mission Home in Labrador in the 1960s. He recalled being punished for speaking Inuktitut: "I still couldn't speak English, although it was Grade Two; I used to speak little bit English. So once in a while when I used to talk Inuktitut, and when I got caught talking Inuktitut, they used to put me in the corner. Stand in the corner until our lessons was over. I stand in the corner lots of times for trying to talk Inuktitut."[44]

Samuel Nui, who was born in Davis Inlet, Labrador, attended the North West River school for one year in the early 1950s. He recalled that he was made to strip naked in front of male and female students for wetting his bed. He was also punished with a belt for bedwetting. Sometimes he was denied food or water for a day. When his mother came to the community for medical treatment, he was not allowed to see her.[45]

Patricia Kemuksiak recalled being taken by force from her grandmother's house to the school in North West River:

> We hung onto our grandmother and we wouldn't let go and they tore us out of her arms and brought us to North West River into the foreign dorm.
>
> My sister who was about a year old went into the infants' home and me and my brother went to the junior dorm in North West River; however, we were in the same dorm but we were separated and hardly saw each other because we were separated by boys and girls.

She found school life to be highly regimented: "We were scheduled and scheduled and scheduled to death. Everything went on a schedule and a bell. And if people didn't like the food we ate, because the food was really bad there, food was shoved down their throat until they threw up." She recalled it as an austere and loveless institution: "We were fed, clothed and had a bed, but there was no love, no caring, and no support. I had a lot of anger for being put there in the dorm or the orphanage, some people called it, and I felt abandoned. I tried to maintain contact with my brother and sister, but it was difficult. I prayed a lot to go home, constantly prayed."[46]

From the students' perspective, there was little to distinguish life in the Labrador residential schools from life in the residential schools that operated in the rest of the country. Nevertheless, residential schools in Labrador were excluded from the Indian Residential Schools Settlement Agreement. That did not preclude the TRC from hearing from former students of Labrador residential schools who had relevant experiences to share with the Commission in its efforts to "tell the complete history" and legacy of residential schools in Canada.

In 2010, the Newfoundland and Labrador Court of Appeal certified a class action suit launched by former students of the Labrador schools for abuses that occurred in the schools. The Newfoundland Court of Appeal upheld that decision in 2011.[47] In January 2015, it was announced that the parties had agreed to submit the case to mediation.[48]

Conclusion

Residential schooling in northern Canada was, at most times and places, not a segregated system but part of a system of public education. And yet, like the better-known segregated systems in southern Canada, these schools disrupted the intergenerational transmission of values and skills and imparted few if any of the skills needed for employment.

There were a number of unique elements to the northern experience. Perhaps one of the most unusual was the number of former residential school students who served in the legislature of the Northwest Territories. These former students, some of whom served as cabinet ministers, mounted a direct challenge to the thinking of education officials. They clearly identified the system's failings and proposed remedies that were distinctly northern.

The harm done by residential schooling in the North remains. The students who were adults in Akaitcho Hall in 1975 may well have been the same young men and women who were disoriented, bullied, and abused as children in the large hostels in the mid-1960s. Although some were not abused or treated roughly themselves, they all lived in a milieu where abuse, whether in the classroom or the hostel, was all too common. When they returned to their communities, they were estranged from their parents, their language, and their culture. Many of their parents, the generation still in a state of shock from the upheavals of the 1940s through the 1960s, could not knit their communities back together again. The removal of children added to the damage already done by other economic and demographic changes. And jobs—which were the main inducement to parents to give up their young people—generally failed to materialize. But despite these hardships, many Survivors found the courage and the energy to begin to pull their lives and their communities back together.

Notes

An era of neglect:

Canadian government policy in the North before 1950

1. *Canadian Geographic*, "Historical Maps of Canada, 1873," http://www.canadiangeographic. ca/mapping/historical_maps/1873.asp.
2. Morrison, *True North*, 3, 21–22, 29; McMillan and Yellowhorn, *First Peoples*, 5–9.
3. Coates, *Canada's Colonies*, 66–99.
4. Grant, *Sovereignty or Security?*, 10.
5. Carney, "Relations in Education," 33.
6. Morrison, *True North*, 105.
7. Morrison, *True North*, 109.
8. Grant, *Sovereignty or Security?*, 14.
9. Morrison, *True North*, 75.
10. Grant, *Sovereignty or Security?*, 13–15.
11. Carney, "Relations in Education," 34.
12. Grant, *Sovereignty or Security?*, 16.
13. Carney, "Relations in Education," 124.
14. Canada, Aboriginal Affairs and Northern Development Canada, Treaty No. 8, http://www. aadnc-aandc.gc.ca/eng/1100100028813/1100100028853.
15. Carney, "Relations in Education," 34.
16. Carney, "Relations in Education," 127–128.
17. McCarthy, *From the Great River*, 176.
18. Canada, Aboriginal Affairs and Northern Development Canada, Treaty No. 11, http://www. aadnc-aandc.gc.ca/eng/1100100028916/1100100028947.
19. Morrison, *True North*, 111.
20. TRC, NRA, Deschatelets Archives – Ottawa, HR 8004.C73R 3, Missions indiennes des pères oblates, Procés-verbal de la Troisième Réunion tenue à Ottawa, 24–25 novembre 1937. [OMI-033063]
21. Diubaldo, *Government of Canada*, 34–38; Jenness, *Eskimo Administration*, 32–33.
22. *Quebec Boundaries Extension Act*, Statutes of Canada, 1912, Chapter 45.
23. Diubaldo, "The Absurd Little Mouse," 36.
24. Rompkey, *Story of Labrador*, 37–47; Rompkey, *Grenfell of Labrador*.

Laying the groundwork: Mission schools: 1850 to 1900

1. Choquette, *Oblate Assault*, 38–47; Huel, *Proclaiming the Gospel*, 15–18.
2. Huel, *Proclaiming the Gospel*, 17–24.
3. Quoted in Choquette, *Oblate Assault*, 141–143; Abel, *Drum Songs*, 116–117; McCarthy, *From the Great River*, 47–49.
4. McCarthy, *From the Great River*, 50.
5. Abel, *Drum Songs*, 120.
6. Choquette, *Oblate Assault*, 69.
7. Rutherdale, *Women and White Man's God*, 7–8.
8. Choquette, *Oblate Assault*, 157.
9. McCarthy, *From the Great River*, 160; Carney, "Grey Nuns and Children," 291; Duchaussois, *Grey Nuns in the Far North*, 148.
10. McCarthy, *From the Great River*, 163.
11. McCarthy, *From the Great River*, 159–163.
12. Carney, "Relations in Education," 159.
13. McCarthy, *From the Great River*, 159–163.
14. Duchaussois, *Grey Nuns in the Far North*, 171.
15. McCarthy, *From the Great River*, 164.
16. McCarthy, *From the Great River*, 164.
17. Duchaussois, *Grey Nuns in the Far North*, 148.
18. Duchaussois, *Grey Nuns in the Far North*, 152.
19. McCarthy, *From the Great River*, 162, 236.
20. Huel, *Proclaiming the Gospel*, 111.
21. TRC, NRA, Anglican Church of Canada, General Synod Archives, ACC-MSCC-GS 75-103, series 2.15, box 27, file 8, St. Peter's Mission, Hay River, Diocese of Mackenzie River, Parish History, n.d.; [AAC-087477] TRC, NRA, Anglican Church of Canada, General Synod Archives, ACC-MSCC-GS 75-103, series 2.15, box 27, file 8, Hay River Slides, Alf. J. Vale, n.d. [AAC-087480]
22. McCarthy, *From the Great River*, 165; TRC, NRA, Library and Archives Canada, RG85, Perm. volume 1878, file 630/109-2, part 1, Hay River School St. Peter's Mission, 1900–1923, FA 85-8, private secretary to Alma Marsh, 25 February 1901. [HRU-000204]
23. TRC, NRA, Library and Archives Canada, RG10, volume 6475, file 918-1, part 1, G. Breynat to D. Laird, 29 March 1904, 4. [FPU-000069]
24. TRC, NRA, Library and Archives Canada, RG10, volume 6475, file 918-1, part 1, D. Laird to Frank Pedley, 6 May 1904. [FPU-000070]
25. Coates, *Canada's Colonies*, 150.
26. Library and Archives Canada, RG10, volume 3906, file 3908, W. Bompas to Minister of the Interior, 18 June 1896, quoted in Coates, *Canada's Colonies*, 137–138.
27. Coates, *Canada's Colonies*, 152.
28. Choquette, *Oblate Assault*, 160–161; TRC, NRA, Library and Archives Canada, RG10, volume 6479, file 940-1, part 1, "The Chooutla Indian School," in *Northern Lights* 15, 1 (February 1927). [CAR-011225]

Mission schools of the Northwest Territories: 1900 to 1960

1. For Fort Resolution, see: Carney, "Relations in Education," 60. For Aklavik, see: Canada, *Annual Report of the Department of Indian Affairs, 1927*, 14.

2. Johns, "History of St Peter's Mission," 22; TRC, NRA, Anglican Church of Canada, General Synod Archives, "Eskimo Residential School," in *Northern Lights*, August 1929, 16. [DYK-201365]

3. TRC, NRA, Library and Archives Canada, RG85, Perm. volume 1877, file 630/101-3, part 1, R.C. School Day Resolution 1905–1944, FA 85-8, Extract from minutes of the Fifty-Sixth Session of the Northwest Territories Council, 25 February 1935. [RCN-004681]

4. For the opening date of All Saints, see: Canada, *Annual Report of the Department of Mines and Resources, 1937*, 208. The Hay River residential school is listed in the 1937–1938 Indian Affairs annual report but not the 1938–1939 annual report. Dominion of Canada, *Annual Report of the Department of Mines and Natural Resources, 1938*, 231; *Annual Report of the Department of Mines and Natural Resources, 1939*.

5. For Fort Resolution, see: TRC, NRA, INAC – Departmental Library, "Farewell to St. Joseph's School, Fort Resolution, N.W.T.," *Indian Record*, volume 20, number 5, May 1957. [IMR-000160] For Fort Providence, see: TRC, NRA, Government of Northwest Territories Archives, file 600-1-1, part 4, School Policy [and Hostels], 1959–1961, Archival box 202-1, Archival Acc. G-1979-003, Department of Northern Affairs and National Resources, "Historic Names for Northern Schools and Residences," news release, 2 March 1961. [RCN-010612-0002]

6. Dickerson, *Whose North?*, 41.

7. Carney, "Relations in Education," 60; TRC, NRA, Library and Archives Canada, RG85, Perm. volume1878, file 630/109-2, part 1, Hay River School, St. Peter's Mission, 1900–1923, FA 85-8, letter from St. Peter's Mission Hay River, 25 July 1910. [HRU-000248]

8. John Francis Moran, *Local Conditions in the Mackenzie District, 1922,* Ottawa: F. A. Acland, printer to the King, 1923, 16–17, quoted in Jenness, *Eskimo Administration*, 43–44.

9. Innis, Wherrett, and Moore, "Survey of Education," 70.

10. TRC, NRA, Library and Archives Canada, RG85, volume 1051, file 630/158-9, part 1, "Historic Names for Northern Schools and Residences," 2 March 1961, 3. [RCN-002118]

11. Carney, "Relations in Education," 197.

12. TRC, NRA, Anglican Church of Canada, General Synod Archives – Ottawa, ACC-MSCC-GS 75-103, series 2.15, box 27, file 1, Report of the Joint Delegation and Interview with the Prime Minister, 20 December 1934, 1. [AAC-087280]; TRC, NRA, Library and Archives Canada, RG10, volume 7185, file 1/25-1-7-1, part 1, Harold McGill to church officers, principals of Indian Residential Schools, 22 February 1933. [AEMR-255373]

13. TRC, NRA, No document location, no document file source, J. O. Plourde to T. A. Crerar, 12 June 1940. [GMA-002340]

14. Carney, "Relations in Education," 424.

15. TRC, NRA, Library and Archives Canada, RG85, volume 793, file 6334, part 1, Shingle Point Day and Residential School, 1923–1932, "Application for Admission to Residential School," 1 September 1929. [SPU-000030]

16. TRC, NRA, Library and Archives Canada, RG85, volume 793, file 6334, part 1, Shingle Point Day and Residential School, 1923–1932, H. S. Shepherd to J. A. McDougal, 21 November 1931. [SPU-000164-0005]

17. TRC, NRA, Library and Archives Canada, RG85, volume 793, file 6334, part 1, Shingle Point Day and Residential School, 1923–1932, A. L. Fleming to H. E. Hume, 7 March 1932, 1. [SPU-000167]

18. TRC, NRA, Library and Archives Canada, RG85, volume 793, file 6334, part 1, Shingle Point Day and Residential School, 1923–1932, [illegible] Doyle to H. E. Hume, 10 August 1932. [SPU-000182]

19. TRC, NRA, Library and Archives Canada, RG85, Perm. volume 1883, file 630/219-2, part 3, Shingle Point Anglican School 1935–1936, FA 85-8, "Application for Admission to Residential School," 1 September 1932. [SPU-000053-0001]

20. TRC, NRA, Library and Archives Canada, RG85, Perm. volume 1882, file 630/119-3, part 1, Aklavik, N.W.T. R.C. Residential School, April 1927–January 1940, FA 85-8, Memorandum to H. E. Rowatt, 20 February 1933. [ICU-000922]

21. TRC, NRA, Library and Archives Canada, RG85, Perm. volume 1877, file 630/101-3, part 1, R.C. School Day Resolution, 1905–1944, FA 85-8, H. E. Hume to H. H. Rowatt, 23 September 1933. [RCN-001623-0001]

22. Dickerson, *Whose North?*, 39.

23. Jenness, *Eskimo Administration,* 42.

24. Jenness, *Eskimo Administration*, 30.

25. Jenness, *Eskimo Administration*, 48.

26. Grant, *Sovereignty or Security?,* 18.

27. Carney, "Relations in Education," 60.

28. TRC, NRA, English Language Summary of the Fort Resolution Chronicles, volume 1, 1903–1942, 1. [GNN-000077-0001]

29. Carney, "Relations in Education," 142.

30. Kelcey, *Alone in Silence*, 133–134.

31. 29 January 1926, W242, Microfilm reel 1, Aklavik Histoire Document 12, Archives Deschâtaulets/Grey Nuns, quoted in Kelcey, *Alone in Silence*, 134–135.

32. Kelcey, *Alone in Silence*, 135.

33. Carney, "Relations in Education," 240.

34. TRC, NRA, Library and Archives Canada, RG85, volume 1128, file 250-1-1, part 2B, O. S. Finnie to W. W. Cory, 16 January 1928. [NPC-400544-0000]

35. Archives of the Diocese of Mackenzie-Fort Smith, Yellowknife, Indian Affairs file, G. Breynat to C. Stewart, 25 May 1928, quoted in Carney, "Residential Schooling,"120.

36. TRC, NRA, Library and Archives Canada, RG85, volume 793, file 6334, part 1, Shingle Point Day and Residential School, 1923–1932, W. W. Cory to A. L. Fleming, 3 January 1929. [SPU-000094]

37. TRC, NRA, Library and Archives Canada, RG85, volume 793, file 6334, part 1, Shingle Point Day and Residential School, 1923–1932, O. S. Finnie to W. W. Cory, 21 December 1928. [SPU-000091-0000]

38. TRC, NRA, Library and Archives Canada, RG85, volume 793, file 6334, part 1, Shingle Point Day and Residential School, 1923–1932, W. W. Cory to A. L. Fleming, 3 January 1929. [SPU-000094]

39. TRC, NRA, Library and Archives Canada, RG85, Perm. volume 1877, file 630/101-3, part 1, R.C. School Day Resolution, 1905–1944, FA 85-8, Extract from the Minutes of the 64th Session of the Northwest Territories Council, held on December 29, 1936. [ASU-000003]

40. TRC, NRA, Library and Archives Canada, RG85, Perm. volume 1877, file 630/101-3, part 1, R.C. School Day Resolution, 1905–1944, FA 85-8, L. D. Livingstone to R. A. Gibson, 18 March 1941. [ASU-000009]

41. TRC, NRA, Library and Archives Canada, RG85, volume 226, file 630/119-2, part 1B, Anglican Schools – Aklavik, 1931–1949, R. A. Gibson to L. D. Livingstone, 10 April 1941. [ASU-000011]

42. TRC, NRA, Library and Archives Canada, RG85, volume 226, file 630/119-2, part 3, Anglican Schools – Aklavik, 1951–1952, Laval Fortier to Donald B. Marsh, 12 February 1952. [ASU-000027]

43. TRC, NRA, Library and Archives Canada, RG85, Perm. volume 441, file 630/119-2, part 7, Anglican Schools – Aklavik, N.W.T.,1955–1956, FA 85-1, J. W. Burton to L. A. C. O. Hunt, 23 February 1956. [ASU-000046]

44. G. Breynat to J. Plourde, Commission Oblate des Oeuvres Indiennes, Archives of the Vicariate of the Mackenzie, quoted in Carney, "Relations in Education," 209.

45. Coates, "A Very Imperfect Means,"143.

46. Canada, *Annual Report of the Department of Indian Affairs, 1908,* 398.

47. Canada, *Annual Report of the Department of Indian Affairs, 1908,* 399.

48. TRC, NRA, Library and Archives Canada, RG10, volume 6474, file 916-1, part 1, M. Christianson to H. McGill, 14 August 1936. [FRU-010051]

49. TRC, NRA, Library and Archives Canada, RG10, volume 6475, file 916-5, part 3, J. W. McKinnon to Indian Affairs Branch, 9 August 1947. [FRU-010095]

50. TRC, NRA, Library and Archives Canada, RG85, volume 225, file 630/118-1, part 1, Government School – Fort McPherson, N.W.T., 1900–1950, Extracts from Mr. J. W. McKinnon's Report, dated at Yellowknife, N.W.T., 1 July 1947. [FHU-000315]

51. TRC, NRA, Library and Archives Canada, RG85, volume 226, file 630/119-2, part 3, Anglican Schools – Aklavik, 1951–1952, Inspection Report, J. V. Jacobson, 29 February 1952, 19–24. [ASU-000029]

52. TRC, NRA, Library and Archives Canada, RG22, Perm. volume 877, file 41-4-2, part 1, Schools – Aklavik, N.W.T., May 1951–January 1952, FA 22-1, J. Trocellier to H. A. Young, 8 September 1952. [AKU-001616]

53. TRC, NRA, Library and Archives Canada, RG85, Perm. volume 395, file 630/101-3, part 5, R.C. Schools – Fort Resolution, N.W.T., April 1954–December 1954, FA 85-1, W. G. Devitt to F. J. G. Cunningham, 3 May 1953. [FRU-001955]

54. TRC, NRA, Library and Archives Canada, RG85, Perm. volume 497, file 630/119-1, part 5, Government School – Aklavik, 1956–1958, J. V. Jacobson to M. E. Winter, 13 February 1957. [ASU-000048]

55. TRC, NRA, Library and Archives Canada, RG85, volume 226, file 630/119-2, part 3, Anglican Schools – Aklavik, 1951–1952, Inspection Report, J. V. Jacobson, 29 February 1952, 19–24. [ASU-000029]

56. Phillips, *Canada's North,* 233.

57. Duchaussois, *Grey Nuns in the Far North,* 277.

58. Carney, "Native–Wilderness Equation," 70.

59. Carney, "Residential Schooling," 126.

60. TRC, NRA, Library and Archives Canada, RG85, Perm. volume 222, file 630/110-3, part 2, R.C. Schools – Fort Providence, N.W.T., October 1949–December 1952, FA 85-1, J. W. McKinnon to B. F. Neary, 1 August 1950. [FPU-002381]

61. Djwa, *Politics of the Imagination,* 318–327.

62. Scott, "Fort Providence," in *Collected Poems*, 230–231.

63. Carney, "Residential Schooling," 128.

64. Carney, "Residential Schooling," 129.

65. TRC, AVS, Jane S. Charlie, Statement to the Truth and Reconciliation Commission of Canada, Deline, Northwest Territories, 2 March 2010, Statement Number: 07-NWT-02MR1-002.

66. Elias, "Lillian Elias," 49.

67. TRC, AVS, Samuel Gargan, (Speaking Notes) Statement to the Truth and Reconciliation Commission of Canada, Fort Providence, Northwest Territories, 27 April 2011, Statement Number: SP015.

68. Margaret Oldenburg Papers, http://special.lib.umn.edu/findaid/xml/uarc00512.xml.

69. TRC, NRA, Library and Archives Canada, RG29, volume 926, file 386-1-14, part 1, Margaret Oldenburg to Dr. Pett, 29 [month not identified] 1946. [NPC-600901]

70. TRC, NRA, Library and Archives Canada, RG10, volume 7186, file 139/25-1, J. W. Burton to J. G. Wright, 3 January 1952. [FRU-010106-0001]

71. Elias, "Lillian Elias," 54–55.

72. TRC, AVS, Samuel Gargan, (Speaking Notes) Statement to the Truth and Reconciliation Commission of Canada, Fort Providence, Northwest Territories, 27 April 2011, Statement Number: SP015.

73. TRC, NRA, Library and Archives Canada, RG85, volume 1130, file 254-1, part 1, "Memorandum re Vocational Training of the Eskimo," Diamond Jenness, 26 November 1925, 2–3. [NCA-002168-0001]

74. Jenness was still writing of this failure in 1964; see Jenness, *Eskimo Administration*, 48.

75. TRC, NRA, Library and Archives Canada, RG85, volume 1130, file 254-1, part 1, A. L. Fleming to O. S. Finnie, 22 November 1928. [NCA-002197] For alternative spelling, see: Eber, *When the Whalers*, 115.

76. Eber, *When the Whalers*, 114–115.

77. TRC, NRA, Library and Archives Canada, RG85, volume 1130, file 254-1, part 1, A. L. Fleming to O. S. Finnie, 22 November 1928. [NCA-002197]

78. Geller, *Northern Exposures*, 79.

79. TRC, AVS, Willy Erasmus, Statement to the Truth and Reconciliation Commission of Canada, Fort Good Hope, Northwest Territories, 15 July 2010, Statement Number: 01-NWT-JY10-022.

80. TRC, AVS, Rita Arey, Statement to the Truth and Reconciliation Commission of Canada, Aklavik, Northwest Territories, 12 May 2011, Statement Number: SP019.

81. Elias, "Lillian Elias," 49.

82. TRC, AVS, Samuel Gargan, (Speaking Notes) Statement to the Truth and Reconciliation Commission of Canada, 27 April 2011, Fort Providence, Northwest Territories, Statement Number: SP015.

83. TRC, NRA, Anglican Church of Canada – Ottawa, Diocese of Calgary, General Synod Archives, Peace Messenger [Athabasca], 01/1934–05/1967, *Peace Messenger*, July 1936. [AGS-000209]

84. TRC, NRA, Library and Archives Canada, RG10, volume 6472, file 905-1, part 1, Extract from Report of Inspector H. A. Conroy on the Boarding Schools in Treaty 8 and Mackenzie District, 18 December 1911, 3. [HRU-000890]

85. TRC, NRA, Library and Archives Canada, RG85, volume 793, file 6334, part 1, Shingle Point Day and Residential School, 1923–1932, A. L. Fleming to O. S. Finnie, 23 May 1929. [SPU-000097]

86. TRC, NRA, Anglican Church of Canada – Ottawa, General Synod Archives, IERSC Minutes, 01/33–10/34, 1654–1877, Accession GS-75-103, series 2:15[a], box 18, Missionary Society of the Church of England in Canada, Minutes of Meeting of Indian Residential School Commission, MSCC, 10 January 1933, 5. [AGS-000482]

87. TRC, NRA, No document location, no document file source, Fort Providence Chronicles, 1909–1915, 5 February 1910, 127. [GNN-000613]

88. TRC, NRA, English Language Summary of the Fort Resolution Chronicles – Ottawa, volume 1, 1903–1942, 12–13. [GNN-000077-0001]

89. TRC, NRA, English Language Summary of the Fort Resolution Chronicles – Ottawa, volume 1, 1903–1942, 16–17. [GNN-000077-0001]

90. TRC, NRA, Library and Archives Canada, RG10, volume 6474, file 916-1, part 1, Bishop G. Breynat to W. Cory, 17 November 1927. [FRU-010031]

91. Quoted in Krech, "Nutritional Evaluation," 186.

92. Quoted in Krech, "Nutritional Evaluation," 186.

93. Quoted in Krech, "Nutritional Evaluation," 189.

94. TRC, NRA, Anglican Church of Canada, General Synod Archives – Ottawa, ACC-MSCC-GS 75-103, series 2.15, box 27, file 8, A. J. Vale, "Vale's Vale," 12 April 1946. [AAC-087474]

95. Krech, "Nutritional Evaluation," 189.

96. TRC, NRA, Library and Archives Canada, RG10, volume 6475, file 918-1, part 1, Extract from Report of Mr. H. J. Bury on the Boarding Schools of Treaty No. 8, Northern Section, 5 October 1916. [FPU-000089]

97. TRC, NRA, Library and Archives Canada, RG10, volume 6475, file 918-5, part 1, Extract of monthly report of C. Bourget, M.D., Indian Agent Resolution, N.W.T., 12 February 1924, 1. [FPU-000408]

98. TRC, NRA, Anglican Church of Canada, General Synod Archives – Ottawa, Minutes of the Meetings of Indian Residential School Commission MSCC, 01/1930–11/1932, Accession GS 75-103, series 2:15[a], box 18, Minutes of Meeting of Indian Residential School Commission, MSCC, 16 December 1930, 8. [AGS-000136]

99. TRC, NRA, Library and Archives Canada, RG85, volume 793, file 6334, part 1, Shingle Point Day and Residential School, 1923–1932, A. L. Fleming to H. E. Hume, 7 March 1932, 2. [SPU-000167]

100. TRC, NRA, Library and Archives Canada, RG85, Perm. volume 1877, file 630/101-3, part 1, R.C. School Day Resolution, 1905–1944, FA 85-8, Précis for the Northwest Territories Council: Medical examination of children before admission to schools, 25 April 1939. [RCN-001688]

101. Innis, Wherrett, and Moore, "Survey of Education," 56.

102. TRC, NRA, Library and Archives Canada, RG85, Perm. volume 442, file 630/119-3, part 8, R.C. Schools – Aklavik, N.W.T. 1955–1956, FA 85-1, L. A. C. O. Hunt to Director Northern Administration and Lands Branch, 21 April 1955. [ICU-000550]

103. Canada, *Annual Report of the Department of Indian Affairs, 1913*, Ottawa, 1913, 592.

104. TRC, NRA, No document location, no document file source, Fort Providence Chronicles, 1918–1924, 23 September 1919; 24 September 1919; 21–22, October 1919, 61–63. [GNN-000614-0001]

105. TRC, NRA, No document location, no document file source, Fort Providence Chronicles, 1918–1924, 31 August 1920; 23–24 September; 26 September 1920; 28 September 1920. [GNN-000614-0001]

106. TRC, NRA, No document location, no document file source, Fort Providence Chronicles, 1943–1964, 28 April 1943, 6. [GNN-000616]

107. TRC, NRA, No document location, no document file source, Fort Providence Chronicles, 1943–1964, 2 December 1944, 55. [GNN-000616]

108. TRC, NRA, No document location, no document file source, Fort Providence Chronicles, 1943–1964, 5 February 1945, 61. [GNN-000616]

109. TRC, NRA, No document location, no document file source, Fort Providence Chronicles, 1943–1964, 2 April 1950, 158. [GNN-000616]

110. TRC, NRA, No document location, no document file source, Fort Providence Chronicles, 1943–1964, 30 October 1952, 206; 5 May 1957, 301–302. [GNN-000616]

111. TRC, NRA, GNN, No document location, no document file source, Fort Providence Chronicles, 1943–1964, 10 March 1958, 319. [GNN-000616]

112. TRC, NRA, English Language Summary of the Fort Resolution Chronicles – Ottawa, Volume 1, 1903–1942, 13, 24, 28, 29, 41, 66, 77, 82, 83, 87, 94, 95. [GNN-000077-0001]

113. TRC, NRA, English Language Summary of the Fort Resolution Chronicles – Ottawa, volume 1, 1903–1942, 25. [GNN-000077-0001]

114. TRC, NRA, English Language Summary of the Fort Resolution Chronicles – Ottawa, volume 1, 1903–1942. [GNN-000077-0001]

115. TRC, NRA, Library and Archives Canada, RG10, volume 6472, file 905-1, part 1, J. D. McLean to David Laird, 9 June 1904. [HRU-000870]

116. TRC, NRA, Library and Archives Canada, RG10, volume 6472, file 905-1, part 1, George Bowring to D. C. Scott, 1 February 1918. [HRU-000883]

117. TRC, NRA, Library and Archives Canada, RG85, Perm. volume 809, file 6792, Great Slave Lake District M.H.O.'s Report, April 1930, FA 85-2, John Moran to O. Finnie, 13 October 1930. [HRU-000925-0000]

118. TRC, NRA, Anglican Church of Canada, General Synod Archives – Ottawa, Minutes of the Meetings of Indian Residential School Commission MSCC, 02/35–05/38, 1902–2256, Accession GS 75-103, series 2:15[a], box 19, Minutes of Meeting of Indian Residential School Commission, MSCC, 18 June 1935, 6. [AGS-000533]

119. TRC, NRA, Anglican Church of Canada – Ottawa, Diocese of Calgary, General Synod Archives, Peace Messenger [Athabasca], 01/1934-05/1967, *Peace Messenger*, 1936. [AGS-000209]

120. Johns, "A History of St Peter's Mission," 23.

121. TRC, NRA, Library and Archives Canada, RG10, volume 6472, file 905-1, part 1, Hay River Indian Boarding School, I. O. Stringer, 4 June 1910. [HRU-000878-0001]

122. Library and Archives Canada, RG85, Perm. volume 809, file 6792, Great Slave Lake District M.H.O.'s Report, April 1930, FA 85-2, John Moran to O. Finnie, 13 October 1930. [HRU-000925-0000]

123. Johns, "History of St Peter's Mission," 28.

124. TRC, NRA, Anglican Church of Canada – Ottawa, General Synod Archives, file 24-2, Mabel Jones, 1932–1938 [Shingle Point, Aklavik], 10/33–01/36, Accession M96-7, series 2:1, Diocese of the Arctic, 29 January 1936. [AGS-000547]

125. TRC, NRA, Library and Archives Canada, RG85, volume 906, file 10498, Death of J. Sakaluk – Roman Catholic Mission Pupil, Aklavik, 1939, Royal Canadian Mounted Police Report, D. C. Martin, 8 August 1938. [ICU-000516]

126. TRC, NRA, Anglican Church of Canada – Ottawa, General Synod Archives, file 24-2, Mabel Jones, 1932–1938 [Shingle Point, Aklavik], 10/33–01/36, Accession M96-7, series 2:1, Diocese of the Arctic, Mabel Jones to A. L. Fleming, 3 October 1933, 3. [AGS-000491]

127. TRC, NRA, Library and Archives Canada, RG10, volume 6472, file 905-1, part 1, Extract from Report of Inspector H. A. Conroy on the Boarding Schools in Treaty 8 and Mackenzie District, 18 December 1911. [HRU-000890]

128. TRC, NRA, Library and Archives Canada, RG85, Perm. volume 1879, file 630/109-2, part 3a, Hay River Anglican Residential School, 1935–1937, FA 85-8, Extract from Mr. Meikle's Report on Inspection Trip to Mackenzie River District – June 21 1937, Church of England Mission, Hay River. [HRU-000744]

129. TRC, NRA, Library and Archives Canada, RG10, volume 6472, file 905-5, part 1, T. B. R. Westgate to Secretary, Indian Affairs, 24 June 1924. [HRU-000907]

130. TRC, NRA, Library and Archives Canada, RG10, volume 6472, file 905-1, part 1, Superintendent of Indian Education to D. C. Scott, 29 May 1924. [HRU-000886]

131. TRC NRA, Library and Archives Canada, RG85, Perm. volume 1883, file 630/219-2, part 3, Shingle Point Anglican School 1935–1936, FA 85-8, J. A. Urquhart to Mr. Turner, 17 October 1934. [SPU-000243]

132. TRC, NRA, Library and Archives Canada, RG10, volume 6474, file 915-5, part 1, 1928–1938, Reel C-8790, A. F. MacKenzie to Sister A. McQuillan, 3 March 1931. [ICU-000008]

133. TRC, NRA, Library and Archives Canada, RG85, Perm. volume 1882, file 630/119-3, part 1, Aklavik, N.W.T., R.C. Residential School, April 1927–January 1940, FA 85-8, Chairman, Dominion Lands Branch to H. H. Mowatt, 4 February 1933. [ICU-001211-0000]

134. TRC, NRA, Library and Archives Canada, RG85, Perm. volume 1882, file 630/119-3, part 1, Aklavik, N.W.T., R.C. Residential School, April 1927–January 1940, FA 85-8, H. H. Hume to J. C. Lefebvre, 9 February 1933. [ICU-001214]

135. TRC, NRA, Library and Archives Canada, RG85, Perm. volume 1243, file 333-3/101, part 1, Sanitation – Fort Resolution, N.W.T., 1932–1960, FA 85-3, A. H. Perry, Report of a Survey of the Sanitary Condition at Fort Resolution, Northwest Territories, 2 November 1938, 6–7. [FRU-002309]

136. TRC, NRA Library and Archives Canada, RG10, volume 6475, file 916-5, part 2, Microfilm reel C-8790, J. H. Riopel to Secretary, Indian Affairs Branch, 8 August 1945. [FRU-010092]

137. TRC, NRA, Library and Archives Canada, RG10, volume 6475, file 916-5, part 3, Extract from Annual Report on Fort Resolution Northwest Territories Agency dated 1947–1948. [FRU-010097]

138. TRC, NRA, Library and Archives Canada, RG85, volume 643, file 630/101-1, part 3, J. V. Jacobson, 3 November 1953. [FPU-001529]

139. TRC, NRA, Library and Archives Canada, RG85, Perm. volume 395, file 630/101-3, part 5, R.C. Schools – Fort Resolution, N.W.T., April 1954–December 1954, FA 85-1, L. A. C. O. Hunt to the Director, 16 September 1954. [FRU-001934-0001]

140. Canada, *Annual Report of the Department of Indian Affairs, 1908*, 399.

141. TRC, NRA, Anglican Church of Canada – Ottawa, General Synod Archives, Minutes of the Meetings of Indian Residential School Commission MSCC, 01/1930–11/1932, Accession GS 75-103, series 2:15[a], box 18, Minutes of Meeting of Indian Residential School Commission, MSCC, Held on Tuesday, April 7, 1931, 5; [AGS-000145] Minutes of the Meetings of Indian Residential School Commission MSCC, 02/35–05/38, 1902–2256, Accession GS 75-103, series

2:15[a], box 19, Minutes of Meeting of Indian Residential School Commission, MSCC, Held on Tuesday, May 14, 1935, 7. [AGS-000529]

142. TRC, NRA, No document location, no document file source, Fort Providence Chronicles, 1943–1964, 31 August 1943, 14. [GNN-000616]

143. TRC, NRA, Library and Archives Canada, RG10, volume 6475, file 916-5, part 1, G. Breynat to H. H. McGill, 31 January 1936. [FRU-010052]

144. TRC, NRA, Library and Archives Canada, RG10, volume 6475, file 916-5, part 1, Extract from Radiotelegram from Dr. Bourget, Resolution, N.W.T., 27 December 1935. [FRU-010048]

145. TRC, NRA, English Language Summary of the Fort Resolution Chronicles, volume 1, 1903–1942, 38, 43, 44, 56, 66. [GNN-000077-0001]

146. TRC, NRA, Library and Archives Canada, file 919-1, part 1, Fort Norman Agency – Aklavik Church of England Residential School – General Administration, 1922–1947, FA 10-17, Perm. volume 6476, Microfilm reel C-8792, S. T. Wood to Commissioner, Royal Canadian Mounted Police, 29 November 1922. [AKU-000012]

147. Jenness, *Eskimo Administration*, 48.

148. TRC, NRA, Library and Archives Canada, RG10, volume 6032, file 150-40a, part 1, Headquarters – Compulsory Attendance of Pupils – Indian Schools, 1904–1933, Microfilm reel C-8149, FA 10-17, J. D. McLean to T. W. Harris, 26 May 1921. [AEMR-255301]

149. TRC, NRA, English Language Summary of the Fort Resolution Chronicles, volume 1, 1903–1942, 3. [GNN-000077-0001]

150. TRC, AVS, Willy Erasmus, Statement to the Truth and Reconciliation Commission of Canada, Fort Good Hope, Northwest Territories, 15 July 2010, Statement Number: 01-NWT-JY10-022.

151. TRC, NRA, Library and Archives Canada, RG85, volume 1505, file 600-1-1, part 1, N.W.T. – General Policy file – Education and Schools, 1905–1944, Extract from Act. Sgt. G. T. Makinson's Report – Resolution, N.W.T., 3 July 1937. [FRU-010059]

152. TRC, NRA, Library and Archives Canada, RG10, volume 6475, file 918-1, part 1, [illegible], Office of the General Superintendent, Oblate Catholic Indian Missions to Philip Phelan, 21 October 1941. [FPU-000133]

153. TRC, NRA Library and Archives Canada, RG85, Perm. volume 1877, file 630/101-3, part 1, R.C. School Day Resolution, 1905–1944, FA 85-8, J. Doyle to Mr. Cumming, 16 February 1942. [RCN-001713]

154. TRC, NRA, Library and Archives Canada, RG85, Perm. volume 1877, file 630/101-3, part 1, R.C. School Day Resolution, 1905–1944, FA 85-8, D. J. Martin to Commissioner, RCMP, 15 January 1942. [RCN-001709-0001]

155. TRC, NRA, Library and Archives Canada, RG85, volume 225, file 630/118-1, part 1, Government School – Fort McPherson –N.W.T., 1900–1950, A. S. Dewdney to Gibson, 19 February 1945. [FHU-000267-0001]

156. TRC, NRA, Library and Archives Canada, RG10, volume 6476, file 918-10, part 4, Philip Phelan to Reverend J. Trocellier, 2 November 1951. [FPU-000654]

157. TRC, NRA, Library and Archives Canada, RG85, volume 643, file 630/101-1, part 3, Government School – Fort Resolution, N.W.T., 1953–1960, L. G. P. Waller to P. Phelan, 29 August 1953. [FRU-001447]

158. TRC, NRA, Library and Archives Canada, RG85, volume 707, file 630/100-3, part 6, C. L. Merrill to Reverend J. Trocellier, 20 September 1957. [FPU-001545]

159. TRC, NRA, No document location, no document file source, Fort Providence Chronicles, 20 March 1902; 27 April 1902, 56–57. [GNN-000612]

160. TRC, NRA, English Language Summary of the Fort Resolution Chronicles, volume 1, 1903–1942, 1. [GNN-000077-0001]

161. TRC, NRA, English Language Summary of the Fort Resolution Chronicles, volume 1, 1903–1942, 34. [GNN-000077-0001]

162. TRC, NRA, Library and Archives Canada, RG10, volume 6475, file 918-1, part 1, Royal Canadian Mounted Police Report, Search for Missing Children, R.C. Residential School, Providence, N.W.T., 24 August 1942. [FPU-000140]

Student Life at the Mission Schools

1. French, *Restless Nomad*, 1.
2. French, *My Name*, 17–20.
3. French, *My Name*, 22.
4. French, *My Name*, 24.
5. French, *My Name*, 29.
6. French, *My Name*, 37–38.
7. French, *My Name*, 42.
8. French, *My Name*, 24–25, 43, 52, 79–80.
9. French, *My Name*, 49.
10. French, *My Name*, 82–83.
11. French, *My Name*, 44.
12. French, *My Name*, 21.
13. French, *Restless Nomad*, 1.
14. French, *Restless Nomad*, 5.
15. French, *Restless Nomad*, 14.
16. French, *Restless Nomad*, 3.
17. French, *Restless Nomad*, 4.
18. French, *Restless Nomad*, 178.
19. French, *Restless Nomad*, 19.
20. French, *Restless Nomad*, 93.
21. French, *Restless Nomad*, 76–77.
22. French, *Restless Nomad*, 162.
23. Thrasher, *Thrasher*, 3.
24. Thrasher, *Thrasher*, 11.
25. Thrasher, *Thrasher*, 3–4.
26. Thrasher, *Thrasher*, 13–14.
27. Thrasher, *Thrasher*, 14.
28. Thrasher, *Thrasher*, 28.
29. Thrasher, *Thrasher*, 15.
30. Thrasher, *Thrasher*, 14.
31. Thrasher, *Thrasher*, 45.
32. Thrasher, *Thrasher*, 38.
33. Thrasher, *Thrasher*, 27.
34. Thrasher, *Thrasher*, 28.
35. Thrasher, *Thrasher*, 39.

36. Thrasher, *Thrasher*, 26.
37. Thrasher, *Thrasher*, 30.
38. Blondin-Perrin, *My Heart*, 1.
39. Blondin-Perrin, *My Heart*, 4.
40. Blondin-Perrin, *My Heart*, 5.
41. Blondin-Perrin, *My Heart*, 6.
42. Blondin-Perrin, *My Heart*, 11.
43. Blondin-Perrin, *My Heart*, 12.
44. Blondin-Perrin, *My Heart*, 13.
45. Blondin-Perrin, *My Heart*, 21.
46. Blondin-Perrin, *My Heart*, 29.
47. Blondin-Perrin, *My Heart*, 27.
48. Blondin-Perrin, *My Heart*, 41–42.
49. Blondin-Perrin, *My Heart*, 31.
50. Blondin-Perrin, *My Heart*, 32.
51. Blondin-Perrin, *My Heart*, 89.
52. Blondin-Perrin, *My Heart*, 39.
53. Canadien, *From Lishamie*, 47.
54. Canadien, *From Lishamie*, 50–52.
55. Canadien, *From Lishamie*, 52.
56. Canadien, *From Lishamie*, 56.
57. Canadien, *From Lishamie*, 106.
58. Canadien, *From Lishamie*, 57.
59. Canadien, *From Lishamie*, 57.
60. Canadien, *From Lishamie*, 57.
61. Canadien, *From Lishamie*, 57.
62. Canadien, *From Lishamie*, 65.
63. Canadien, *From Lishamie*, 94.
64. Canadien, *From Lishamie*, 69.
65. Canadien, *From Lishamie*, 179.
66. Canadien, *From Lishamie*, 186.
67. Canadien, *From Lishamie*, 90.
68. Canadien, *From Lishamie*, 84.
69. Canadien, *From Lishamie*, 98.
70. Canadien, *From Lishamie*, 59, 195.
71. Canadien, *From Lishamie*, 176, 178, 213.
72. Canadien, *From Lishamie*, 214.
73. Canadien, *From Lishamie*, 205–206.
74. TRC, AVS, Angus Lennie, (Speaking Notes) Statement to the Truth and Reconciliation Commission of Canada, Tulita, Northwest Territories, 10 May 2011, Statement Number: SP018.

Education for what purpose?

1. Canada, *Annual Report of the Department of Indian Affairs, 1909*, 198.
2. F. H. Kitto, Report of a Preliminary Investigation of the Natural Resources of Mackenzie District and their Economic Development, made during the summer of 1920, Ottawa, Department of the Interior, Natural Resources Intelligence Branch, Section VII, quoted in Fumoleau, *As Long as This Land*, 143.
3. TRC, NRA, Library and Archives Canada, RG10, volume 3952, file 134, 858, J. Macrae to C. Sifton, 7 December 1900, 2. [FRU-002098]
4. Canada, *Annual Report of the Department of Indian Affairs, 1907*, 389.
5. McCarthy, *From the Great River*, 163.
6. H. B. Bury, 7 November 1917, "Report on Indian Affairs – Education," RG10 IABS – 4042 – 336877, 4–7, manuscript, quoted in Carney, "Relations in Education," 91.
7. F. H. Kitto, "Report on the Mackenzie District," 22 December 1920, RG15, a–2, VII, quoted in Carney, "Relations in Education," 92.
8. TRC, NRA, Library and Archives Canada, RG85, volume 1130, file 254-1, part 1, J. I. Doyle to J. Lorne Turner, 13 July 1934. [NCA-005284]
9. TRC, NRA, Library and Archives Canada, RG85, volume 1128, file 250-1-1, part 2b, O. S. Finnie to W.W. Cory, 16 January 1928. [NPC-400544-0000]
10. TRC, NRA, Library and Archives Canada, RG85, Perm. volume 1883, file 630/219-2, part 3, Shingle Point Anglican School 1935, FA 85-8, J. A. Urquhart to Mr. Turner, 17 October 1934. [SPU-000243]
11. TRC, NRA, Library and Archives Canada, RG85, volume 1130, file 254-1, part 1, Extracts from the Minutes of the Fifty-third Session of the Northwest Territories Council held on 17 October 1934. [NCA-005286]
12. TRC, NRA, Library and Archives Canada, RG85, volume 847, file 7770, Education of Lapp Children and Education Policy in General, 1933–1934, Extracts from the Minutes of the Fifty-fourth Session of the Northwest Territories Council, 26 November 1934. [RCN-000103]
13. TRC, NRA, Library and Archives Canada, RG85, volume 1130, file 254-1, part 1, F. E. Porsild to J. Lorne Turner, 22 May 1934. [NCA-005281]
14. TRC, NRA, Library and Archives Canada, RG85, volume 1130, file 254-1, part 1, Diamond Jenness to Council of the Northwest Territories, 11 May 1934. [NCA-006999] Twenty years later the federal government did seek to use the Inuit to strengthen Canada's claims to northern sovereignty. In the 1950s, the federal government relocated Inuit from the eastern side of Hudson Bay to Resolute Bay and Grise Fiord in the High Arctic. The Royal Commission on Aboriginal Peoples concluded in 1994 that the relocation was involuntary, poorly planned and executed, and "inhumane in its design and in its effects." In a special report on the relocation, the Royal Commission noted that "the influence of sovereignty on the relocation serves only to reinforce the Commission's conclusions about the inappropriateness" of the relocation. Following the Commission's report the federal government set up a $10-million compensation fund and in 2010 formally apologized for the relocation. Tester and Kulchyski, *Tammarniit (Mistakes)*, 133, 160; Canada, Aboriginal and Northern Affairs Canada, "Backgrounder – Apology," http://www.aadnc-aandc.gc.ca/eng/1100100015426/1100100015427.
15. "Old Crow," *The Living Message*, May 1938, 136, quoted in Rutherdale, *Women and the White Man's God*, 48.

16. TRC, NRA, Library and Archives Canada, RG85, Perm. volume 1877, file 630/101-3, part 1, R.C. School Day Resolution, 1905–1944, FA 85-8, Memorandum for Northwest Territories Council – Education – N.W.T., 10 January 1939. [RCN-001679]

17. Geller, *Northern Exposures*, 135–164.

18. Finnie, *Canada Moves North*, 74.

19. Finnie, *Canada Moves North*, 75.

20. Finnie, *Canada Moves North*, 77.

21. Finnie, *Canada Moves North*, 78.

22. TRC, NRA, Library and Archives Canada, RG85, Perm. volume 1877, file 630/101-3, part 1, R.C. School Day Resolution, 1905–1944, FA 85-8, Mary Mack to R. A. Hoey, 15 July 1942. [FRU-000878-0003]

23. TRC, NRA, Library and Archives Canada, RG85, Perm. volume 1877, file 630/101-3, part 1, R.C. School Day Resolution 1905–1944, FA 85-8, S. Lapointe to R. A. Hoey, 20 July 1942. [FRU-000878-0001]

24. TRC, NRA, Library and Archives Canada, RG85, Perm. volume 1877, file 630/101-3, part 1, R.C. School Day Resolution, 1905–1944, FA 85-8, E. Kristoff to R. A. Hoey, 17 September 1942. [RCN-001719-0006]

25. TRC, NRA, Library and Archives Canada, RG85, Perm. volume 1877, file 630/101-3, part 1, R.C. School Day Resolution, 1905–1944, FA 85-8, H. W. Shepherd to R. A. Hoey, 17 September 1942. [RCN-001719-0007]

26. Innis, Wherrett, and Moore, "Survey of Education," 61.

27. Innis, Wherrett, and Moore, "Survey of Education," 61.

28. Innis, Wherrett, and Moore, "Survey of Education," 62.

29. Innis, Wherrett, and Moore, "Survey of Education," 67.

30. Innis, Wherrett, and Moore, "Survey of Education," 82.

31. Innis, Wherrett, and Moore, "Survey of Education," 71–75.

32. Morrison, *True North*, 151.

33. Diubaldo, *Government of Canada*, 90.

34. TRC, NRA, Library and Archives Canada, RG85, Perm. volume 1877, file 630/101-3, part 1, R.C. School Day Resolution, 1905–1944, FA 85-8, R. A. Gibson to Major McKeand, 11 May 1944. [RCN-001769]

35. TRC, NRA, Library and Archives Canada, RG85, Perm. volume 1877, file 630/101-3, part 1, R.C. School Day Resolution, 1905–1944, FA 85-8, W. F. Lothian to Major McKeand, 1 June 1944. [RCN-001770]

36. TRC, NRA, Library and Archives Canada, RG85, Perm. volume 1877, file 630/101-3, part 1, R.C. School Day Resolution, 1905–1944, FA 85-8, P. D. Baird to Major McKeand, 26 June 1944. [RCN-001771]

37. TRC, NRA, Library and Archives Canada, RG22, volume 165, file 5-2-1-1, part 1, Education in Canada's Northland, 12 December 1954, 2. [NCA-014503]

38. Grant, *Sovereignty or Security?*, 199.

39. TRC, NRA, Library and Archives Canada, RG22, volume 165, file 5-2-1-1, part 1, Education in Canada's Northland, 12 December 1954. [NCA-014503]

40. Innis, Wherrett, and Moore, "Survey of Education," 78.

41. Innis, Wherrett, and Moore, "Survey of Education," 63–64.

42. Innis, Wherrett, and Moore, "Survey of Education," 82.

43. TRC, NRA, Library and Archives Canada, RG85, volume 1506, file 600-1-1, part 2a, J. G. Wright to Mr. Gibson, 19 November 1946. [NCA-005728]

44. TRC, NRA, Library and Archives Canada, RG85, volume 229, file 630/158-9, part 1, Government Hostel – Chesterfield Inlet, 1929–1953, Extracts from S. J. Bailey's Report, Eastern Arctic Patrol, 27 July 1948. [CIU-000189]

45. TRC, NRA, Library and Archives Canada, RG85, volume 1072, file 254-1, part 2a, S. J. Bailey, Western Arctic Inspection Flight: Report on Education, 9 April 1950. [NCA-005694]

46. TRC, NRA, Library and Archives Canada, RG85, volume 1130, file 254-1, part 1, Henry Cook to F. S. G. Cunningham, 9 August 1952. [NCA-005288-0001]

47. TRC, NRA, Library and Archives Canada, RG22, volume 254, file 40-8-1, part 3, Report of the First Meeting of the Sub-Committee on Eskimo Education Held in Room 302, Vimy Building, 26 September 1952. [NCA-006031-0000]

48. TRC, NRA, Library and Archives Canada, RG85, Perm. volume 1072, file 254-1, part 2, Eskimo Education [incl. Sub-Committee on Eskimo Education] 1952–1953, FA 85-3, E. M. Hinds, January 9, 1953. [RCN-011606]

49. TRC, NRA, Library and Archives Canada, RG22, volume 254, file 40-8-1, part 3, Report of the Second Meeting of the Sub-Committee on Eskimo Education Held in the Library of the Vimy Building, on Friday, 1 April 1953. [NPC-400761-0001]

50. TRC, NRA, Library and Archives Canada, RG85, volume 229, file 630/158-9, part 1, Government Hostel – Chesterfield Inlet, 1929–1953, J. G. Wright to Director, 29 December 1952. [CIU-000553]

51. TRC, NRA, Library and Archives Canada, RG22, volume 165, file 5-2-1-1, part 1, Education in Canada's Northland, 12 December 1954, 5. [NCA-014503]

The mission era in the Yukon

1. Coates, *Canada's Colonies*, 85, 92.

2. Coates, *Canada's Colonies*, 130–131.

3. TRC, NRA, Library and Archives Canada, RG22, volume 165, file 5-2-1-1, part 1, Education in Canada's Northland, 12 December 1954, 1. [NCA-014503]

4. Tizya, "Comment," 103.

5. Coates, "A Very Imperfect Means," 132–149.

6. Coates, "'Betwixt and Between,'" 152.

7. For the appeal, see: Coates, "'Betwixt and Between,'" 152. For the new school, see: TRC, NRA, Library and Archives Canada, RG10, volume 6479, file 940-1, part 1, "The Chooutla Indian School," *Northern Lights*, volume 15, number 1, February 1927. [CAR-011225]

8. Coates, "'Betwixt and Between,'" 152.

9. Yukon Territorial Archives, Anglican Church, New Series, file 2, Notes of Interview, February 26, 1909, quoted in Coates, *Best Left as Indians*, 138.

10. TRC, NRA, Library and Archives Canada, RG10, volume 6479, file 940-1, part 1, J. D. McLean to A. Henderson, 13 April 1908. [CAR-011062]

11. TRC, NRA, Library and Archives Canada, RG10, volume 3962, file 147, 654-1 2, A. W. Vowell and A. E. Green to Secretary, Indian Department, 14 August 1908. [CAR-017386]

12. TRC, NRA, Anglican Diocese of Yukon Fonds, Yukon Archives – Ottawa, COR 260, F. 3, Lists of Pupils and Staff at Chooutla [Carcross] IRS, 1909–1926, Acc. 88/128, Anglican Church,

Diocese of the Yukon Records, Assistant Secretary Indian Affairs to W. E. Meara, 13 October 1908. [DYK-015668]

13. TRC, NRA, Library and Archives Canada, RG10, volume 6479, file 940-1, part 1, I. Stringer to Secretary, Indian Affairs, 22 March 1911; Secretary, Indian Affairs to I. O. Stringer, 22 March 1911. [CAR-011075]

14. Cruikshank, *Life Lived*, 71.

15. TRC, NRA, Library and Archives Canada, RG10, volume 6479, file 940-1, part 1, E. E. Stockton to Deputy Superintendent General, Indian Affairs, 29 November 1912. [CAR-011098]

16. Cruikshank, *Life Lived,* 70.

17. TRC, NRA, Library and Archives Canada, RG29, Perm. volume 2779, file 822-1-X900, part 1a, Medical and Dental Arrangements, Yukon Region, Whitehorse, Y.T., September 1905–August 1963, FA 29-143, I. O. Stringer to Honourable Commissioner of the Yukon Territory, 12 April 1912. [CAR-017301]

18. TRC, NRA, Anglican Church of Canada – Ottawa, General Synod Archives, "School News," *Northern Lights*, volume 2, number 1, September 1913, 2. [DYK-201302]

19. TRC, NRA, Anglican Church of Canada – Ottawa, General Synod Archives, Northern Lights, Anglican Church of Canada, "School News," *Northern Lights*, volume 4, number 1, February 1916, 5–6. [DYK-201312]

20. TRC, NRA, Anglican Church of Canada – Ottawa, General Synod Archives, ACC–MSCC–GS 75-103, series 2.15, box 21, file 1, Report of the Indian and Eskimo Commission to the Executive Committee of the MSCC for the Year Ending 30 June 1917, 3. [AAC-083304]

21. TRC, NRA, Library and Archives Canada, RG10, volume 6479, file 940-1, part 1, J. Hawksley, Report on the Carcross Indian Residential School, 9 July 1929. [CAR-011233-0001]

22. Tiyza, "Comment," 103–104.

23. Coates, "'Betwixt and Between,'" 162.

24. TRC, NRA, Library and Archives Canada, RG10, volume 6481, file 940-10, part 5, J. Hawksley to A. F. MacKenzie, 27 February 1931. [CAR-011293]

25. TRC, NRA, Library and Archives Canada, Yukon Territorial Records, RG91, volume 11, file 2335, part 6, J. Hawksley to A. F. MacKenzie, 30 August 1932. [CAR-015262]

26. TRC, NRA, Library and Archives Canada, RG10, volume 6479, file 940-1, part 2, G. Binning to Secretary, Department of Indian Affairs, 2 July 1936. [CAR-010617]

27. Quoted in King, *School at Mopass,* 37.

28. TRC, NRA, Anglican Church of Canada – Ottawa, General Synod Archives, "School News," *Northern Lights*, volume 2, number 1, September 1913. [DYK-201302]

29. TRC, NRA, Library and Archives Canada, RG10, volume 6479, file 940-1, part 1, J. Hawksley "Report on the Carcross Indian Residential School," 9 July 1929. [CAR-011233-0001]

30. TRC, NRA, Library and Archives Canada, RG10, volume 6479, file 940-1, part 1, J. Hawksley to A. F. Mackenzie, 25 March 1931. [CAR-011264]

31. TRC, NRA, Library and Archives Canada, RG10, volume 6479, file 940-5, part 5, T. B. R Westgate to Secretary, Indian Affairs, 5 October 1935. [CAR-012469]

32. TRC, NRA, Library and Archives Canada, RG10, volume 6479, file 940-1, part 2, H. C. M. Grant to Superintendent of Indian Affairs, 5 February 1940. [CAR-011309]

33. TRC, NRA, Library and Archives Canada, RG10, volume 3920, file 116818, H. Reed to Assistant Commissioner, 28 June 1895. [EDM-003376]

34. TRC, NRA, Library and Archives Canada, RG10, volume 6480, file 940-5, part 7, H. C. M. Grant to Superintendent of Indian Affairs, 1 February 1949. [CAR-013291]

35. TRC, NRA, Library and Archives Canada, RG10, volume 6479, file 940-1, part 2, T. B .R. Westgate to Secretary, Indian Affairs Branch, 16 October 1942. [CAR-011306]

36. TRC, NRA, Library and Archives Canada, RG10, volume 6479, file 940-1, part 2, F. B. Roth to J. E. Gibben, 30 September 1942. [CAR-011315-0000]

37. TRC, NRA, Library and Archives Canada, RG10, volume 6479, file 940-1, part 2, T. B. R. Westgate to Secretary, Indian Affairs Branch, 16 October 1942. [CAR-011306]

38. TRC, NRA, Library and Archives Canada, RG10, volume 6480, file 940-5, part 9, H. A. Alderwood to R. A. Hoey, 17 May 1944. [CAR-012026]

39. TRC, NRA, Library and Archives Canada, RG85, Perm volume 1336, file 560-3-1, part 1, Care of Children – Yukon [General] 1954, FA 85-4, Laval Fortier to R. G. Robertson, 28 January 1954. [CAR-201404]

40. TRC, NRA, Library and Archives Canada, RG10, volume 6479, file 940-1, part 2, D. J. Martin to Commissioner, Royal Canadian Mounted Police, 31 March 1943. [CAR-011311]

41. TRC, NRA, Anglican Church of Canada – Ottawa, General Synod Archives, ACC MSCC GS 75-103, series 2.15, box 21, file 1, H. A. Alderwood, Indian School Administration, Missionary Society of the Church of England in Canada, Quarterly Report to the Executive Committee, 14 November 1946, 4. [AAC-083308]

42. TRC, NRA, Library and Archives Canada, RG10, volume 6481, file 940-23, part 2, R. J. Meek to Unknown, 8 May 1953. [CAR-011298]

43. TRC, NRA, Library and Archives Canada, RG10, file 951/6-1, part 4, volume 8691, R. J. Meek, Re: New Building, Carcross Indian Residential School, 1 February 1954. [CAR-015461]

44. TRC, NRA, Library and Archives Canada, Burnaby file 801/25-2-940, volume 1, 12/1953-12/1956, Admission and Discharge – Carcross IRS, RG10-151, V1989-90/101, box 38, C. T. Stanger to M. G. Jutras, 7 February 1956. [YKS-003442-0001]

45. TRC, NRA, Library and Archives Canada, Burnaby file 801/25-2-929, volume 2, Admission and Discharge – Whitehorse IDS, RG10-151, V1989-90/101, box 38, M. G. Jutras to W. S. Arneil, 8 March 1956. [YKS-003482]

46. King, *School at Mopass*, 37.

47. TRC, NRA, Library and Archives Canada, Yukon Territorial Records, RG91, volume 11, file 2335, part 6, J. Hawksley to A. F. Mackenzie, 20 July 1932. [CAR-015340]

48. TRC, NRA, Library and Archives Canada, RG10, volume 6481, file 940-10, part 5, R. J. Meek to Indian Affairs, 29 August 1947. [CAR-011279]

49. TRC, NRA, Library and Archives Canada, file 801/25-1-940, volume 1, Education – Carcross IRS, 07/1957-02/1962, RG10-151, V1989-90/101, box 36, M. G. Jutras to E. Nielson, 21 January 1959. [YKS-003318]

50. Coates, *Best Left as Indians*, 192.

51. TRC, NRA, Anglican Church of Canada, General Synod Archives, Northern Lights, Anglican Church of Canada, *Northern Lights*, volume 1, January 1913. [DYK-201301]

52. King, *School at Mopass*, 15, 18.

53. King, *School at Mopass*, 15.

54. Yukon Territorial Archives, Anglican Church, Moosehide File, Sarah Jane Essau to Bishop, 31 August 1919, quoted in Coates, *Best Left as Indians*, 154.

55. Yukon Territorial Archives, Anglican Church Carmacks–Little Salmon File, "Report of Missionary Work Carried on from May 23 to August 31 1934 in and about Carmacks," quoted in Coates, *Best Left as Indians*, 154.

56. TRC, NRA, Library and Archives Canada, file 630/211-1, part 1, Indian School – Carcross, Y.T., FA 85-4, Perm. volume 1444, I. O. Stringer to Secretary, Indian Affairs, 26 July 1918. [CAR-014704]

57. TRC, NRA, Library and Archives Canada, RG10, volume 6479, file 940-1, part 1, D. C. Scott to I. O. Stringer, 7 September 1918. [CAR-011143]

58. TRC, NRA, Library and Archives Canada, Yukon Territorial Records, RG91, volume 11, file 2335, part 6, J. Hawksley to Principal, Chooutla Indian School, 27 May 1933. [CAR-015290]

59. TRC NRA, Library and Archives Canada, Yukon Territorial Records, RG91, volume 11, file 2335, part 6, J. Hawksley to Principal, Chooutla Indian School, 10 August 1933. [CAR-015296]

60. TRC, NRA, Library and Archives Canada, RG10, volume 6481, file 940-24, part 1, Re: Carcross Indian Residential School (Anglican) Yukon, 28 November 1935. [CAR-011635-0002]

61. TRC, NRA, Library and Archives Canada, file 921-1, part 1, Yukon Agency – Whitehorse Day School – General Admin., 1911–1949, FA 10-17, volume 6477, Microfilm reel C-8793, R. J. Meek to Unknown, 14 October 1946. [BAP-000307-0001]

62. TRC, NRA, Library and Archives Canada, file 921-1, part 1, Yukon Agency – Whitehorse Day School – General Admin., 1911–1949, FA 10-17, volume 6477, Microfilm reel C-8793, R. J. Meek to R. A. Hoey, 5 September 1946. [BAP-000306]

63. TRC, NRA, Library and Archives Canada file 921-1, part 1, Yukon Agency – Whitehorse Day School – General Admin., 1911–1949, FA 10-17, volume 6477, Microfilm reel C-8793, R. J. Meek to R. A. Hoey, 5 September 1946. [BAP-000306]

64. TRC, NRA, Library and Archives Canada–Ottawa, file 921-1, part 1, Yukon Agency – Whitehorse Day School – General Admin., 1911–1949, FA 10-17, volume 6477, Microfilm reel C-8793, R. J. Meek to Unknown, 14 October 1946; [BAP-000307-0001] M. Hackett to P. E. Moore, 24 January 1947. [BAP-000315]

65. TRC, NRA, Library and Archives Canada, file 921-1, part 1, Yukon Agency – Whitehorse Day School – General Admin., 1911–1949, FA 10-17, volume 6477, Microfilm reel C-8793, B. F. Neary to R. J. Meek, 19 October 1946; [BAP-000308] B. F. Neary to W. A. Geddes, 25 January 1947. [BAP-000313]

66. TRC, NRA, Library and Archives Canada file 921-1, part 1, Yukon Agency – Whitehorse Day School – General Admin., 1911–1949, FA 10-17, volume 6477, Microfilm reel C-8793, W. A. Geddes to B. F. Neary, 5 February 1947. [BAP-000316]

67. TRC, NRA, Library and Archives Canada, file 921-1, part 1, Yukon Agency – Whitehorse Day School – General Admin., 1911–1949, FA 10-17, volume 6477, Microfilm reel C-8793, B. F. Neary to R. J. Meek, 11 February 1947; [BAP-000317] B. F. Neary to R. J. Meek, 4 March 1947. [BAP-000319]

68. TRC, NRA, Library and Archives Canada, file, 921-1, part 1, Yukon Agency – Whitehorse Day School – General Admin., 1911–1949, FA 10-17, volume 6477, Microfilm reel C-8793, R. J. Meek to Unknown, 14 October 1946. [BAP-000307-0001]

69. TRC, NRA, Library and Archives Canada, file 921-1, part 1, Yukon Agency – Whitehorse Day School – General Admin., 1911–1949, FA 10-17, volume 6477, Microfilm reel C-8793, C. A. F. Clark to B. F. Neary, 16 May 1947. [BAP-000321]

70. TRC, NRA, Library and Archives Canada, file 921-1, part 1, Yukon Agency – Whitehorse Day School – General Admin., 1911–1949, FA 10-17, volume 6477, Microfilm reel C-8793, H. I. Lee to R .J. Meek, 18 August 1947. [BAP-000336]

71. TRC, NRA, Library and Archives Canada, file 921-1, part 1, Yukon Agency–Whitehorse Day School–General Admin., 1911–1949, FA 10-17, volume 6477, Microfilm reel C-8793, R. J. Meek to Indian Affairs, 18 August 1947. [BAP-000338]

72. TRC, NRA, Library and Archives Canada, file 921-1, part 1, Yukon Agency – Whitehorse Day School – General Admin., 1911–1949, FA 10-17, volume 6477, Microfilm reel C-8793, B. F. Neary to R. J. Meek, 23 October 1947. [BAP-000350]

73. TRC, NRA, Library and Archives Canada, file 921-1, part 1, Yukon Agency – Whitehorse Day School – General Admin., 1911–1949, FA 10-17, volume 6477, Microfilm reel C-8793, R. J. Meek to Indian Affairs, 8 October 1947. [BAP-000347]

74. TRC, NRA, Library and Archives Canada, file 921-1, part 1, Yukon Agency – Whitehorse Day School – General Admin., 1911–1949, FA 10-17, volume 6477, Microfilm reel C-8793, R. J. Meek to Indian Affairs Branch, 25 October 1947. [BAP-000352]

75. TRC, NRA, Library and Archives Canada, file 921-1, part 1, Yukon Agency – Whitehorse Day School – General Admin., 1911–1949, FA 10-17, volume 6477, Microfilm reel C-8793, R. J. Meek to Indian Affairs, 11 August 1948. [BAP-000380]

76. TRC, NRA, Library and Archives Canada, file 921-1, part 1, Yukon Agency – Whitehorse Day School – General Admin., 1911–1949, FA 10-17, volume 6477, Microfilm reel C-8793, Proposed Agreement Between Indian Affairs Branch of the Department of Mines and Resources and the Reverend H. I. Lee of Whitehorse, 1 September 1948. [BAP-000397-0001]

77. TRC, NRA, Library and Archives Canada, file 921-1, part 1, Yukon Agency – Whitehorse Day School – General Admin., 1911–1949, FA 10-17, volume 6477, Microfilm reel C-8793, R. J. Meek to Indian Affairs, 23 March 1948. [BAP-000369]

78. TRC, NRA, Library and Archives Canada, file 929-5, part 3, Yukon Agency – Whitehorse Day School – Building Maintenance – Supplies – Accounts, 1947–1950, FA 10-17, volume 6477, Microfilm reel C-8793, R. J. Meek to Indian Affairs Branch, Ottawa, 2 July 1947; [BAP-000453] file 929-5, part 3, Yukon Agency – Whitehorse Day School – Building Maintenance – Supplies – Accounts, FA 10-17, volume 6477, Microfilm reel C-8793, purchase order, 14 July 1947. [BAP-000502]

79. TRC, NRA, Library and Archives Canada, file 929-11, part 1, Yukon Agency – Whitehorse Day School – Vocational Training – Accounts, 1949–1950, FA 10-17, volume 6478, Microfilm reel C-8793, R. J. Meek to Indian Affairs Branch, 23 December 1949. [BAP-000269]

80. TRC, NRA, Library and Archives Canada, RG10, volume 8762, file 906/25-1-005, part 1, R. J. Meek to Indian Affairs Branch, 8 February 1950, 3. [BAP-090013]

81. TRC, NRA, Library and Archives Canada, file 929-23, part 1, Yukon Agency – Whitehorse Day School – Death of Pupils, 1922–1951, FA 10-17, volume 6478, Microfilm reel C-8793, P. Phelan to R. J. Meek, 1 March 1951. [BAP-000303]

82. TRC, NRA, Library and Archives Canada, file 929-23, part 1, Yukon Agency – Whitehorse Day School – Death of Pupils, 1922–1951, FA 10-17, volume 6478, Microfilm reel C-8793, R. J. Meek to Indian Affairs Branch, 7 March 1951. [BAP-000305]

83. TRC, NRA, Library and Archives Canada, file 929-5, part 3, Yukon Agency – Whitehorse Day School – Building Maintenance – Supplies – Accounts, 1947–1950, FA 10-17, volume 6477, Microfilm reel C-8793, H. Lee to J. A. Simmons, 14 February 1959. [BAP-000567]

84. TRC, NRA, Library and Archives Canada, file 929-5, part 3, Yukon Agency – Whitehorse Day School – Building Maintenance, B. F. Neary to the Director, Indian Affairs, 23 February 1950. [BAP-000570]

85. TRC, NRA, Yukon Archives – Ottawa, Gov 2209 f. 8, series 1, Whitehorse Indian Mission School, 1950–1955, Finding Aid – Yukon Records Office Files, 1901–1977, L. S. Lee to Praying Friends, April 1952. [BAP-001085]

86. TRC, NRA, Yukon Archives – Ottawa, Gov 2209 f. 8, series 1, Whitehorse Indian Mission School, 1950–1955, Finding Aid – Yukon Records Office Files, 1901–1977, L. S. Lee to Praying Friends, April 1952. [BAP-001085]

87. TRC, NRA, INAC – Main Records Office – Ottawa, file 906/36-4-005, volume 1, School Land, Yukon District, Whitehorse School, 1947–1954, locator X314-667, R. F. Davey to F. Fraser, 14 July 1954. [BAP-000652]

88. TRC, NRA, Library and Archives Canada, RG10, volume 8762, file 906/25-1-005, part 1, W. G. Brown to R. G. Robertson, 14 September 1954. [BAP-090021]

89. TRC, NRA, Yukon Archives – Ottawa, Gov 2209 f. 8, Series 1, Whitehorse Indian Mission School, 1950–1955, Finding Aid – Yukon Records Office Files, 1901–1977, R. G. Robertson to F. H. Collins, 17 August 1955. [BAP-001038-0000]

90. TRC, AVS, (Daukaly) Hammond Dick, Statement to the Truth and Reconciliation Commission of Canada, Watson Lake, Yukon, 25 May 2011, Statement Number: 2011-0309.

91. TRC, NRA, Library and Archives Canada, Burnaby file 25-2-929, Admission and Discharge, 12/1952–12/1956, V-1989-90/101, boxes 1–58, box 38, R. J. Meek to Superintendent of Education, 30 September 1954. [BAP-000822]

92. TRC, NRA, Library and Archives Canada, file 906/25-1-005, part 1, Yukon Agency – Correspondence Regarding Indian Schools and Education, 1950–1959, FA 10-28, volume 8762, Microfilm reel C-9703, E. R. Lee to J. W. Pickersgill, 1 March 1955. [BAP-000067-0001]

93. TRC, NRA, Library and Archives Canada, Burnaby file 25-2-929, Admission and Discharge, 12/1952–12/1956, V-1989-90/101, boxes 1–58, box 38, W. S. Arneil to M. G. Jutras, 17 June 1955. [BAP-000607]

94. TRC, NRA, Yukon Archives – Ottawa, Gov 2209 f. 8, series 1, Whitehorse Indian Mission School, 1950–1955, Finding Aid – Yukon Records Office Files, 1901–1977, E. R. Lee to H. M. Jones, 8 September 1955. [BAP-001032]

95. TRC, NRA, Yukon Archives – Ottawa, Gov 2209 f. 8, series 1, Whitehorse Indian Mission School, 1950–1955, Finding Aid – Yukon Records Office Files, 1901–1977, L. R. Shields to W. D. Robertson, 9 September 1955. [BAP-001030]

96. TRC, NRA, Anglican Church of Canada – Ottawa, General Synod Archives, file 1, Visit Reports of the Superintendent, 02/54–12/54, pages 004126–004227, Accession GS 75-103, series 2:15, box 24, Superintendent's Visit to Chooutla School, Carcross, Y.T., 3–6 December 1954, 3. [DYK-201620]

97. TRC, NRA, Anglican Diocese of Yukon Fonds – Ottawa, Yukon Archives, COR 262, f.11, Indian School Administration, 1956–1960, Anglican Church Diocese of Yukon [box 14], series I–I.1.c., folder 11 of 18, H. G. Cook to T. Greenwood, 12 July 1956. [BAP-000005]

98. TRC, NRA, Anglican Diocese of Yukon Fonds – Ottawa, Yukon Archives, COR 262, f. 11, Indian School Administration, 1956–1960, Anglican Church Diocese of Yukon [box 14], series I–I.1.c., folder 11 of 18, H. G. Cook to H. M. Jones, 1 August 1956; [BAP-000009] TRC, NRA, Anglican Diocese of Yukon Fonds – Ottawa, Yukon Archives, COR 262, f. 11, Indian School Administration, 1956–1960, Anglican Church Diocese of Yukon [box 14], series I–I.1.c., folder 11 of 18, Bishop of Brandon to T. Greenwood, 7 August 1956. [BAP-000012]

99. TRC, NRA, Document location unknown – Ottawa, Protestant Hostel, file. 25-1-943, volume 1, Aug./58–Dec./60, E. R. Lee to M. G. Jutras, 1 May 1959. [YKS-003094]

100. TRC, NRA, Anglican Diocese of Yukon Fonds – Ottawa, Yukon Archives, file 11, Indian School Administration, 1956–1960, Anglican Church – Diocese of Yukon Records [box 14], series I-I-1.c, folder 11 of 18, COR 262, H. G. Cook to Director, Indian Affairs Branch, 8 January 1960. [DYK-010169]

101. TRC, NRA, Anglican Diocese of Yukon Fonds – Ottawa, Yukon Archives, COR 262, f. 11, Indian School Administration, 1956-1960, Anglican Church Diocese of Yukon [box 14], series I-I.1.c., folder 11 of 18, Bishop of Yukon to E. Fairclough, 19 June 1959. [BAP-000033]

102. TRC, NRA, INAC – Resolution Sector – IRS Historical Files Collection – Ottawa, 853/25-1, 1956–1968, volume 2, H. C. Montgomery to H. M. Jones, 10 May 1960. [BAP-090005]

103. TRC, NRA, INAC – Resolution Sector – IRS Historical Files Collection – Ottawa, file 853/25-1, volume 2 (Ctrl #49-5), H. M. Jones to H. C. Montgomery, 19 May 1960. [NCA-009361-0001]

104. TRC, NRA, Document location unknown, Protestant Hostel, file 25-1-943, volume 2, Jan/61–Feb/62, R. F. Davey to Indian Commissioner of British Columbia, 4 January 1961. [YKS-003168]

105. TRC, NRA, Library and Archives Canada, RG10, volume 7182, file 1/25-1, part 12, Teachers Permanent Indian Day – Residential Schools, 30 September 1962. [RCM-000205]

106. For the date of the Carcross closing, see: TRC, NRA, Library and Archives Canada – Burnaby, RG10-151, V1989-90/101, file 801/6-1-011, volume 2, Carcross IRS, 06/1955–06/1960, Treasury Board Document, 3 March 1969. [CAR-011355-0001] For the date of the Lower Post closing, see: TRC, NRA, Library and Archives Canada, RG10, box 66, Acc. 1988-1989/057, General Correspondence Lower Post Students Residence, 1965–1978, G. K. Gooderham to Department Secretariat, 2 May 1975. [LOW-041388]

Section 2 – Introduction

1. See, for example: King, *School at Mopass,* 34–36.
2. For a fuller discussion of the process of population concentration, see: Duffy, *Road to Nunavut,* and Damas, *Arctic Migrants.*
3. Grygier, *Long Way from Home,* xxi.

The federal government rethinks its northern policy

1. TRC, NRA, National Capital Regional Service Centre – LAC, volume 2, file 600-1, locator #062-94, Education of Eskimos (1949–1957), Department of Northern Affairs and National Resources to Northern Administration and Land branch, 8 April 1958. [NCA-016925]
2. Duffy, *Road to Nunavut,* 3–4.
3. Coates, "Best Left as Indians," 179–204.
4. *Reference whether "Indians" includes "Eskimo",* [1939] SCR 104, 05 April 1939, http://scc-csc.lexum.com/scc-csc/scc-csc/en/item/8531/index.do, accessed 20 May 2014. For details of issue see: Diubaldo, "Absurd Little Mouse," 34–40.
5. Coates, *Canada's Colonies,* 167–176.
6. Coates, *Canada's Colonies,* 189–190.
7. Coates, *Canada's Colonies,* 176–180.

8. Crowe, *History of the Original Peoples*, 180–181.

9. Canada, Department of Northern Affairs and National Resources, *Annual Report, 1955*, 11.

10. Coates, *Canada's Colonies*, 225–226; Yukon Archives/Yukon Legislative Assembly, "History of the Yukon Legislative Assembly," The Legislature Speaks, Yukon Legislature: http://yukonlegislaturespeaks.ca/index.php/history, accessed 14 March 2014.

11. *The Beaver* was a magazine first published by the Hudson's Bay Company in 1920. Initially used to promote the "progress" created by the HBC in Canada, by the 1930s it was mainly a magazine devoted to teaching all (southern) Canadians about the country's "northlands"; indeed, from the 1930s the subtitle of the magazine was "A Magazine of the North."

12. The first article in the series outlines the purpose of the series. See Margaret Mead, "Enter the European: I – Into the South Pacific," June 1953, 4. Subsequent articles in the series include Charles Wagley, "Enter the European: II – Into Brazil – Half of South America," September 1953; Paul A. W. Wallace, "Enter the European: III – Into the United States," December 1953; H. B. Hawthorn, "Enter the European: IV – Among the Indians of Canada," Summer 1954; D. B. Marsh, "Enter the European: V – Among the Eskimos: Enter ... The Anglican Missionaries," Winter 1954; Arthur Thibert, O.M.I., "Enter the European: V – Among the Eskimos: Enter ... The Roman Catholic Missionaries," Winter 1954; P. A. C. Nichols, "Enter the European: V – Among the Eskimos: Enter ... The Fur Traders," Winter 1954; and Jean Lesage, "Enter the European: V – Among the Eskimos (Part II)," Spring 1955.

13. Mead, "Into the South Pacific," 9; Wagley, "Into Brazil"; Wallace, "Into the United States"; Hawthorn, "Among the Indians of Canada"; Jenness, "Among the Eskimos."

14. Marsh, "Enter ... The Anglican Missionaries," 33.

15. Thomson, *Jean Lesage*, 82–85.

16. Lesage, "Among the Eskimos (Part II)," 4.

17. Lesage, "Among the Eskimos (Part II)," 5.

18. Lesage, "Among the Eskimos (Part II)," 4.

19. Lesage, "Among the Eskimos (Part II)," 5.

20. Lesage, "Among the Eskimos (Part II)," 7.

21. Lesage, "Among the Eskimos (Part II),"4.

22. Lesage, "Among the Eskimos (Part II)," 8.

23. Lesage, "Among the Eskimos (Part II)," 5.

24. Lesage, "Among the Eskimos (Part II)," 5.

25. Lesage, "Among the Eskimos (Part II)," 6.

26. Lesage, "Among the Eskimos (Part II)," 6.

27. Lesage, "Among the Eskimos (Part II)," 6.

28. Canada, Department of Northern Affairs and National Resources, *Annual Report, 1955*.

29. Canada, Department of Northern Affairs and National Resources, *Annual Report, 1955*, 20–27.

30. Canada, Department of Northern Affairs and National Resources, *Annual Report, 1955*, 18.

31. Canada, Department of Northern Affairs and National Resources, *Annual Report, 1955*, 19.

32. TRC, NRA, Government of Northwest Territories Archives, file T-600-1-1, part 2a, Education and Schools – N.W.T. [General and Policy] 1968–1969, Archival box 203-3, Archival Acc. G-1979-003, 28 January 1968. [RCN-011441-0001]

33. TRC, NRA, Government of Northwest Territories Archives, file A-600-1-1, part 5, Education, Schools Policy N.W.T., 1961–1965, Archival box 202-2, Archival Acc. G-1979-003, "Religious Affiliation of Teaching Staff," undated. [RCN-009985-0001]

34. Canada, Department of Northern Affairs and National Resources, *Annual Report, 1955*, 19.

35. TRC, NRA, National Capital Regional Service Centre – LAC, volume 2, file 600-1, locator #062-94, Education of Eskimos (1949–1957), Department of Northern Affairs and National Resources to Northern Administration and Land branch, 8 April 1958. [NCA-016925]

36. TRC, NRA, Library and Archives Canada, RG85, volume 711, file 630/158-1, part 5, Government School – Chesterfield Inlet N.W.T., 1956–1957, "Boarding Schools for Eskimos – Chesterfield Inlet," 8 August 1958. [CIU-000485]

37. Canada, Department of Northern Affairs and National Resources, *Annual Report, 1955*, 18.

38. Canada, *Annual Report of the Department of Indian Affairs, 1956*, 51.

39. Library and Archives Canada, Indian Affairs Annual Reports, 1864–1990 History, http://www.bac-lac.gc.ca/eng/discover/aboriginal-heritage/first-nations/indian-affairs-annual-reports/Pages/introduction.aspx, accessed 10 December 2014.

40. Canada, Advisory Committee on Northern Development, *Government Activities*, 71.

41. Farish and Lackenbauer, "High Modernism," 532–539.

42. Canada, Advisory Committee on Northern Development, *Government Activities*, 71.

43. For 1949 figures, see: TRC, NRA, National Capital Regional Service Centre – LAC, volume 2, file 600-1, locator #062-94, Education of Eskimos (1949–1957), Department of Northern Affairs and National Resources to Northern Administration and Land branch, 8 April 1958. [NCA-016925] For 1959 figure, see: TRC, NRA, Library and Archives Canada, RG85, Perm. volume 1468, file 630/125-9, part 1, Govt. Hostel [R.C.] Inuvik, N.W.T. 1956–December 1959, FA 85-4, 1959–1960 Program, Inuvik, NWT, 10 August 1959. [RCN-008488]

44. TRC, NRA, Library and Archives Canada, RG22, Perm. volume 1019, file 40-2-17, part 9, Schools – N.W.T. – General Building ... Maintenance of ... Personnel of ... January 1964–June 1965, FA 22-3, "A Five-Year Education Plan for the Northwest Territories and Northern Quebec – 1965–1970," schedule B. [RCN-009392-0001]

45. TRC, NRA, Library and Archives Canada, RG22, Perm. volume 1019, file 40-2-17, part 9, Schools – N.W.T. – General Building ... Maintenance of ... Personnel of ... January 1964–June 1965, FA 22-3, "A Five-Year Education Plan for the Northwest Territories and Northern Quebec – 1965–1970," 13. [RCN-009392-0001]

46. Canada, *Annual Report of the Department of Indian Affairs, 1968*, 26.

47. TRC, NRA, INAC – Departmental Library – Ottawa, "Farewell to St. Joseph's School, Fort Resolution, N.W.T.," *Indian Record*, volume 20, number 5, May 1957. [IMR-000160]

48. TRC, NRA, Library and Archives Canada, RG85, Perm. volume 1062, file 630/125-8, part 2, Govt. Hostel [Anglican – Inuvik – N.W.T.] September 1959–February 1961, FA 85-3, R. G. Robertson to D. B. March, 9 October 1959. [SHU-000155]

49. TRC, NRA, Government of Northwest Territories Archives, file 600-1-1, part 4, School Policy [and Hostels], 1959–1961, Archival box 202-1, Archival Acc. G-1979-003, Department of Northern Affairs and National Resources, "Historic Names for Northern Schools and Residences," news release, 2 March 1961. [RCN-010612-0002] See McCarthy, *From the Great River*, 159, for opening date of Fort Providence.

50. TRC, NRA, Library and Archives Canada, RG85, Perm. volume 1376, file 660-14, part 2, Canadian Association of School Superintendents and Inspectors January 1958–June 1962, FA 85-4, "Speech to the Canadian Associations of School Superintendents and Inspectors," Citizenship and Immigration Minister Richard Bell. [RCN-012875]

51. TRC, NRA, Government of Northwest Territories Archives, file 600-1-1, part 4, School Policy [and Hostels], 1959–1961, Archival box 202-1, Archival Acc. G-1979-003, Department of

Northern Affairs and National Resources News Release, "Historic Names for Northern Schools and Residences," 2 March 1961. [RCN-010612-0002]

52. TRC, NRA, Library and Archives Canada, RG85, volume 711, file 630/158-1, part 5, Government School – Chesterfield Inlet N.W.T., 1956–1957, Boarding Schools for Eskimos – Chesterfield Inlet, 8 August 1958. [CIU-000485]

53. TRC, NRA, Library and Archives of Canada, R776-0-5 (RG55), volume 290, TB #626127, May-14-1964, Department of Northern Affairs and National Resources to Treasury Board, "Details of request to the Honourable the Treasury Board," 20 April 1964. [120.10656A]

54. TRC, NRA, Government of Northwest Territories Archives, Akaitcho Hall Reports, 1969–1970, Archival box 9-2, Archival Acc. G1995-004. [AHU-003844-0003]

55. Dickerson, *Whose North?*, 42–44.

56. TRC, NRA, Library and Archives Canada, RG22, volume 880, file 41-9-2, part 2, W. E. Winter to B. G. Sivertz and J. V. Jacobson, 16 July 1957. [NCA-014404-0000]

57. TRC, NRA, Library and Archives Canada, RG22, Perm. volume 872, file 40-10-4, part 3, Educational Policy in the Northwest Territories April 1955–December 1957, FA 22-1, W. E. Winter to B. G. Sivertz, 22 August 1957. [RCN-008257]

58. For the period of disruption and transition from intermittent contact to the government-commercial period, see McClellan, *Part of the Land*.

59. Canada, *Annual Report of the Department of Indian Affairs Branch, 1951*, 12.

60. TRC, LAC, Library and Archives Canada, RG22, volume 318, file 40-2-18, part 1, F. G. Cunningham to Deputy Minister, 24 February 1956. [NCA-014010]

61. TRC, NRA, Yukon Archives, GOV 2209, f.9, series 1, volume 9, Proposed New Whitehorse Indian Baptist Mission Hostel, 1956–1963, FA – Yukon Records Office Files, 1901–1977, J. L. Coudert to J. W. Pickersgill, 12 November 1956. [BAP-001197-0001]

62. TRC, NRA, National Capital Regional Service Centre – LAC, file 1/25-1, volume 15 (locator #H4-77), Yukon, G. R. Cameron to E. A. Côté, 26 May 1966. [NCA-001030]

63. TRC, NRA, Library and Archives Canada, file 801/25-2, volume 3, Admission and Discharge Residential Schools, 03/1961–11/1962, RG10-151, V1989-90/101, box 36, W. E. Grant to H. Murphy, 2 March 1961. [CAR-090008]

The federal day schools

1. TRC, NRA, Government of Northwest Territories Archives, Government of Northwest Territories Legislative Library, Joseph Katz, *Educational Environments of School-Hostel Complexes in the Northwest Territories* (Vancouver, BC: Education Division, Canadian Department of Northern Affairs and National Resources, July 1965), 4. [RCN-013107]

2. TRC, NRA, Government of Northwest Territories Archives, Government of Northwest Territories Legislative Library, Joseph Katz, *Educational Environments of School-Hostel Complexes in the Northwest Territories* (Vancouver, BC: Education Division, Canadian Department of Northern Affairs and National Resources, July 1965), 5. [RCN-013107]

3. Canada, J. W. McKinnon to Special Joint Committee, *Minutes of Proceedings and Evidence*, 1947, 1142.

4. See for example: Canada, Department of Northern Affairs and National Resources, *Annual Report, 1959*, 25.

5. King, *School at Mopass*, 48–49.

6. King, *School at Mopass,* 49–50.

7. King, *School at Mopass,* 56.

8. King, *School at Mopass,* 59.

9. Mouat, "Education in the Arctic District," 6.

10. TRC, NRA, Library and Archives Canada, RG85, Perm. volume 1895, file 620-1-1, part 6, Information Re: School Curriculum Incl. Printed Material, 1969–1970, FA 85-8, L. G. P. Waller for R. F. Davey to R. Kruse, 30 September 1969. [RCN-001551]

11. LeFrancois, "Native Education in Yukon," vii.

12. TRC, NRA, Library and Archives Canada, RG10, Acc. 2003-00196-4, file AQR630/313-1, box 19, volume 1, "Federal School – Payne Bay, P.Q.," A. Meldrum to C. M. Bolger, 9. [PBH-000086-0001]

13. TRC, NRA, Library and Archives Canada, RG85, volume 708, file 630/105-7, part 3, High School Facilities – Yellowknife [Public and Separate Schools], 1958–1959, "Yellowknife Composite High School and Vocational School, Proposed Program, 1958–1959." [AHU-000363] For the Churchill school, see: Canada, *Annual Report of the Department of Indian Affairs, 1967,* 24.

14. TRC, NRA, Library and Archives Canada, RG85, box 125, Acc. 1997-98/076, file 630/105-10, part 2, Govt. Hostel – Yellowknife, N.W.T. February 1959–December 1959, FA 85-52, J. M. Black to Chief Superintendent of Schools, 1 December 1959. [AHU-000588]

15. Canada, *Annual Report of the Department of Indian Affairs, 1967,* 24.

16. TRC, NRA, Library and Archives Canada, RG85, Perm. volume 1468, file 630/125-9, part 1, Govt. Hostel [R.C.] Inuvik, N.W.T. 1956–December 1959, FA 85-4, "1959–1960 Program, Inuvik, NWT," 10 August 1959. [RCN-008488]

17. TRC, NRA, Government of Northwest Territories Archives, file T-600-1-1, part 1b, Education and Schools in the N.W.T. General Policy 1966–1968, Archival box 203-1, Archival Acc. G-1979-003, "Information to Members of Council – Number 8, Change of School Year in Keewatin." [RCN-011201]

18. TRC, NRA, Library and Archives Canada, RG85, Perm. volume 1434, file 600-1-1, part 20, Education – Schools, N.W.T. [General and Policy File] August 1963–November 1964, FA 85-4, R. A. J. Phillips to Gordon, 21 January 1964, 2. [RCN-006677]

19. TRC, NRA, Library and Archives, RG85, Perm. volume 1468, file 630/125-1, part 1, Govt. School at Inuvik, N.W.T. 1956–December 1959, FA 85-4, E. W. Lyall to Jacobson, 25 October 1959. [RCN-008532]

20. TRC, NRA, Library and Archives Canada, RG85, Perm. volume 1468, file 630/125-1, part 1, Govt. School at Inuvik, N.W.T. 1956–December 1959, FA 85-4, Administrator of the Mackenzie, Department of Northern Affairs and National Resources, Northern Administration and Lands Branch to J. V. Jacobsen, 25 November 1959. [RCN-009843]

21. TRC, NRA, Library and Archives Canada RG85, Perm. volume 644, file 630/158-1, part 6, Govt. School – Chesterfield Inlet, N.W.T. October 1957–May 1959, FA 85-1, Dickson for J. V. Jacobsen to Director, 11 May 1959. [CIU-002037]

22. Pupils of the Spence Bay Federal School, *Spence Bay – 1967.*

23. Pupils of the Spence Bay Federal School, *Spence Bay – 1967.*

24. TRC, NRA, Library and Archives Canada, RG 85, box 162, Acc. 1997-98/076, file 1010-7, part 3, Roman Catholic Church – Gen. File [Incl. Indian and Eskimo Welfare Com.] December 1960–March 1970, FA 85-52, J. M. Rousselière – Les Missionnaires Oblats de Marie Immaculée to Côté, 20 November 1967. [CIU-001786-0001]

25. Phillips, *Canada's North,* 240.

26. TRC, NRA, Government of Northwest Territories Archives, file 630-100/12-1, part 2, Reports and Returns Fort Smith Hostel – Breynat Hall 1962–1965, Archival box 222-1, Archival Acc. G-1979-003, W. G. Booth to B. C. Gillie, 12 July 1963. [BTU-000723] For report of being allowed to speak Aboriginal language at Lapointe Hall in Fort Simpson, see: Blondin-Perrin, *My Heart Shook,* 146.

27. TRC, AVS, Margaret Leishman, Statement to the Truth and Reconciliation Commission of Canada, K'atl'Odeeche, Northwest Territories, 8 March 2012, Statement Number: SP056.

28. TRC, NRA, INAC – Resolution Sector – IRS Historical Files Collection – Ottawa, file 600-1-6, volume 6, Hostel Management – N.W.T. [General and Policy], March 1964–January 1965, IRSRC Historical Files, "Staff Fluent in Native Languages of the Pupils," 29 August 1964. [RCN-002549-0001]

29. TRC, NRA, Library and Archives Canada, RG85, Acc. 1997-98/076, box 131, file 680-1-15, volume 4, Excerpt from NWT Hansard (no date, but context indicates spring 1970), 95–96. [CVC-000558-0002] For Williamson's position: Northern Research Portal, "R. G. Williamson fonds," http://scaa.usask.ca/gallery/northern/en_finding_aid_display.php?filename=williamson&title=Robert%20Williamson%20fonds, accessed 8 March 2014.

30. TRC, NRA, Library and Archives Canada RG85, Acc. 1997-98/076, box 131, file 680-1-15, volume 4, R. Ritcey to Regional Superintendent of Schools, Churchill, Manitoba, 26 March 1970. [CVC-000560]

31. TRC, NRA, Library and Archives Canada, RG85, Acc. 1997-98/076, box 131, file 680-1-15, volume 4, W. I. Mouat to R. J. Carney, 2 April 1970. [CVC-000561]

32. TRC, NRA, Library and Archives Canada, RG85, Acc. 1997-98/076, box 131, file 680-1-15, volume 4, B. C. Gillie to Commissioner, 22 April 1970. [CVC-000563]

33. TRC, NRA, Library and Archives Canada 779/25-1-1, volume 1, 04/70–02/71, D. A. Davidson to G. D. Cromb, 9 November 1970. [BQL-002898-0001]

34. Eva Aariak, "Remembering Jose Kusugak," http://arcticcollege.ca/josekusugak/?p=291.

35. Macpherson, *Dreams & Visions,* 278.

36. Ipellie, "He Scared the Hair," 60–63.

37. TRC, NRA, Government of Northwest Territories Archives, Cambay [Cambridge Bay] – General, 1969–1970, Archival box 5-3, Archival Acc. G-1995-004, N. J. Macpherson to Principal and Staff, Territorial School, Cambridge Bay, N.W.T., 20 April 1970. [CBS-000861]

38. NWT Hansard (5 February 1979), 528, 533–34, 539. In the orthography of the time, Piita Irniq's name was spelled "Peter Ernerk."

39. TRC, NRA, DIAND HQ, file 40-2-185, volume 1, 05/1966–02/1969, C. M. Bolger to C. M. Whitton, 7 October 1966. [AEMR-019430E]

40. TRC, NRA, DIAND HQ, file 40-2-185, volume 1, 05/1966–02/1969, D. B. Marsh to C. M. Bolger, 12 December 1966. [AEMR-019430D]

41. "Priest Calls Department Anti-Catholic," *Ottawa Citizen,* 10 June 1961, quoted in Carney, "Relations in Education," 487.

42. TRC, NRA, INAC – Resolution Sector – IRS Historical Files Collection – Ottawa, file 853/25-1, volume 2 (Ctrl #49-5), "Report to the Chief of the Education Division, Indian Affairs Branch, On the Experiment With Integration of Indian Students (R.C.) Into Whitehorse Schools, 1960-1961," E. Cullinane, 1961. [NCA-009389-0001]

43. TRC, NRA, INAC – Resolution Sector – IRS Historical Files Collection – Ottawa, 853/25-1, 1956–1968, volume 2, RCAP, E. A. Cullinane to J. E. Ingot, 24 January 1962. [CDH-000060]

44. TRC, NRA, Library and Archives Canada, RG10, box 366, Acc. 1999-01431-6, file 906/25-7, part 1, W. E. Grant to A/Indian Commissioner for British Columbia, 5 June 1961. [NCA-010764-0002]

45. TRC, NRA, Library and Archives Canada, RG85, volume 1338, file 600-1-1, part 19, D. W. Hepburn, "Northern Education: Facade for Failure," *Variables: The Journal of the Sociology Club* (University of Alberta) 2, no. 1 (February 1963): 16–21, 16. [NCA-005960]

46. TRC, NRA, Library and Archives Canada, RG85, volume 1338, file 600-1-1, part 19, D. W. Hepburn, "Northern Education: Facade for Failure," *Variables: The Journal of the Sociology Club* (University of Alberta) 2, no. 1 (February 1963): 16–21, 17. [NCA-005960]

47. TRC, NRA, Library and Archives Canada, RG85, volume 1338, file 600-1-1, part 19, D. W. Hepburn, "Northern Education: Facade for Failure," *Variables: The Journal of the Sociology Club* (University of Alberta) 2, no. 1 (February 1963): 16–21, 18. [NCA-005960]

48. TRC, AVS, Petah Inukpuk, Statement to the Truth and Reconciliation Commission of Canada (simultaneous translation), Inuvik, Northwest Territories, 30 June 2011, Statement Number: SP149.

49. TRC, AVS, Petah Inukpuk, Statement to the Truth and Reconciliation Commission of Canada (simultaneous translation), Inuvik, Northwest Territories, 30 June 2011, Statement Number: SP149.

50. See, for example, TRC, AVS, Beatrice Bernhardt, Statement to the Truth and Reconciliation Commission of Canada, Inuvik, Northwest Territories, 30 June 2011, Statement Number: SP150; and Piita Irniq, quoted in Legacy of Hope Foundation, *We Were So Far Away*, 109.

51. NWT Hansard (28 January 1970), 955–56.

52. TRC, NRA, Government of Northwest Territories – Education, Culture and Employment, file 73-500-400/B, volume 1, Inuvik Hostel – Grollier Hall [R.C.] – Quarterly Returns [Fort McPherson], 09/69–12/71, Transfer No. 0330, box 8-25, "Statistics on Students Leaving a Particular and Special Hostel: Grollier Hall," 1971. [GHU-001200]

53. TRC, NRA, Government of Northwest Territories – Education, Culture and Employment, Quarterly Reports from Staff, 1987–1988, Transfer No. 1530, box 15, "Semester 2 Final Marks – 1986–1987." [AHU-004913-0001]

54. TRC, NRA, Government of Northwest Territories – Education, Culture and Employment, Quarterly Reports from Staff, 1987–1988, Transfer No. 1530, box 15, "Semester I, Mid-Term Marks, 1987–88." [AHU-004914-0001]

55. TRC, NRA, Government of Northwest Territories – Education, Culture and Employment, Correspondence – Kitikmeot Region, 1990–1992, Transfer No. 1530, box 10, "Kitikmeot Dropouts 1990–1991," 16 June 1991. [AHU-004019-0002]

56. Duffy, *Road to Nunavut,* 125.

57. Dickerson, *Whose North?,* 128–129.

58. Lillian Elias, quoted in Legacy of Hope Foundation, *We Were So Far Away*, 51.

59. Quassa, *We Need to Know*, 29.

60. Piita Irniq, quoted in Legacy of Hope Foundation, *We Were So Far Away*, 111.

61. TRC, AVS, Eddie Dillon, Statement to the Truth and Reconciliation Commission of Canada, Inuvik, Northwest Territories, 1 July 2011, Statement Number: SP151.

62. Peterson, "Sir Joseph Bernier Federal Day School," 8.

63. Peterson, "Sir Joseph Bernier Federal Day School," 8.

64. Peterson, "Sir Joseph Bernier Federal Day School," 9.

65. Peterson, "Sir Joseph Bernier Federal Day School," 9–11.

66. For an example, see TRC, AVS, Elijah Nashook, Statement to the Truth and Reconciliation Commission of Canada (simultaneous translation), Inuvik, Northwest Territories, 1 July 2011, Statement Number: SP151.

67. John Amagoalik quoted in McGregor, *Inuit Education*, 110.

68. Amagoalik, *Changing the Face of Canada*, 43–46.

69. TRC, AVS, David Simailak, Statement to the Truth and Reconciliation Commission of Canada, Baker Lake, Nunavut, 15 November 2011, Statement Number: SP032.

70. TRC, AVS, Marjorie Ovayuak, Statement to the Truth and Reconciliation Commission of Canada, Inuvik, Northwest Territories, 30 June 2011, Statement Number: SP150.

71. Duffy, *Road to Nunavut,* 102.

72. Nungak, "Experimental Eskimos," 16. Back issues of *Inuktitut* are now available online, at https://www.itk.ca/publication/magazine/Inuktitut. See also the short feature on this event on the Inuit Tapiriit Kanatami website, https://www.itk.ca/historical-event/experimental-eskimo-zebedee-nungak-leaves-puvirnituq-nunavik, accessed 31 January 2013; and the documentary film *Experimental Eskimos*, reviewed here: http://www.imdb.com/title/tt1414861/plotsummary, accessed 31 January 2013.

73. Nungak, "Experimental Eskimos," 16.

74. Ittinuar, *Teach an Eskimo*, 2008.

75. Ittinuar, *Teach an Eskimo,* 65.

The large hostels

1. TRC, NRA, Government of Northwest Territories – Education, Culture and Employment, Student Residence – Attendance Stats. 09/69–06/73, Transfer No. 0274, box 4-20, "Enrolment at Stringer Hall – By settlement – Quarter ending June 30, 1970." [SHU-000588]

2. TRC, NRA, Government of Northwest Territories – Education, Culture and Employment, Student Residence – Attendance Stats. 09/69–06/73, Transfer No. 0274, box 4-20, "Enrolment for Akaitcho Hall – by Settlement, Quarter Ending December 31, 1970." [AHU-003842]

3. TRC, NRA, INAC – Archival Unit – Ottawa, file 630/500-10, "Pupils attending Pre-Vocational School, Churchill, Man. From Arctic District," 30 September 1964. [CVC-001217-0005]

4. Distance calculator, Yellowknife to Iqaluit, http://www.distance-calculator.co.uk/world-distances-yellowknife-to-iqaluit.htm; Air Miles calculator, Inuvik to Taloyoak, http://www.airmilescalculator.com/distance/yev-to-yyh/.

5. TRC, NRA, Library and Archives Canada, RG85, Perm. volume 1468, file 630/125-9, part 1, Govt. Hostel [R.C.] Inuvik, N.W.T. 1956–December 1959, FA 85-4, "1959–1960 Program, Inuvik, NWT," 10 August 1959. [RCN-008488]

6. TRC, NRA, Library and Archives Canada, RG85, Perm. volume 709, file 630/105-10, part 1, Govt. Hostel – Yellowknife, N.W.T. April 1957–January 1959, FA 85-1, J. V. Jacobson to Director, 11 October 1957. [RCN-008265]

7. See "Line of Authority in the Hostel" in Clifton, *Inuvik Study*, 54, 67.

8. TRC, NRA, Library and Archives Canada, RG85, Perm. volume 1443, file 630/125-8, part 4, Govt. Hostel [Anglican] Inuvik, N.W.T. [Stringer Hall] April 1963–October 1965, FA 85-4, B. G. Sivertz to Deputy Minister, 9 October 1963. [IKU-000612]

9. TRC, NRA, INAC – Resolution Sector – IRS Historical Files Collection – Ottawa, file 600-1-6, volume 6, Hostel Management – N.W.T. [General and Policy], March 1964–January 1965, C. M. Bolger to Administrator of the Arctic, 5 November 1964. [RCN-002539]

10. TRC, NRA, Government of Northwest Territories Archives, Government of Northwest Territories Legislative Library, Joseph Katz, *Educational Environments of School-Hostel Complexes in the Northwest Territories* (Vancouver, BC: Education Division, Canadian Department of Northern Affairs and National Resources, July 1965), 15. [RCN-013107]

11. TRC, NRA, Government of Northwest Territories Archives, file 630.116, part 1, Hostel Facilities – Chesterfield Inlet, 1963, Archival box 37, Archival Acc. N-1994-009, I. Mouat to Sister Arcand, 31 March 1967. [CIU-001776-0001]

12. TRC, NRA, Government of Northwest Territories Archives, Government of Northwest Territories Legislative Library, Joseph Katz, *Educational Environments of School-Hostel Complexes in the Northwest Territories* (Vancouver, BC: Education Division, Canadian Department of Northern Affairs and National Resources, July 1965), 16. [RCN-013107]

13. TRC, NRA, Library and Archives Canada, RG85, Acc. 1997-98/076, box 131, file 680-1-15, volume 1, "Memo – Churchill School Data," undated. [CVC-001896-0000] For diagram showing layout of Akaitcho Hall dormitory, see: TRC, NRA, Library and Archives Canada, RG 29, volume 2989, file 851-6-4, part 3a, Akaitcho Hall, Yellowknife, Sketch of Girls Dormitory, October 1960. [120.16375A]

14. TRC, NRA, Library and Archives Canada, RG85, Perm. volume 1051, file A-630/158-9, part 1, Govt. Hostel [R.C.] – Chesterfield Inlet, October 1959–April 1961, FA 85-3, "Criteria for Selecting Children to Attend Hostels and Residential Schools," 19 October 1960. [CIU-000090-0001]

15. TRC, NRA, INAC – Resolution Sector – IRS Historical Files Collection – Ottawa, file 600-1-6, volume 2, Hostel Management – N.W.T. General and Policy, May 1960–December 1960, R. A. Bishop to Administrator of the Mackenzie, 10 May 1960, 2. [RCN-000655]

16. TRC, NRA, Library and Archives Canada, RG22, Perm. volume 1061, file 250-3-20, part 1, R.C. Hostel – Inuvik (N.W.T.) 1957, FA 22-3, B. G. Sivertz to Deputy Minister, 22 June 1959. [IKU-001224-0001]

17. Norm Burgess, quoted in Macpherson, *Dreams & Visions*, 332.

18. TRC, AVS, Eric Anautalik, Statement to the Truth and Reconciliation Commission of Canada, Baker Lake, Nunavut, 15 November 2011, Statement Number: SP032.

19. TRC, AVS, Dora Fraser, Statement to the Truth and Reconciliation Commission of Canada, Winnipeg, Manitoba, 19 June 2010, Statement Number: 02-MB-19JU10-012.

20. TRC, AVS, Beatrice Bernhardt, Statement to the Truth and Reconciliation Commission of Canada, 30 June 2011, Inuvik, Northwest Territories, Sharing Panel: SP150.

21. Quassa, *We Need to Know*, 25–26.

22. Watt, "Eyewitness Says," *Winnipeg Free Press.*

23. TRC, NRA, Library and Archives Canada, RG85, Perm. volume 1376, file 660-14, part 2, Canadian Association of School Superintendents and Inspectors January 1958–June 1962, FA 85-4, "Speech to the Canadian Association of School Superintendents and Inspectors," Citizenship and Immigration Minister Richard Bell. [RCN-012875]

24. TRC, NRA, Government of Northwest Territories Archives, file 630-100/12-1, part 2, Reports and Returns Fort Smith Hostel – Breynat Hall 1962–1965, Archival box 222-1, Archival Acc. G-1979-003, W. G. Booth to B. C. Gillie, 12 July 1963. [BTU-000723]

25. Tagoona, "Education," 53–55.

26. TRC, AVS, Norman Attungala, Statement to the Truth and Reconciliation Commission of Canada (simultaneous translation), Baker Lake, Nunavut, 15 November 2011, Statement Number: SP032.

27. Lillian Elias, quoted in Legacy of Hope Foundation, *We Were So Far Away*, 60.

28. Piita Irniq, quoted in Legacy of Hope Foundation, *We Were So Far Away*, 98.

29. TRC, AVS, Eric Anautalik, Statement to the Truth and Reconciliation Commission of Canada (simultaneous translation), Baker Lake, Nunavut, 15 November 2011, Statement Number: SP032.

30. TRC, AVS, Mary Charlie, Statement to the Truth and Reconciliation Commission of Canada, Watson Lake, Yukon, 25 May 2011, Statement Number: SP021.

31. TRC, AVS, Agnus Lennie, Statement to the Truth and Reconciliation Commission of Canada, Tulita, Northwest Territories, 10 May 2011, Statement Number: SP018.

32. TRC, AVS, Towkie Karpit, Statement to the Truth and Reconciliation Commission of Canada, Pangnirtung, Nunavut, 13 February 2012, Statement Number: SP045.

33. Apphia Agalakti Siqpaapik Awa, quoted in Wachowich, *Saqiyuq*, 106.

34. TRC, AVS, Peggy Tologanak, Statement to the Truth and Reconciliation Commission of Canada, Iqaluit, Nunavut, 25 March 2011, Statement Number: SP008.

35. TRC, NRA, Library and Archives Canada, RG85, Acc. 1997-98/076, box 131, file 680-1-15, volume 1, "Memo – Churchill School Data," undated, 4. [CVC-001896-0000]

36. TRC, AVS, Norma Yakeleya, Statement to the Truth and Reconciliation Commission of Canada, Tulita, Northwest Territories, 10 May 2011, Statement Number: SP018.

37. TRC, AVS, Peggy Tologanak, Statement to the Truth and Reconciliation Commission of Canada, Iqaluit, Nunavut, 25 March 2011, Statement Number: SP008. Many of these items are now of significant commercial value. Handmade, hand-tanned moccasins can cost over $500, while parkas can cost over $1,000. For examples, see: Tlicho Online Store, http://onlinestore.tlicho.ca/.

38. TRC, AVS, Marjorie Jack, Statement to the Truth and Reconciliation Commission of Canada, Watson Lake, Yukon, 25 May 2011, Statement Number: SP021.

39. See TRC, AVS, Candace Ikey, Statement to the Truth and Reconciliation Commission of Canada, Kuujjuaq, Quebec, 16 March 2011, Statement Number: SP003.

40. TRC, AVS, David Simailak, Statement to the Truth and Reconciliation Commission of Canada, Baker Lake, Nunavut, 15 November 2011, Statement Number: SP032.

41. TRC, AVS, Helen Naedzo Squirrel, Statement to the Truth and Reconciliation Commission of Canada, Tulita, Northwest Territories, 10 May 2011, Statement Number: SP018.

42. Piita Irniq, quoted in Legacy of Hope Foundation, *We Were So Far Away*, 99.

43. TRC, AVS, Anna Kasudluak, Statement to the Truth and Reconciliation Commission of Canada (simultaneous translation), Inuvik, Northwest Territories, 30 June 2011, Statement Number: SP149.

44. Ralph Ritcey, quoted in Macpherson, *Dreams & Visions*, 330.

45. TRC, NRA, Government of Northwest Territories Archives, file 630-100/12-1, part 2, Reports and Returns Fort Smith Hostel – Breynat Hall 1962–1965, Archival box 222-1, Archival Acc. G-1979-003, W. G. Booth to B. C. Gillie, 12 July 1963. [BTU-000723]

46. TRC, AVS, Anna Kasudluak, Statement to the Truth and Reconciliation Commission of Canada (simultaneous translation), Inuvik, Northwest Territories, 30 June 2011, Statement Number: SP149.

47. TRC, AVS, Veroha Dewar, Statement to the Truth and Reconciliation Commission of Canada (simultaneous translation), Iqaluit, Nunavut, 25 March 2011, Statement Number: SP008.

48. TRC, AVS, Eva Lapage, Statement to the Truth and Reconciliation Commission of Canada, Halifax, Nova Scotia, 29 October 2011, Statement Number: 2011-2919.

49. TRC, NRA, INAC – Archival Unit – Ottawa, file 630/500-10, "Churchill Pupil Residence, Routine and Rules," 30 September 1964. [CVC-001217-0008]

50. TRC, AVS, Peggy Tologanak, Statement to the Truth and Reconciliation Commission of Canada, Iqaluit, Nunavut, 25 March 2011, Statement Number: SP008.

51. TRC, AVS, Peggy Tologanak, Statement to the Truth and Reconciliation Commission of Canada, 25 March 2011, Iqaluit, Nunavut, Statement Number: SP008.

52. TRC, AVS, Veronica Dewar, Statement to the Truth and Reconciliation Commission of Canada (simultaneous translation), 25 March 2011, Iqaluit, Nunavut, Statement Number: SP008.

53. Piita Irniq, quoted in Legacy of Hope Foundation, *We Were So Far Away*, 100.

54. AVS, TRC, Rebecca Williams, Statement to the Truth and Reconciliation Commission of Canada, Halifax, Nova Scotia, 28 October 2011, Statement Number: SC076.

55. Clifton, *Inuvik Study*, 60.

56. Clifton, *Inuvik Study*, 61.

57. See for example: TRC, AVS, Marjorie Ovayuak, Statement to the Truth and Reconciliation Commission of Canada, Inuvik, Northwest Territories, 30 June 2011, Statement Number: SP150.

58. TRC, AVS, Beatrice Bernhardt, Statement to the Truth and Reconciliation Commission of Canada, Inuvik, Northwest Territories, 30 June 2011, Statement Number: SP150.

59. TRC, AVS, Eddie Dillon, Statement to the Truth and Reconciliation Commission of Canada, Inuvik, Northwest Territories, 1 July 2011, Statement Number: SP151.

60. TRC, AVS, Beatrice Bernhardt, Statement to the Truth and Reconciliation Commission of Canada, Inuvik, Northwest Territories, 30 June 2011, Statement Number: SP150.

61. TRC, AVS, Peggy Tologanak, Statement to the Truth and Reconciliation Commission of Canada, Iqaluit, Nunavut, 25 March 2011, Statement Number: SP008.

62. TRC, AVS, Jeannie Evalik, Statement to the Truth and Reconciliation Commission of Canada, Cambridge Bay, Nunavut, 11 April 2011, Statement Number: SP009.

63. TRC, AVS, Marjorie Ovayuak, Statement to the Truth and Reconciliation Commission of Canada, Inuvik, Northwest Territories, 30 June 2011, Statement Number: SP150.

64. TRC, AVS, Judi Kochon, Statement to the Truth and Reconciliation Commission of Canada, Tulita, Northwest Territories, 10 May 2011, Statement Number: SP018.

65. TRC, NRA, Library and Archives Canada, RG85, volume 708, file 630/105-7, part 3, High School Facilities – Yellowknife [Public and Separate School], 1958–1959, A. J. Boxer to J. M. Black, "Progress Report – Yellowknife Hostel. Initial Period to New Year," 9 December 1958, 5. [AHU-000005-0000]

66. TRC, NRA, Government of Northwest Territories Archives, file 630-105/12-1,2,3, Akaitcho Hall, Yellowknife, 1961–1965, Archival box 229-1, Archival Acc. G-1979-003, N. J. Macpherson to W. G. Booth, 22 November 1963. [AHU-001404-0001]

67. TRC, NRA, Government of Northwest Territories Archives, Confidential, Hostels, 1971–1974, Archival box 8-24, Archival Acc. G1995-004, "Ukkivik Residence, Frobisher Bay, Northwest Territories: A Report and Recommendations," 24 December 1973, 5. [FBS-000431]

68. Blondin-Perrin, *My Heart Shook*, 134.

69. TRC, NRA, Government of Northwest Territories Archives, Government of Northwest Territories Legislative Library, Joseph Katz, *Educational Environments of School-Hostel Complexes in the Northwest Territories* (Vancouver, BC: Education Division, Canadian Department of Northern Affairs and National Resources, July 1965), 17, 22. [RCN-013107]

70. TRC, NRA, Government of Northwest Territories Archives, Confidential, Hostels, 1971–1974, Archival box 8-24, Archival Acc. G1995-004, "Ukkivik Residence, Frobisher Bay, Northwest Territories: A Report and Recommendations," 24 December 1973, 4–5. [FBS-000431]

71. TRC, NRA, Library and Archives Canada, RG85, Perm. volume 1374, file 630/158-9, part 7, Govt. Hostel [R.C.] Chesterfield Inlet, N.W.T. February 1960–September 1962, FA 85-4, R. Bélair to A. Bishop, 28 September 1961. [CIU-001666]

72. TRC, NRA, Library and Archives Canada, RG85, Perm. volume 1374, file 630/158-9, part 7, Govt. Hostel [R.C.] Chesterfield Inlet, N.W.T. February 1960–September 1962, FA 85-4, R. A. Bishop to R. Bélair, 31 May 1962. [CIU-001692]

73. TRC, NRA, Library and Archives Canada, RG85, Perm. volume 1374, file 630/158-9, part 7, Govt. Hostel [R.C.] Chesterfield Inlet, N.W.T. February 1960–September 1962, FA 85-4, R. Bélair to R. A. Bishop, 22 July 1962. [CIU-001700]

74. TRC, NRA, Library and Archives Canada, RG85, Perm. volume 1442, file 630/125-8, part 3, Govt. Hostel [Anglican] [Inuvik – N.W.T.] March 1961–March 1963, 85-4, L. Holman to B. Sivertz, 27 October 1961. [SHU-000185-0000]

75. TRC, NRA, INAC – Resolution Sector – IRS Historical Files Collection – Ottawa, file 600-1-6, volume 3, Hostel Management – N.W.T. [General and Policy], January 1961–October 1961, L. Holman to B. G. Sivertz, undated. [RCN-000785-0005]

76. TRC, NRA, Government of Northwest Territories – Education, Culture and Employment, file 73-500-400/A, volume 1, Inuvik Hostel – Grollier Hall [R.C.] – Quarterly Returns [Fort McPherson], 09/69–12/71, Transfer No. 0330, box 8-25, M. Thomson to Regional Director, Northern Region Medical Services, Government of Canada, 27 October 1970. [SHU-000594]

77. TRC, NRA, CGS Records Warehouse, Iqaluit, Government of Nunavut, Akaitcho Hall Correspondence, 1988–1989 Kitikmeot Region [Kugluktuk] – box 202, T. Gavac to D. Harvey, 30 May 1990, 4. [AHU-004004]

78. Quassa, *We Need to Know*, 29–30.

79. TRC, NRA, INAC – Resolution Sector – IRS Historical Files Collection – Ottawa, file 600-1-6, volume 2, Hostel Management – N.W.T. General and Policy, May 1960–December 1960, F. A. G. Carter to A. Renaud, "Facilities for Medical Care and General Health at Hostels in the Northwest Territories," 9 May 1960, 2. [RCN-000653]

80. TRC, NRA, Library and Archives Canada, RG85, volume 708, file 630/105-7, part 3, High School Facilities – Yellowknife [Public and Separate School], 1958–1959, "Public Health Services to Yellowknife Composite School," 20 January 1959. [AHU-000387]

81. TRC, NRA, Library and Archives Canada, RG85, Acc. 1997-98/076, box 131, file 680-1-15, volume 1, "Memo – Churchill School Data," undated, 3. [CVC-001896-0000]

82. TRC, NRA, INAC – Resolution Sector – IRS Historical Files Collection – Ottawa, file 600-1-6, volume 2, Hostel Management – N.W.T. General and Policy, May 1960–December 1960, R. A. Bishop to Administrator of the Mackenzie, 10 May 1960. [RCN-000655]

83. TRC, NRA, Library and Archives Canada, RG85, Perm. volume 1374, file 630/111-8, part. 2, Gov't. Hostel [Anglican] Fort Simpson, N.W.T. December 1961–December 1963, FA 85-4, B. Sales to W. Karashowski, 21 December 1963. [BPU-000052-0002] See also: TRC, NRA, Library and Archives Canada, RG85, Perm. volume 1441, file 630/111-8, part 3, Govt. Hostel [Angli-

can] – Fort Simpson, N.W.T. January 1964–December 1965, FA 85-4, "Memorandum for the Director," 7 January 1964. [BPU-000262]

84. TRC, NRA, Library and Archives Canada, RG85, box 143, Acc. 1997-98/076, file 1000/125, part 5, Inuvik, N.W.T. – General File February 1959–December 1967, FA 85-52, J. V. Jacobsen to the Director, "Memorandum for the Director: Measles – Inuvik," 7 December 1959. [IKU-001287]

85. TRC, NRA, Library and Archives Canada, RG85, box 143, Acc. 1997-98/076, file 1000/125, part 5, Inuvik, N.W.T. – General File February 1959–December 1967, FA 85-52, P. E. Moore to Deputy Minister, National Health, Deputy Minister, Northern Affairs and National Resources, "G" Division, R.C.M.P. Regional Superintendent, Foothills Region Chief, Epidemiology, "Urgent Report: Influenza Epidemic," 13 October 1960. [IKU-001315]

86. TRC, NRA, Library and Archives Canada, RG85, box 143, Acc. 1997-98/076, file 1000/125, part 5, Inuvik, N.W.T. – General File February 1959–December 1967, FA 85-52, P. E. Moore to Deputy Minister, Northern Affairs and National Resources, "Urgent Report: Influenza," 28 April 1961. [IKU-001339]

87. TRC, NRA, Library and Archives Canada, RG29, volume 1245, file 312-2-13, volume 2, Report of Medical Health Officer, 26 April 1963. [NPC-600531]

88. TRC, NRA, Anglican Church of Canada, General Synod Archives, ACC-MSCC-GS 75-103, series 2-15, box 30, file 3, "News Letter," May 1966. [AAC-084515]

89. TRC, NRA, Library and Archives Canada, file A3725-2-017, part 1, 1970–1971, Management Services – Whitehorse, Student residence: Indian-Eskimo Affairs Branch, "Whitehorse Student Residence Indian-Eskimo Affairs Branch," A. G. Massé, B. Stanton, S. Meggs, Department of Indian Affairs and Northern Development, Management Services, August 1971, 10. [YHU-090221]

90. TRC, NRA, Government of Northwest Territories Archives, Government of Northwest Territories Legislative Library, Joseph Katz, *Educational Environments of School-Hostel Complexes in the Northwest Territories* (Vancouver, BC: Education Division, Canadian Department of Northern Affairs and National Resources, July 1965), 20. [RCN-013107]

91. TRC, NRA, Government of the Northwest Territories Archives, file 630.012, part 1, Hostels – Churchill, 1964, Archival box 31, Archival Acc. N1994-009, J. Poste to R. L. Graves, 25 November 1964; [CVC-002131] R. L. Graves to A. Whitton, 2 December 1964. [CVC-002144-0001]

92. TRC, NRA, Government of Northwest Territories Archives Pupil Residence – General, 1974–1978 Archival box 3-3, Archival Acc. G1995-004, M. Tatty to B. Lewis, 7 December 1978. [AHU-003901]

93. TRC, NRA, Library and Archives Canada, RG 29, volume 2984, file 851-5-X600, part 10a, J. H. Rocks to R. J. Orange, 3 May 1965. [NPC-620584]

94. TRC, NRA, Government of Northwest Territories Archives, file 311/125B, part 1, School Buildings – Inuvik, 1959–1968, Archival box 87-1, Archival Acc. G1979-003, J. H. Rooks to Superintendent of Schools, Inuvik, Northwest Territories, 5 May 1965. [IKU-001507]

95. TRC, NRA, Library and Archives Canada, RG85, Perm. volume 1441, file 630/111-8, part 3, Govt. Hostel [Anglican] – Fort Simpson, N.W.T. January 1964–December 1965, FA 85-4, T. E. Jones to F. A. G. Carter, 20 October 1965. [BPU-000367]

96. TRC, NRA, Government of Northwest Territories Archives, Directorate School Policy – Education [volume 1], part 1, 05/68–12/69, Archival box 262, Archival Acc. G1999-046, B. C. Gillie to S. M. Hodgson, 21 April 1969. [FNU-001685]

97. TRC, NRA, Government of Northwest Territories – Education, Culture and Employment, file 73-500-402, volume 2, Fort McPherson Hostel [Anglican] – Quarterly Returns [Fort McPher-

son], 01/72–12/76, Transfer No. 0330, box 8-21, R. L. Ha[illegible]ey to J. A. Coady, 27 February 1973. [FHU-002368-0001]

98. TRC, NRA, Government of Northwest Territories – Education, Culture and Employment, file 73-500-402, volume 2, Fort McPherson Hostel [Anglican] – Quarterly Returns [Fort McPherson], 01/72–12/76, Transfer No. 0330, box 8-21, R. J. Morrison to S. M. Hodgson, 27 November 1975. [FHU-002398-0002]

99. Blondin-Perrin, *My Heart Shook*, 95.

100. Canadien, *From Lishamie*, 251.

101. Canadien, *From Lishamie*, 253.

102. TRC, AVS, Richard Kaiyogan, Statement to the Truth and Reconciliation Commission of Canada, Inuvik, Northwest Territories, 30 June 2011, Statement Number: SC091.

103. TRC, AVS, Florence Barnaby, Statement to the Truth and Reconciliation Commission of Canada, Winnipeg, Manitoba, 15 June 2010, Statement Number: 02-MB-16JU10-014.

104. TRC, AVS, Willy Carpenter, Statement to the Truth and Reconciliation Commission of Canada, Tuktoyaktuk, Northwest Territories, 20 September 2011, Statement Number: 2011-0353.

105. TRC, AVS, Steve Lafferty, Statement to the Truth and Reconciliation Commission of Canada, Fort Smith, Northwest Territories, 6 May 2011, Statement Number: 2011-0392.

106. TRC, AVS, Brenda Jancke, Statement to the Truth and Reconciliation Commission of Canada, Cambridge Bridge, Nunavut, 11 April 2011, Statement Number: SP009.

107. TRC, AVS, Bernice Lyall, Statement to the Truth and Reconciliation Commission of Canada, Cambridge Bay, Nunavut, 11 April 2011, Statement Number: SP009.

108. TRC, NRA, Library and Archives Canada, RG85, volume 708, file 630/105-7, part 3, High School Facilities – Yellowknife [Public and Separate School], 1958–1959, F. J. G. Cunningham to Sivertz, 27 January 1958. [RCN-000641] For Akaitcho biography see: Helm and Gillespie, "Akaitcho," 209.

109. TRC, NRA, Library and Archives Canada, RG22, Perm. volume 864, file 40-2-136, part 2, Hostels in N.W.T. and Y.T. – General January 1959–December 1960, FA 22-1, P. Piché to B. G. Sivertz, 16 July 1960. [RCN-008605-0003]

110. TRC, NRA, Government of Northwest Territories Archives, file 600-1-1, part 4, School Policy [and Hostels], 1959–1961, Archival box 202-1, Archival Acc. G-1979-003, Department of Northern Affairs and National Resources News Release, "Historic Names for Northern Schools and Residences," 2 March 1961. [RCN-010612-0002]

111. Archives Canada, "Whitehorse Diocese collection," http://www.archivescanada.ca/english/search/ItemDisplay.asp?sessionKey=1143412449030_206_191_57_196&l=0&lvl=2&v=0&coll=1&itm=268856&rt=1&bill=1.

112. TRC, NRA, Government of Northwest Territories – Education, Culture and Employment, Schools Registers and Hostels Forms 1961–1974 [Ukkivik Hostel], Transfer No. 0274, box 4-23, "Student Residence Quarterly Return," September 1971. [FBS-000001]

113. TRC, NRA, INAC – Archival Unit – Ottawa, file 630/500-10, D. Marsh to B. Thorsteinsson, 9 September 1964. [CVC-001210-0001]

114. TRC, NRA, INAC – Archival Unit – Ottawa, file 250/25-23, volume 1, R. L. Kennedy to R. Haramburu, 26 November 1964. [CVC-000415-0001]

115. TRC, NRA, INAC – Archival Unit – Ottawa, file 250/25-23, volume 1, Director to Deputy Minister, 3 December 1964. [CVC-000415-0000]

116. TRC, NRA, INAC – Archival Unit – Ottawa, file 630/500-10, volume 3, J. Dufour to F. Dunford, 19 May 1970. [CVC-001236]

117. TRC, NRA, INAC – Resolution Sector – IRS Historical Files Collection – Ottawa, file 600-1-6, volume 6, Control 440-10, Director, Ottawa to Administrator of the Mackenzie, "Regulations in Pupil Residence," 27 January 1965. [NCA-016417]

118. TRC, NRA, Library and Archives Canada, RG85, Acc. 1997-98/076, box 131, file 680-1-15, volume 4, F. Dunford to R. Ritcey, 26 May 1970. [CVC-000504]

119. TRC, NRA, Government of Northwest Territories Archives, file T-600-1-1, part 2a, Education and Schools – N.W.T. [General and Policy] 1968–1969, Archival box 203-3, Archival Acc. G-1979-003, "Report on the Inter-relation of Religious Organizations and the Northern Education Program," 28 January 1968, 3–4. [RCN-011441-0001]

120. TRC, NRA, Anglican Church of Canada, General Synod Archives ACC-MSCC-GS 75-103, series 2.15, box 25, file 14, H. G. Cook to Principals, 4 September 1959. [AAC-087024]

121. Honigmann and Honigmann, *Arctic Townsmen*, 180.

122. TRC, NRA, Beaufort-Delta Education Council Warehouse, Inuvik, NWT, Grollier Try-Action File 1984–88, "Additional facilities and Equipment Provided by Father Ruyant," J. Maher to D. Ramsden, undated. [GHU-000675-0001]

123. TRC, NRA, Beaufort-Delta Education Council Warehouse, Inuvik, NWT, Grollier Try-Action File 1984–88, M. Ruyant to J. Maher, 27 February 1987. [GHU-000673]

124. Cross Country Ski de Fond, "History of TEST," http://www.cccski.com/About/History/Photos-and-Stories/The-History-of-T-E-S-T—%281%29.aspx#.UvukJV6Lnv0.

125. TRC, NRA, Library and Archives Canada, RG85, volume 708, file 630/105-7, part 3, High School Facilities – Yellowknife [Public and Separate School], 1958–1959, A. J. Boxer to J. M. Black, "Progress Report – Yellowknife Hostel. Initial Period to New Year," 9 December 1958. [AHU-000005-0000]

126. TRC, NRA, Library and Archives Canada, RG85, Perm. volume 1373, file 630/105-10, part 3, Govt. Hostel – Yellowknife, N.W.T. January 1960–August 1962, FA 85-4, "Superintendent's Hostel Report, Akaitcho," G. H. Needham, 7 February 1961, 3. [AHU-000684-0001]

127. TRC, NRA, Library and Archives Canada, RG85, box 125, Acc. 1997-98/076, file 630/105-10, part 2, Govt. Hostel – Yellowknife, N.W.T February 1959–December 1959, FA 85-52, J. M. Black to Chief Superintendent of Schools, 1 December 1959. [AHU-000588]

128. TRC, NRA, Library and Archives Canada, RG85, Acc. 1997-98/076, box 131, file 680-1-15, volume 1, "Memo – Churchill School Data," undated. [CVC-001896-0000]

129. TRC, NRA, Library and Archives Canada, RG85, volume 1266, file 1000/158, part 2, "Welfare Teacher's Monthly Report," E. Herauf, 18 March 1957. [CIU-000444]

130. TRC, NRA, Library and Archives Canada, RG85, volume 1348, file 1000/158, part 3, W. G. Devitt for J. V. Jacobsen to T. Chaput, 20 January 1959. [CIU-000521]

131. TRC, NRA, Anglican Church of Canada, General Synod Archives ACC-MSCC-GS 75-103, series 2-15, box 30, file 3, "Residential Schools & Hostels, Division of M.S.C.C., Newsletter Spring – 1963." [AAC-084493]

132. Quassa, *We Need to Know*, 29, 36.

133. TRC, AVS, David Simailik, Statement to the Truth and Reconciliation Commission of Canada, Baker Lake, Nunavut, 1 July 2011, Statement Number: SP032.

134. TRC, AVS, Alex Alikashuak, Statement to the Truth and Reconciliation Commission of Canada, Winnipeg, Manitoba, 16 June 2010, Statement Number: 02-MB-16JU10-137.

135. TRC, AVS, Betsy Annahatak, Statement to the Truth and Reconciliation Commission of Canada, Halifax, Nova Scotia, 28 October 2011, Statement Number: 2011-2896.

136. TRC, NRA, Library and Archives Canada, RG85, volume 708, file 630/105-7, part 3, High School Facilities – Yellowknife [Public and Separate School], 1958–1959, A. J. Boxer to J. M. Black, 9 December 1958, 4. [AHU-000005-0000]

137. TRC, NRA, INAC – Resolution Sector – IRS Historical Files Collection – Ottawa, file 600-1-6, volume 8, Hostel Management N.W.T. [General and Policy], July 1965–April 1966, D. G. Davis for F. A. G. Carter to C. Gilles, 8 October 1965. [BTU-000294]

138. TRC, NRA, Government of Northwest Territories Archives, Government of Northwest Territories Legislative Library, Joseph Katz, *Educational Environments of School-Hostel Complexes in the Northwest Territories* (Vancouver, BC: Education Division, Canadian Department of Northern Affairs and National Resources, July 1965), 8. [RCN-013107]

139. TRC, NRA, INAC – Resolution Sector – IRS Historical Files Collection – Ottawa, file 600-1-6, volume 6, Hostel Management – N.W.T. [General and Policy], March 1964–January 1965, "Staff Fluent in Native Languages of the Pupil," 29 August 1964. [RCN-002549-0001]

140. TRC, NRA, Government of Northwest Territories Archives, Pupil Residence – General, 1974–1978, Archival box 3-3, Archival Acc. G1995-004, J. MacEachern to L. Gilberg, 17 January 1977, 4. [LHU-000676-0002]

141. TRC, NRA, Government of Northwest Territories Archives, Pupil Residence – General, 1973–1978, Archival box 4-2, Archival Acc. G1995-004, B. Lewis to Deputy Commissioner, 1 December 1977. [LHU-000684]

142. TRC, NRA, Government of Northwest Territories Archives, Pupil Residence – General, 1973–1978, Archival box 4-2, Archival Acc. G1995-004, R. L. Julyan to R. W. Halifax, 28 December 1977, 7. [LHU-000685-0001]

143. Repeal 43 Committee, "School Corporal Punishment," http://www.repeal43.org/school-corporal-punishment/.

144. TRC, NRA, Library and Archives Canada, RG85, volume 708, file 630/105-7, part 3, High School Facilities – Yellowknife [Public and Separate School], 1958–1959, A. J. Boxer to J. M. Black, 9 December 1958, 5. [AHU-000005-0000]

145. TRC, NRA, Government of Northwest Territories Archives, file 630-105/12-1,2,3, Akaitcho Hall, Yellowknife, 1961–1965, Archival box 229-1, Archival Acc. G-1979-003, A. J. Boxer to W. G. Booth, 19 December 1962; [AHU-001319] TRC, NRA, Government of Northwest Territories Archives, file 0000, Akaitcho Hall General, 1965–1968, Archival box 3, Archival Acc. N1994-009, "Report of Informal Investigation into Conditions in Girls' Dormitory, Akaitcho Hall," N. J. Macpherson, 18 December 1964. [AHU-003821-0001]

146. Clifton, *Inuvik Study*, 55.

147. Clifton, *Inuvik Study*, 52.

148. King, *School at Mopass*, 77–78.

149. TRC, NRA, Library and Archives Canada, RG10, volume 13836, file 1/1-18-7, part 3, 1958–1965, I. M. McCoy to R. F. Davey, 26 June 1964. [CAR-010114]

150. Peterson, "Sir Joseph Bernier Federal Day School," 5.

151. TRC, NRA, INAC – Resolution Sector – IRS Historical Files Collection – Ottawa, 853/1-13, 1965–1967, volume 2, 18 January 1966. [YKS-003126-0003]

152. TRC, NRA, Unknown Education, Whitehorse Hostel, 25-1-014, volume 2, Nov/63–June/68, D. S. Fraser to L. Badine, 22 February 1966. [YKS-000131]

153. TRC, NRA, Government of Northwest Territories Archives, file 630-105-10, part 5, Government Hostel, [Akaitcho Hall] Yellowknife, N.W.T., 1966–1969, Archival box 228-1, Archival Acc.

G-1979-003, R. Haggart, "A Friend Must Be Approved," *The Telegram*, Toronto, 3 March 1969. [AHU-001617-0001]

154. TRC, NRA, Government of Northwest Territories Archives, file 630-105-10, part 5, Government Hostel, [Akaitcho Hall] Yellowknife, N.W.T, 1966–1969, Archival box 228-1, Archival Acc. G-1979-003, J. Chrétien to A. Gillespie, 28 March 1969. [AHU-001624]

155. TRC, NRA, Government of Northwest Territories Archives, file 630-105-10, part 5, Government Hostel, [Akaitcho Hall] Yellowknife, N.W.T, 1966–1969, Archival box 228-1, Archival Acc. G-1979-003, Government of Northwest Territories press release, 1 April 1969. [AHU-001629]

156. TRC, NRA, Government of Northwest Territories Archives, file 630-105-10, part 5, Government Hostel, [Akaitcho Hall] Yellowknife, N.W.T, 1966–1969, Archival box 228-1, Archival Acc. G-1979-003, S. M. Hodgson to J. Chrétien, 2 April 1969. [AHU-001630-0000]

157. TRC, NRA, Government of Northwest Territories Archives, file 630-105-10, part 5, Government Hostel, [Akaitcho Hall] Yellowknife, N.W.T, 1966–1969, Archival box 228-1, Archival Acc. G-1979-003, N. J. Macpherson, "Statement of Events at Akaitcho Hall, Saturday, February 22, 1969," 24 February 1969. [AHU-001596-0003]

158. TRC, NRA, Government of Northwest Territories Archives, file 630-105-10, part 5, Government Hostel, [Akaitcho Hall] Yellowknife, N.W.T, 1966–1969, Archival box 228-1, Archival Acc. G-1979-003, J. Chrétien to S. M. Hodgson, 10 April 1969. [AHU-001631]

159. TRC, NRA, Government of Northwest Territories Archives, Akaitcho Hall Reports, 1969–1970, Archival box 9-2, Archival Acc. G1995-004, "Akaitcho Hall – Yellowknife." [AHU-003837] For reference to twenty-seven-page document see: TRC, NRA, Government of Northwest Territories Archives, file 630-105-10, part 5, Government Hostel, [Akaitcho Hall] Yellowknife, N.W.T, 1966–1969, Archival box 228-1, Archival Acc. G-1979-003, R. Haggart, "A Friend Must Be Approved," *The Telegram*, Toronto, 3 March 1969, 1. [AHU-001617-0001]

160. TRC, NRA, Government of Northwest Territories – Education, Culture and Employment, AKH Staff Handbook, 1981–1982, Transfer No. 1419, box 11, M. Marykuca to All Staff, 3 March 1981. [AHU-003013]

161. TRC, NRA, INAC – Resolution Sector – IRS Historical Files Collection – Ottawa, file 600-1-6, volume 11, Hostel Management – N.W.T. [General and Policy], August 1967–April 1969, L. Holman to B. C. Gillie, 28 March 1969. [SHU-000037-0001]

162. TRC, NRA, Beaufort-Delta Education Council Warehouse, Inuvik, NWT, General Children Correspondence [box 44], L. Holman to R. Buie, 30 October 1967. [SHU-000796]

163. TRC, NRA, INAC – Resolution Sector – IRS Historical Files Collection – Ottawa, file 600-1-6, volume 11, Hostel Management – N.W.T. [General and Policy], August 1967–April 1969, L. Holman to B. C. Gillie, 28 March 1969. [SHU-000037-0001]

164. TRC, NRA, Government of Northwest Territories – Education, Culture and Employment, file 73-500-400/A, volume 3, Inuvik Hostel Stringer Hall [Anglican] – Quarterly Returns [Inuvik], 01/73–04/72, Transfer No. 0330, box 8-3, P. Stewart and forty-nine others to D. C. Danks, 15 November 1974. [SHU-000489-0001]

165. TRC, NRA, Government of Northwest Territories – Education, Culture and Employment, file 73-500-400/A, volume 3, Inuvik Hostel Stringer Hall [Anglican] – Quarterly Returns, Inuvik, 01/73–04/72, Transfer No. 0330, box 8-3, H. Firth and three others to Dear Sir, 22 November 1974. [SHU-000623]

166. TRC, NRA, Government of Northwest Territories Archives, Pupil Residence – General, 1974–1978, Archival box 3-3, Archival Acc. G1995-004, J. F. Blewett to Director, Department of Education, 6 December 1974. [SHU-000625]

167. TRC, NRA, Beaufort-Delta Education Council Warehouse, Inuvik, NWT, [Grollier Hall] Student Files Pre: 1991 K-Z, E. Lavoie to J. and [name redacted], 10 October 1989. [GHU-000573-0003]

168. TRC, NRA, Beaufort-Delta Education Council Warehouse, Inuvik, NWT, [Grollier Hall] Student Files: 1989–1993, A-I, 1/2, "Grollier Hall Incident Report," 27 November 1991. [GHU-000445-0016]

169. TRA, NRA, Government of Northwest Territories Archives, Pupil Residence – General, 1973–1978, Archival box 4-2, Archival Acc. G1995-004, G. Black, 28 February 1973, 2. [FNU-001748]

170. TRC, NRA, Government of Northwest Territories Archives, Pupil Residence – General, 1973–1978, Archival box 4-2, Archival Acc. G1995-004, R. L. Julyan to R. W. Halifax, 28 December 1977. [LHU-000685-0001]

171. TRC, NRA, INAC – Archival Unit – Ottawa, file 250/25-23, volume 1, unsigned to Bishop Marsh, 9 September 1965. [CVC-000450]

172. TRC, NRA, Library and Archives Canada – Burnaby Yukon Hostel, file No. 25-1-012, volume 3, July/65–Aug/66, A. W. Ratcliffe to Indian Commissioner for B.C., 27 July 1965, 2. [YHU-090129]

173. TRC, NRA, Library and Archives Canada, file A3725-2-017, part 1, 1970–1971, Management Services – Whitehorse, Student residence: Indian-Eskimo Affairs Branch, "Whitehorse Student Residence Indian-Eskimo Affairs Branch," A. G. Massé, B. Stanton, S. Meggs, Department of Indian Affairs and Northern Development, Management Services, August 1971, 7–9. [YHU-090221]

174. TRC, NRA, Government of Northwest Territories – Education, Culture and Employment, file 73-500-402, volume 2, Fort McPherson Hostel [Anglican] – Quarterly Returns [Fort McPherson], 01/72–12/76, Transfer No. 0330, box 8-21, L. Donovan to Mr. Mayne, 15 January 1976. [FHU-002394]

175. TRC, NRA, Government of Northwest Territories Archives, Pupil Residence – General, 1973–1978, Archival box 4-2, Archival Acc. G1995-004, R. L. Julyan to R. W. Halifax, 28 December 1977. [LHU-000685-0001]

176. TRC, NRA, Government of Northwest Territories Archives, Government of Northwest Territories Legislative Library, Joseph Katz, *Educational Environments of School-Hostel Complexes in the Northwest Territories* (Vancouver, BC: Education Division, Canadian Department of Northern Affairs and National Resources, July 1965), 10. [RCN-013107]

177. TRC, NRA, Government of Northwest Territories Archives, Government of Northwest Territories Legislative Library, Joseph Katz, *Educational Environments of School-Hostel Complexes in the Northwest Territories* (Vancouver, BC: Education Division, Canadian Department of Northern Affairs and National Resources, July 1965), 19. [RCN-013107]

178. Clifton, *Inuvik Study*, 71.

179. Clifton, *Inuvik Study*, 67, 74.

180. TRC, NRA, Library and Archives Canada, RG85, volume 1445, file 630/500-10, volume 2, J. G. Ratz to Administrator of the Arctic, 5 October 1965. [CVC-000981]

181. TRC, NRA, Library and Archives Canada, RG85, volume 1445, file 630/500-10, volume 2, A. Stevenson to Director, 5 October 1965; [CVC-000987] A. Stevenson to Director, 15 October 1965. [CVC-000968]

182. TRC, NRA, INAC – Archival Unit – Ottawa, file N-5150/C6-3, volume 1, 1/72–4/74, R. Ritcey to F. Dunford, 17 January 1972. [CVC-000288]

183. TRC, NRA, INAC – Archival Unit – Ottawa, file N-5150/C6-3, volume 1, 1/72–4/74, R. Ritcey to J. Dalgetty, 23 August 1972; [CVC-000244] W. Eliott to J. A. Provins, 27 August 1972. [CVC-002453-0001]

184. TRC, NRA, Government of Northwest Territories – Education, Culture and Employment, file 73-500-402, volume 2, Fort McPherson Hostel [Anglican] – Quarterly Returns [Fort McPherson], 01/72–12/76, Transfer No. 0330, box 8-21, J. A. Coady to J. Simon, 11 December 1974. [FHU-002382]

185. TRC, NRA, Government of Northwest Territories Archives, CR#70-820-000, Pupil Residences – General, 01/72–06/74, Archival box 260, Archival Acc. G1999-046, S. M. Hodgson to J. Simon, 13 June 1974. [FHU-003783]

186. TRC, NRA, Government of Northwest Territories – Education, Culture and Employment, file 73-500-402, volume 2, Fort McPherson Hostel [Anglican] – Quarterly Returns [Fort McPherson], 01/72–12/76, Transfer No. 0330, box 8-21, N. J. Macpherson to Member of the Executive for Education, 21 April 1976. [FHU-002403]

187. TRC, NRA, Government of Northwest Territories Archives, Confidential, Hostels, 1971–1974, Archival box 8-24, Archival Acc. G1995-004, L. P. Holman to J. Coady, 19 June 1972. [SHU-000488]

188. TRC, NRA, Government of Northwest Territories Archives, file 630-105-10, part 5, Government Hostel, [Akaitcho Hall] Yellowknife, N.W.T, 1966–1969, Archival box 228-1, Archival Acc. G-1979-003, B. C. Gillie, Signed for K. W. Hawkins to D. W. Simpson, 27 December 1966. [AHU-001529]

189. TRC, NRA, Government of Northwest Territories Archives, file 630/105-10, part 6, Government Hostel [Akaitcho Hall] Yellowknife, N.W.T, 1958–1961, Archival box 228-2, Archival Acc. G-1979-003, undated letter from E. Nind, 23 July 1970. [AHU-001636-0001]

190. TRC, NRA, CGS Records Warehouse, Iqaluit, Government of Nunavut, Akaitcho Hall Correspondence, 1988–1989 Kitikmeot Region [Kugluktuk] – box 202, M. Pardy to M. McLeod, 19 January 1988. [AHU-003972]

191. TRC, NRA, INAC – Resolution Sector – IRS Historical Files Collection – Ottawa, file 853/25-1, volume 2 (Ctrl #49-5), F. Barnes to R. F. Davey, 1 October 1960. [NCA-009383]

192. TRC, NRA, Library and Archives Canada – Burnaby, Protestant Hostel, file 25-2-943, volume 1, Aug/60–Feb/62, F. Barnes to W. Grant, 4 October 1960. [YHU-090125]

193. TRC, NRA, Library and Archives Canada – Burnaby, Admissions/Discharges R.C. Hostel, 25-2-941, volume 4, Sept/60–Dec/62, E. A. Cullinane to W. E. Grant, 2 May 1961. [CDH-090003]

194. TRC, NRA, Unknown Education, Whitehorse Hostel, 25-1-014, volume 2, Nov/63–June/68, M. Piché to A. Fry, 1 March 1965. [YKS-000125]

195. TRC, NRA, Library and Archives Canada – Burnaby, file 801/25-8, volume 11, Education Assistance, 10/1964–06/1968, FA 10-151, V1989-90/101, Archival box 42, 14 October 1964. [CDH-200617]

196. TRC, NRA, Library and Archives Canada – Burnaby, file 801/25-2-14, volume 2, Admission and Discharge – R.C. Hostel, 05/1967–01/1969, FA 10-151, V1989-90/101, Archival box 38, G. Michaud to Indian Affairs Branch, 28 November 1967. [CDH-001202]

197. TRC, NRA, Beaufort-Delta Education Council Warehouse, Inuvik, NWT, Drop Outs 1967–1968, 600-1-3 [box 44], L. P. Holman to R. Buie, 4 December 1967. [SHU-000798]

198. TRC, NRA, Beaufort-Delta Education Council Warehouse, Inuvik, NWT, General Children Correspondence [box 44], L. P. Holman to R. Buie, 14 February 1968; [SHU-000803] L. P. Holman to R. Buie, 16 February 1968. [SHU-000804]

199. TRC, NRA, Government of Northwest Territories – Education, Culture and Employment, Rafferty – General Correspondence, 1985, Transfer No. 1530, box 14, J. Rafferty to E. Duggan, 26 March 1985. [AHU-003940]

200. TRC, AVS, Peggy Tologanak, Statement to the Truth and Reconciliation Commission of Canada, Iqaluit, Nunavut, 25 March 2011, Statement Number: SP008.

201. TRC, NRA, Government of Northwest Territories Archives, Confidential, Hostels, 1971–1974, Archival box 8-24, Archival Acc. G1995-004, L. Holman to J. Coady, 7 September 1972. [IKU-001764]

202. TRC, NRA, Anglican Church of Canada, Diocese of the Arctic, General Synod Archives, file 110-09, Stringer Hall, Accession M96-7, series 2:1, Notice of missing boys, 1972. [AGS-000341]

203. TRC, NRA, Government of Northwest Territories Archives, Confidential, Hostels, 1971–1974, Archival box 8-24, Archival Acc. G1995-004, Leonard Holman to J. Coady, 14 July 1972. [SHU-000486] For distance, see: Inuvik to Tuktoyaktuk Highway, http://actionplan.gc.ca/en/initiative/inuvik-tuktoyaktuk-highway.

204. TRC, AVS, Lavinia Brown, Statement to the Truth and Reconciliation Commission of Canada, Winnipeg, Manitoba, 16 June 2010, Statement Number: SC093.

205. King, *School at Mopass*, 78.

206. TRC, NRA, Government of Northwest Territories – Education, Culture and Employment, Staff Meetings, 1990–1991, Transfer No. 1530, box 17, "Coping with Death," 16 January 1992; [AHU-005021] Government of Northwest Territories – Education, Culture and Employment, Akaitcho Hall Administration, 1992–1993, Transfer No. 1531, box 5, Script for radio interview, 17 June 1992; [AHU-004037-0001] Government of Northwest Territories – Education, Culture and Employment, Misc. Correspondence, 1991–1994, Transfer No. 1531, box 5, Feltham to Paradis, 27 April 1992. [AHU-004036-0003]

207. For examples, see: TRC, NRA, Government of Northwest Territories Archives, file 630-105/10, 12-1, part 1, Sir John Franklin School, Akaitcho Hall, 1959–1960, Archival box 228-8, Archival Acc. G-1979-003, A. J. Boxer to W. G. Booth, 5 October 1959; [AHU-001109] A. J. Boxer to J. M. Black, 6 October 1959; [AHU-001110] A. J. Boxer to J. M. Black, 22 October 1959. [AHU-001112-0002]

208. TRC, NRA, Government of Northwest Territories Archives, file 630-105/10, 12-1, part 1, Sir John Franklin School, Akaitcho Hall, 1959–1960, Archival box 228-8, Archival Acc. G-1979-003, A. J. Boxer to W. G. Booth, 2 February 1960. [AHU-001154]

209. Nickerson, *Legal Drinking Age*, 20.

210. TRC, NRA, Government of Northwest Territories Archives, file 630-105/12-1-1, part 3, General, Reports Akaitcho Hall, Yellowknife, 1961–1966, Archival box 229-3, Archival Acc. G-1979-003, A. J. Boxer to Staff, 22 November 1965. [AHU-001471-0001]

211. TRC, NRA, Government of Northwest Territories Archives, Akaitcho Hall Reports, 1971–1972, Archival box 9-3, Archival Acc. G1995-004, A. J. Boxer to N. Macpherson, 18 October 1971. [AHU-003301-0003]

212. Clifton, *Inuvik Study*, 72.

213. Clifton, *Inuvik Study*, 72.

214. TRC, NRA, Government of Northwest Territories Archives, CR# 71-602-000, Pupil Residence – General, 04/1968–12/71, Archival box 266, Archival Acc. G1999-046, J. F. Blewett to Director, Department of Education, 4 March 1971. [AHU-003855-0002]

215. TRC, NRA, Government of Northwest Territories Archives, Akaitcho Hall Students, 1972–1973, Archival box 9-16, Archival Acc. G1995-004, A. J. Boxer to W. Stapleton, 21 February 1973. [AHU-004832]

216. TRC, NRA, Beaufort-Delta Education Council Warehouse, Inuvik, NWT, Residences – General – Correspondence [box 42], [name redacted] to J. Maher, 27 October 1986. [GHU-001316]

217. TRC, NRA, CGS Records Warehouse, Iqaluit, Government of Nunavut, Cambridge Bay – 1984–1987 Kitikmeot Region [Kugluktuk] – box 139, M. McLeod to [name redacted], 17 February 1987. [AHU-004546-0016]

218. TRC, NRA, Government of Northwest Territories Archives, file 630-105/10, 12-1, part 1, Sir John Franklin School, Akaitcho Hall, 1959–1960, Archival box 228-8, Archival Acc. G-1979-003, A. J. Boxer to W. G. Booth, 5 October 1959. [AHU-001109]

219. TRC, NRA, Government of Northwest Territories Archives, file 630-105/12-1-1, part 3, General, Reports Akaitcho Hall, Yellowknife, 1961–1966, Archival box 229-3, Archival Acc. G-1979-003, B. C. Gillie to N. J. Macpherson, 24 June 1966. [AHU-001507]

220. TRC, NRA, Government of Northwest Territories – Education, Culture and Employment, Student Information, 1970–1971, Transfer No. 1419, box 21, A. J. Boxer and R. L. Toutant to J. Walker, 20 June 1971; [AHU-003264] A. J. Boxer and R. L. Toutant to R. Graves, 20 June 1971; [AHU-003262] A. J. Boxer and R. L. Toutant to E. Shorn, 20 June 1971; [AHU-003261] A.J. Boxer and R.L Toutant to J. Coady, 20 June 1971; [AHU-003263]. A. J. Boxer and R. L. Toutant to H. Darkes, 20 June 1971. [AHU-003265]

221. TRC, NRA, Beaufort-Delta Education Council Warehouse, Inuvik, NWT, Grollier Hall 1965–66 [box 12], M. Ruyant to R. M. Buie, 5 December 1966. [GHU-001290]

222. TRC, NRA, Beaufort-Delta Education Council Warehouse, Inuvik, NWT, Refusals 600-1-4-1 [box 44], L. P. Holman to R. Buie, 9 October 1967. [SHU-000791]

223. TRC, NRA, Beaufort-Delta Education Council Warehouse, Inuvik, NWT, Refusals, 1969–1970 [box 25], R. Buie to P. Castle, 25 July 1968. [SHU-000812]

224. TRC, NRA, Government of Northwest Territories Archives, Pupil Residence – General, 1974–1978, Archival box 3-3, Archival Acc. G1995-004, P. Ernerk to Minister of Education, 15 December 1976. [AHU-003892-0001]

225. TRC, NRA, Government of Northwest Territories – Education, Culture and Employment, Residences 1976–1977 [Akaitcho Hall], Transfer No. 0349, box 25-1, "Student Residence Quarterly Return, Akaitcho Hall, 30 June 1977," 10. [AHU-000881]

226. TRC, NRA, CGS Records Warehouse, Iqaluit, Government of Nunavut, Cambridge Bay – 1984–1987, Kitikmeot Region [Kugluktuk] – box 139, J. Rafferty to [names redacted], 22 October 1984. [AHU-004550-0002]

227. TRC, NRA, CGS Records Warehouse, Iqaluit, Government of Nunavut, Spence Bay – Active and Former Students, 1984-1987, Kitikmeot Region [Kugluktuk] – box 139, J. Rafferty to [names redacted], 20 December 1984. [AHU-004522-0006]

228. TRC, NRA, Beaufort-Delta Education Council Warehouse, Inuvik, NWT, [Grollier Hall] Student Files Pre: 1991 K-Z, "Contract between Grollier Hall and [name redacted]," 11 October 1989. [GHU-000489-0001]

229. See for example: TRC, NRA, Beaufort-Delta Education Council Warehouse, Inuvik, NWT, [Grollier Hall] Student Files 1992-1995: A-K, B. Lavoie to [name redacted], 21 January 1992; [GHU-000431-0007] B. Lavoie to [name redacted] 22 January 1992; [GHU-000434-0004] [Grollier Hall] Student Files 1992–1995: F-T, D. Mitchell to Whom it May Concern, 12 February 1992; [GHU-000476-0008] [Grollier Hall] Student Files [1989–1993]: K-W, 2/2, D. Mitchell to B.

Larocque, 18 September 1992; [GHU-000610-0011] [Grollier Hall] Student Files: 1989–1993, A-I, 1/2, B. Lavoie to [names redacted], 21 September 1992; [GHU-000319-0017] [Grollier Hall] Student Files [1989–1993]: K-W, 2/2, B. Lavoie to [name redacted], 21 September 1992. [GHU-000623-0005]

230. TRC, NRA, Government of Northwest Territories – Education, Culture and Employment, Akaitcho Hall, 1977–1982, Transfer No. 0342, box 1, M. Marykuca to M. S. Naidoo, 23 January 1980. [AHU-003905-0001]

231. TRC, NRA, Government of Northwest Territories – Education, Culture and Employment, Akaitcho Hall, 1979–1981, Transfer No. 0340, box 4, C. J. Dent to T. Butters, 4 February 1980. [AHU-003907]

232. TRC, NRA, Government of Northwest Territories – Education, Culture and Employment, Meetings [Advisory Board – Student, Staff, Heads, SJF Staff], 1980–1986, Transfer No. 1531, box 4, "Akaitcho Hall Report for Community Education Committee Meeting," R. Menagh, 5 May 1982. [AHU-005009-0000]

233. TRC, NRA, Government of Northwest Territories – Education, Culture and Employment, Akaitcho Hall, 1977–1982, Transfer No. 0342, box 1, D. Palfrey to D. Patterson, 14 June 1982. [AHU-003928]

234. TRC, NRA, Government of Northwest Territories – Education, Culture and Employment, Parents Concerns, 1982, Transfer No. 1419, box 11, untitled report of committee of parents from the Keewatin Region, D. Palfrey, 8 June 1982. [AHU-003927-0001]

235. TRC, NRA, Government of Northwest Territories – Education, Culture and Employment, Quarterly Reports from Staff, 1987–1988, Transfer No. 1530, box 15, D. Gibson, "Quarterly Report – Boys Dorm," 31 December 1987. [AHU-004964]

236. TRC, NRA, Government of Northwest Territories – Education, Culture and Employment, Misc. Correspondence, 1991–1994, Transfer No. 1531, box 5, "Akaitcho Hall – Draft Proposal Interim Plan Re: Alcohol/Drug involved Students," 7 November 1990. [AHU-004036-0008]

237. TRC, NRA, Government of Northwest Territories – Education, Culture and Employment, Akaitcho Hall, 1992–1994, Transfer No. 0247, box 9, T. Gavac to J. Antoine, 12 March 1992. [AHU-004033-0000]

238. TRC, NRA, Government of Northwest Territories – Education, Culture and Employment, 114 GNWT Policies and Information, 1991,Transfer No. 1530, box 9, J. Martin to M. Mercredi, 12 June 1991. [AHU-004020]

239. TRC, NRA, Government of Northwest Territories – Education, Culture and Employment, Quarterly Reports for Staff, 1992–1993, Transfer No. 1530, box 15, "Akaitcho Hall Girls Dormitory, March 1992," M. Paradis, March 1992. [AHU-004879-0000]

240. TRC, NRA, Government of Northwest Territories – Education, Culture and Employment, Admissions/Dismissals [Procedures – Reports – Correspondence], 1992–1993, Transfer No. 1530, box 14, V. J. Feltham to M. Mercredi, 30 November 1992; [AHU-005264] L. Klasen, 30 November 1992. [AHU-005263]

241. TRC, NRA, INAC – Resolution Sector – IRS Historical Files Collection – Ottawa, 853/1-13, 1965–1967, volume 2, M. Brodhead to Area Personal [sic] Officer, 28 September 1966. [YHU-090123]

242. TRC, NRA, Library and Archives Canada – Burnaby Admissions and Discharges, Yukon Hostel, file 25-2-012, volume 2, Apr/67–Dec/68, K. W. Johnson to Edith Josie, 8 September 1967. [YKS-003192]

243. TRC, NRA, Library and Archives of Canada, R776-0-5 (RG55), volume 290, TB 626127, May-14-1964, "Details of request to the Honourable the Treasury Board," 20 April 1964. [120.10656A]

244. TRC, CAR, Anglican Church of Canada, Diocese of the Arctic, Diocese of the Arctic fonds, 1850-1999, series 2, D. B. Marsh Records, 930-1984; Predominant 1950–1972, sub-series 2-6, Diocesan files. 1938-1983, Accession, M96-7 box 92, file 1a. D. Marsh to B. Thorsteinsson, 9 September 1964. [39b-c000095-d0175-002]

245. TRC, CAR, Anglican Church of Canada, Diocese of the Arctic, Diocese of the Arctic fonds, 1850–1999, series 2, D. B. Marsh Records, 930-1984; Predominant 1950–1972, sub-series 2-6, Diocesan files 1938–1983, Accession M96-7, box 92, file 1a, D. Marsh to B. Thorsteinsson, 10 August 1964. [39b-c000095-d0175-004]

246. TRC, NRA, INAC – Archival Unit – Ottawa N-5150-/C6-4, R. Ritcey to J. R. Witty, 5 December 1973. [CVC-000041]

247. TRC, NRA, INAC – Archival Unit – Ottawa, file 250/25-23, volume 1, E. A. Côté to Executive Assistant to the Minister, 28 July 1964. [CVC-000467-0000]

248. TRC, NRA, Library and Archives Canada, RG85, Perm. volume 685, file A 680-1-15, part 1, Vocational Training – Churchill, March 1964–March 1965, FA 85-1, Regional Administrator to Arctic Administration, Ottawa, 11 March 1965. [CVC-002449]

249. TRC, NRA, Library and Archives Canada, RG85, Acc. 1997-98/076, box 131, file 680-1-15, volume 1, J. B. H. Gunn to Administrator of the Arctic, 7 December 1966. [CVC-001853]

250. TRC, NRA, Library and Archives Canada, RG85, Acc. 1997-98/076, box 131, file 680-1-15, volume 1, CBC Radio News script, 29 December 1966. [CVC-001844]

251. TRC, NRA, Library and Archives Canada, RG22, Perm. volume 1271, file 40-2-136, part 4, Hostels in N.W.T. and Y.T. – General January 1965–December 1966, FA 22-31, A. Laing to D. B. Marsh, 19 July 1966. [RCN-009554]

252. TRC, NRA, Government of Northwest Territories Archives, file A-630/169-1, part 4, Govt. School Facilities, Frobisher Bay, N.W.T. 1968–1969, Archival box 249-9, Archival Acc. G1979-003, "Frobisher Bay Academic and Occupational School," W. W. Buell, 17 December 1968. [FBS-000402] For date of the opening of Ukkivik see: TRC, NRA, Government of Northwest Territories – Education, Culture and Employment, Schools Registers and Hostels Forms 1961–1974 [Ukkivik Hostel], Transfer No. 0274, box 4-23, "Student Residence Quarterly Return," September 1971. [FBS-000001]

253. TRC, NRA, Government of Northwest Territories Archives, file A-630/138-1, part 1, Education Facilities – Schools Igloolik, N.W.T. Govt. School 1959–1969, Archival box 246-1, Archival Acc. G-1979-003, J. Kadlutsiak and others, petition, 13 November 1968. [IGS-000360] TRC, NRA, Library and Archives Canada, RG22, Perm. volume 940, file 40-8-9, part 4, Education – Eskimos December 1968–September 1971, FA 22-1, M. O'Connell to J. Chrétien, 20 January 1969. [RCN-009722]

254. TRC, NRA, Government of Northwest Territories Archives, Confidential, Hostels, 1971–1974, Archival box 8-24, Archival Acc. G1995-004, C. D. King to Regional Superintendent of Education, Government of the Northwest Territories, 19 October 1971, 3. [FBS-000419]

255. TRC, NRA, Government of Northwest Territories Archives, Confidential, Hostels, 1971–1974, Archival box 8-24, Archival Acc. G1995-004, N. J. Macpherson to R. McKenzie, 27 October 1971, 2. [FBS-000420]

256. TRC, NRA, Government of Northwest Territories Archives, Confidential, Hostels, 1971–1974, Archival box 8-24, Archival Acc. G1995-004, C. D. King to W. W. Buell, 6 June 1972. [FBS-000424]

257. TRC, NRA, Government of Northwest Territories Archives, Personnel [Vol. 2], Part 2, 01/72–12/72, Archival box 258, Archival Acc. G1999-046, R. McKenzie to W. W. Buell, 19 June 1972. [FBS-000436]

258. TRC, NRA, Government of Northwest Territories Archives, Confidential, Hostels, 1971–1974, Archival box 8-24, Archival Acc. G1995-004, J. A. Earle to N. J. Macpherson, 22 November 1972. [FBS-000427]

259. TRC, NRA, Government of Northwest Territories Archives, Pupil Residence – General, 1973–1978, Archival box 4-2, Archival Acc. G1995-004, W. G. Devitt to Deputy Commissioner, 28 November 1972. [FBS-000541]

260. TRC, NRA, Government of Northwest Territories Archives, Confidential, Hostels, 1971–1974, Archival box 8-24, Archival Acc. G1995-004, Ukkivik students to R. Pilot, 26 November 1972. [FBS-000429]

261. TRC, NRA, Government of Northwest Territories Archives, Confidential, Hostels, 1971–1974, Archival box 8-24, Archival Acc. G1995-004, "Ukkivik Residence, Frobisher Bay, Northwest Territories: A Report and Recommendations," undated, 4. [FBS-000431]

262. TRC, AVS, Mary Olibuk Tatty, Statement to the Truth and Reconciliation Commission of Canada, Rankin Inlet, Nunavut, 21 March 2011, Statement Number: 2011-0156.

263. TRC, NRA, Government of Northwest Territories Archives, file 630-105/10, 12-1, part 1, Sir John Franklin School, Akaitcho Hall, 1959–1960, Archival box 228-8, Archival Acc. G-1979-003, A. J. Boxer to J. M. Black, 25 November 1959. [RCN-009845-0001]

264. TRC, NRA, Government of Northwest Territories Archives, Akaitcho Hall Students, 1971–1972, Archival box 9-15, Archival Acc. G1995-004, A. J. Boxer to W. Stapleton, 13 November 1971. [AHU-004772]

265. TRC, NRA, Government of Northwest Territories Archives, Confidential, Hostels, 1971–1974, Archival box 8-24, Archival Acc. G1995-004, L. P. Holman to J. Coady, 6 November 1971. [SHU-000482-0000]

266. TRC, NRA, Government of Northwest Territories – Education, Culture and Employment, Akaitcho Hall, 1977–1982, Transfer No. 0342, box 1, M. Marykuca to R. L. Toutant, 7 December 1977. [AHU-004173-0001]

267. TRC, NRA, Library and Archives Canada – Burnaby, file 801/25-8, volume 7, Education Assistance, 01/1961–03/1962, FA 10-151, V1989-90/101, Archival box 41, W. E. Grant to Indian Commissioner for B.C., 28 February 1962. [CDH-200703-0000]

268. TRC, NRA, Library and Archives Canada – Burnaby, file 801/25-2-14, volume 2, Admission and Discharge – R.C. Hostel, 05/1967–01/1969, FA 10-151, V1989-90/101, Archival box 38, G. Michaud to Indian Affairs Branch, 15 January 1968. [CDH-001220]

269. TRC, NRA, Government of Northwest Territories – Education, Culture and Employment, Quarterly Reports, 1988–1990, Transfer No. 1530, box 7, "Akaitcho Hall Chaplains Report for November/December 1989," December 1980. [AHU-004895]

270. Joseph Jean Louis Comeau worked at Grollier Hall from 1959 to 1965: *R. v. Comeau* [1998] NWTJ 34 (NTSC). Martin Houston worked there from 1960 to 1962: TRC, ASAGR, Aboriginal Affairs and Northern Development Canada, Walter Rudnicki to Director, Indian Affairs, 17 August 1962 [AANDC-234696]; Aboriginal Affairs and Northern Development Canada, Royal Canadian Mounted Police Report, Western Arctic Division, Division File Number 628-626-1,

Code 0559, re: Martin Houston, 29 August 1962. [AANDC-234684] George Maczynski worked there from 1966 to 1967: TRC, NRA, Beaufort-Delta Education Council Warehouse, Inuvik, NWT, Payroll, 1959 to 1966 [box 1], M. Ruyant to Department of Northern Affairs and National Resources, Payroll list of employees at the hostel for September 1966, September 1966 [GHU-002427]; Beaufort-Delta Education Council Warehouse, Inuvik, NWT, Payroll, 1967 to 1970 [box 1]; Department of Northern Affairs and National Resources, Northern Administration: Paylist – Hostel, May 1967. [GHU-002435] Paul Leroux worked there from 1967 to 1979: Taylor, "Grollier Man Pleads Not Guilty," http://www.nnsl.com/frames/newspapers/1997-11/nov28_97sex.html. All four were convicted of abusing students at Grollier Hall.

271. Peterson, "Sir Joseph Bernier Federal Day School," 7.

272. TRC, NRA, Government of Northwest Territories Archives file 630-118/10-1,2,3, part 1a, Fort McPherson Reports, General and Supplies, 1963-1967, Archival box 239-1, Archival Acc. G-1979-003, O. G. Tucker to H. Darkes, 26 March 1964. [FHU-001914] TRC, ASAGR, Aboriginal Affairs and Northern Development Canada, Your File 20 – Perdue, Donald Arthur, T. E. Jones to B. Thorsteinsson, 24 June 1964. [AANDC-765642]

273. *R. v. Frappier* [1990] YJ 163 (Territorial Court).

274. *The Province*, "Accused of 22 Sex Offences,.

275. "Data for the TRC – October 7, 2014," electronic document received from the Indian Residential Schools Adjudication Secretariat attached to email from Shelley Trevethan to Kim Murray, 10 October 2014.

276. TRC, AVS, Paul Voudrach, Statement to the Truth and Reconciliation Commission of Canada, Inuvik, Northwest Territories, 30 June 2011, Statement Number: SP150.

277. TRC, AVS, Beatrice Bernhardt, Statement to the Truth and Reconciliation Commission of Canada, Inuvik, Northwest Territories, 30 June 2011, Statement Number: SP150.

278. TRC, AVS, Veronica Dewar, Statement to the Truth and Reconciliation Commission of Canada (simultaneous translation), Iqaluit, Nunavut, 25 March 2011, Statement Number: SP008.

279. TRC, AVS, Margaret Bouvier, Statement to the Truth and Reconciliation Commission of Canada, K'atl'Odeeche, Northwest Territories, 8 March 2012, Statement Number SP056.

280. TRC, AVS, Paul Voudrach, Statement to the Truth and Reconciliation Commission of Canada, Inuvik, Northwest Territories, 30 June 2011, Statement Number: SP150.

281. TRC, AVS, Veronica Dewar, Statement to the Truth and Reconciliation Commission of Canada (simultaneous translation), Iqaluit, Nunavut, 25 March 2011, Statement Number: SP008.

282. See TRC, AVS, Andre Tautu, Statement to the Truth and Reconciliation Commission of Canada, Inuvik, Northwest Territories, 30 June 2011, Statement Number: SP150.

283. TRC, AVS, Elijah Nashook, Statement to the Truth and Reconciliation Commission of Canada (simultaneous translation), Inuvik, Northwest Territories, 1 July 2011, Statement Number: SP151.

284. TRC, AVC, Paul Voudrach, Statement to the Truth and Reconciliation Commission of Canada, Inuvik, Nunavut, 30 June 2011, Statement Number: SP150.

285. TRC, AVS, Jimmie Itulu, Statement to the Truth and Reconciliation Commission of Canada (simultaneous translation), Iqaluit, Nunavut, 25 March 2011, Statement Number: SP008.

286. TRC, AVS, Eric Idlaut, Statement to the Truth and Reconciliation Commission of Canada (simultaneous translation), Iqaluit, Nunavut, 25 March 2011, Statement Number: SP008.

287. TRC, AVS, Agnes Chief, Statement to the Truth and Reconciliation Commission of Canada, Watson Lake, Yukon, 25 May 2011, Statement Number: SP021.

288. TRC, NRA, Library and Archives Canada, RG85, Perm. volume 1283, file 303/100, part 6, Town Planning – Fort Smith, N.W.T. 1959–1960, FA 85-4, Administrator of the Mackenzie, Department of Northern Affairs and National Resources to Director to Department of Northern Affairs and National Resources, 22 June 1960. [GCU-000211]

289. TRC, NRA, Government of Northwest Territories Archives, file 600-1-1, part 1a, Education, Schools – General Policy, 1962–1969, Archival box 202-4, Archival Acc. G-1979-003, P. Piché to R.J. Orange, 27 May 1964. [GCU-000178]

290. Pigott, "Leadership Factory," *National Post.* Becker, "Priests Hope for College Grads," *Montreal Gazette.*

291. Van Camp, "Bishop Paul Piché," 169.

292. Van Camp, "Bishop Paul Piché," 170.

293. Pigott, "Leadership Factory," *National Post.*

294. TRC, NRA, Sisters of Charity [Grey Nuns] Edmonton Archives – Alberta Fort Smith – Grandin College, 1968–1980, Historical: Documents – 19, L146 – B01, Grandin College News Letter, 30 April 1981, 3, 6. [GNN-000699]

295. TRC, NRA, Library and Archives Canada, RG85, box 162, Acc. 1997-98/076, file 1010-7-4, part 1, Roman Catholic Church – Grandin Hall – Fort Smith, N.W.T. 1964–December 1967, FA 85-52, Director, Department of Northern Affairs and National Resources to Commissioner of the Northwest Territories, 30 September 1964. [GCU-000018]

296. TRC, NRA, Library and Archives Canada, RG85, box 162, Acc. 1997-98/076, file 1010-7-4, part 1, Roman Catholic Church – Grandin Hall – Fort Smith, N.W.T. 1964–December 1967, FA 85-52, "Financial Assistance to Church Educational Institutions and the Control of Educational Policy in the Northwest Territories," E. A. Côté, 12 March 1965. [GCU-000048-0001]

297. TRC, NRA, Library and Archives Canada, RG85, Perm. volume 1466, file 630/106-1, part 4, Govt. School [Indian] Rae N.W.T. October 1964–October 1968, FA 85-4, P. Piché to F. A. G. Carter, 11 April 1966. [GCU-000183]

298. TRC, NRA, Library and Archives Canada, RG85, box 162, Acc. 1997-98/076, file 1010-7-4, part 1, Roman Catholic Church – Grandin Hall – Fort Smith, N.W.T. 1964–December 1967, FA 85-52, S. M. Hodgson to E. A. Côté, 20 December 1967. [GCU-000137]

299. TRC, NRA, Diocese of Mackenzie – Yellowknife, NWT, Grandin College – Administration Files Miscellaneous Papers, Buell for R. Orange to P. Piché, 29 November 1967. [GCU-800198]

300. Blondin-Andrew, "New Ways," 64.

301. Mountain, "Saved from Grollier Hall," http://www.nnsl.com/northern-news-services/stories/papers/nov12_07mountain.html.

302. Van Camp, "Bishop Paul Piché," 169; Pigott, "Leadership Factory," *National Post.*

303. Pigott, "N.W.T. 'Leadership Factory" Alumni," http://www.cbc.ca/news/canada/north/story/2008/05/19/nwt-grandin.html; Mathisen, "Grand Reunion," http://www.nnsl.com/northern-news-services/stories/papers/may20_08gra3-nwt.html.

304. Geens, "Behchoko Priest," http://www.nnsl.com/frames/newspapers/2006-06/jun26_06b.html.

305. TRC, NRA, Diocese of Mackenzie – Yellowknife, NWT Grandin College – Administration Files Grandin's Progress Reports, "Grandin College: Report on the Year 1972–1973," undated. [GCU-800229]

306. TRC, NRA, Diocese of Mackenzie – Yellowknife, NWT, Grandin College – Administration Files Rapports Financiers, C. N. Deharveng, "Some short reflections on Grandin College," 7 October 1983. [GCU-800245]

307. TRC, NRA, Diocese of Mackenzie – Yellowknife, NWT, Grandin College – Administration Files Miscellaneous Papers, Letter Sent on Behalf of Bishop P. Piché and his Diocesan Council, 4 June 1985. [GCU-800247]

308. Raithby, "Residential Schools Returning?," *News North.*

309. Quassa, *We Need to Know*, 36–37.

310. John Amagoalik, quoted in McGregor, *Inuit Education*, 110.

311. John Amagoalik, quoted in McGregor, *Inuit Education*, 110.

312. Quassa, *We Need to Know*, 36–37.

313. Irniq, "Remembering Ralph Ritcey's," http://www.nunatsiaqonline.ca/archives/31219/opinionEditorial/letters.html.

314. TRC, AVS, Eddie Dillon, Statement to the Truth and Reconciliation Commission of Canada, Inuvik, Northwest Territories, 1 July 2011, Statement Number: SP151.

The small hostels

1. TRC, NRA, INAC – Resolution Sector – IRS Historical Files Collection – Ottawa, file 600-1-6-1, volume 1, Small Hostel – N.W.T. General, February 1960–May 1961, "Memorandum for the Administrator of the Arctic: Small Hostels," Director to the Administrator of the Arctic, 21 April 1960. [RCN-004411-0000]

2. TRC, NRA, Library and Archives Canada, RG85, Perm. volume 1949, file A-600-1-6-1, part 1, Small Hostel N.W.T. [General File] 1960–1961, FA 85-8, "Guide to the Operation and Maintenance of Small Hostels in the Eastern Arctic," 21 November 1960. [RCN-003468-0001]

3. TRC, NRA, Library and Archives Canada, RG85, volume 645, file 630/158-9, part 6, Government Hostel [Roman Catholic] Chesterfield Inlet, N.W.T., 1959–1960, Brief summary of references made in minutes of the sub-committee on Eskimo education, no date; [RCN-005922] RG85, Perm. volume 541, file 630/145-2, part 5.2, Anglican Schools – Coppermine [Incl. Tent Hostel] November 1955–June 1956, FA 85-1, R. G. Robertson to D. B. Marsh, 15 March 1956; [CPU-000295-0000] RG85, Perm. volume 644, file 630/145-2, part 7, Anglican Schools – Coppermine, N.W.T. [Incl. Tent Hostel] November 1957–December 1959, FA 85-1, "Donald the Arctic" (D. B. Marsh) to B. G. Silvertz, 28 September 1959. [CPU-000437-0000]

4. TRC, NRA, Library and Archives Canada, RG22, Perm. volume 386, file 41-15,-2, part 1, School – Coppermine [N.W.T] November 1950–February 1956, FA 22-3, 16 August 1952. [CPU-001146]

5. TRC, NRA, Library and Archives Canada, RG85, Perm. volume 644, file 630/145-2, part 7, Anglican Schools – Coppermine, N.W.T. [Incl. Tent Hostel] November 1957–December 1959, FA 85-1, R. G. Robertson to J. R. Sperry, 29 November 1959, 4. [CPU-000356] For start date, see: TRC, NRA, Government of Northwest Territories Archives, file 630-145/22-2, Reports and Returns, Coppermine Tent Hostel School, 1954–1956, Archival box 247-3, Archival Acc. G-1979-003, "Report on the Coppermine Experimental Tent Hostel," David S. Wilson, undated. [CPU-001206-0002]

6. TRC, NRA, Library and Archives Canada, RG85, Perm. volume 541, file 630/145-2, part 5.2, Anglican Schools – Coppermine [Incl. Tent Hostel] November 1955–June 1956, FA 85-1, L. A. C. O. Hunt to Director, 8 March 1956; [CPU-000294] D. S. Wilson, "Report of the Coppermine Experimental Tent Hostel," undated. [CPU-000295-0001]

7. TRC, NRA, Library and Archives Canada, RG85, Perm. volume 541, file 630/145-2, part 5.2, Anglican Schools – Coppermine [Incl. Tent Hostel] November 1955–June 1956, FA 85-1, L. A. C. O. Hunt to The Director, 23 March 1956. [CPU-000299]

8. TRC, NRA, Library and Archives Canada, RG85, Perm. volume 401, file 630/145-2, part 4, Anglican Schools – Coppermine, N.W.T. [Incl. Tent Hostel] March 1955–October 1955, FA 85-1, L. A. C. O. Hunt to The Director, 20 April 1955; [CPU-000205] RG85, Perm. volume 541, file 630/145-2, part 5.2, Anglican Schools – Coppermine [Incl. Tent Hostel] November 1955–June 1956, FA 85-1, L. A. C. O. Hunt to Director, 8 March 1956; [CPU-000294] D. Marsh, "Report on the Tent Hostel Coppermine," 1 April 1956. [CPU-000304]

9. TRC, NRA, Library and Archives Canada, RG85, Perm. volume 541, file 630/145-2, part 5.2, Anglican Schools – Coppermine [Incl. Tent Hostel] November 1955–June 1956, FA 85-1, "Donald the Arctic" (D. B. Marsh), "Report on the Tent Hostel Coppermine," 8 April 1956. [CPU-000304]

10. TRC, NRA Library and Archives Canada, RG85, Perm. volume 644, file 630/145-2, part 7, Anglican Schools – Coppermine, N.W.T. [Incl. Tent Hostel] November 1957–December 1959, FA 85-1, Director to Administrator of the Mackenzie, Fort Smith, N.W.T., 26 September 1959. [CPU-000436]

11. Indian Residential Schools Settlement, "List of Residential Schools," http://www.residentialschoolsettlement.ca/schools.html. Aside from the hostels on the settlement agreement, there were small hostels at Fort Liard and Fort Good Hope; see: TRC, NRA, Government of Northwest Territories – Education, Culture and Employment, Residences 1976–77 – Quarterly Returns [Akaitcho Hall, Ukkivik, Lapointe Hall, Grollier Hall, Fort Liard, Chief Jimmy Bruneau], 10/75–07/77, Transfer No. 0349, box 25-1, "Attendance, April, May, June, 1976," 30 June 1976. [RCN-012401]

12. TRC, NRA, Library and Archives Canada, RG85, Perm. volume 701, file 106-5-3, part 1, Inspection Trips [Including Reports] re: Education Division 1962–1963, FA 85-1, Maguire to Rancier, "Report to Mr. Rancier, Mrs. Maguire's Trip to Keewatin District," 5 February 1962, 3. [RCN-006477]

13. TRC, NRA, Library and Archives Canada, RG85, Perm. volume 1436, file 610-1, part 20, School Teachers and Welfare Teachers – N.W.T. [General File] 1963–1964, FA 85-4, A. Emmett to W. G. Devitt, 28 October 1963. [IGS-000275]

14. TRC, NRA, Government of Northwest Territories Archives, CR #71-601-700 School Services – Pond Inlet, 07/67–12/71, Archival box 265, Archival Acc. G1999-046, "An Account of Pond Inlet Until 1967," D. Davies, June 1967, 3, 4. [POS-000174]

15. TRC, NRA, Government of Northwest Territories Archives, file 630.135, part 1, School Facilities Hostel – Eskimo Point, 1962, Archival box 37, Archival Acc. N1994-009, P. B. Gorlick to Regional Administrator, Churchill, Manitoba, "Bathing Facilities, Small Hostels, Baker Lake and Eskimo Point," 18 May 1965. [EPS-000372]

16. TRC, NRA, Government of Northwest Territories Archives, Cambridge Bay – Hostel, 1970, Archival box 9-14, Archival Acc. G1995-004, F. S. Ellis to N. J. Macpherson, 17 January 1970, 2. [CBS-000200]

17. TRC, NRA, Library and Archives Canada, RG85, Perm. volume 701, file 106-5-3, part 1, Inspection Trips [Including Reports] re: Education Division 1962–1963, FA 85-1, Maguire to Rancier, "Report to Mr. Rancier, Mrs. Maguire's Trip to Keewatin District," 5 February 1962, 3. [RCN-006477]

18. TRC, NRA, INAC – Resolution Sector – IRS Historical Files Collection – Ottawa, file 600-1-6, volume 12, A. Stevenson to Director, Territorial Relations Branch, "Hostel Mother and Assistants Remuneration," 23 June 1969. [GWR-000243-0000]

19. TRC, NRA, Library and Archives Canada, RG85, Perm. volume 711, file 630/158-9, part 5, Government Hostel [Roman Catholic] Chesterfield Inlet, N.W.T. 1956–1959, FA 85-1, E. N. Grantham to Jacobson, 24 September 1957, 3. [RCN-005285]

20. TRC, NRA, Government of Northwest Territories Archives, file A-630/167-1, part 2, Education Facilities – Schools Lake Harbour, N.W.T. 1960–1966, Archival box 249-7, Archival Acc. G1979-003, K. Kristensen to Devitt, 15 June 1964, 2. [LHS-000052]

21. Library and Archives Canada, RG18, Accession 1985–86/048, box 55, file TA 500-8-1-12, RCMP, "Conditions Amongst Eskimos Generally, Annual Report Ending December 31, 1965."

22. TRC, NRA, Library and Archives Canada, RG85, Perm. volume 1949, file A-600-1-6-1, part 1, Small Hostel N.W.T. [General File] 1960–1961, FA 85-8, "Guide to the Operation and Maintenance of Small Hostels in the Eastern Arctic," undated, 21 November 1960, foreword. [RCN-003468-0001]

23. TRC, NRA, Library and Archives Canada, RG85, Perm. volume 1949, file A-600-1-6-1, part 1, Small Hostel N.W.T. [General File] 1960–1961, FA 85-8, A. Schalburg to R. Hanna, Attached "Memorandum to Mr. R. Hanna: Addendum to Memorandum on Guide to the Operation and Maintenance of Small Hostels in the Eastern Arctic," 21 November 1960. [RCN-003468-0001]

24. TRC, NRA, Government of Northwest Territories Archives, file 610.105, part 1, Teachers – Baker Lake, 1962–1969, Archival box 31, Archival Acc. N1994-009, W. I. Mouat, "Principal's Report, School Year 1961–62, 3 August 1962," 4. [BLS-000260]

25. TRC, NRA, Library and Archives Canada, RG85, Perm. volume 1470, file 630/1023-1, part 1, Govt. School – Broughton Island N.W.T. 1959–June 1967, FA 85-4, O. Larson to B. Thorsteinson, "Principal's Half-Yearly Progress Report," 31 January 1965, 2–5. [BIS-000174-0001]

26. TRC, NRA, Library and Archives Canada, RG85, Perm. volume 1949, file A-600-1-6-1, part 1, Small Hostel N.W.T. [General File] 1960–1961, FA 85-8, "Guide to the Operation and Maintenance of Small Hostels in the Eastern Arctic," undated, 2. [RCN-003468-0001]

27. TRC, NRA, Library and Archives Canada, RG85, Perm. volume 1949, file A-600-1-6-1, part 1, Small Hostel N.W.T. [General File] 1960–1961, FA 85-8, "Guide to the Operation and Maintenance of Small Hostels in the Eastern Arctic," undated, 1–2. [RCN-003468-0001]

28. TRC, NRA, Government of Northwest Territories Archives, file 610.105, part 1 Teachers – Baker Lake, 1962–1969, Archival box 31, Archival Acc. N1994-009, I. Mouat, "Principal's Report, School Year 1961–62," 3 August 1962, 2–3. [BLS-000260]

29. TRC, NRA, Government of Northwest Territories Archives, file A-630/159-1, part 1, Education Facilities – Schools Baker Lake, N.W.T. Government School, 1960–1966, Archival box 248-6, Archival Acc. G-1979-003, "Principal's Report, 1962–63," I. Mouat, 29 June 1963, 3. [BLS-000425-0001]

30. TRC, NRA, Library and Archives Canada, RG85, Perm. volume 1951, file A.1000/153, part 1, Settlement and Areas Eskimo Point 1960–1964, FA 85-8, M. P. Walsh, "Report of Community Principal on the Community of Eskimo Point and on the Work of the School (including Estimates Material 1961–1962)," 11. [EPS-000255]

31. TRC, NRA, Library and Archives Canada, RG10, Accession 2003-00196-4, box 19, file AQR630/313-1, volume 1, A. Meldrum, "Federal School – Payne Bay, P.Q.," 4. [PBH-000086-0001]

32. TRC, NRA, Library and Archives Canada, RG85, Perm. volume 1436, file 610-1, part 20, School Teachers and Welfare Teachers – N.W.T. [General File] 1963–1964, FA 85-4, A. Emmett to W. G. Devitt, 28 October 1963, 3. [IGS-000275]

33. TRC, NRA, Library and Archives Canada, RG10, Accession 2003-00196-4, box 23, file AQR1000-302, part 1, A. Stevenson to Regional Administrator, Arctic Quebec, 11 September 1967. [GWR-000237-0001]

34. Desrosiers, "Examen de la Politique de Scolarisation," 108.

35. TRC, NRA, Government of Northwest Territories Archives, CR #71-601-700 School Services – Pond Inlet, 07/67–12/71, Archival box 265, Archival Acc. G1999-046, D. Davies, "An Account of Pond Inlet Until 1967," June 1967, 8–9. [POS-000174]

36. TRC, NRA, Government of Northwest Territories Archives, Pupil Residence – General, 1974–1978, Archival box 3-3, Archival Acc. G1995-004, H. J. Mayne to B. Lewis, 31 December 1976, 1–2. [CBS-000233]

37. TRC, NRA, Government of Northwest Territories – Education, Culture and Employment, Hostel Contract, 1988–1991, Transfer – Nunavut, box 74, "Hostel Contract Questionnaire, Cambridge Bay Hostel, April 1989," D. Wilson to K. Friesen, 28 April 1989. [CBS-000116]

38. TRC, NRA, Government of Northwest Territories Archives, CR #71-601-700 School Services – Pond Inlet, 07/67–12/71, Archival box 265, Archival Acc. G1999-046, "An Account of Pond Inlet Until 1967," D. Davies, June 1967. [POS-000174]

39. TRC, NRA, INAC – Resolution Sector – IRS Historical Files Collection – Ottawa, file 600-1-6, volume 10, Hostel Management – N.W.T. [General and Policy], August 1967–September 1968, A. Stevenson to Director, 23 January 1968. [RCN-002857]

40. TRC, NRA, INAC – Resolution Sector – IRS Historical Files Collection – Ottawa, file 600-1-6-1, volume 1, Small Hostel – N.W.T. General, February 1960–May 1961, "Memorandum for the Administrator of the Arctic: Small Hostels," Director to the Administrator of the Arctic, 21 April 1960. [RCN-004411-0000]

41. TRC, NRA, Government of Northwest Territories Archives, file A-630/138-11, part 1, Education Facilities – Schools Small Hostels – Igloolik, 1962–1969, Archival box 245-6, Archival Acc. G-1979-003, W. G. Devitt to A. Stevenson, "Hostel Furnishings," 2 August 1963. [IGS-000055]

42. TRC, NRA, Library and Archives Canada, RG85, Perm. volume 1436, file 610-1, part 20, School Teachers and Welfare Teachers – N.W.T. [General File] 1963–1964, FA 85-4, A. Emmett to W. G. Devitt, 28 October 1963, 4. [IGS-000275]

43. TRC, NRA, Government of Northwest Territories Archives, file A-600-1-6, part 1, Hostel Arrangements, 1964–1968, Archival box 204-4, Archival Acc. G-1979-003, S. Schuurman to W. Zuk, October 1964, 2. [IGS-000071]

44. TRC, NRA, Government of Northwest Territories Archives, file 630.105, part 1, School Facilities Hostel – Baker Lake, 1962, Archival box 37, Archival Acc. N1994-009, A. Stevenson to Regional Administrator, 9 June 1965. [BLS-000501]

45. TRC, NRA, INAC – Resolution Sector – IRS Historical Files Collection – Ottawa, file 600-1-6, volume 10, Hostel Management – N.W.T. [General and Policy], August 1967–September 1968, W. I. Mouat for J. B. H. Gunn to Administrator of the Arctic, 30 January 1968. [RCN-002847]

46. TRC, NRA, Government of Northwest Territories Archives, Cambridge Bay – Hostel, 1970, Archival box 9-14, Archival Acc. G1995-004, F. S. Ellis to N. J. Macpherson, 17 January 1970. [CBS-000200]

47. TRC, NRA, Library and Archives Canada, RG85, volume 1375, file 630/302-11, part 1, C. M. Bolger to Director, "Hostels – Great Whale River," 21 December 1961. [GWR-000155]

48. TRC, NRA, Library and Archives Canada, RG85, volume 1375, file 630/302-11, part 1, Director to Devitt, 8 August 1962. [GWR-000175-0001]

49. TRC, NRA, Government of Northwest Territories Archives, file A-600-1-6-1, part 2, Small Hostel, N.W.T, 1962–1965, Archival box 205-4, Archival Acc. G-1979-003, R. L. Kennedy to Director, 25 November 1963. [RCN-009195]

50. TRC, NRA, Government of Northwest Territories Archives, file A-630/166-11, part 1, Education Facilities – School Small Hostel Cape Dorset 1962–1965, Archival box 249-6, Archival Acc. G1979-003, B. W. Lewis to McKee, 27 September 1963. [CPS-000228]

51. TRC, NRA, Government of Northwest Territories Archives, file A-630/166-11, part 1, Education Facilities – School Small Hostel Cape Dorset 1962–1965, Archival box 249-6, Archival Acc. G1979-003, B. Shasstein to Administrator of the Arctic, 28 November 1963. [CPS-000232]

52. TRC, NRA, Library and Archives Canada, RG85, Perm. volume 1463, file 600-1-5, part 7, Expansion of Educational Facilities in the Northwest Territories 1966–1968, FA 85-4, D. W. Simpson to Administrator of the Arctic, 27 February 1967. [RCN-004116]

53. TRC, NRA, Government of Northwest Territories Archives, file A-630/136-1, part 1, Education Facilities – Schools Pond Inlet Govt. School 1960–1969, Archival box 245-4, Archival Acc. G-1979-003, W. Berry to Regional Administrator, Frobisher Bay, N.W.T., 17 February 1965. [POS-000140-0001]

54. TRC, NRA, Library and Archives Canada, RG85, Perm. volume 1470, file 630/1023-1, part 1, Govt. School – Broughton Island N.W.T. 1959–June 1967, FA 85-4, O. Larson to B. Thorsteinson, "Principal's Half-Yearly Progress Report," 31 January 1965, 5–6. [BIS-000174-0001]

55. TRC, NRA, Government of Northwest Territories Archives, file A-630/138-1, part 1, Education Facilities – Schools Igloolik, N.W.T. Govt. School 1959–1969, Archival box 246-1, Archival Acc. G-1979-003, W. M. Zuk to the Regional Administrator, 7 October 1964. [IGS-000292]

56. TRC, NRA, Government of Northwest Territories Archives, file A-600-1-6, part 1, Hostel Arrangements, 1964–1968, Archival box 204-4, Archival Acc. G-1979-003, S. Schuurman to W. Zuk, October 1964, 3. [IGS-000071]

57. TRC, NRA, Government of Northwest Territories Archives, file A-630/138-11, part 1, Education Facilities – Schools Small Hostels – Igloolik, 1962–1969, Archival box 245-6, Archival Acc. G-1979-003, C. E. McKee to Administrator of the Arctic, 28 January 1965. [IGS-000079-0000]

58. TRC, NRA, Library and Archives, Canada, RG10, 2003-0196-4, box 19, file AQR-630/314-1, "George River Seasonal School Report," J. Ryan, November 1960. [FGR-000015-0001]

59. TRC, NRA, Library and Archives Canada, RG10, Accession 2003-00196-4, box 19, file AQR630/313-11, volume 1, A. Meldrum to Regional Superintendent of Schools, "Department of Northern Affairs and National Resources, Pupil Residence Quarterly Return," 1 April 1962. [PBH-000121]

60. TRC, NRA, Library and Archives Canada, RG10, Accession 2003-00196-4, box 19, file AQR630/313-11, volume 1, [illegible] to Devitt, 22 May 1963. [PBH-000116]

61. TRC, NRA, Library and Archives Canada, RG85, Perm. volume 1949, file A-600-1-6, part 1, Hostel Management – N.W.T. [General and Policy] 1960–1964, FA 85-8, Memorandum from Acting Director, Northern Administration Branch, Department of Northern Affairs and National Resources to Administrator of the Arctic, 16 December 1963; [RCN-003695] RG10, Accession 2003-00196-4, box 19, file AQR630/313-1, volume 1, L. Beauchamp to Regional Administrator, 14 October 1964. [PBH-000114]

62. TRC, NRA, Government of Northwest Territories Archives, file AQR 630/174-11, volume 1, Education Facilities – Small Hostels – Belcher Islands, 1963–1968, Archival box 250-4, Archival

Acc. G-1979-003, P. H. Zacharias to Northern Administration Branch, "Pupil Residence Quarterly Return, Belcher Islands Residence," 31 March 1964. [BES-000002]

63. TRC, NRA, Government of Northwest Territories Archives, file AQR 630/174-1, part 1, Education Facilities – Small Hostels – Belcher Islands, 1963–1968, Archival box 2500-4, Archival Acc. G-1979-003, "Extract from Mr. Neve's Report of a Visit to the Belcher Islands from January 22 to February 7, 1964," file A-1000/174, undated. [BES-000146]

64. TRC, NRA, Government of Northwest Territories Archives, file AQR-633/174-1, part 2, School Statistics – Belcher Islands, 1961–1969, Archival box 256-5, Archival Acc. G-1979-003, "Enrolment Form, Belcher Islands, Federal Day School," M. C. Sutton, September 1964. [BES-000011]

65. TRC, NRA, Government of Northwest Territories Archives, file AQR 630/174-1, part 1, Education Facilities – School Belcher Islands, 1960–1969, Archival box 250-3, Archival Acc. G1979-003, H. Helbecque to Northern Administrator, Great Whale River, 24 November 1964. [BES-000036]

66. TRC, NRA, Library and Archives Canada, RG85, Perm. volume 1462, file 600-1-1, part 23, Education and Schools N.W.T. General and Policy April 1967–April 1968, FA 85-4, J. Cann to J. Bowie, 25 January 1968. [BES-000174]

67. TRC, NRA, Government of Northwest Territories Archives, file 610.105, part 1, Teachers – Baker Lake, 1962–1969, Archival box 31, Archival Acc. N1994-009, I. W. Mouat, "Principal's Report, School Year 1961–62," 3 August 1962. [BLS-000260]

68. TRC, NRA, Government of Northwest Territories Archives, file A-630/159-1, part 1, Education Facilities – Schools Baker Lake, N.W.T. Government School, 1960–1966, Archival box 248-6, Archival Acc. G-1979-003, "Principal's Report, 1962–63," I. W. Mouat, 29 June 1963, 3. [BLS-000425-0001]

69. TRC, NRA, Library and Archives Canada, RG85, volume 1353, file 1000/304, part 8, C. M. Bolger to Director, 27 April 1962. [PHQ-007467]

70. TRC, NRA, Government of Northwest Territories Archives, file A-633/153-1, part 1, School Statistics – Eskimo Point, N.W.T. 1959–1966, Archival box 253-5, Archival Acc. G-1979-003, Promotion Form, Eskimo Point Junior Class, B. M. Davies, 10 July 1963 (eleven of twenty-three students at Clearwater); [EPS-000070] Promotion Form, Eskimo Point Junior Class, B. M. Davies, 10 July 1963 (seventeen of thirty-three students at Clearwater); [EPS-000071] Promotion Form, Eskimo Point Senior Class, David M. Davies, 10 July 1963 (five of twenty-eight students at Clearwater). [EPS-000072]

71. TRC, NRA, Library and Archives Canada, RG29, volume 2939, file 851-1-X600, part 2a, H. N. Colburn to J. H. Wiebe, 19 July 1963. [NPC-621706]

72. TRC, NRA, Government of Northwest Territories Archives, file A-600-1-6, part 1, Hostel Arrangements, 1964–1968, Archival box 204-4, Archival Acc. G-1979-003, A. Stevenson to J. H. Wiebe, 26 October 1964. [RCN-010871]

73. TRC, NRA, Library and Archives Canada, RG85, box 15, Accession 1985-86/220, file A1000/153, part 2, Settlements and Area – Eskimo Point February 1967–October 1969, FA 85-15, "Report on Situation at Eskimo Point," 19 March 1967. [EPS-000402-0001]

74. TRC, AVS, [name redacted], Statement to the Truth and Reconciliation Commission of Canada, Cambridge Bay, Nunavut, 11 April 2011, Statement Number: SP009.

75. Carolyne Nivixie, quoted in Legacy of Hope Foundation, *We Were So Far Away*, 118.

76. TRC, AVS, Eric Anautalik, Statement to the Truth and Reconciliation Commission of Canada (simultaneous translation), Baker Lake, Nunavut, 15 November 2011, Statement Number: SP032.

77. TRC, AVS, Sarah Peryouar, Statement to the Truth and Reconciliation Commission of Canada, Baker Lake, Nunavut, 15 November 2011, Statement Number: SP032.

78. See TRC, AVS, Mary Lareau, Statement to the Truth and Reconciliation Commission of Canada, Baker Lake, Nunavut, 15 November 2011, Statement Number: SP032. TRC, AVS, Jimmy Itulu, Statement to the Truth and Reconciliation Commission of Canada, Iqaluit, Nunavut, 25 March 2011, Statement Number: SP008.

79. TRC, AVS, Annie Agligoetok, Statement to the Truth and Reconciliation Commission of Canada, Cambridge Bay, Nunavut, 11 April 2011, Statement Number: SP009.

80. Dora Fraser, Statement to the Truth and Reconciliation Commission of Canada, Winnipeg, Manitoba, 19 June 2010, Statement Number: 02-MB-19JU10-012.

81. TRC, AVS, Sarah Peryouar, Statement to the Truth and Reconciliation Commission of Canada, Baker Lake, Nunavut, 15 November 2011, Statement Number: SP032.

82. TRC, NRA, Library and Archives Canada, RG85, box 15, Accession 1985-86/220, file 1000/138, part 2, General File Re: Settlements and Areas in N.W.T. and Y.T. Igloolik March 1969–August 1969, FA 85-15, "Igloolik, N.W.T.," J. Waye, February 1969. [IGS-000094-0001]

83. TRC, NRA, Government of Northwest Territories Archives, file A-630/138-1, part 1, Education Facilities – Schools Igloolik, N.W.T. Govt. School 1959–1969, Archival box 246-1, Archival Acc. G-1979-003, Administrator of the Arctic to Mowat, 24 July 1969. [IGS-000368]

84. TRC, NRA, Government of Northwest Territories – Education, Culture and Employment, Students Residences [1983–1987] Misc. LEA [Local Education Authorities] RIMS ID #1201, box 9, "Department of Education, Government Northwest Territories, Student Residences," undated. [RCN-007186]

85. TRC, NRA, Government of Northwest Territories – Education, Culture and Employment, M. Farrow to J. Larocque, 11 May 1995. [FBS-000439] "Did You Reside at Kivalliq Hall" (advertisement), http://www.myvirtualpaper.com/doc/nortext/120316_nnlayout_1-36_vr/2012031401/11.html#10.

86. The Truth and Reconciliation Commission of Canada was not able to find a document confirming the date of the opening for this hostel. For confirmation that it was in operation by 1992, see: TRC, NRA, Government of Northwest Territories – Education, Culture and Employment, Ukkivik – Future Plans [Capital Planning], 1995, Transfer – Nunavut, box 21, "Baffin Divisional Board of Education: Analysis of Funding Levels for Residences," 25 November 1995. [FBS-000566-0005]

87. TRC, NRA, Government of Northwest Territories – Education, Culture and Employment, Ukkivik – Future Plans [Capital Planning], 1995, Transfer – Nunavut, box 21, untitled consultant's report, 2 February 1995, 6. [FBS-000451]

88. TRC, NRA, Library and Archives Canada, RG85, file 632-108-1, volume 1, box 22, Quarterly Attendance Report/Fort Franklin – NWT, 09/1967–12/1968, "Pupil Residence Quarterly Return, Fort Franklin," 30 September 1967; [FFS-000001-0001] Government of Northwest Territories – Education, Culture and Employment, file 73-600-303, volume 2, School Services – Fort Franklin, 01/72–09/73, Transfer No. 0330, box 9, J. A. Coady to N. Macpherson, 22 March 1973. [FFS-000018]

89. TRC, NRA, Government of Northwest Territories – Education, Culture and Employment, Miscellaneous Hostel Reports RIMS ID #1209, box 9, "Student Residences (Hostels)," undated. [RCN-007183]

90. TRC, NRA, Government of Northwest Territories – Education, Culture and Employment, Students Residences [1983–1987] Misc. LEA [Local Education Authorities] RIMS ID #1201, box 9, "Department of Education, Government of the Northwest Territories, Students Residences," undated. [RCN-007186]

91. TRC, NRA, CGS Records Warehouse, Iqaluit, Government of Nunavut, 4235 – Residence – Homeboarding NU Education – box 168, T. Stewart to D. Wilson, 12 May 1996. [CBS-001201-0001]

Territorial administration: 1969 to 1997

1. TRC, NRA, Government of Northwest Territories – Education, Culture and Employment, Residences 1976–77 – Quarterly Returns [Akaitcho Hall, Ukkivik, Lapointe Hall, Grollier Hall, Fort Liard, Chief Jimmy Bruneau], 10/75–07/77, Transfer No. 0349, box 25-1, "Enrolment in Residences by Age, Oct., Nov., Dec.," 1976. [RCN-012407]

2. NWT Hansard (13 January 1969), 15.

3. TRC, NRA, Government of Northwest Territories Archives, CR #71-602-000, Pupil Residence – General, 04/1968–12/71, Archival box 266, Archival Acc. G1999-046, G. Devitt to Director of Education, 5 December 1969. [CIU-001807]

4. TRC, NRA, Government of Northwest Territories Archives, Inuvik Hostel: Grollier Hall [R.C.], 1972–1976, Archival box 1-5, Archival Acc. G2000-014, J. R. Sperry to S. M. Hodgson, 10 January 1975. [SHU-000821]

5. TRC, NRA, Government of Northwest Territories – Education, Culture and Employment, ECE [02330-6, 004508], Government of Northwest Territories, Yellowknife, NWT, Peter L. McKlusky to Territorial Auditor, 17 December 1975. [SHU-000074-0000]

6. TRC, NRA, Government of Northwest Territories – Education, Culture and Employment, Miscellaneous Hostel Reports, RIMS ID #1209, box 9, "Student Enrolment in Hostels, 1967–1975." [RCN-007181]

7. Jenness, *Eskimo Administration,* 130–132.

8. The figures were provided by Director of Education B. C. Gillie to the Legislative Assembly; NWT Hansard (11 February 1971), 503.

9. TRC, NRA, Government of Northwest Territories – Education, Culture and Employment, Residences 1976–77 – Quarterly Returns [Akaitcho Hall, Ukkivik, Lapointe Hall, Grollier Hall, Fort Liard, Chief Jimmy Bruneau], 10/75–07/77, Transfer No. 0349, box 25-1, "Enrolment in Residences by Age," 30 June 1977. [RCN-012415]

10. NWT Hansard (20 January 1975), 515.

11. TRC, NRA, Government of Northwest Territories – Education, Culture and Employment, Student Residence –Attendance Stats. 09/69–06/73, Transfer No. 0274, box 4-20, "Student Residence Enrolment – age 12 and under." [RCN-012596-0001]

12. TRC, NRA, Government of Northwest Territories Archives, Pupil Residence – General, 1973–1978, Archival box 4-2, Archival Acc. G1995-004, R. L. Julyan to R. W. Halifax, 28 December 1977. [LHU-000685-0001] TRC, NRA, Government of Northwest Territories – Education,

Culture and Employment, Miscellaneous Hostel Reports, RIMS ID #1209, box 9, "Student Enrolment in Hostels, 1967–1975." [RCN-007181]

13. TRC, NRA, Government of Northwest Territories – Education, Culture and Employment, Student Residence Enrolment and Semi-annual Attendance, 1985–1986 [Deh Cho Hall], Transfer No. 1201, box 9-1, M. Letcher, "Student Residence Quarterly Return, Deh Cho Hall, Fort Simpson," December 1985. [LHU-000286]

14. TRC, NRA, Government of Northwest Territories Archives, D. Patterson, "Northwest Territories Education Annual Report: 1987," 18. [FNU-001846]

15. Thompson, "Dehcho Hall to Close," http://www.nnsl.com/frames/newspapers/2009-01/jan26_09h.html.

16. TRC, NRA, Government of Northwest Territories – Education, Culture and Employment, Staff Meetings, 1991–1993, Transfer No. 1419, box 10, "Akaitcho Hall Enrolment Projection." [AHU-005118-0001]

17. TRC, NRA, Government of Northwest Territories – Education, Culture and Employment, Misc. Correspondence, 1991–1994, Transfer No. 1531, box 5, C. McLean to J. Stad, 24 June 1994. [AHU-004085]

18. TRC, NRA, Beaufort–Delta Education Council Warehouse, Inuvik, NWT, Grollier Try-Action File 1984–88, J. Maher to LEA's Inuvik Region Chairperson, "Operational Guidelines, Grollier Hall," 30 October 1986. [GHU-000661]

19. TRC, NRA, Beaufort–Delta Education Council Warehouse, Inuvik, NWT, Grollier Try-Action File 1984–88, D. Croteau to D. Patterson, 26 June 1986. [GHU-000637]

20. TRC, NRA, Beaufort–Delta Education Council Warehouse, Inuvik, NWT, Grollier Try-Action File 1984–88, J. Maher to E. Lavoie, 28 July 1987. [GHU-000713]

21. TRC, NRA, Government of Northwest Territories – Education, Culture and Employment, Grollier Hall [495-6], 1987–1990, Transfer No. 0246, box 3, G. Joyce to P. Murray, 15 March 1990; [GHU-000770-0001] G. Joyce to P. Murray, 12 April 1990. [GHU-000770-0000]

22. TRC, NRA, Government of Northwest Territories – Education, Culture and Employment, Student Accommodation in the Inuvik Region, 1995 Transfer – Active, Avery of Cooper Consulting to Department of Education, "Student Accommodation in the Inuvik Region," February 1995, 10. [GHU-000718-0000]

23. TRC, NRA, Government of Northwest Territories – Education, Culture and Employment, Ukkivik – Future Plans [Capital Planning], 1995, Transfer – Nunavut, box 2, L. Levy to H. Hunt, 26 April 1995. [FBS-000452]

24. TRC, NRA, no document location, no document file source, B. Pusharenko, Inuvik, NWT, "Demolition of Former Residential School Called For to Put Bad Memories to Rest," *Edmonton Journal*, 13 August 1998. [GNN-000298-0026]

25. TRC, NRA, Library and Archives Canada – Burnaby, Admissions and Discharges, Carcross IRS, 801/25-2-11, March 1966–June 1969, A. H. Friesen to E. J. Underwood, 27 June 1968. [YHU-090040]

26. TRC, NRA, Library and Archives Canada – Burnaby, file 801/6-1-011, volume 2, Carcross IRS, 06/1955–06/1960, RG10-151, V1989-90/101, Treasury Board Document, 3 March 1969. [CAR-011355-0001]

27. TRC, NRA, INAC – Resolution Sector – IRS Historical Files Collection – Ottawa, file 801/25-1, volume 6, 06/1972–12/1973, "Education Yukon," 11 December 1972. [YKS-005103]

28. TRC, NRA, Anglican Diocese of Yukon Fonds, Yukon Archives, COR 301, file 9, Anglican Church Series IV.3, box 53, "New Policy for Student Dormitories," *Whitehorse Star*, 18 August 1970. [CDH-090069-0001]

29. TRC, NRA, Library and Archives Canada, volume 2, 04/71–02/80, Student Residence, PARC, I. P. Kirkby to G. D. Cromb, 24 November 1971. [YKS-002862, 25-13]

30. TRC, NRA, Yukon Archives, GOV 2404, file 5[a], Ferguson to Levirs, Superintendent of Education, "Whitehorse Student Residences," 18 August 1971. [CDH-090068-0001]

31. TRC, NRA, Library and Archives Canada, RG10, box 66, Acc. 1988-1989/057, General Correspondence Lower Post Students Residence, 1965–1978, G. K. Gooderham to Department Secretariat, 2 May 1975. [LOW-041388]

32. Canada, *Annual Report of the Department of Indian Affairs*, 1985, 54.

33. TRC, NRA, INAC – Resolution Sector – IRS Historical Files Collection – Ottawa, E4974-1, volume 1, 10/1979 –10/1987, B. Zizman to J. McArthur, 7 May 1985, 3. [YKS-005141]

34. TRC, NRA, Library and Archives Canada, RG85, Perm. volume 1462, file 600-1-1, part 23, Education and Schools N.W.T. General and Policy, April 1967–April 1968, FA 85-4, "Hostels Homewreckers," undated article from unidentified publication (internal evidence indicates that it is from after 1967). [RCN-012280-0001] For information on Gibson's appointment see: Gibson and Renison, *Bull of the Woods*, 285.

35. TRC, NRA, INAC – Archival Unit – Ottawa, file 250/25-23, volume 2, R. G. Williamson to A. Laing, 23 August 1967, 4. [CVC-000370-0004]

36. TRC, NRA, Government of Northwest Territories Archives, file T-600-1-1, part 1b, Education and Schools in the N.W.T. General Policy 1966–1968, Archival box 203-1, Archival Acc. G-1979-003, [illegible] to B. Sivertz, 5 January 1967. [RCN-011088] For Williamson's position, see: University of Saskatchewan, Northern Research Portal, "R. G. Williamson fonds": http://scaa.usask.ca/gallery/northern/en_finding_aid_display.php?-filename=williamson&title=Robert%20Williamson%20fonds.

37. Baffin Region Eskimo Advisory Council Conference et al., *Baffin Region Eskimo Advisory Council Conference.*

38. "Telegram from Coppermine Conference," http://www.capekrusenstern.org/docs/itc_coppermine_1970.pdf. The statement was sent by telegram to Prime Minister Pierre Elliott Trudeau. A copy of this well-known eight-page document appears on Capekrusenstern.org, a privately managed online repository of mainly western Arctic public documents.

39. Yukon Native Brotherhood, *Education of Yukon Indians*, 1.

40. Yukon Native Brotherhood, *Education of Yukon Indians*, 1.

41. Council for Yukon Indians, *Together Today*, 20–21.

42. Dene Nation, "Dene Declaration," 3–4.

43. NWT Hansard (2 February 1971), 44–45; NWT Hansard (11 February 1971), 500–508.

44. Kakfwi and Overvold, "Schools," 142.

45. Kakfwi and Overvold, "Schools," 147.

46. Berger, *Northern Frontier*, 90–91.

47. TRC, NRA, INAC – Resolution Sector – IRS Historical Files Collection – Ottawa, file 600-1-6, volume 12, Hostel Management , N.W.T. [General and Policy], 06/1969–11/1970, F. Dunford to K. Bowles, 4 November 1970. [RCN-001355]

48. See: Inuit Tapirisat of Canada, "Education."

49. Curley, "On Education," 29.

50. NWT Hansard (14 January 1975), 122.

51. NWT Hansard (4 March 1991), 290.

52. Hamilton, *Arctic Revolution*, 110–111.

53. NWT Hansard (11 February 1971), 499.

54. TRC, NRA, Government of Northwest Territories – Education, Culture and Employment, Fort Simpson Lapointe Hall [RC], 01/72–12/72, Transfer No. 0330, box 8-2, NWT Hansard, 1972, 683. [LHU-000637-0001]

55. TRC, NRA, Government of Northwest Territories – Education, Culture and Employment, Uk-kivik – Future Plans [Capital Planning], 1995, Transfer – Nunavut, box 21, untitled consultant's report, 2 February 1995, 6. [FBS-000451]

56. Zoe, "Strong Like Two People," 17.

57. TRC, NRA, Government of Northwest Territories – Education, Culture and Employment, Hostel Enrolments of the NWT / Stats. File, 09/71–06/74, Transfer No. 0274, box 4-31, "Students in Pupil Residences, by ages – for the quarter ending September 30, 1971."[RCN-012577]

58. Tolley, "Chief Jimmy Bruneau School," 60; TRC, NRA, Government of Northwest Territories – Education, Culture and Employment, Hostel Enrolments of the NWT – Stats. File, 09/71–06/74, Transfer No. 0274, box 4-31, "Students in Pupil Residences, by ages – for the quarter ending September 30, 1972."[RCN-012593]

59. TRC, NRA, Government of Northwest Territories Archives, Hostel Enrolment, 1974, Archival box 9-10, Archival Acc. G1995-004, "Pupil Residence Enrolment by Grade, Quarter Ending September 30, 1973"; [RCN-012612-0000] Archival box 9-11, Archival Acc. G1995-004, "Students in Pupil Residences, by ages – for the quarter ending September 30, 1974." [RCN-012618]

60. Tolley, "Chief Jimmy Bruneau School," 60.

61. Sharp, *Yukon Rural Education*, 12, 15–17, 82.

62. TRC, NRA, National Capital Regional Service Centre, Library and Archives Canada, file 801/25-1, volume 7 (locator N338-402), P. B. Lesaux to H. B. Robinson, 29 May 1974. [NCA-017354-0000]

63. TRC, NRA, Library and Archives Canada, R776-0-5 (RG55), volume 1639, DIAND 1975, part 1, TB 739089, Treasury Board, "Authority to Enter into a Service Contract," Mr. & Mrs. Coad, 16 September 1975; [NPC-521960] Mr. & Mrs. Aucoin, 16 September 1975. [NPC-521959]

64. TRC, NRA, INAC – Resolution Sector – IRS Historical Files Collection – Ottawa, E4974-1, volume 1, 10/1979–10/1987, B. Zizman to J. McArthur, 7 May 1985, 3. [YKS-005141]

65. Sharp, *Yukon Rural Education*, 39.

66. Canada, Indian and Northern Affairs Canada, *Umbrella Final Agreement*, 240–41, 259.

67. TRC, NRA, Government of Northwest Territories – Education, Culture and Employment, Private Boarding, 1981–1983, Transfer No. 1419, box 11, D. Mandeville to T. Curley, 23 September 1980. [AHU-004181]

68. TRC, NRA, Government of Northwest Territories – Education, Culture and Employment, Hostel Policies, 1978–1986, Transfer No. 0341, box 3, E. J. Duggan to H. Simms, 11 October 1984. [AHU-003937]

69. TRC, NRA, Government of Northwest Territories – Education, Culture and Employment, 110 Akaitcho Hall Advisory Board, 1986–1989, Transfer No. 1530, box 14, J. C. R. Williams to D. Patterson, 25 February 1987. [AHU-004188]

70. TRC, NRA, Government of Northwest Territories – Education, Culture and Employment, General – Homeboarding [496-1], 1988–1990, Transfer No. 0246, box 3, "Schedule of home boarding rates." [AHU-004194-0001]

71. TRC, NRA, Government of Northwest Territories – Education, Culture and Employment, Future Plans [Capital Planning], 1995, Transfer – Nunavut, box 21, "Options for Educational Residences at Iqaluit," 2 February 1995, 17–18. [FBS-000451]

72. TRC, NRA, Government of Northwest Territories – Education, Culture and Employment, Future Plans [Capital Planning], 1995, Transfer – Nunavut, box 21, "Options for Educational Residences at Iqaluit," 2 February 1995, 11–12, 14, 18. [FBS-000451]

73. TRC, NRA, Government of Northwest Territories – Education, Culture and Employment, Future Plans [Capital Planning], 1995, Transfer – Nunavut, box 21, "Options for Educational Residences at Iqaluit," 2 February 1995, 18. [FBS-000451]

74. TRC, NRA, Government of Northwest Territories – Education, Culture and Employment, Akaitcho Hall, 1992–1994, Transfer No. 0247, box 9, "The Akaitcho Hall Review, June 1992," 23. [AHU-004040-0001]

75. Ritcey, "School in the South," 21.

76. Kaplansky, *Inuit in the South*.

77. Curley, "Boarding House System," 56–61.

78. For example, Kaplansky, *Inuit in the South*.

79. NWT Hansard (9 February 1983), 201–203.

The residential school experience in Arctic Québec and Labrador

1. Diubaldo, "Absurd Little Mouse," 34–40.

2. Vick-Westgate, *Nunavik*, 59–60.

3. Indian Residential Schools Settlement, "List of Residential Schools," http://www.residential-schoolsettlement.ca/schools.html#Qu%C3%A9bec.

4. Macpherson, *Dreams & Visions*, 76–77.

5. TRC, NRA, Library and Archives Canada, RG85, file 633-1, volume 13, box 22, Statistics re: Education 06/1969–09/1973, "Transfer Plans – Educational Activity – Arctic District," 19 March 1970, 2. [RCN-009771-0001]

6. Vick-Westgate, *Nunavik*, 54.

7. Clemens, "Canadian Colonialism," 59–60.

8. Clemens, "Canadian Colonialism," 120.

9. TRC, NRA, Library and Archives Canada, file 380/6-2-007, volume 1, C. L'Heureux to W. J. McGuire, 22 March 1972; [PHQ-005693] INAC – Archival Unit – Ottawa, file 5150/C6-1, volume 1, D. Davidson to the Secretary-Treasurer, "Junior High School – Hearne Hall," 27 March 1973. [CVC-000615-0000]

10. Vick-Westgate, *Nunavik*, 75.

11. Clemens, "Canadian Colonialism," 93–94; Cram, "Native Education Programs," 52.

12. Kaplansky, *Inuit in the South*, 15–16.

13. Commission Scolaire Kativik School Board, *Symposium '85*, 65, 122.

14. McMillan and Yellowhorn, *First Peoples*, 287; Nunatsiavut Government, "Labrador Inuit," http://www.nunatsiavut.com/visitors/labrador-inuit/.

15. McMillan and Yellowhorn, *First Peoples*, 118–119.

16. Williamson, "Moravian Mission," 32.

17. Williamson, "Moravian Mission," 33.

18. Williamson, "Moravian Mission," 32.

19. Williamson, "Moravian Mission," 34.

20. Williamson, "Moravian Mission," 35.

21. Rompkey, *Grenfell of Labrador,* 23.

22. Rompkey, *Grenfell of Labrador,* 40.

23. Rompkey, *Grenfell of Labrador,* 126.

24. Rompkey, *Grenfell of Labrador,* 156.

25. Kennedy, "Impact of the Grenfell Mission," 201.

26. Cadigan, *Newfoundland and Labrador,* 191; Paddon, *Labrador Doctor,* 170.

27. Rompkey, *Grenfell of Labrador,* 234.

28. Rompkey, *Grenfell of Labrador,* 275.

29. Rompkey, *Story of Labrador,* 116.

30. Paddon, *Labrador Doctor,* 177–180.

31. Rompkey, *Story of Labrador,* 107.

32. Rompkey, *Story of Labrador,* 103.

33. MacKenzie, "Indian Act," 164.

34. Hanrahan, *Lasting Breach,* 235–236.

35. CBC News, "N.L. Residential School Lawsuit," http://www.cbc.ca/news/canada/newfoundland-labrador/n-l-residential-school-lawsuit-can-proceed-1.921137.

36. See: *Anderson v. Canada (Attorney General),* 2011 NLCA 82, para 1.

37. TRC, AVS, Rose Oliver, Statement to the Truth and Reconciliation Commission of Canada, Halifax, Nova Scotia, 27 October 2011, Statement Number: 2011-2878.

38. TRC, AVS, Rosalie Webber, Statement to the Truth and Reconciliation Commission of Canada, Halifax, Nova Scotia, 26 November 2011, Statement Number: 2011-2891.

39. TRC, AVS, Matilda Lampe, Statement to the Truth and Reconciliation Commission of Canada, Goose Bay, Newfoundland and Labrador, 20 September 2011, Statement Number: 2011-4249.

40. TRC, AVS, Rosie Mitsuk, Statement to the Truth and Reconciliation Commission of Canada, Hopedale, Newfoundland and Labrador, 23 September 2011, Statement Number 2011-2160.

41. TRC, AVS, Joanna Michel, Statement to the Truth and Reconciliation Commission of Canada, Goose Bay, Newfoundland and Labrador, 20 September 2011, Statement Number 2011-4248.

42. TRC, AVS, Sophie Keelan, Statement to the Truth and Reconciliation Commission of Canada, Halifax, Nova Scotia, 28 October 2011, Statement Number: 2011-2887.

43. TRC, AVS, Marjorie Goudie, Statement to the Truth and Reconciliation Commission of Canada, Halifax, Nova Scotia, 27 November 2011, Statement Number: 2011-2892.

44. TRC, AVS, Abraham Nochasak, Statement to the Truth and Reconciliation Commission of Canada, Hopedale, Newfoundland and Labrador, 23 September 2011, Statement Number 2011-2162.

45. TRC, AVS, Samuel Nui, Statement to the Truth and Reconciliation Commission of Canada, Halifax, Nova Scotia, 27 October 2011, Statement Number: 2011-2860.

46. TRC, AVS, Patricia Kemuksigak, Statement to the Truth and Reconciliation Commission of Canada, Inuvik, Northwest Territories, 1 July 2011, Statement Number: SP151.

47. CBC News, "Labrador Residential School Lawsuit Approved," http://www.cbc.ca/news/canada/newfoundland-labrador/labrador-residential-school-lawsuit-approved-1.1026425; "Labrador Residential School Lawsuit Postponed," http://www.cbc.ca/news/canada/newfoundland-labrador/labrador-residential-school-lawsuit-postponed-1.2839624.

48. Canadian Press, "Newfoundland and Labrador Residential Schools Suit," http://www.thetelegram.com/News/Local/2015-01-26/article-4020691/Newfoundland-and-Labrador-residential-schools-suit-moves-to-mediation/1.

Bibliography

Primary Sources

1. Truth and Reconciliation Commission Databases

The endnotes of this report often commence with the abbreviation TRC, followed by one of the following abbreviations: ASAGR, AVS, CAR, IRSSA, NRA, RBS, and LAC. The documents so cited are located in the Truth and Reconciliation Commission of Canada's database, housed at the National Centre for Truth and Reconciliation. At the end of each of these endnotes, in square brackets, is the document identification number for each of these documents. The following is a brief description of each database.

Active and Semi-Active Government Records (ASAGR) Database: The Active and Semi-Active Government Records database contains active and semi-active records collected from federal governmental departments that potentially intersected with the administration and management of the residential school system. Documents that were relevant to the history and/or legacy of the system were disclosed to the Truth and Reconciliation Commission of Canada (TRC) in keeping with the federal government's obligations in relation to the Indian Residential Schools Settlement Agreement (IRSSA). Some of the other federal government departments included, but were not limited to, the Department of Justice, Health Canada, the Royal Canadian Mounted Police, and National Defence. Aboriginal Affairs and Northern Development Canada undertook the responsibility of centrally collecting and producing the records from these other federal departments to the TRC.

Audio/Video Statement (AVS) Database: The Audio/Video Statement database contains video and audio statements provided to the TRC at community hearings and regional and national events held by the TRC, as well as at other special events attended by the TRC.

Church Archival Records (CAR) Database: The Church Archival Records database contains records collected from the different church/religious entities that were involved in administration and management of residential schools. The church/religious entities primarily included, but were not limited to, entities associated with the Roman Catholic Church, the Anglican Church of Canada, the Presbyterian Church in Canada, and the United Church of Canada. The records were collected as part of the TRC's mandate, as set out in the Indian Residential Schools Settlement Agreement, to "identify sources and create as complete an historical record as possible of the IRS system and legacy."

Indian Residential Schools School Authority (IRSSSA) Database: The Indian Residential Schools School Authority database is comprised of individual records related to each residential school, as set out by the IRSSA.

National Research and Analysis (NRA) Database: The National Research and Analysis database contains records collected by the National Research and Analysis Directorate, Aboriginal Affairs and Northern Development Canada, formerly Indian Residential Schools Resolution Canada (IRSRC). The records in the database were originally collected for the purpose of research into a variety of allegations, such as abuse in residential schools, and primarily resulted from court processes such as civil and criminal litigation, and later the Indian Residential Schools Settlement Agreement (IRSSA), as well as from out-of-court processes such as Alternative Dispute Resolution. A majority of the records were collected from Aboriginal Affairs and Northern Development Canada. The collection also contains records from other federal departments and religious entities. In the case of some records in the database that were provided by outside entities, the information in the database is incomplete. In those instances, the endnote in the report reads, "No document location, no document file source."

Red, Black and School Series (RBS) Database: The Red, Black and School Series database contains records provided by Library and Archives Canada to the TRC. These three sub-series contain records that were originally part of the "Headquarters Central Registry System," or records management system, for departments that preceded the current federal department of Aboriginal Affairs and Northern Development Canada. The archival records are currently related to the Department of Indian Affairs and Northern Development fonds and are held as part of Library and Archives Canada's collection.

Library and Archives Canada (LACAR) Archival Records Container (File) and Document Databases – The LAC Records Container (File) and Document databases contain records collected from Library and Archives Canada (LAC). The archival records of federal governmental departments that potentially intersected with the administration and management of Indian Residential Schools were held as part of Library and Archives Canada's collection. Documents that were relevant to the history and/or legacy of the Indian Residential School system were initially collected by the Truth and Reconciliation Commission, in conjunction with Aboriginal Affairs and Northern Development Canada, as part of their mandate, as set out in the Indian Residential Schools Settlement Agreement. The collection of records was later continued by Aboriginal Affairs and Northern Development Canada, based on the federal government's obligation to disclose documents in relation to the Indian Residential Schools Settlement Agreement.

The report also drew on the following papers that were contributed to the Commission by Rodney Clifton.

> Pupils of the Spence Bay Federal School. *Spence Bay – 1967.* 1967. Rodney A. Clifton papers, Truth and Reconciliation Commission of Canada Archives.
> Clifton, Rodney. *Inuvik Study, 1967,* unpublished paper, Rodney A. Clifton papers, Truth and Reconciliation Commission of Canada Archives.

2. Indian Affairs Annual Reports, 1864–1997

Within this report, *Annual Report of the Department of Indian Affairs* denotes the published annual reports created by the Government of Canada and relating to Indian Affairs over the period from 1864 to 1997.

The Department of Indian Affairs and Northern Development was created in 1966. In 2011, it was renamed Aboriginal Affairs and Northern Development. Before 1966, different departments were responsible for the portfolios of Indian Affairs and Northern Affairs.

The departments responsible for Indian Affairs were (in chronological order):

- The Department of the Secretary of State of Canada (to 1869)
- The Department of the Secretary of State for the Provinces (1869–1873)
- The Department of the Interior (1873–1880)
- The Department of Indian Affairs (1880–1936)
- The Department of Mines and Resources (1936–1950)
- The Department of Citizenship and Immigration (1950–1965)
- The Department of Northern Affairs and National Resources (1966)
- The Department of Indian Affairs and Northern Development (1966 to the present)

The exact titles of Indian Affairs annual reports changed over time, and were named for the department.

3. Library and Archives Canada

RG10 (Indian Affairs Records Group) The records of RG10 at Library and Archives Canada are currently part of the R216, Department of Indian Affairs and Northern Development fonds. For clarity and brevity, in footnotes throughout this report, records belonging to the RG10 Records Group have been identified simply with their RG10 information. Where a copy of an RG10 document held in a TRC database was used, the TRC database holding that copy is clearly identified, along with the RG10 information connected with the original document.

4. Other Archives

University of Minnesota Archives

Margaret Oldenburg Papers, 1917–1930. http://special.lib.umn.edu/findaid/xml/uarc00512.xml.

5. Government Publications

Berger, Thomas R. *Northern Frontier, Northern Homeland: The Report of the Mackenzie Valley Pipeline Inquiry: Volume One*. Ottawa: Minister of Supply and Services Canada, 1977.

Canada. Advisory Committee on Northern Development. *Government Activities in the North – 1958*. Ottawa: Advisory Committee on Northern Development, 1959.

Canada. Aboriginal Affairs and Northern Development Canada. "Map of Distribution of Independent Assessment Process (IAP) Admitted Claims, data from September 19, 2007 to September 30, 2013." https://www.aadnc-aandc.gc.ca/eng/1353515018482/1353515056754 (accessed 16 November 2014).

Canada. Aboriginal Affairs and Northern Development Canada. "Treaty No. 11." http://www.aadnc-aandc.gc.ca/eng/1100100028916/1100100028947.

Canada. Aboriginal Affairs and Northern Development Canada. "Treaty No. 8." http://www.aadnc-aandc.gc.ca/eng/1100100028813/1100100028853.

Canada. Aboriginal and Northern Affairs Canada. "Backgrounder – Apology for Inuit High Arctic Relocation." http://www.aadnc-aandc.gc.ca/eng/1100100015426/1100100015427.

Canada. Department of Northern Affairs and National Resources. *Annual Report,* 1955. Ottawa: Queen's Printer, 1955.

Canada. Department of Northern Affairs and National Resources. *Annual Report,* 1959. Ottawa: Queen's Printer, 1959.

Canada. *The High Arctic Relocation: A Report on the 1953-55 Relocation*. Ottawa: Royal Commission on Aboriginal Peoples, 1994.

Canada. Indian and Northern Affairs Canada. *Umbrella final agreement between the government of Canada, the Council for Yukon Indians and the government of the Yukon*. Ottawa: 1993.

Canada. Infrastructure Canada. "Inuvik to Tuktoyaktuk Highway." http://actionplan.gc.ca/en/initiative/inuvik-tuktoyaktuk-highway (accessed 30 September 2014).

Canada. Parliament. Special Joint Committee of the Senate and the House of Commons appointed to examine and consider the Indian Act. Minutes of Proceedings and Evidence, 1946–1948.

Canada. Royal Canadian Mounted Police. "Conditions Amongst Eskimos Generally: Annual Report Ending December 31, 1965." Library and Archives Canada, RG18, Acc. 1985-86/048, box 55, file TA 500-8-1-12, 1965.

Diubaldo, Richard. *The Government of Canada and the Inuit 1900–1967*. Ottawa: Indian and Northern Affairs Canada, 1985.

Hanrahan, Maura. *The Lasting Breach: The Omission of Aboriginal People From the Terms of Union Between Newfoundland and Canada and its Ongoing Impacts*. Report prepared for the Royal Commission on Renewing and Strengthening Our Place in Canada. Newfoundland, March 2003.

LeFrancois, Roger, for HLA Consultants. "Native Education in Yukon." Consultant report for the Yukon Joint Commission on Native Education and Training, August 1987.

Madill, Dennis F.K. *Treaty Research Report – Treaty Eight (1899)*. Treaties and Historical Research Centre, Indian and Northern Affairs Canada, 1986. http://www.aadnc-aandc.gc.ca/eng/1100100028809/1100100028811.

Northwest Territories. Legislative Assembly. *Debates*, 13 January 1969; 28 January 1970; 2 February 1971; 11 February 1971; 14 January 1975; 20 January 1975; 5 February 1979; 9 February 1983; 4 March 1991.

Nunatsiavut Government. "Labrador Inuit: The Pride of Nunatsiavut." http://www.nunatsiavut.com/visitors/labrador-inuit/ (accessed 23 March 2014).

NWT Hansard: see Northwest Territories, Legislative Assembly, *Debates*.

Peterson, Katherine. "Sir Joseph Bernier Federal Day School – Turquetil Hall; Investigation Report." Report to Government Leader, Government of the Northwest Territories, Yellowknife, November 1994.

Sharp, Robert. *Yukon Rural Education: An Assessment of Performance.* Whitehorse: Department of Education, Government of Yukon, 1985.

Yukon. Archives and Legislative Assembly. "History of the Yukon Legislative Assembly." http://yukonlegislaturespeaks.ca/index.php/history (accessed 14 March 2014).

6. Legal Cases

Anderson v. Canada (Attorney General) [2011] NLCA 82.

R. v. Frappier [1990] YJ 163 (Territorial Court).

Reference whether "Indians" includes "Eskimo" [1939] SCR 104.

7. Other Sources

Indian Residential Schools Settlement. "Official Court Website." http://www.residentialschoolsettlement.ca/ (accessed 23 March 2014).

Secondary Sources

1. Books and Published Reports

Abel, Kerry. *Drum Songs: Glimpses of Dene History.* Montreal and Kingston: McGill-Queen's University Press, 1993.

Amagoalik, John. *Changing the Face of Canada: The Life Story of John Amagoalik.* In *Life Stories of Northern Leaders: Vol. 2.* Edited by Louis McComber. Iqaluit: Nunavut Arctic College, 2007.

Baffin Region Eskimo Advisory Council Conference, et al. *Baffin Region Eskimo Advisory Council Conference. Frobisher Bay, NWT, April 16ᵗʰ–20ᵗʰ 1968.* Copy of unpublished proceedings in Library of Department of Aboriginal Affairs and Northern Development, consulted November 2012.

Blondin-Perrin, Alice. *My Heart Shook Like a Drum: What I Learned at the Indian Mission School, Northwest Territories.* Ottawa: Borealis Press, 2009.

Briggs, Jean L. *Never in Anger: Portrait of an Eskimo Family.* Cambridge: Harvard University Press, 1970.

Cadigan, Sean T. *Newfoundland and Labrador: A History.* Toronto: University of Toronto Press, 2009.

Canadien, Albert. *From Lishamie.* Penticton, British Columbia: Theytus Books, 2010.

Choquette, Robert. *The Oblate Assault on Canada's Northwest.* Ottawa: University of Ottawa Press, 1995.

Coates, Ken. *Best Left as Indians: Native-White Relations in the Yukon Territory, 1840–1973.* Montreal and Kingston: McGill-Queen's University Press, 1991.

Coates, Kenneth. *Canada's Colonies: A History of the Yukon and Northwest Territories.* Toronto: James Lorimer and Company, 1985.

Commission scolaire Kativik. *Symposium '85: 1978–1985.* Dorval: Commission scolaire Kativik, 1986.

Council for Yukon Indians. *Together Today for our Children Tomorrow.* Whitehorse: Council for Yukon Indians, 1977. http://www.eco.gov.yk.ca/pdf/together_today_for_our_children_tomorrow.pdf. (accessed 31 January 2013).

Crowe, Keith J. *A History of the Original Peoples of Northern Canada.* Revised edition. Montreal and Kingston: McGill-Queen's University Press, 1991.

Cruikshank, Julie, in collaboration with Angela Sidney, Kitty Smith, and Annie Ned. *Life Lived like a Story: Life Stories of Three Yukon Native Elders.* Vancouver: University of British Columbia Press, 1991.

Damas, David. *Arctic Migrants, Arctic Villagers: The Transformation of Inuit Settlement in the Central Arctic.* Montreal and Kingston: McGill-Queen's University Press, 2002.

Dickerson, Mark. *Whose North? Political Change, Political Development, and Self-Government in the Northwest Territories.* Vancouver: University of British Columbia Press and The Arctic Institute of North America, 1992.

Djwa, Sandra. *The Politics of the Imagination: A Life of F.R. Scott.* Vancouver: Douglas and McIntyre, 1989.

Duchaussois, J.R. *The Grey Nuns in the Far North (1867–1917).* Toronto: McClelland and Stewart, 1919.

Duffy, R. Quinn. *The Road to Nunavut: The Progress of the Eastern Arctic Inuit Since the Second World War.* Montreal and Kingston: McGill-Queen's University Press, 1988.

Eber, Dorothy. *When the Whalers Were Up North: Inuit memories from the Eastern Arctic.* Kingston: McGill-Queen's, 1989.

Finnie, Richard. *Canada Moves North.* New York: Macmillan, 1942.

French, Alice. *My Name is Masak.* Winnipeg: Peguis Publishers, 1976.

French, Alice. *The Restless Nomad.* Winnipeg: Pemmican Publications, 1991.

Fumoleau, René. *As Long As This Land Shall Last: A History of Treaty 8 and Treaty 11, 1870–1939.* Toronto: McClelland and Stewart, 1973.

Geller, Peter. *Northern Exposures: Photographing and Filming the Canadian North, 1920–45.* Vancouver: University of British Columbia Press, 2004.

Gibson, Gordon, and Carol Renison. *Bull of the Woods: The Gordon Gibson Story.* Vancouver: Douglas and McIntyre, 1980.

Grant, Shelagh D. *Sovereignty or Security? Government Policy in the Canadian North 1936–1950.* Vancouver: University of British Columbia Press, 1988.

Grygier, Pat Sandiford. *A Long Way from Home: The Tuberculosis Epidemic Among the Inuit.* Montreal and Kingston: McGill-Queen's University Press, 1994.

Hamilton, John David. *Arctic Revolution: Social Change in the Northwest Territories 1935–1994.* Toronto: Dundurn Group, 1994.

Honigmann, John and Irma. *Arctic Townsmen: Ethnic Backgrounds and Modernization.* Ottawa: Canadian Research Centre for Anthropology, St. Paul University, 1970.

Huel, Raymond J. A. *Proclaiming the Gospel to the Indians and Métis*. Edmonton: University of Alberta Press, 1996.

Ittinuar, Peter Freuchen. *Teach an Eskimo How to Read ... Conversations with Peter Freuchen Ittinuar*. Edited by Thierry Rodon. Life Stories of Northern Leaders 4. Iqaluit: Nunavut Arctic College, 2008.

Jenness, Diamond. *Eskimo Administration: Vol. 2: Technical Paper No. 14*. Montreal: Arctic Institute of North America, 1964.

Kaplansky, Marsha. *Inuit in the South*. Special issue of *Inuktitut Magazine*. Ottawa: Inuit Tapirisat of Canada, 1981.

Kelcey, Barbara E. *Alone in Silence: European Women in the Canadian North before 1940*. Montreal and Kingston: McGill-Queen's University Press, 2001.

King, A. Richard. *The School at Mopass; A Problem of Identity*. New York: Holt, Rinehart and Winston, 1967.

Legacy of Hope Foundation. *We Were So Far Away: The Inuit Experience of Residential Schools*. Ottawa: Legacy of Hope Foundation, 2010.

Macpherson, Norman. *Dreams & Visions: Education in the Northwest Territories From Early Days To 1984*. Yellowknife: Northwest Territories Education, 1991.

McCarthy, Martha. *From the Great River to the Ends of the Earth: Oblate Missions to the Dene, 1847–1921*. Edmonton: University of Alberta Press and Western Canadian Publishers, 1995.

McClellan, Catharine, with Lucie Birkel, et al. *Part of the Land, Part of the Water: A History of the Yukon Indians*. Vancouver: Douglas and McIntyre, 1987.

McGregor, Heather E. *Inuit Education and Schools in the Eastern Arctic*. Vancouver: University of British Columbia Press, 2010.

McMillan, Alan, and Eldon Yellowhorn. *First Peoples in Canada*. Vancouver: Douglas and McIntyre, 2004.

Morrison, William R. *True North: The Yukon and Northwest Territories*. Toronto: Oxford University Press, 1998.

Nickerson, Christy. *The Legal Drinking Age: A Review of the Research Literature*. Alberta: Alberta Alcohol and Drug Abuse Commission, 2001.

Paddon, W.A. *Labrador Doctor: My Life with the Grenfell Mission*. Toronto: J. Lorimer, 1989.

Peake, Frank A. *The Bishop Who Ate His Boots: A Biography of Isaac O. Stringer*. Toronto: Anglican Church of Canada, 1966.

Phillips, R. A. J. *Canada's North*. Toronto: Macmillan of Canada, 1967.

Quassa, Paul. *We Need to Know Who We Are: The Life Story of Paul Quassa*. Edited by Louis McComber. Translated by Letia Qiatsuk. Life Stories of Northern Leaders 3. Iqaluit: Nunavut Arctic College, 2008.

Rompkey, Ronald. *Grenfell of Labrador*. Toronto: University of Toronto Press, 1991.

Rompkey, William. *The Story of Labrador*. Montreal and Kingston: McGill-Queen's University Press, 2003.

Rutherdale, Myra. *Women and the White Man's God: Gender and Race in the Canadian Mission Field*. Vancouver: University of British Columbia Press, 2002.

Scott, F. R. *The Collected Poems of Frank Scott*. Toronto: McClelland and Stewart, 1981.

Tester, Frank, and Peter Kulchyski. *Tammarniit (Mistakes): Inuit Relocation in the Eastern Arctic, 1939–63*. Vancouver: University of British Columbia Press, 1994.

Thomson, Dale C. *Jean Lesage: La Révolution Tranquille*. Saint-Laurent: Macmillan of Canada, 1984.

Thrasher, Anthony Apakark. *Thrasher: Skid Row Eskimo.* Toronto: Griffin House, 1976.

Vick-Westgate, Ann. *Nunavik: Inuit-Controlled Education in Arctic Quebec.* Northern Lights Series. Calgary: University of Calgary Press, 2002.

Wachowich, Nancy, in collaboration with Apphia Agalakti Awa, Rhoda Kaukjak Katsak, and Sandra Pikujak Katsak. *Saqiyuq: Stories from the Lives of Three Inuit Women.* Montreal and Kingston: McGill-Queen's University Press, 1999.

Yukon Native Brotherhood. *Education of Yukon Indians: a Position Paper,* January 1972. A copy consulted in the library of Aboriginal Affairs and Northern Development Canada, September 2012. Also available as an appendix to *Together Today for our Children Tomorrow.* http://www.eco.gov.yk.ca/pdf/together_today_for_our_children_tomorrow.pdf (accessed 31 January 2013).

2. Book Chapters and Journal Articles

Blondin-Andrew, Ethel. "New Ways of Looking for Leadership." In *Leading in an Upside-Down World: New Canadian Perspectives on Leadership,* edited by J. Patrick Boyer, 59–70. Toronto: Dundurn Press, 2003.

Carney, Robert. "The Grey Nuns and the Children of Holy Angels: Fort Chipewyan, 1874–1924." In *Proceedings of the Fort Chipewyan and Fort Vermilion Bicentennial Conference,* edited by P.A. McCormack and R. Geoffrey Ironside. Edmonton: Boreal Institute for Northern Studies University of Alberta, 1990.

Carney, Robert. "The Native-Wilderness Equation: Catholic and Other School Orientations in the Western Arctic." *Canadian Catholic Historical Association: Study Sessions* 48 (1981): 61–77.

Carney, Robert. "Residential Schooling at Fort Chipewyan and Fort Resolution, 1874–1974." In *Western Oblate Studies 2: Proceedings of the Second Symposium on the History of the Oblates in Western and Northern Canada,* edited by R.[-J.-A.] Huel with Guy Lacombe, 115–138. Lewiston, New York: Edwin Mellon Press, 1992.

Coates, Kenneth. "Best Left as Indians: The Federal Government and the Indians of the Yukon, 1894–1950." *Canadian Journal of Native Studies* 4, no. 2 (1984): 179–204.

Coates, Kenneth. "'Betwixt and Between': The Anglican Church and the Children of the Carcross (Chooutla) Residential School, 1911–1954." In *Interpreting Canada's North: Selected Readings,* edited by Kenneth S. Coates and William R. Morrison, 150–167. Toronto: Copp Clark Pitman, 1989.

Coates, Kenneth. "A Very Imperfect Means of Education: Indian Day Schools in the Yukon Territory, 1890–1955." In *Indian Education in Canada.* Volume 1. *The Legacy,* edited by Jean Barman, Yvonne Hebert, and Don McCaskill, 132–149. Vancouver: University of British Columbia Press, 1986.

Cram, J.M. "Native Education Programs in the Canadian North." *Revue d'Études canadiennes/ Canadian Studies* 21, no. 2 (December 1986): 7–17.

Curley, Tagak. "Boarding House System." *Inuit Today* 5, no. 3 (March 1976): 56–61.

Curley, Tagak. "Inuit In Our Educational System: Part III." *Inuit Today* 5, no. 2 (February 1976): 19–25.

Curley, Tagak. "On Education." *Inuit Today* 3, no. 7 (September 1974): 29.

"Dene Declaration." In *Dene Nation: The Colony Within*, edited by Mel Watkins, 3–4. Toronto: University of Toronto Press, 1977.

Diubaldo, R.J. "The Absurd Little Mouse: When Eskimos Became Indians." *Journal of Canadian Studies* 16, no. 2 (1981): 34–40.

Ekho, Naqi, and Uqsuralik Ottokie. "Childrearing Practices." In *Interviewing Inuit Elders Volume 3*, edited by Jean L. Briggs. Iqaluit: Nunavut Arctic College, 2000.

Elias, Lillian. "Lillian Elias." In *We Were So Far Away: The Inuit Experience of Residential Schools*. Ottawa: Legacy of Hope, 2010.

Farish, Matthew, and Whitney Lackenbauer. "High Modernism in the Arctic: Planning Frobisher Bay and Inuvik." *Journal of Historical Geography* 35, no. 3 (2009): 517–44.

Hawthorn, H. B. "Enter the European: IV – Among the Indians of Canada." *Beaver* (Summer 1954).

Helm, June, and Beryl C. Gillespie. "Akaitcho (ca. 1786–1838)." *Arctic Profiles* 36, no. 2 (1983): 208–209.

Innis, H. A., G. J. Wherrett, and Andrew Moore. "Survey of Education in the Mackenzie School District." Arctic Survey. *Canadian Journal of Economics and Political Science* 11, 1 (February 1945).

Inuit Tapirisat of Canada. "Education." *Inuktitut Magazine* 48 (July 1981).

Ipellie, Alootook. "He Scared the Hair off my Head." *Inuit Today* 6, no. 3 (March 1975): 60–63.

Jenness, Diamond. "Enter the European: V – Among the Eskimos. Enter the European... Among the Eskimos." *Beaver* (Winter 1954).

Johns, Robert. "A History of St Peter's Mission and of Education in Hay River, NWT Prior to 1950." *Musk-Ox* 13 (1973): 22–32.

Kakfwi, Steve, and Bob Overvold. "The Schools." In *Dene Nation: The Colony Within*, edited by Mel Watkins, 142–148. Toronto: University of Toronto Press, 1977.

Kennedy, John C. "The Impact of the Grenfell Mission on Southeastern Labrador Communities." *Polar Record* 24, no. 149 (July 1988): 199–206.

Krech, Shepard, III. "Nutritional Evaluation of a Mission Residential School Diet: The Accuracy of Informant Recall." *Human Organization* 37 (1978): 186–190.

Lesage, Jean. "Enter the European: V – Among the Eskimos (Part II)." *Beaver* (Spring 1955).

MacKenzie, David. "The Indian Act and the Aboriginal Peoples of Newfoundland at the Time of Confederation." *Newfoundland and Labrador Studies* 25, no. 2 (2010): 161–182.

Marsh, D. B. "Enter the European: V – Among the Eskimos: Enter... The Anglican Missionaries." *Beaver* (Winter 1954).

Mead, Margaret. "Enter the European: I – Into the South Pacific." *Beaver* (June 1953).

Mouat, Ivan W. "Education in the Arctic District." *Musk-Ox* 7 (1970): 1–9.

Nichols, P.A.C. "Enter the European: V – Among the Eskimos: Enter...The Fur Traders." *Beaver* (Winter 1954).

Nungak, Zebedee. "Experimental Eskimos." *Inuktitut Magazine* 87 (2000): 3–16.

Ritcey, Ralph. "School in the South in the '60s and '70s." *Inuktitut Magazine* 87 (2000): 18–28.

Tagoona, Armand. "Education." *Inuit Today* 6, no. 5 (June 1977): 53–55.

Thibert, O.M.I., Arthur. "Enter the European: V – Among the Eskimos: Enter...The Roman Catholic Missionaries." *Beaver* (Winter 1954).

Tizya, Clara. "Comment." In *The Education of Indian Children in Canada: A Symposium, written by Indian Affairs Education Division, with comments by Indian People*, edited by L. G. P. Waller. Toronto: Ryerson Press, 1965.

Tolley, Chuck. "Chief Jimmy Bruneau School." In *Sharing Our Success: More Case Studies in Aboriginal Schooling*, edited by George Taylor Fulford, with Helen Raham and Jackie Moore Daigle, 59–90. Kelowna: Society for the Advancement of Excellence in Education, 2007.

Van Camp, Rosa. "Bishop Paul Piché." *Arctic Profiles* 42, no. 2 (1989): 168–170.

Wagley, Charles. "Enter the European: II – Into Brazil – Half of South America." *Beaver* (September 1953).

Wallace, Paul A. W. "Enter the European: III – Into the United States." *Beaver* (December 1953).

Williamson, H. Anthony. "The Moravian Mission and its Impact on the Labrador Eskimo." *Arctic Anthropology* 2, no. 2 (1964): 32–36.

Zoe, John B. "Strong Like Two People." In *Trails of Our Ancestors: Building a Nation*, edited by John B. Zoe. Behchoko: Tlicho Community Services Agency, 2007.

3. Online Sources

Archives Canada. "Roman Catholic Church, Whitehorse Diocese collection." http://www.archivescanada.ca/english/search/ItemDisplay.asp?sessionKey=1143412449030_206_191_57_196&l=0&lvl=2&v=0&coll=1&itm=268856&rt=1&bill=1 (accessed 16 March <YEAR?>).

Canadian Geographic. "Historical Maps of Canada, 1873." http://www.canadiangeographic.ca/mapping/historical_maps/1873.asp.

Cross Country Canada. "The History of T.E.S.T." 28 December 2010. http://www.cccski.com/About/History/Photos-and-Stories/The-History-of-T-E-S-T—%281%29.aspx#.UvukJV6Lnv0 (accessed 12 February 2014).

"*The Experimental Eskimos* (2009) Plot Summary." Internet Movie Database (IMDb). http://www.imdb.com/title/tt1414861/plotsummary (accessed 31 January 2013).

Inuit Tapiriit Kanatami. "'Experimental Eskimo' Zebedee Nungak leaves Puvirnituq, Nunavik." https://www.itk.ca/historical-event/experimental-eskimo-zebedee-nungak-leaves-puvirnituq-nunavik (accessed 31 January 2013).

Inuktitut Magazine. https://www.itk.ca/publication/magazine/Inuktitut.

Legacy of Hope Foundation. *We Were So Far Away; The Inuit Experience Of Residential Schools Curatorial Text/Timeline.* Ottawa: Legacy of Hope Foundation, 2010. http://www.legacyofhope.ca/downloads/we-were-so-far-away-curatorial-booklet.pdf.

Nunavut Arctic College. "Remembering Jose Kusugak. Premier Aariak Honours the Passing of Jose Kusugak." http://arcticcollege.ca/josekusugak/?p=291 (accessed 14 March 2014).

Repeal 43 Committee. "School Corporal Punishment." http://www.repeal43.org/school-corporal-punishment/ (accessed 16 January 2014).

"Telegram from Coppermine Conference – July 16th, 1970, to Prime Minister Pierre E. Trudeau." http://www.capekrusenstern.org/docs/itc_coppermine_1970.pdf (accessed 7 January 2013).

Tlicho Online Store. http://onlinestore.tlicho.ca/ (accessed 15 October 2014).

University of Saskatchewan. Northern Research Portal. "R. G. Williamson fonds." http://scaa.usask.ca/gallery/northern/en_finding_aid_display.php?filename=williamson&title=Robert%20Williamson%20fonds (accessed 8 March 2014).

4. Newspapers and Broadcast Media

Becker, Jane. "Priests Hope For College Grads Among North's Eskimos, Indians." *Montreal Gazette*, 2 October 1965.

St. John's Telegram. "Newfoundland and Labrador Residential Schools Suit moves to mediation." 26 January 2015. http://www.thetelegram.com/News/Local/2015-01-26/article-4020691/Newfoundland-and-Labrador-residential-schools-suit-moves-to-mediation/1 (accessed 7 February 2015).

CBC News. "Labrador residential school lawsuit approved: Feds in 'scheme to obliterate aboriginal languages, traditions and beliefs,' suit alleges." 22 December 2011. http://www.cbc.ca/news/canada/newfoundland-labrador/labrador-residential-school-lawsuit-approved-1.1026425 (accessed 23 March 2014).

CBC News. "Labrador Residential School Lawsuit Postponed." 18 November 2014. http://www.cbc.ca/news/canada/newfoundland-labrador/labrador-residential-school-lawsuit-postponed-1.2839624 (accessed December 2014).

CBC News. "N.L. residential school lawsuit can proceed: Class action seeks compensation for aboriginal students who were abused." 8 June 2010. http://www.cbc.ca/news/canada/newfoundland-labrador/n-l-residential-school-lawsuit-can-proceed-1.921137 (accessed 23 March 2014).

CBC News. "N.W.T. 'leadership factory' alumni reunite to celebrate experience." 19 May 2008. http://www.cbc.ca/news/canada/north/story/2008/05/19/nwt-grandin.html (accessed 10 February 2014).

Geens, Jennifer. "Behchoko priest receives Order of Canada." *Northern News Services*, 26 June 2006. http://www.nnsl.com/frames/newspapers/2006-06/jun26_06b.html (accessed 20 March 2014).

Irniq, Piita. "Remembering Ralph Ritcey's Compassion and Love." *Nunatsiaq Online.* 5 December 2003. http://www.nunatsiaqonline.ca/archives/31219/opinionEditorial/letters.html (accessed 27 January 2011).

Mathisen, Herb. "Grand Reunion for Grandin College." *Northern News Services,* 20 May 2008. http://www.nnsl.com/northern-news-services/stories/papers/may20_08gra3-nwt.html (accessed 10 February 2014).

Mountain, Antoine. "Saved from Grollier Hall." *Northern News Services*, 12 November 2007. http://www.nnsl.com/northern-news-services/stories/papers/nov12_07mountain.html accessed 8 March 2014.

Nunatsiaq News [advertisement]. "Did you reside at Kivalliq Hall between 1985 and 1997." 16 March 2012. http://www.myvirtualpaper.com/doc/nortext/120316_nnlayout_1-36_vr/2012031401/11.html#10 (accessed 23 March 2014).

Pigott, Catherine. "The Leadership Factory: Grandin College never turned out a priest or a nun, but it produced an elite North of 60." *National Post*, 4 Dec 1999.

Province (Vancouver). "Accused of 22 Sex Offences." 21 July 1993.

Raithby, Heather. "Residential schools returning? Stephen Kakfwi says boarding schools create a sense of community and push students to excel." *News North*, 15 January 1990.

Taylor, Glenn. "Grollier Man Pleads Not Guilty to Sex Offences." *Northern News Services*, 28 November 1997. http://www.nnsl.com/frames/newspapers/1997-11/nov28_97sex.html (accessed 17 April 2012).

Thompson, Roxanna. "Dehcho Hall to close its doors." *Northern News Services*, 26 January 2009. http://www.nnsl.com/frames/newspapers/2009-01/jan26_09h.html (accessed 28 February 2014).

Watt, Erik. "Eyewitness says: Kidnap children to fill school." *Winnipeg Free Press*, 30 September 1959.

5. Theses

Carney, Robert. "Relations in Education Between the Federal and Territorial Governments and the Roman Catholic Church in the Mackenzie District, Northwest Territories, 1867–1961." PhD dissertation, University of Alberta, 1971.

Clemens, Lisbeth. "Canadian Colonialism: Inuit Schooling in Northern Quebec prior to 1975." MA thesis, McGill University, 1984.

Desrosiers, Martin. "Examen de la Politique de Scolarisation du Gouvernement Fédéral dans l'Àrctique Canadien, 1930 à 1970." MA thesis, Université du Québec à Montréal, 2006.

King, David Paul. "The History of the Federal Residential Schools for the Inuit Located in Chesterfield Inlet, Yellowknife, Inuvik and Churchill, 1955–1970." MA thesis, Trent University, 1998.